God delivers

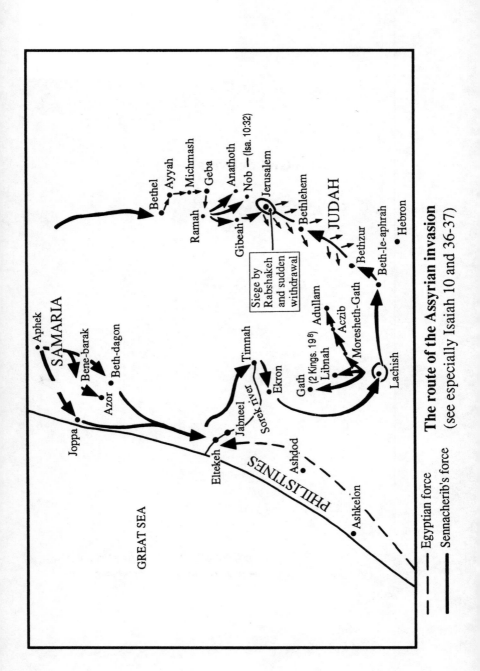

The route of the Assyrian invasion
(see especially Isaiah 10 and 36-37)

Siege by Rabshakeh and sudden withdrawal

Bethel
Ayyah
Michmash
Geba
Ramah
Gibeah
Anathoth
Nob — (Isa. 10:32)
Jerusalem
Bethlehem
JUDAH
Bethzur
Beth-le-aphrah
Hebron

Aphek
SAMARIA
Bene-barak
Beth-dagon
Azor
Joppa

Timnah
Jabneel
Sorek river
Ekron
Eltekeh
Ashdod
Ashkelon
PHILISTINES

Adullam
Aczib
(2 Kings. 19⁸)
Moresheth-Gath
Gath
Libnah
Lachish

GREAT SEA

- - - Egyptian force
—— Sennacherib's force

God delivers

Isaiah simply explained

by

Derek Thomas

EVANGELICAL PRESS

EVANGELICAL PRESS
Grange Close, Faverdale North, Darlington, DL3 OPH, England

© Evangelical Press 1991
First published 1991
Second Impression 1998

British Library Cataloguing in Publication Data available

ISBN 0-85234-290-X

Unless otherwise indicated, Scripture quotations in this publication are
from the Holy Bible, New International Version. Copyright © 1973, 1978,
1984, International Bible Society. Published by Hodder & Stoughton.

Printed and bound in Great Britain by Creative Print & Design,
Ebbw Vale, Wales.

To the members and friends of
Stranmillis Evangelical Presbyterian Church

Contents

Preface

A tension exists in this book between a competent handling of the text of Isaiah and the overall length of the book. In conforming to the style of the *Welwyn Commentary Series* there has been a need to keep the comments brief — summarizing even to an extent that some might find excessive. Students of Isaiah need no reminder that it contains sixty-six chapters, and to comment on every verse (let alone every word) would necessitate a commentary twice the size of this one. Some may feel that this could have been achieved by omitting certain illustrative material, but it can be argued that it is precisely such passages that have made the *Welwyn Commentary Series* the success that they have proved to be. Commentaries, after all, are not usually meant for reading from cover to cover, but for reference. This series is designed differently.

I have tried, therefore, to keep three boundaries in mind: firstly, the need to sustain an interest in the *whole* of Isaiah, and not just its well-known parts; secondly, to be helpful by way of illustrating the text of Isaiah, thus providing a few windows to let in light; and thirdly, to keep to the publisher's request that the result be of moderate length, contained in one volume.

The balance is, of course, a matter of judgement — a fallible one in my own case. Those anxious for greater light can consult two giants in the understanding of Isaiah: John Calvin and Edward J. Young.[1] Their commentaries have been at my side throughout the writing of this book and their towering genius and sensitivity are (to use the current, but misused phrase) awesome!

I must express thanks to a number of people, including Ernest Brown for his constant encouragement in its production, Peter McClintock whose patient skills in computing have once again proven invaluable, and the publishers for their valuable insights and suggestions. Most of all I am grateful to the members and friends of Stranmillis Evangelical Presbyterian Church, who listened for just about a year or so to a series of expositions from Isaiah; it is to them I owe the most gratitude for their love and faithfulness. It is to them that I dedicate this book.

Derek Thomas
Belfast,
1991

Introduction

Isaiah, whose name means 'Jehovah (Yahweh) has saved' or 'Salvation is of the Lord', saw in his lifetime the power of God at work amongst his people. An Indian summer which lasted for some fifty years ended with the death of Uzziah in 740 B.C. Thereafter, for both Israel in the north and Judah in the south (Isaiah's home territory), there followed a century of invasion by predatory Assyrian kings: Tiglath-Pileser III, Shalmaneser V, Sargon II and Sennacherib. These kings were ambitious and ruthless. They sought after territory ferociously and without any compasssion, dealing swiftly with any sign of rebellion by means of brutal force and mass transplantation of the population.

Isaiah witnessed the collapse of the northern kingdom of Israel under the Assyrian onslaught. The fault, according to Isaiah, lay in their sustained rebellion against God. Ministering in the southern kingdom of Judah, in the city of Jerusalem itself, he saw his own country brought to the edge of disaster. But the Lord intervened and saved them. Isaiah could testify to the fact that 'Jehovah has saved'. But Judah did not learn the lesson well. In the not too distant future the Babylonians would capture Jerusalem and take the people of God into captivity. Isaiah gave warning of this to Hezekiah — an otherwise good king, but for a lapse of faith which brought this catastrophic judgement upon Judah (39:5-7). The king's response was merely one of relief that it would not take place in his own lifetime.

It is with this Babylonian captivity — perhaps the greatest trial for the Old Testament church after the captivity in Egypt — that the rest of the book of Isaiah is concerned. The prophet's message is one of judgement suffused with the promise of restoration. The exile would prove to be a terrible ordeal, but God would not abandon his promise, his covenant. He would restore the people to their land once more. Isaiah's vision of a restored Jerusalem, however, transcends the historical realities of the Old Testament. Judah's return from captivity was to be a foreshadowing of a far greater splendour: the recovery of the heavens and the earth to the glory that was originally intended, but which had been ruined by the Fall and the introduction of sin into the beauty that God had created — a transformation so spectacular and magnificent that it makes Isaiah's prophecy thrilling and captivating reading. Truly, the Lord delivers!

An Old Testament prophet

As is often the case with the prophets, we know next to nothing about the man himself. What we do know is that he was born into a noble family, and that he had access to the highest courts of the land (7:3). He could fraternize with priests (8:2), and more particularly with the nation's leaders and decision-makers.

Tradition claims that he was a cousin of King Uzziah, but there is no proof of this. Married, with at least two sons, Isaiah was undoubtedly the greatest preacher of the eighth century B.C., exercising a ministry which lasted for at least forty years: from a time before King Uzziah's death in 740 B.C. to Sennacherib's invasion of Jerusalem in 701 B.C.

Decline into apostasy

Isaiah's appearance as God's messenger could not have been more timely. Judah was rapidly descending into apostasy, following the disastrous path of her northern neighbour, Israel. Following relatively peaceful reigns under Asa and his son Jehoshaphat came the reign of Jehoram. His marriage to Ahab's daughter was the catalyst for decline and departure from the ways of God. After eight years of his rule the Philistines attacked, taking captive all his house except his wife Athaliah and son Ahaziah (2 Kings 8:16-24; 2 Chron. 21:16-17).

Ahaziah ruled for less than a year before he was killed in battle (8:25 - 9:29). Athaliah then took the throne, continued to enforce Baal worship and killed all the royal family except Ahaziah's young son Joash, who was hidden by his aunt.

When only seven, Joash was crowned and Athaliah killed, as a result of a conspiracy by the priest Jehoiada. During his forty-year reign, Joash instituted sweeping reforms. The temple of Baal was destroyed, although some of the high places remained. Solomon's temple was repaired and sacrifices begun (11:4 - 12:8). However, when Jehoiada the priest died, the officials of Judah persuaded Joash to return to Baal-worship. The next year Jerusalem was invaded and Joash was wounded. Some of his officials killed him because he had earlier killed the son of Jehoiada who had prophesied against him (2 Chron. 24:17-25).

Joash's son, Amaziah, assumed the throne in 796 B.C. and ruled twenty-nine years. He, like so many before him, followed the Lord, 'but not wholeheartedly' (2 Chron. 25:2). He challenged Israel to battle and was soundly beaten. Jerusalem's walls were partially destroyed and its treasures plundered. Amaziah was taken captive (around 790 B.C.) and his sixteen-year-old son Uzziah (who was also called Azariah) became co-regent and ruled for fifty-two years (2 Kings 14; 2 Chron. 25).

Judah was at its lowest point. It is at such points that God steps in to save. He raises up a man of God called Isaiah — God delivers!

God's messenger

Isaiah was to know four of Judah's kings intimately: Uzziah, Jotham, Ahaz and Hezekiah, each with their weaknesses and compromises. If there was already trouble in Judah when Isaiah began his ministry, it was as nothing compared with the threat that was emerging from the north. First there was a coalition of forces from Israel and Syria. Later came a threat by Assyria — an empire which by now was at the height of its power and brutality. Its expansionist policies threatened the existence of Judah. Military might was not going to be enough to save them. They needed the power of God to prevent total disaster. This was to be Isaiah's contribution: calling a wayward people back to the Lord and the security of his covenant promises to the faithful.

Isaiah was, then, a man who lived through troubled times: as for example, when Ahaz turned to Assyria for help against the threat of Israel and Syria. When Israel and Syria were destroyed by the Assyrians, Judah's troubles multiplied. Had it not been for Isaiah's ministry, the very existence of Judah (and the promise of a Saviour which was bound up with it) would have been in total jeopardy.

Isaiah knew times of blessing too. When Hezekiah assumed the throne of Judah there was a reversal of ways, from apostasy to revival. Hezekiah was a good king; but at the end of his life, after having witnessed a spectacular recovery from illness which added fifteen years to his life, Hezekiah then did a very stupid thing. In a moment of pride, he showed all his treasures to envoys from Babylon — an empire rapidly overtaking that of Assyria. The folly proved costly and after his death, about a century later, the Babylonians attacked (fulfilling Isaiah's prophecy) Judah was overthrown and the temple destroyed.

A timely message

As we have seen, living in troubled and unstable times is something Isaiah knew all about. His prophecy has something very relevant to say for the times we live in. The importance of his prophecy can be seen from two points of view: first, the fact that the New Testament refers to the writings of Isaiah at least sixty-six times, more than any other Old Testament book except the Psalms; and, second, the use made of the prophecy by Jesus himself.

Jesus began his public ministry by quoting some words from Isaiah 61 (Luke 4:16-21). And Isaiah's portrayal of the Suffering Servant in the latter chapters of the prophecy is seen by our Lord as a representation of himself and the work of redemption he came to accomplish — a work which begins 'in eternity past' and ends 'in eternity future'. There is also a suggestion that Isaiah may have been a carpenter, something which would identify him more closely with the Saviour (44:14).[1] Small wonder that Jerome referred to Isaiah as 'the Evangelical Prophet'.

In that way, Isaiah unites the central message of both Old and New Testaments and enables us to see that the message of the Bible — that God saves sinners through faith in Jesus Christ — is a unity. Indeed, so plain is the gospel message set forth in Isaiah's prophecy that Philip Melancthon, preaching at the funeral service of Martin Luther, could claim that the pure gospel had been most clearly set forth by five men: Isaiah, John the Baptist, Paul, Augustine and Luther![2] For Melancthon, at least, Isaiah was a preacher of the gospel *par excellence!*

Isaiah's message is relevant and timely because at its heart is a currently neglected truth which an apostate church and a godless society need to hear: namely, that God can turn and become our enemy (63:10). Isaiah's prophecy serves as a witness against the people for ever (30:8; cf. Deut. 31:19,26). The Lord is a God of judgement (see, e.g, 34:2,8; and the reference in 61:2 to 'the day of vengeance'). The heart of the message lies in covenant retribution; Israel had broken the covenant.

Prophecy is the interpretation of history from the standpoint of God's covenant word and promise. That was the key to the ministry of the prophets: they interpreted history on the basis of what God had said in his covenant. God is faithful to his word — always — no matter what the consequences for himself or for his people. He is faithful in the blessings he sends, but he is no less faithful in chastisement and judgement. The events predicted for Israel and Jerusalem and their terrible consequences formed the most undeniable proofs that God does what he has promised. Yet God's ultimate purpose here was not judgement but rather mercy. Even in the midst of trial, God's people — those who trust what he is doing — could yet praise him for what he would yet do for them. A day would dawn when they would sing,

> 'Although you were angry with me,
>   your anger has turned away
>   and you have comforted me.
> Surely God is my salvation;
>   I will trust and not be afraid.
> The Lord, the Lord, is my strength and my song;
>   he has become my salvation...
> Give thanks to the Lord, call on his name;
>   make known among the nations what he has done,
>   and proclaim that his name is exalted.
> Sing to the Lord, for he has done glorious things;
>   let this be known to all the world'

(12:1-5).

Instead of a desolate city Jerusalem will be called 'Hephzibah'—
'My delight is in her' and 'Beulah' — married (62:4). Such is God's
unfailing love to his people.

Knowing truths like this will make us strong. It is Isaiah's
conviction that the church needs to remember the consequences of
God's holy character and live accordingly if she is to experience
blessing and revival. In a moving passage, God speaks of the church
as 'the people I formed for myself, that they may proclaim my
praise' (43:21). The church is meant to be filled with the praises of
God. Peter takes up this verse and underlines it; we were meant to
'declare the praises of him who called [us] out of darkness into his
wonderful light' (1 Peter 2:9-10). It is not God's faithfulness, but
ours, that is in question.

Focus

The covenant of grace and the doctrine of the remnant

Before we make a start on the text of Isaiah we need to get one or two things in focus to help us see straight. Isaiah's message assumes we know something of the rest of the Bible, in particular the early books setting out God's dealings with Israel. From the early chapters of the Bible it becomes clear that God is determined to take and keep a people for himself. Nothing else explains why God bothered with such an unattractive crowd as the slaves in Egypt, the incessant grumblers of Moses' day, or the apostate and thankless men and women of Isaiah's time. It is only the covenant love of God that explains it (Deut. 7:7-9). Even when the apex of rebellion was reached in the worship of the golden calf, God did, to be sure, make a fresh start within the family of Abraham (Exod. 32), but he did not abandon the core of his promise to the patriarch.

God has predetermined to save and none can thwart it; he has chosen a people to serve him and praise him, a people that he calls out of bondage into a loving relationship with himself, a people predestined to serve him faithfully and willingly. It is God's commitment to his word of promise — his covenant — that holds Isaiah's message together and that gave such a basis of hope for the true people of God who heard his message:

> '"Though the mountains be shaken
>   and the hills be removed,
> yet my unfailing love for you will not be shaken
>   nor my covenant of peace be removed,"
>   says the Lord, who has compassion on you'

(54:10).

A pattern of electing grace becomes visible through the pages of history.

The doctrine of election finds eloquent expression in Isaiah (e.g. 41:9). It is this that lies behind our understanding of the chastisements that come upon Israel and Judah. It is, Isaiah tells us, a refining process. God is sifting the wheat from the chaff.

Central to Isaiah's message is the doctrine of the *remnant*: they are not all Israel who are of Israel; God's covenant promise finds its fulfilment in those who remained true to him. So central is this to Isaiah that it finds expression in the opening chapter:

> 'Unless the Lord Almighty
>   had left us some survivors,
> we would have become like Sodom,
>   we would have been like Gomorrah'

(1:9).

The number of the faithful within Judah were pitifully small. They are compared to a flag-pole on a hilltop (30:17), the stump of a felled tree (6:13), the gleanings of the field or a few olives left at the top of a tree (17:6). They are a band of disciples maintaining the truth of God (8:16-18). Through the chastening experience of exile, the remnant emerged. God will not cast his elect away:

> 'But you, O Israel, my servant,
>   Jacob, whom I have chosen,
>   you descendants of Abraham my friend,
> I took you from the ends of the earth,
>   from its farthest corners I called you.
> I said, "You are my servant";
>   I have chosen you and have not rejected you'

(41:8-9; cf. 42:18 - 44:5).

It is part of the overall plan and purpose of Almighty God to redeem his remnant church by means of his Servant-Son, Jesus, who is called from the womb (49:1,5), named by God (49:1) and kept in his hand (49:2). In him the covenant principle will find expression: God with us — *Immanuel*! (7:14).

Through the Servant-Messiah, the remnant will come to Zion to worship (2:2-4; 56:3-8; 60:3) bringing their treasures and gifts

(60:5; 61:6), together with *the scattered remnant of the nations* (49:22; 60:4). The remnant of the nations (45:20) joins with the remnant of Israel (19:24-25; 66:18-23).

This is the new Israel in which peace prevails (9:4-7; 11:6-9); heavenly bodies have their light increased (30:26); where there is no longer day and night (60:20), for the sun and moon are replaced by God's glory. The mountain of the temple will rise above all the other mountains (2:2), and a feast will be spread on it (25:6-8). It is here (once more in figurative language) that the temple will be re-established (2:2-4), and sacrifices will again be offered (56:7). This is not a restoration of Solomon's temple, but of the Garden of Eden! The wilderness becomes a fruitful field (32:15), the desert blossoms as the rose (or 'crocus' 35:1), the dry places yield springs of water (35:7). Tame, domesticated animals are envisaged in this Israel (11:6-9; 35:9).

And with all this comes also the idea of rejection: only the elect, those who demonstrate their election by a life of faith in God's promise, will be redeemed. The rebellious will be cast away (66:24). This, too, is part of his covenant; it is the 'curse of the covenant' (Deut. 28 - 29; Lev. 26:14-39). As for the covenant people of God, theirs is a glorious future of unimaginable beauty and wonder: 'They', God assures us, 'will see my glory' (66:18).

All things will be restored for the remnant people, and the Lord will be their crown of glory (28:5).

FIGURE 1 - Israel and Judah c.750 B.C.

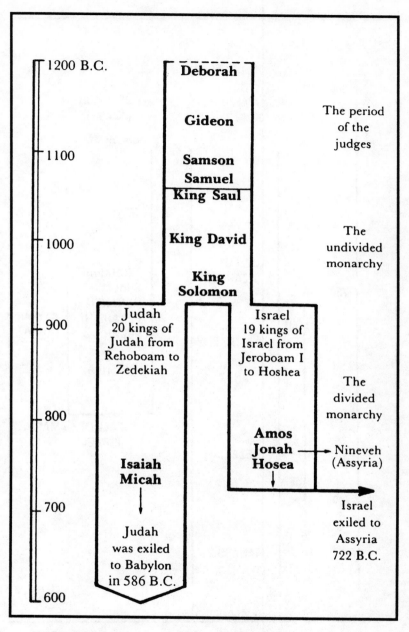

FIGURE 2 - The prophets of the 8th century B.C.

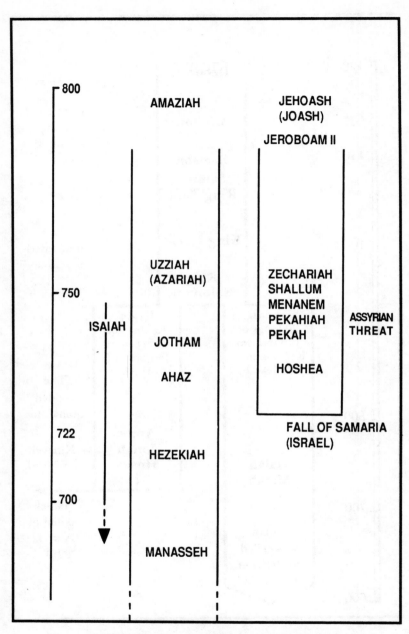

FIGURE 3 - The period of Isaiah

1.
Crisis in the church

Please read Isaiah 1

We all live somewhere: in a certain dwelling, in a certain street, in a certain village, town or city. Knowing precisely where we live is important if we are to find our way about and get home again. Bible books have their 'addresses' too. The books of the prophets were written in very definite periods of church history; well-defined problems brought about much of what the prophets said. Isaiah, like all the others, preached his message in a historical setting. At certain points in this book we shall need to know the background in order to understand his message. The opening verse of Isaiah tells us that we need to engage in a history lesson! **'The vision concerning Judah and Jerusalem that Isaiah son of Amoz saw during the reigns of Uzziah, Jotham, Ahaz and Hezekiah, kings of Judah'** (1:1).

Exciting times

Isaiah lived in the capital city of Jerusalem in the southern kingdom of Judah, with his wife and two children. There could hardly have been a more exciting time in which to live than the eighth century B.C.

1. A time of war

The ten northern tribes, collectively known as Israel, were about to disappear for ever by the onslaught of the mighty empire of Assyria, led by a succession of ruthless kings: Tiglath-Pileser III (745-727), Shalmaneser V (727-722), Sargon II (722-705) and Sennacherib (705-681). The first twenty years or so of Isaiah's ministry would see the northern kingdom dispose of six kings through internal squabbles; some reigns, like those of Zechariah, Shallum and Menahem, lasted only for a few months, and ended in bloody assassination.

Nor was Judah exempt from these things. The relationship between Israel and Judah was difficult and sometimes spilt over into outright hostility. In the reign of Amaziah, Uzziah's father and predecessor, war broke out between the two nations and Jerusalem was ransacked. Amaziah was taken captive by Israeli soldiers. The fact is that Amaziah had begun well, but became proud and boastful of his attainments (2 Chron. 25:19). God showed him mercy. He returned and reigned with Uzziah for a while but was eventually assassinated, by his own people, at Lachish (2 Chron. 25:27).

2. A time of political change

Before any of the above happened, both Israel and Judah had known an Indian summer which had lasted for about fifty years and in which both territories had been free from large-scale aggression. This came to an end in 740 B.C. when King Uzziah died (6:1).

Uzziah (also known as Azariah) came to the throne at the age of sixteen. He was a good king, at least to begin with (2 Chron. 26:4). But like his father Amaziah, Uzziah too became proud (2 Chron. 26:16). We are never so vulnerable as when we believe we are strong in ourselves. It is written of Uzziah that when he 'became powerful, his pride led to his downfall. He was unfaithful to the Lord his God, and entered the temple of the Lord to burn incense on the altar of incense' (2 Chron. 26:16). When he was discovered Uzziah 'became angry' (2 Chron. 26:19), and was smitten with leprosy. Sin and guilt rendered him incapable of self-control. Uzziah, like Jeroboam I (1 Kings 13) offered incense upon the altar. His confrontation with Azariah the high priest, together with eighty other priests, makes dramatic reading. His internment and leprosy bear a sad testimony to the sins that can befall a man in his mature years.

The reign of Jotham, Uzziah's son, was a good one (2 Chron. 27). He was both a powerful military leader (like David) and a builder (like Solomon).

3. A time of religious apostasy

The reign of Ahaz (also known as Jehoahaz) stands out by way of contrast as possessing no redeeming feature at all! Like Manasseh (two kings later) he was faithless (2 Chron. 28). He closed the temple, used temple money to pay tribute to Assyria and indulged in Canaanite religion — even to the extent of burning alive his own children in ritualistic fires. His reign marked the beginning of Judah's downfall. God is faithful in every way. His holy character brings judgement upon Judah and 'humbles' them.

Desperate people do desperate things, and Judah was besieged by the northern kingdom of Israel in coalition with Syria and driven to make a deal with Egypt to the south, as a means of withstanding the aggression of Assyria. There was nothing of faith in it and Isaiah said so (ch. 7). King Ahaz was not a man of faith and was judged for his unbelief. The northern regions (**'Galilee'**, 9:1) fell in *c*.734 and the rest of Israel in 722. Assyria was now at the gates of Jerusalem and the need for faithful leadership had never been greater. At such a time as this, God raised up one of Judah's best kings, Hezekiah.

4. A time of revival

Hezekiah was the greatest king since David. During his reign Judah experienced both revival and renewal. The political and spiritual turmoil of the northern kingdom affected Judah also, and when Assyria came marching into Israel, taking villages, towns and cities with considerable ease, Judah feared the worst and panicked. The Assyrian threat is one that will occupy Isaiah's message for almost the entire first half of the book. The fact that we now know that Assyria would fall to Babylon without a fight before gaining its much sought-after prize of Jerusalem does not lessen the reality of the threat it posed to the Lord's people. Hezekiah was tempted more than once to counter the threat of Assyria by unfaithful means. It is to the considerable credit and faithfulness of Isaiah that Hezekiah was kept from doing what his sinful heart tempted him to do.

Perhaps you sometimes wonder if the Bible has any relevance to today's situation. As I write these lines the ancient kingdom of Babylon (modern Iraq) is threatening to destroy Israel and bring the entire world into conflict. In Africa there are several bloody wars taking place. In Eastern Europe, political changes once thought unimaginable have taken place. And in my own province of Northern Ireland murder and political intrigue are features of daily occurrence. Isaiah lived through days when nations were at war and fell, when kings were murdered, when tyrants threatened to destroy the world and when politicians were doing anything but asking for the Lord's help. Isaiah has a message for today!

Rebellion

Isaiah's entire message is bounded, as between two book-ends, by the word **'rebelled'** (1:2; 66:24). Five times in this first chapter, God charges the Old Testament church with rebellion (1:2,5,20,23,28) and he repeats the charge on eleven other occasions.[1] Behind the accusation lies a history of unfaithfulness to God's covenant, his solemn promise entered into with his people. To understand this, we need to go back to the time of Moses and the calling of Israel to be God's covenant people.

After God had entered into a covenant with Moses on Mt Sinai, the people rebelled. An entire generation died in the wilderness. God led Israel on from Sinai as they journeyed through the wilderness towards Canaan. Just before they entered Canaan, a land given to Israel by God, a renewal ceremony took place on the plains of Moab (Deut. 1:5). Moses reflected on the law, which God had given, in the hearing of a second generation (Deut. 8:2-5). God had spoken! He had revealed how his people should live so as to glorify him. Not only that, but every day brought fresh glimpses of God's faithfulness and unfailing provision.

In an unforgettable moment the solemnity of what they were doing was reinforced. Blessings lay ahead for the obedient; but just as surely there were curses for those who did not obey (Deut. 27 - 28). At the end of this ritual, Deuteronomy records that Israel became witnesses to this covenant (Deut. 30:19; 31:28; 32:1). On the plains of Moab, Moses called upon 'heaven and earth' to testify to the truth of God's warning. Here, in Isaiah, God calls upon them again to bear witness to the rightness of his accusation: **'Hear, O heavens! Listen, O earth!'** (1:2). This is Isaiah's message to Judah: they have broken God's covenant (24:5). Watching a family break up is a very sad thing. God's **'children'** have rebelled: they are become by turn sinful, guilty, evil and corrupt (1:4).

If you are a Christian, but your life is not what it should be; if you have slipped into worldly ways; if your walk with God is not an obedient one, then be prepared for a stern rebuke and a call to repentance as you read Isaiah!

Hardness

Isaiah describes Judah's condition by using the picture of a man who has been beaten almost to death, and yet wants more. He will not listen to the voice of rebuke and chastisement. Judah's heart is hardened.[2]

Behind these words lies the terrible history of Sennacherib's invasion of Judah (see chs 36 - 37). Jerusalem, though sorely threatened, remained unconquered. But almost everything else in Judah fell. The Taylor prism records that forty-six walled towns were captured, together with 'innumerable villages' and a fifth of a million people. Jerusalem was like a **'hut in a field of melons'** (1:8), or to borrow F. F. Bruce's paraphrase, 'a tool-shed in an abandoned allotment'.[3] They had come within an inch of the fate of Sodom and Gomorrah, that is, of extinction! (1:9).

We are not to feel sorry for Judah. They deserved what they received, and more. They deserved to be judged more severely than Sodom and Gomorrah, because they should have known better. But they did not know:

> **'The ox knows his master,**
> **the donkey his owner's manger,**
> **but Israel does not know,**
> **my people do not understand'**

(1:3).

Imagine the pain when a child grows up and turns on loving parents! This was what Judah did. All too often this is the sin that lies so close to our hearts.

Even at this early stage in Isaiah we are meant to catch a glimpse of Jesus! Using three particular words, Isaiah describes Judah's condition as 'beaten' (1:5), 'injured' (1:5) and full of 'wounds and bruises' (1:6). These are precisely the words used to describe what will become of the suffering Servant of Isaiah 53, where Jesus in prophecy is said to have been 'stricken', 'smitten', and to have 'infirmities' and 'wounds' (53:4-5). Already, the divine substitute appears: Jesus, 'by whose wounds we are healed', is the burden of Isaiah's message.

Self-righteousness

Several times the prophets engage in a sustained outburst against formal, empty religion (1 Sam. 15:22; Jer. 7:21-23; Hosea 6:6; Amos 5:21-24; Micah 6:6-8, and here in Isa. 1:10-20). When it comes to worship, there comes a time when God's patience runs out. On the eve of Jesus' death, the Saviour boiled over with righteous fury at the travesty of commercialism in the temple and the self-righteous attitude of the Pharisees (Matt. 21:12-17; 23:1-39).

Religion had several features in Isaiah's day: first, there were the **'offerings'** (1:11,13). These were the daily services which involved animal sacrifices. They were obviously kept punctiliously! Then there were the festivals, or **'convocations'** (1:13). There were the **'assemblies'** (1:13), a bit like our rallies and conferences. The traditional gatherings laid down in the law were not enough. They had to devise additional ones. Finally there were times of public prayer (1:15).

What was wrong with all these? Nothing at all! But here they give God no pleasure (1:11). The sound of these folk coming to the temple is likened to that of a noisy rabble (1:12). Their offerings are **'meaningless'** (1:13). God **'hates'** their conferences (1:14); and he refuses to listen to their prayers (1:15).

Do not misunderstand Isaiah, for he is not saying that God hates Old Testament worship. After all, this pattern had been laid down, more or less, by God himself. No! God hates this particular worship by these particular people. Why? The answer is given in verse 17 (and repeated in 1:23):

> **'Learn to do right!**
> **Seek justice,**
> **encourage the oppressed.**
> **Defend the cause of the fatherless,**
> **plead the case of the widow.'**

If there is one thing that a close study of the prophets will tell us, it is that true faith will manifest itself in deeds of faith. For Jesus it was a matter of everyday gardening: a good vine will produce grapes (John 15).⁴ If some branches seem to be reluctant to do so, a gardener worth his salt will cut off those branches and burn them.

Be honest! What do the words 'do right' and 'justice' say to you? Perhaps you think of the 'social gospel', of folk who have very little time for personal issues of faith and repentance and what they would call 'pietistic' religion and who instead concentrate entirely upon the effect of the Christian message upon society. There is no doubt that this was once very fashionable, particularly in the early part of the twentieth century.

Evangelicals have been quite right to mistrust a Christian message which does not first of all seek to make sinners right with God. But have they been right to forget about the social implications altogether? The prophets would say, 'No'! 'Let justice roll down like a river, righteousness like a never-failing stream!' (Amos 5:24). The world can never be changed unless the gospel is preached. But that does not mean that Christians are to be indifferent to social and political matters. Christians should be concerned about the oppressed and downtrodden. Some, it is true, have taken the gospel and made it to mean something different. To get involved in liberation movements in the Third World is to preach the gospel, they say. They are wrong. But that does not mean we are to be unconcerned about the oppressed. During the revival of the eighteenth century that swept through Britain under the preaching of men like George Whitefield, John Wesley, Howell Harris and Daniel Rowland, the effect was that thousands were converted. In turn these converted Christians reformed prisons, infused clemency into penal laws, abolished the slave trade and gave leadership to nationwide education of children.

Let's talk about it

God has presented his case against Judah: they are rebels, hard-hearted and self-righteous! What comes next is a wonderful demonstration of the grace of God. He calls upon Judah to **'reason'** with him (1:18). There are two distinct components here: God's *invitation to talk* and his *offer of mercy*.

Have you noticed how people will talk about anything except their relationship with God? In the part of the world where I live elaborate rituals have to take place before politicians can feel free even to sit down and talk. They must first engage in 'talks about talks'. God is anxious to get down to business straight away. He wants to talk about his charges against Judah and see whether or not they are fair. It is not that there is any doubt about their accuracy; he simply wants Judah to admit it.

At the very start of the book, it is as though Isaiah is saying to us, 'When did you last talk to God about your sin, about God's threat to punish it unless it is atoned for by Jesus Christ, or about heaven and hell? If you go on ignoring the problem for ever, you may find it is too late to talk!'

God's invitation to talk is accompanied by a word of grace. In unforgettable terms he uses the violent picture of a murder:

> **'Though your sins are like scarlet,**
> **they shall be as white as snow;**
> **though they are red as crimson,**
> **they shall be like wool'**

(1:18).

'Scarlet' and 'crimson' are the colour of blood on a murderer's hands (cf. 1:15,21). You may recall how Lady Macbeth's conscience at the murder of Duncan caused her to sleepwalk at night. Wringing her hands in a gesture of washing, she lamented: '"Will all the perfumes of Arabia not cleanse this hand of mine?"'[5] Death is an appropriate metaphor; it is the wages of sin (Rom. 6:23).

Behind this entire opening chapter lies the image of Deuteronomy 30, where Israel were witnesses to God's covenant. In words reminiscent of Deuteronomy 30:15-20, God's offer of mercy is couched in terms of blessings and curses. Those who obey God's invitation will be blessed (1:19); but those who remain hardened and stubborn will be destroyed (1:20). Jesus echoed the same warning to the Jews of his day who did not believe his testimony: 'I have come in my Father's name, and you do not accept me ... But do not think I will accuse you before the Father. Your accuser is Moses, on whom your hopes are set' (John 5:43,45).

Warning!

Things were not well in the church of Isaiah's day. God's bride had become a **'harlot'** (1:21). As in an earlier day, so now, the glory has departed (1 Sam. 4:21). Instead of reflecting the beauty of the Lord, she was mirroring the marks of the beast (see Rev. 17). The prophet Micah, a contemporary of Isaiah, says much the same thing, summarizing the church's condition thus: 'You who hate good and love evil' (Micah 3:2).

What has already been traced in 1:2-17 is now underlined: God's Old Testament church had no love for spiritual things — a fact portrayed by its utter lack of concern for social justice (1: 23, cf. 1:17).

When Christians grow cold and formal in their faith, they can expect to be chastised (Heb. 12:7-13). Indeed, it is part of the New Testament's use of the book of Isaiah to show that Jesus, too, was chastised by the Father: chastised, that is, for no sin of his own, but in our place as our substitute (Isa. 53:10,12; Acts 2:23; Rom. 8:32). We are to 'consider him who endured such opposition from sinful men...' (Heb. 12:3), recalling that the same Father is using the same method with us. Rebellious Christians can expect to pass through the Refiner's fire (1:24-25). **'I will turn my hand against you; I will thoroughly purge away your dross and remove all your impurities'** (1:25).

A former minister in Belfast, greatly used by God and much loved, used to say to his congregation: 'We become agitated when the foundations are shaking beneath us, and at such times we turn to God for help and reassurance, only to find that God is the One doing the shaking!' This is Isaiah's message, too.

The love of God is holy and his justice is tempered with mercy. God's enemies can expect no mercy if they remain impenitent. They will be destroyed (1:24). The Lord's people, however, can expect to be redeemed, though the dross must first be removed (1:27). The judgement falls upon believer and unbeliever alike. But for the unbeliever there is no hope: **'But rebels and sinners will both be broken, and those who forsake the Lord will perish'** (1:28). Using the metaphors of **'oaks'** (1:29) and **'gardens'** (1:30), suggesting by turns man's strength and works, Isaiah predicts their

complete downfall: the tree had no leaves and the garden no water:
'Both will burn together, with no one to quench the fire' (1:31).
Right at the beginning of this prophecy is a warning to the impenitent sinner which, later, will toll as a funeral bell: 'There is no peace
for the wicked' (48:22; 57:21).

These are only general statements so far; they will become
explicit as we study Isaiah further. Behind these warnings of
chastisements, as we shall see, lies the coming of Assyrian and
Babylonian forces to destroy Jerusalem and take God's people into
captivity. This would mark Israel's lowest point in all her long
history. Already the theme is set: the church has become apostate
and God is angry. There is a course which leads to restoration and
it lies in the way of repentance. Failing this, there is no hope, 'but
only a fearful expectation of judgement and of raging fire that will
consume the enemies of God' (Heb. 10:27).

But all is not lost. God's judgements are tempered with mercy;
and blossoming from this chapter are indications of the righteous
rule of the Messiah, pictured in terms of the justice that prevailed in
David's day — restoring the judges as in the days of old (1:26). Jesus
will introduce the **'City of Righteousness, the Faithful City'**
(1:26). What could not be found in Isaiah's day — justice and good
counsel — will be found abundantly in him and the church which
mirrors him.

Facing difficulties as we do, we are like the disciples in the upper
room to whom Jesus said, 'You do not realize now what I am doing,
but later you will understand' (John 13:7). The Refiner's fire is not
pleasant (Heb. 12:11), but it is necessary. Our task is to trust him and
pray, 'Lord, give me grace to turn away from the cold indifference
that marks too much of my life and produce in me the fruits of
righteousness.' At the very start of this prophecy, Isaiah has set the
tone of his message which prevails to the very last page. There is
abundant hope for repentant sinners and it lies in the provision of a
suffering Servant who takes the sinner's place, thus providing a way
of redemption. Trusting Jesus for our pardon and deliverance is the
only way to be safe from the wrath to come. Those who despise this
message — and there were plenty who did in Isaiah's day (cf. 53:1)
as there are today — can expect no mercy. Unrepentant sinners will
find no cause for joy in this book!

Summary

God is about to take Judah, his apostate church, and shake her. It will prove a devastating experience; but for those who heed his offer of grace and mercy, it will prove a blessing. God desires to revive and reform the church.

2.
Things to come

Please read Isaiah 2

If Isaiah's first vision (1:1) was of Judah's present sinful condition, his second vision (2:6-22) is of their impending judgement. It is on 'things to come' that the prophet wants our attention to be focused. Knowing what lies ahead is important if we are to make sustained and careful progress. He begins with a short, but spectacular, picture of Judah's glorious future (2:1-4). It is almost identical to a message delivered by Micah — Isaiah's contemporary in Jerusalem (cf. Micah 4:1-3). G. K. Chesterton wrote in a child's picture book,

> Stand up, and keep your childishness,
> Read all the pedant's creeds and strictures
> But don't believe in anything
> That can't be told in coloured pictures![1]

A picture is what the prophet now paints.

The mountain of the Lord

The picture may well be based on a scene familiar enough to the inhabitants of Jerusalem — **'the mountain of the Lord'** (2:2). Every year pilgrims would make their way to the city to celebrate the annual feasts. At Passover time in Jesus' day, for example, the population of Jerusalem could be swelled from 50,000 to around 200,000. The sight of folk in festive spirit filling the temple area of Jerusalem was common enough and it is easy for us to visualize how

Isaiah could use this as illustrative of what God was going to do in the future — but on an even bigger scale, involving not just Judah or even Israel, but the entire world.

An examination of the 'picture' reveals the following points.

1. The supremacy of Jerusalem's God

Mt Zion is seen in a position of elevation:

> **'The mountain of the Lord's temple will be**
> **established**
> **as chief among the mountains;**
> **it will be raised above the hills,**
> **and all nations will stream to it'**
>
> (2:2).

There is both a geographical and spiritual reference here. Geographically, Mt Hermon in northern Galilee was the highest mountain in Palestine, rising to 9,200 feet. Its snow-capped peaks were a sight of great beauty. Mt Zion, on the other hand, was a mere 2,400 feet above sea level. The psalmist alludes to this difference when he describes days spent in Jerusalem as being so magnificent that it was as though the dew of Mt Hermon had fallen upon Mt Zion (Ps. 133:3). He refers to it again in another psalm:

> 'The mountains of Bashan are majestic mountains;
> rugged are the mountains of Bashan.
> Why gaze in envy, O rugged mountains,
> at the mountain where God chooses to reign,
> where the Lord himself will dwell for ever?'
>
> (Ps. 68:15-16).

Just as geographically Mt Zion was nowhere near the size and greatness of Mt Hermon, so to many Zion had little spiritual significance. Other mountains, with their religious associations, were dominant in Isaiah's day, including Mt Sinai, with its connections with the giving of the law. But a day will dawn when Zion will surpass all others. It is this spiritual significance of certain mountains in Palestine that lies behind Jesus' interrogation of the woman of Samaria (John 4:21-24). The point made there is relevant here

too: it is not the literal Mt Gerizim (important for the Samaritans) or
Mt Zion that ultimately matters, but whether or not God is worshipped 'in spirit and in truth' (John 4:24). A time will come when
the God who has revealed himself in Jerusalem will be shown to be
far greater than any other 'god' currently worshipped elsewhere.
The God of Israel is not just some local deity. He is the God of the
whole earth.

2. The universality of God's saving purpose

It is a fatal mistake to think that the Old Testament confines its
interest to Israel and the Jews. Israel were an elect nation and the
Jews a chosen people (41:8-10), but even in the Old Testament
God's purposes were international. The inclusion of Ruth, a
Moabitess, in the genealogy of Jesus Christ shows that (Matt. 1:5).
Later in the prophecy, Isaiah reproves the Jews for their lack of
evangelism to the foreigners and strangers who gathered in Jeru-
salem (42:18-25). Isaiah sees a day when the nations will 'flow' to
Jerusalem, and

> **'Many peoples will come and say,**
>
> **"Come, let us go up to the mountain of the Lord,**
> **to the house of the God of Jacob.**
> **He will teach us his ways,**
> **so that we may walk in his paths."**
> **The law will go out from Zion,**
> **the word of the Lord from Jerusalem'**

(2:3).

But, the number of those who came to faith during the Old
Testament period was small. The devil had blinded the nations (cf.
Luke 10:18). It is not without significance that Luke records those
present on the Day of Pentecost who received the Holy Spirit:
'Parthians, Medes and Elamites; residents of Mesopotamia, Judea
and Cappadocia, Pontus and Asia, Phrygia and Pamphylia, Egypt
and the parts of Libya near Cyrene; visitors from Rome (both Jews
and converts to Judaism); Cretans and Arabs' (Acts 2:9-11).

3. God is the bringer of peace

The reference to the transformation of weapons of warfare into farming implements (2:4) has been inscribed on a wall-mounting in the United Nations office in New York. Those uninterested in the prophet's spiritual applications have seen here a reference to world peace. Behind it lies a belief in the inherent goodness of man, a belief that has received a severe blow in this, the bloodiest of all centuries. Peace is God's concern, it is true. The central mission of the Mediator is to bring peace; so much so that he is called the Prince of Peace (9:6; cf. 11:6-10). Reconciliation has been God's purpose since the Fall in Eden. Restoring sinful man into a relationship of peace with God is what the gospel is all about. 'Therefore, since we have been justified through faith, we have peace with God through our Lord Jesus Christ' (Rom. 5:1). Having been made right with God, and only then, we are in a position to be made right with our neighbour. The healing of the breach between Jews and Gentiles is something Ephesians 2:11-22 focuses upon. Those who were formerly enemies are, in Christ, brought into the one family of God; former adversaries are now brothers and sisters, sharing the same promise of heaven (Eph. 2:19). This, at least in part, is what Isaiah can see in the future.

4. The Gentiles are to gather at the great festival assembly of God

The imagery here is of a festival gathering. It is reminiscent of the assembly that gathered at Sinai (Deut. 4:10; 9:10; 10:4; 18:16) and marked the climax of God's redemption, constituting the people as the people of God. Numbers 10:1-10 provides for the blowing of two silver trumpets for the gathering of later assemblies at the door of the tent of meeting. Later renewals of the covenant were made by an assembed Israel (cf. Josh. 8:30-35). And three times a year the people were ordered to gather together for the feasts of the sacred calendar (see Lev. 23). Other such gatherings include the succession of Solomon (1 Chron. 28 - 29); the dedication of Solomon's temple (2 Chron. 5:2); and the assembly called by Nehemiah after the exile (Neh. 8).[2]

Isaiah uses, then, a well-defined form to picture the greatness and solemnity of what God is going to do. The ingathering of the nations (cf. Ps. 87) is to be the climax of what Israel had been led to expect every time they met for the great occasions of worship.

How are we to understand this passage?

Several questions now arise.

1. When is all this to come about?

What do the words, **'In the latter days...'** mean? Some insist that the expression 'latter days' always refers to the second coming of Christ, but we can see that this is not the case from a glance at the very first recorded instance of its use in the Bible, when Jacob blessed his sons: 'Then Jacob called for his sons and said: "Gather round so that I can tell you what will happen to you *in days to come*"' (Gen. 49:1). The NIV translators have foreseen the problem by not using the expression 'latter days' at this point.[3] Jacob was not speaking about what would happen to his sons at the second coming of Christ, and still less about the twentieth century! In fact, in the case of Judah, he did refer to the *first* coming of Christ (Gen. 49:10). The rest of his remarks had to do with events in the near future.

The phrase **'will be established'** needs to noted carefully. E. J. Young insists that this 'describes a condition that will already be in existence when the latter days begin to run their course'.[4] This is crucial, for it means that Isaiah's prophecy is fulfilled, at least in part, at the moment when the 'last days' begin. The question remains: when do the 'last days' begin? New Testament writers, it seems, were conscious that they were living 'in the last days'. In his Pentecost sermon, Peter cites a prophecy from Joel:

'No, this is what was spoken by the prophet Joel:

"In the last days, God says,
  I will pour out my Spirit on all people.
Your sons and daughters will prophesy,
    your young men will see visions,
    your old men will dream dreams"'

(Acts 2:16-17).

As far as Peter is concerned, he is saying in effect: 'We are in the last days now.' The writer of Hebrews had a similar view of things (Heb. 1:2; 9:26). So did the apostle John: 'Dear children, this is the last hour; and as you have heard that the antichrist is coming, even now many antichrists have come. This is how we know it is the last hour' (1 John 2:18). What Isaiah sees — the supremacy of Judah's God over the gods of the world, the nations coming to put their trust in him and the peace that issues between people as a result of coming to faith in God — all this has already begun to take place in the New Testament. The coming of Jesus Christ, the bringer of peace, is to bring about the salvation of the nations.

2. Are we to understand this prophecy literally?

Some, who mistakenly think the latter days are necessarily at the end of the New Testament era, expect a quite literal fulfilment of these words, even to the extent of Mt Zion 'rising up' over the other mountains of Palestine! Prophecies like this one[5] are viewed as a sign that the people of Israel will at some time in the future be regathered in the land of Canaan, will enjoy prosperity and blessing, and will live under the benevolent rule of their Messiah in a millennial reign.[6] It must be remembered that the picture in (2:2) is of a river 'flowing' *up* a mountain! This is an illustration!

Others, from a quite different perspective, insist that since nothing of the magnitude depicted by Isaiah has yet taken place, we can expect to see a 'golden age', some time in the future, when a vast number of people will be converted. 'Since [these passages] cannot refer to a post-adventual reign of Christ and because nothing that has taken place in history does justice to the glory of the prophetic vision, the golden age must be yet future, but prior to Messiah's return.'[7]

Though the prophecy urges us to be optimistic about what grace will accomplish, the fact that New Testament writers are conscious of living 'in the last days' precludes either of these views. When the first token Gentiles responded to Jesus' invitation, he prophesied that in being lifted up on the cross he would draw all men to himself (John 12:32, using the same verb as in the Septuagint of Isa. 2:2). It would seem that, as often happens with prophetic pictures, the image of the future runs on into eternity. What Isaiah sees is

something which first began to see fulfilment at Pentecost, but every
conversion and revival since has been a fulfilment of it too. Eventually, however, what is in view is heaven: or more precisely, 'the new
heavens and the *new earth*'. Prophets saw into the future and we are,
in one sense, to take them literally. There is coming a time when
'The earth will be full of the knowledge of the Lord as the waters
cover the sea' (11:9). And when shall this be?

> 'Behold, I will create
>   new heavens and a new earth.
> The former things will not be remembered,
>   nor will they come to mind'
>
> (65:17).

3. What, then, is the point of the picture?

Verse 5 seems to give the clue: **'Come, O house of Jacob, let us
walk in the light of the Lord.'** Isaiah is living in a day when the
temple stands in the midst of Jerusalem in all its splendour and
beauty; but the people have no delight in God's law. There is, as
chapter 1 has outlined, the smell of apostasy in the air. Isaiah, the
evangelical preacher, sees the people and cries, 'Let us walk in the
ways of God!'[8]

Apocalypse: the Day of the Lord!

By way of contrast to the opening vision of future blessing, the rest
of the chapter is a vision of judgement. This matter will receive
fuller attention in chapters 24-27.

Three times the prophet alludes to a 'day' (2:11,12,17): 'the day
of the Lord'. Isaiah is going to pick up the phrase again in chapter
13 (where it refers in 13:6 to a day not far away and in 13:9 to a day
in the distant future). Other prophets too use this expression (Amos
5:18; Zeph. 1:14-15; Mal. 4:5). History is marching forwards. It
begins with 'the first day' (Gen. 1:5) and ends with 'the last day'
(e.g. John 6:39). Time is not cyclical or confused. Behind the events
that take place is the guiding, steering hand of the Captain. That is
why prophets like Isaiah, who walked closely with God, walked
with the end of the world on their minds.

Few things excite more interest than a study of the 'last things'. Eschatology is an area to which the prophets too were fond of alluding, so much so, that sermon-tasters in Amos' day began to look forward to 'the day of the Lord'. It seems they had a carnal interest in prophecy. Amos has to tell them that it will be a day of 'darkness, not light' (Amos 5:18). There is a dual aspect to it: there will be the salvation of the redeemed; but equally there will be judgement of the ungodly. The Bible is constantly dividing the world into two camps: the saved and the lost, the sheep and the goats, the children of God and the children of the devil, etc. The prophets are no different and part of what lies behind this fearful message is a warning that those who are not right with God can only expect to be judged.

Scanning contemporary Judah, the prophet can see nothing that would attract the nations to God. Instead he sees superstition and false alliances (2:6), wealth and armaments (2:7) and idols (2:8). Isaiah's word for 'idols' is worth noting (Heb. *'elilim*). It literally means 'worthless' (cf. Job 13:4) and, sarcastically, has been translated 'godlets'![9] Judah has everything — except faith in God! This she has cast away (2:6).

What will the day of judgement be like? What can they expect? Two matters are highlighted.

1. It is terrible!

In the time of the judges the Israelites hid in caves from the Midianites (Judg. 6:1-6). They are urged to do so again in an attempt to hide from God's wrath (2:10,19,21; cf. Matt. 24:16). The prophet is not suggesting that it will be possible to escape God's wrath. He merely wants to convey just how awful an event it will be. God's wrath is a consuming fire (Heb. 10:27; 12:29). Three times Isaiah mentions the **'dread of the Lord'** (2:10,19,21).

2. It is humbling

Isaiah refers to the **'majesty'** of God (2:10); the same word when ascribed to man is referred to as **'pride'** (2:11,17). Pride is an attempt by man to reckon himself majestic. Pride, when it manifests itself, is invariably followed by a fall, as both Uzziah and Hezekiah were to learn (2 Chron. 26:16; 32:26; cf. Prov. 16:18). God hates it

(Prov. 8:13). **'The arrogance of man will be brought low and the pride of men humbled; the Lord alone will be exalted in that day'** (2:17).

Give up!

It is hard to imagine a greater contrast than that between the two pictures presented in this chapter. One is of unprecedented blessing and the other of fearful judgement. Little wonder that the chapter ends with a plea to 'give up on man' (a literal translation of **'Stop trusting in man'**, 2:22). The verse is worthy of closer examination for it summarizes the burden of the prophet: **'Stop trusting in man, who has but a breath in his nostrils. Of what account is he?'** The words 'trusting' and 'of what account' correspond exactly to the words 'rejected' and 'esteemed' in Isaiah 53:3:

'He was despised and *rejected* by men,
    a man of sorrows, and familiar with suffering.
Like one from whom men hide their faces
    he was despised, and we *esteemed* him not.'

They gave up on the very One they should have relied upon. The sinner's epitaph is that he trusted in everyone (and everything) except the Son of God!

Summary

Isaiah has depicted the glories and the woes that are coming. There are those who will make their way to a celebration in Zion; they are the redeemed of the Lord. But there are others who have rejected Christ, God's Messiah, and are doomed. The wise will sit up and learn the lesson: 'Come... let us walk in the light of the Lord' (2:5). Are you walking in it?

3.
Progressing backwards

Please read Isaiah 3 and 4

But it seems that something has happened that
has never happened before; though we know
not just when, or why, or how, or where.
Men have left God not for other gods, they say,
but for no gods; and this has never happened before
That men both deny gods and worship gods,
professing first Reason,
And then Money, and Power, and what they call
Life, or Race, or Dialectic.
The Church disowned, the tower overthrown, the
bells upturned, what have we to do
But stand with empty hands and palms upturned
in an age which advances progressively backwards?

(T. S. Eliot).

If T. S. Eliot detected signs of decay in his own society, Solomon gives us the reason behind it: 'Righteousness exalts a nation, but sin is a disgrace to any people' (Prov. 14:34). It is Judah's disgrace that is highlighted in Isaiah 3. Having abandoned God's ways, she can expect to meet his wrath. God is coming to judge: he is about to take hold of the earth and shake it! (2:21). He is even now entering the courtroom (3:13-14). From time to time, the church needs a good shaking. Now is such a time, Isaiah says.

Essentially, what we have in chapter 3 is God's demolition of Judah: the leading features of a disintegrating society together with

the reasons for it. And it is important to remember that these features
are not simply the things for which they will be judged; these things
are themselves the very judgements of God. When God abandons
people to their sins, he is already judging them (cf. Rom. 1:18, 24-
32). Two features are singled out for attention.

1. Crippling of the leadership

Stable government is a blessing. Just as an old man will lean upon
his cane, so a nation can lean upon its leaders (3:1). There are times
when entire nations have been rallied by skilled statesmen whose
wise policy and deft handling of affairs have led people into
righteous patterns of behaviour. When a nation is about to be
overthrown, God removes such leadership. He brings confusion
into every area of the nation's life: the military, judiciary, church,
administration, craftsmanship (mechanical and scientific enterprise) — these are some of the areas singled out by the prophet (3:2-
4). The 'staff' has been removed from Judah. '**Judah is falling**'
(3:8). Instead, the leadership is given to children (3:4,12) and
women! (3:12). It is a tragedy when the leadership of any nation or
institution is given into the hands of the inexperienced, the incom-
petent, the unwise, or the weak.

2. Crippling of the social order

Verse 1 of chapter 3 mentions economic paralysis. Things were
already difficult in Jerusalem, but about 100 years after this time the
invasion by Assyria would make conditions so bad that some in
Jerusalem would be forced to eat their own children! Economic
policy is linked to divine chastisement. One feature of their social
behaviour is worthy of notice: '**The young will rise up against the
old**' (3:5). Disregard of parents was something God legislated for in
the Ten Commandments (Exod. 20:12). It is a sign of God's
abandonment when disobedient children are in the ascendancy (cf.
Rom. 1:30).

    Anarchy — this is the description of Judah in Isaiah's time. The
book was never more relevant than it is to our own day. Having
elevated the individual to be the measure of all things, modern man
is guided by his own darkened heart; there is nothing to respect or
obey, there are no principles to live or die for. Personal feeling,

personal advancement, personal autonomy are the shrines at which he worships. Good government is a blessing that God gives (Rom. 13:1-7). Rulers are meant to be ministers of good to those who obey as well as terror to the wicked. Government is meant to ensure order, liberty, freedom of worship and to promote justice. When such leaders are absent, as they were in Judah (3:7), it is a time of much trouble.

Parading sin

The reasons for Judah's disintegration are now given. Reasons in the plural, yes; but ultimately there is only one: God has been provoked (3:8-9). Things are done openly, brazenly! 'They do not hide it.' A generation has arisen who has forgotten how to blush with shame. As in our own century, sin is paraded openly in the streets. Things once done in secret are now public matters. The cause for the deterioration in Judah was sin. **'They parade their sin like Sodom'** (3:9). The prophet could have said that and closed the book, but like all good evangelical preachers he goes on to expose the sin; he spells it out in detail and applies it to the consciences of his hearers. The passage under consideration is a continuation of Isaiah's second vision (2:6-22). To capture the full extent of the prophet's condemnation we shall need to return to material in the second chapter.

1. The sin of superstition

'They are full of superstitions from the East; they practise divination like the Philistines and clasp hands with pagans' (2:6). The law had expressly forbidden the practice of divination: 'Let no one be found among you who sacrifices his son or daughter in the fire, who practises divination or sorcery, interprets omens, engages in witchcraft, or casts spells, or who is a medium or spiritist or who consults the dead' (Deut. 18:10-11). Three types are mentioned in Ezekiel 21: *rhabdomancy*: throwing sticks or bones in the air to see which way they fell; *hepatoscopy*: examining the markings on the liver of a sacrifice, and *idolatry*: consulting images. It is something Isaiah will take up again in 47:13. Religion had become superstition. Like so many today, they dabbled in it 'just in case'.

2. Materialism

> 'Their land is full of silver and gold;
>   there is no end to their treasures.
> Their land is full of horses;
>   there is no end to their chariots'

(2:7).

Here are people who live for their possessions. They spend their lives in the pursuit of material things. It is the same today. Communism — the religion of materialism — has been demonstrated to be bankrupt. But capitalism can become the servant of mammon. Never has the West had so much and yet been so poor. Death is the final blow to materialism. As David was to say on the eve of his death, 'But who am I, and who are my people, that we should be able to give as generously as this? Everything comes from you, and we have given you only what comes from your hand. We are aliens and strangers in your sight, as were all our forefathers. Our days on earth are like a shadow, without hope' (1 Chron. 29:14-15). To live in the light of this insight is wise.

3. Idolatry

'Their land is full of idols' (2:8). Idolatry is worship in which the honour due to God, and due to him alone, is given to some of his creatures, or some invention of his creatures. You do not have to abandon God entirely to be guilty of idolatry. The Israelites never forsook God entirely, even when they worshipped the golden calf. 'These are your gods,' they said and a feast was kept in honour of the calf as a feast 'unto the Lord' (Exod. 32:4-5). Likewise when Jeroboam asked the ten tribes to commit idolatry, he never asked them to abandon Jehovah. He suggested instead that it was too far to come to Jerusalem, so calves were set up in Dan and Bethel (1 Kings 12:28-29). The idolatrous calf was a 'stepping stone' to 'aid' them in worshipping God, in much the same way that Mary or the relics of saints are 'aids' in Roman Catholicism. Idolatry is the natural tendency of a man's heart. This accounts for the spectacular success of Catholicism. Whatever the outward form, it is wrong. 'I am the Lord; that is my name! I will not give my glory to another or my praise to idols' (42:8). Idolatry is robbery: it robs God of his glory.

4. *Sensuality, sex and self-esteem*

In a scathing attack upon three interrelated vices Isaiah explodes on women (3:16-26). They are vain, arrogant, self-centred and narcissistic. They love beauty, but not 'the beauty of holiness' which shines in God (Ps. 50:2). They walk with their necks stretched out (3:16). 'Whenever dress and splendour are carried to excess,' says Calvin, 'there is evidence of ambition and many vices are connected with it; for whence comes luxury in men and women but from pride?' Peter reminds his readers that women are to be modest in dress, concerned more with godliness (1 Peter 3:3-4).

However much we may be startled by these words from Isaiah to the women of Jerusalem, they are positively complimentary by comparison with the words of Amos. He had the audacity to refer to them as 'cows of Bashan'! (Amos 4:1). In 1558 John Knox could write in similar vein. He published a tract entitled *The First Blast of the Trumpet against the Monstrous Regiment of Women*! Elizabeth I, who came to power that same year, was so shocked by it that she had Knox permanently debarred from the realm. The 'petticoat regiment' of Jerusalem no doubt felt the same about Isaiah. It takes courage to be God's spokesman in days of decline.

All these factors have aroused the wrath of God. Judah has violated the covenant and must face the consequences (cf. Deut. 28). Few things come across so clearly in the Bible as God's declared opposition to sin. God is the Judge and he has now taken his seat (3:13; cf. Ps. 75:7). He is the Judge of all (Heb. 12:23). Merely scan through Bible history and you will see it time and again: the expulsion of Adam and Eve from Eden; the flood in Noah's time; the destruction of Sodom and Gomorrah; the plagues of Egypt; the result of the rebellion of folk like Nadab, Abihu, Koran, Dathan and Abiram; the Assyrian invasion; the Babylonian captivity; and in the New Testament, just in case we mistakenly get the idea that somehow this is 'all Old Testament', we are told the chilling story of the judicial death of Ananias and Sapphira — for lying! It has to be this way, for God is morally just.

But is there no hope for a fallen society? Does the sinner have anywhere to turn? Yes! Isaiah's message is double-edged: of doom for unrepentant sinners and of hope for those who turn to God. Like a golden thread woven through the tapestry of this book is the promise of a Saviour, the 'Servant of the Lord', the 'Prince of Peace', who will save a remnant, the election of grace.

Running along in harmony with this theme is another: that it is God's purpose to advance his church by intermittent judgements. This is his winnowing work. Lean times are sifting times. Thus God has shaken Judah and, perhaps, ourselves too as we read these words of Scripture. Our lives, just as theirs, are too often out of shape. We too need to be shaken so that we may see sense and walk in the light (2:5). And to help us do that, Isaiah introduces us once more to the Saviour and the promises of the gospel which are 'Yes' and 'Amen' in him (2 Cor. 1:20). Following hard on chapter 3 is a chapter which promises renewal and advancement. Persevering through Isaiah's prophecy can be so wonderfully encouraging to Christians who are looking for grace to help them live for God.

The Branch (4:2-6)

Carmarthen is a town in South-West Wales. As a boy it was the nearest 'big' town to where I lived. I loved going there on a Saturday afternoon and wandering through its many streets. It was noted for an old oak tree which, it has been said, grew from an acorn planted on 19 May 1659 by a schoolmaster named Adams, of the old Queen Elizabeth Grammar School, in order to mark the end of the Commonwealth and the town's proclamation of Charles II as king. Mythology had cast a spell upon the fate of the town (supposedly dating back to the Arthurian legend of Merlin in the twelfth century) if ever the tree died. Should it fall, the town would be flooded: 'When Merlin's tree shall tumble down, then shall Carmarthen town.' For many years the town council went to great lengths to secure it from falling. It was just a stump of decaying bark when I was growing up. Now it is gone and the town is still there.[1]

Judah was like this decaying tree in so many ways. Its life seemed almost at an end. But from it would emerge a 'Branch' that would give it fresh life and renewal.

At first sight the expression, **'Branch of the Lord'** (4:2) is a little strange. Other prophets used the phrase also (Jer. 23:5; 33:15; Zech. 3:8; 6:12). It is the picture of something sprouting and coming up out of the ground, or a twig which grows from the trunk of a tree. Since the context is that of a vineyard (3:14; 5:1) it is a tree that he has in mind from which a branch grows. What is only hinted at here is made explicit later. This Branch comes from the stump of Jesse's house (11:1).[2] The Branch is an offshoot of David (Jer. 23:5-6; 33:15-16). It is the son God promised to David when he entered into a covenant with him (2 Sam. 7:11-16). Even with all the threats that have just been issued against Judah, God has not forgotten his promise. The house of David will continue to grow; eventually the Branch will emerge as promised.

The judgement is a refiner's fire (4:4). What emerges through the fire will be pure. In fact, Isaiah uses language that is reminiscent of what God had promised to Moses. 'Cloud', 'fire' and 'shelter' are all words recalling Israel's desert wanderings, when a pillar of cloud and fire guided and protected the people: 'By day the Lord went ahead of them in a pillar of cloud to guide them on their way and by night in a pillar of fire to give them light, so that they could travel by day or night. Neither the pillar of cloud by day nor the pillar of fire by night left its place in front of the people... Then Moses stretched out his hand over the sea, and all that night the Lord drove the sea back with a strong east wind and turned it into dry land. The waters were divided, and the Israelites went through the sea on dry ground, with a wall of water on their right and on their left' (Exod. 13:21-22; 14:21-22).

From Moses to David to Isaiah's day, God remained faithful to his word. God is a God who can be trusted. He is a shelter in the time of storm for those who know him.

The Lord's our Rock. In him we hide,
A shelter in the time of storm
Secure whatever ill betide,
A shelter in the time of storm

(Vernon Charlesworth).

Summary

When a nation finds itself as crippled as this one there is only one remedy. Looking to Jesus is Isaiah's answer to those who discover that their lives are out of sorts. Like Judah, when our own nation has departed from God and is ripe for judgement, running headlong into certain destruction, the only remedy is revival and restoration. It proceeds from God's righteous Branch: Jesus Christ!

4.
God: the fruit-picker!

Please read Isaiah 5

According to A. W. Tozer, 'The church's mightiest influence is felt when she is different from the world in which she lives.'[1] The lack of vigorous consecration in the lives of God's people no doubt accounts for the church's relative ineffectiveness today. Holiness is one of the great needs of our time.

Holiness was a frequent theme in the preaching of Jesus. One of his parables relates the story of a man with a fig tree (Luke 13:6-9). For three years in succession the owner of the fig tree came seeking fruit, but found none. Eventually he ordered that the tree be cut down, but the gardener intervened, pleading that a stay of execution be granted for a year, during which time he would do all in his power to induce it to bring forth fruit. If after a year the tree was still fruitless, the tree could be cut down. The owner's patience was not to last indefinitely.

Another parable tells the story of a farmer whose vineyard is in the hands of tenants (Matt. 21:33-44). When the time of harvest comes, the farmer sends his servants to collect his portion, only to have them abused, beaten and even killed. Last of all, the farmer sends his son, who is shamefully killed. The net result is that the vineyard is taken away from these tenants and given to others.

Whether or not Jesus' parables are directly based on Isaiah 5, the message is identical: sooner or later, God's patience with sinners runs out.[2] He expects his people to be fruitful.

God's disappointment?

Isaiah's parable repeats an indictment against the Old Testament church that we have already heard in chapter 1. We have also seen God's church likened to a vineyard (3:14). Here the charge is in the form of a **'song'** (5:1) and we are meant to believe it is going be a love-song. But it isn't; it is a formal indictment of Judah's sinful ways.

Vineyards have only one purpose: to produce grapes for the year's vintage. The owner has gone to the lengths of hewing out a wine vat out of solid rock (5:2) into which he will place the grapes for crushing and extracting the juice. An allusion to this process can be found in 16:10: 'No one treads out wine at the presses, for I have put an end to the shouting.'

What is the Christian life essentially about? Isaiah's answer is consistent with the rest of the Bible: God wants his people to be holy. In every born-again heart, God has planted a desire for holiness: to walk as close to God as is possible, letting our lives be changed by the Holy Spirit's transforming power. At its very heart lies the idea of separation: thus Christians are to be different, reflecting the fact that they are no longer what they once were. Holiness, fruit-bearing to use Isaiah's picture here, is an urgent priority, for without it we shall not see God (Heb. 12:14). Some have notions that heaven can be attained without it, but they are mistaken. 'A "saint" in whom nothing can be seen but worldliness or sin' writes J. C. Ryle, 'is a kind of monster not recognized in the Bible!'[3]

Unfruitful trees can expect to be cut down. John the Baptist taught this (Matt. 3:10), and so did Jesus (Matt. 7:19). This is the explanation of the curious incident of the cursing of the fig tree, when, seeing the tree devoid of figs, Jesus said, 'May you never bear fruit again!' (Matt. 21:19). Jesus did not lose his temper, as has sometimes been implied. The fig tree was a symbol for Israel, who had rejected God's Son. 'This is to my Father's glory, that you bear much fruit, showing yourselves to be my disciples... You did not choose me, but I chose you and appointed you to go and bear fruit — fruit that will last' (John 15:8,16).

What God looks for

Three particular features are discernible as examples of what the Divine Fruit-picker is looking for.

1. A concerned people

The prophet returns in verse 7 to a theme mentioned in the first chapter (1:17). His people are to show kindness to the helpless and needy. Far from helping the needy, they are exploiting them, robbing them of their land (5:8) and accepting bribes (5:23).

2. A consistent people

A powerful play on words in the Hebrew makes a very telling point (5:7). God wants **'justice'** (Hebrew: *mishpat*) but finds **'bloodshed'** *(mispah)*; he looks for **'righteousness'** *(zedaqah)* but finds **'distress'** *(se'aqah)*. The words sound so alike, but in each case what sounds like the real thing is actually only a pretence. The grapes may have looked sweet, but they tasted sour. God hates pretence in religion. He wants consistency.

3. A Christlike people

God looked for righteousness and justice. These are qualities manifested by the Saviour (1 John 2:1; 1 Peter 3:18). God wants his people to be like his Son in holiness. We are to follow in his steps (1 Peter 2:21).

Real privileges

Judah had received every motivation possible. Such is God's remonstrance to them:

> **'What more could have been done for my vineyard**
>   **than I have done for it?**
> **When I looked for good grapes,**
>   **why did it yield only bad?'**

(5:4).

The vineyard had been carefully dug and cleared of stones (5:2). These same stones may well have been used to build the **'watchtower'**, where the vinedresser could live permanently in the summer to guard against thieves and marauders. Every indication is given of the exhaustive work that had gone into this vineyard. And still it only produced 'bad grapes'. The vines were also chosen with great care. The word **'choicest'** in 5:2 is the Hebrew word *sorek*. It was in the 'valley of Sorek' that Samson fell in love with a woman called Delilah (Judg. 16:4). These vines may well have come from Sorek and be what we would call today 'named varieties'. Even with all these privileges and tender care, these vines still produced only sour grapes. There is something unnatural about it.

God had chosen Israel to be his elect nation (41:8-10). He had entered into covenant with Abraham and promised wonderful things. But they had been so ungrateful. The grumblings in the desert (cf. Exod. 14:11) had now taken root in their hearts. It now appeared as though most (but not all) were either backslidden or entirely unregenerate.

The application is relevant to church members today. God has fulfilled his promise. His Son has come and secured salvation for his people. God could not have done more than he has done. It is unimaginable that a greater price could be paid for our salvation than the judgement that fell upon his own Son at Calvary. It is more than likely that you profess to be a Christian or you would not be reading this book! Where is the fruit of your faith? There are many who claim that once they are saved 'they are always saved' — irrespective of the works that should accompany faith. This is a fallacy. The doctrine of perseverance must always take into account those who merely claim to have been converted, but in reality they have not. The seed sown on the ground in Jesus' parable in some cases grew to a great height. But the fact that it died before producing fruit revealed that it was not genuine (Matt. 13:3-9,18-23). How much fruit can be seen in your heart?

Real problems!

I wonder if you have said to yourself, 'If it wasn't for these problems I would be the most fruitful Christian in the world!' The people of Judah were fond of excusing their fruitlessness by blaming it on the difficulties that filled their lives. The parable mentions three of them. Firstly, the fence that surrounded the vineyard was broken (5:5). Wild beasts were a problem in much the same way as stray sheep and cows can be in a field of corn today. Secondly, briers and thorns were hampering the growth of the vines (5:6) and thirdly, there was a drought (5:6). The result was that a ten-acre vineyard produced only a few gallons of wine (5:10; a **'bath'** is about eight gallons), and in the future, sheep and lambs would graze where once these vines were planted (5:17). The vineyard was all but destroyed. The psalmist paints a similar picture when he says,

> 'You brought a vine out of Egypt;
>   you drove out the nations and planted it.
> You cleared the ground for it,
>   and it took root and filled the land.
> The mountains were covered with its shade,
>   the mighty cedars with its branches.
> It sent out its boughs to the Sea,
>   its shoots as far as the River.
> Why have you broken down its walls
>   so that all who pass by pick its grapes?
> Boars from the forest ravage it
>   and the creatures of the field feed on it'
>
>   (Ps. 80:8-13)

The six woes (5:8-23)

What kind of fruit did Judah produce? Six woes spell it out (5:8,11,18,20,21,22).

1. *Greed* is demonstrated in their desire for more and more property (5:8), disregarding the law which safeguarded the poor and ultimately proclaimed that all land belonged to God (Lev. 25:23). We are only pilgrims on earth and materialistic greed is a denial of it (Heb. 11:13; 1 Peter 2:11).

2. *Drunkenness* was a problem then, as now (5:11-12). It accounts for much evil in the world. Other prophets systematically condemn it (Amos 4:1-3; 6:6-7). Isaiah was familiar with the disgusting

spectacle of a drunk who could only 'stagger around in his own vomit' (19:14), and with men who knew how to mix cocktails (5:22). The picture of men and women living for pleasure and escapism (5:11-12) is a familiar enough one. In this drunken stupor, they cannot think straight. They are beyond reason (cf. 1:18). 'Men were not born to eat and drink, and wallow in luxury,' writes Calvin, 'but to obey God, to worship him devoutly, to acknowledge his goodness, and to endeavour to do what is pleasing in his sight. But when they give themselves up to luxury, when they dance, and sing, and have no other object in view than to spend their life in the highest mirth, they are worse than beasts: for they do not *consider* for what end God created them, in what manner he governs this world by his providence, and to what end all the actions of our life ought to be directed.'[4]

3. *Cynicism* in religious matters is another feature. Scoffers, such as those depicted in verse 19, drag sin along behind them like oxen pulling on heavy carts. When the yoke of God is 'easy' and 'light' (cf. Matt. 11:30), they prefer the burdensome oppression of sin around their necks. Such is the extent of their cynicism that they mock the promises and warnings of God (5:19). In their blasphemous taunts, they show that they despise God.

4. *Distortion* is another feature. The perversion of the sinful heart is that it calls **'evil good, and good evil'** (5:20). 'Doctrine and ethics are close partners' remarks E. J. Young.[5] The unbeliever, in attempting to justify his ways, stands reality on its head! In the darkness of his heart he has convinced himself that his ways are right. This leads to the next woe.

5. *Foolishness.* Sin believes itself to be always in the right (5:21). The beginning of wisdom is to acknowledge God and his ways (Ps. 111:10; Prov. 9:10), but men and women who lack true wisdom lean back upon themselves. Believing themselves to be wise, they are, in fact, fools (Ps. 14:1; 53:1; Matt. 7:26).

6. *Corruption* is the final feature. Returning to the drunkards in Judah, a further woe is pronounced upon them: they are cheaters who will accept a bribe and call it justice (5:22-23; cf. 10:1-2).

Behind all this lies the love of money — the root of all evil (1 Tim. 6:10).

This is Judah's fruit: a sixfold catalogue of corruption! The vine is diseased. This is a theme to which the prophets refer to again and again. Jeremiah called Israel 'a corrupt, wild vine' (Jer. 2:21), and Hosea called her a 'spreading vine' (Hosea 10:1). To every woe is attached a judgement. Thus the houses are to be laid waste (5:9), the arrogant will be humbled (5:15) and the drunkards will die of thirst (5:13,24). God's anger will burn against them and he will strike them down (5:25). The grave will open wide and receive them (5:14). God's hand is stretched out against them. He raises a banner on the hilltop as a sign of the approaching army. God's patience has run out. Assyria will come and destroy them. The picture is awesome. The enemy comes in power and appears invincible (5:26-27). We shall glimpse Assyria's legendary military might again, but the point we need to catch here is that *God has sent them*. God is shaking the foundations!

Isaiah sees bodies lying in heaps on the streets (5:25), and all because

'The Lord's anger burns against his people;
his hand is raised and he strikes them down.
The mountains shake,
and the dead bodies are like refuse in the streets.
Yet for all this, his anger is not turned away,
his hand is still upraised'

(5:25).

We shall see this hand again. For now the message is clear: for those who insist on pursuing a life outside of Jesus Christ, there isn't a ray of hope. As Jesus said, 'Every plant that my heavenly Father has not planted will be pulled up by the roots' (Matt. 15:13).

Christians must make sure that they abide in Christ (John 15:4-6; NIV 'remain'). J. C. Ryle paraphrases what Jesus is saying in John 15 like this: 'Abide in me. Cling to me. Stick fast to me. Live the life of close and intimate communion with me. Get nearer and nearer to me. Roll every burden on me. Cast your whole weight on me. Never let go your hold on me for a moment...'[6]

Summary

Isaiah has depicted an unholy church. This is a contradiction in terms. Authentic Christian holiness is a visible manifestation of the inward life of Christ in our hearts. It was evidently missing in the church of the prophet's day. And God is angry with his people. He is shaking the foundations. Is this what may be happening in our day?

5.
Isaiah meets God

Please read Isaiah 6

Some day we shall meet God. It will be an awesome occasion when we shall stand before him for judgement. Should we find ourselves there with no covering for our sins, it will be to hear the Lord casting us away from his presence. If, however, our sins have been washed 'as white as snow' (1:18) it will be to hear his Son bid us welcome: to enjoy the glory of heaven for ever. Forgiveness is something we must secure *before* we die if we are to make sure of heaven. The purpose of Isaiah 6 is, partly, to inform us that the prophet was a forgiven man.

It would seem that Isaiah was already serving as a prophet (he had received revelation from God while Uzziah was alive, see 1:1). Though it is sometimes portrayed this way, it is not necessary to think of Isaiah 6 as an account of Isaiah's conversion experience. That would imply that the prophet had been ministering in Jerusalem as an unconverted man (in much the same way that John Wesley or Thomas Chalmers had been before God awakened them). Isaiah's visit to the temple was part of his ongoing desire to walk with his Lord and seek his will.[1] What happened that day in the temple was a deepening of everything that he already knew about God and himself as God's servant.

The chapter opens with a precise reference to a date: it is the year 739 B.C. It may also have been the Day of Atonement (the **'live coal'** (6:6) was something which was used on that day, Lev. 16:12). Dates in the Old Testament can be a little tricky, but Isaiah pin-points with total accuracy the time when he met with God in the temple: it was in **'the year that King Uzziah died'**.

There is more to this than just a passing interest in dates. It was a year that stood out as a turning-point in the history of nations. In the northern kingdom, Jeroboam had also died. And further north still an empire was spreading, whose ferocity was to destroy Israel entirely and terrorize Judah to the point of near collapse. Led by one of its most able kings, Tiglath-Pileser III, Assyria saw its opportunity with a weakened kingdom of Syria, a fragmented Israel and a frightened Judah. The hapless Palestinian kingdoms looked around for potential allies and thus Egypt — once their bitterest enemy — emerges as a 'friend'. Egypt had no love for Judah or Israel, but neither did she want Assyria on her doorstep. But all this is still future at this stage.

Uzziah had come to the throne at the age of sixteen and reigned for half a century. Under his leadership Judah had expanded. He was also a good king, starting out, unlike his father Amaziah, to follow the Lord wholeheartedly (2 Chron. 26:5,15; cf. 25:2). However, towards the end of his life, Uzziah committed an act of sacrilege by offering incense on the altar of incense in the temple (2 Chron. 26:16). He was confronted by Azariah the priest and eighty other priests and firmly rebuked. As a judgement, he was to suffer leprosy for the rest of his life (2 Chron. 26:18-21).

It is in this very temple that Isaiah was now worshipping God, no doubt conscious of the events that had taken place a few years earlier. Perhaps, as Sinclair Ferguson suggests, he was thinking, 'This is where Uzziah came that day; there is where he went in order to reach the incense altar. Here is where Azariah and the priests must have come...'[2] It was just then that he was 'lifted out of time into eternity'. Such astonishing things can happen when we worship God! And Isaiah is eager to relate an experience to us that utterly devastated him. He was never the same man again.

The throne of God

What happened that day was akin to what the apostle Paul saw, but could *not* relate (see 2 Cor. 12:2-6), and what the apostle John saw, and *did* relate (Rev. 1:9-19). It was a vision of God. Isaiah saw **'the Lord seated on a throne, high and exalted, and the train of his robe filled the temple'** (6:1). It is important that at the very start we identify who 'the Lord' is that Isaiah saw. In John's Gospel, Isaiah 6:10 is quoted:

'He has blinded their eyes
and deadened their hearts,
so they can neither see with their eyes,
nor understand with their hearts,
nor turn — and I would heal them'

(John 12:40).

According to John, 'Isaiah said this because he saw Jesus' glory and spoke about him' (John 12:41). It was Jesus whom Isaiah encountered in the temple. The God of the Old Testament, so often disparaged and vilified, is none other than Jesus Christ! The apostle John could tell you that he too saw a similar vision of Jesus Christ (Rev. 1:9-19). He could also tell you that this Jesus was both 'with God' and '*was* God' (John 1:1). The mystery of the Trinity tells us that there is more to God than Jesus Christ, but that Jesus Christ is the only God there is. God, in the mystery and unity of his triune being, is revealing a little about himself through the Son.

Jesus (God) is sovereign. The vision is of a throne which is 'high and exalted'. This tells us two things straight away.

First, *God is not to be trifled with.* We live in an age when talk about God is cheap and irreverent. Worship is cheapened by concentrating on what are felt to be human needs. Entertainment takes the place of worship. Who believes these days that folk like Ananias and Sapphira could be struck down dead for telling a lie about the price of some property they had sold? (Acts 5:1-11). But the God Isaiah encountered in the temple that day was awesome.

Second, it is a matter of enormous encouragement to a prophet who must visit the king's palace to know that *the ultimate authority belongs to God.* To have this etched onto our hearts can make all the difference to a Christian worker. In days of pressure, when we may have to face difficult situations, it is this kind of knowledge that strengthens us. It is this that made Daniel strong: he could face the lions' mouths secure in the knowledge that God was in control (Dan. 6:22). For Isaiah the facts were simple: God is in control, he is one to be reckoned with, he is the only God there is. These themes dominate his entire ministry. They were etched on his heart that day he visited the temple. 'The more we know of God,' Gresham Machen once said, 'the more unreservedly we will trust him; the greater our progress in theology, the simpler and more childlike will be our faith.' Isaiah would agree with him.

God is great

Take a look at the **'seraphs'** (6:2). Seraphs are angelic beings not mentioned elsewhere. The 'living creatures' of Revelation 4:6-9 are also said to have 'six wings' and may be identical. What is signifi-cant is not so much who they are, but what they are doing.

'With two wings they covered their faces' suggests that they could not gaze directly at God's glory; they cover their faces with two of their wings. This suggests restraint. There are things about God that he keeps to himself. God is incomprehensible: not in the sense that he cannot be known at all, but that he cannot be known fully. There are aspects of him that defy our understanding. God has revealed only that which we need to know. Some Christians are not content with the mystery of God. They keep on asking questions when a veil has been firmly drawn. It is the way of wisdom to learn from the seraphs a measure of restraint in his presence. God is answerable to no one. There is a time to stop asking questions and get down to worshipping him. 'If angels,' Calvin remarks, 'are overwhelmed by the majesty of God, how great will be the rashness of men if they venture to intrude so far! Let us, therefore, learn that our enquiries concerning God ought never to go beyond what is proper and lawful, that our knowledge may soberly and modestly taste what is far above our capacity.'[3]

'With two they covered their feet' suggests further that they were attempting to cover, not just their feet, but their bodies also, as though they wanted to blot themselves out of the picture entirely. Whenever I get discouraged, an older, more experienced Christian tells me, 'Put yourself out of the picture and see none but Jesus only.' It is seraphic advice. Worship ought to be like that, where we lose ourselves in him. Modern worship services pander too often to the needs of man. True worship exalts God.

This feature also suggests unapproachability. It is not just that we are sinners. That makes matters more difficult, but the separation is there already. These seraphs were sinless, yet they felt unable to come too close to God. There is something about him that calls upon the seraphs to keep their distance. What astonishing closeness to God Christians enjoy! Calling him 'Our Father' only underlines the wonderful grace of God that he allows us, through faith in his Son, to come so close!

'With two they were flying' suggests a picture of humming birds! It is possible to see the seraphs moving to and fro at God's bidding, ready to do whatever he asks.

God is near

'The whole earth is full of his glory,' cried the seraphs, by which they meant that God is near. 'Glory' means God showing us that he is near. For those who have no desire to think that God is aware of what they are doing, this is not good news. But for those who have experienced something of his love and forgiveness it is a wonderful truth. God is the Holy One 'among you' (12:6). He is with us, around us, and in us. That means we are to be on our guard. We want him to search us as did the psalmist in Psalm 139 when he thought about this truth also:

'O Lord, you have searched me
  and you know me.
You know when I sit and when I rise;
  you perceive my thoughts from afar.
You discern my going out and my lying down;
  you are familiar with all my ways...
Search me, O God, and know my heart;
  test me and know my anxious thoughts'

(Ps. 139:1-3,23).

God is holy

The seraphs proclaim the holiness of God: **'Holy, holy, holy is the Lord Almighty'** (6:3). This threefold repetition is the Bible's way of underlining its importance. 'Holy' in Hebrew has the basic idea of being separate or different. Applied to God it conveys all that makes God who he is: that which makes him God and not man. The separation is one of exaltation and therefore implies the need to worship and adore him. It carries with it, too, the thought that, unlike us, God is pure and that means trouble for sinners whose sin is unatoned for. That the vision of God's holiness impressed Isaiah greatly can be seen from his use on twenty-five occasions of the expression 'the Holy One of Israel'.[4] This is hardly surprising because one day when he was worshipping God, the entire temple had shaken and filled up with smoke. Isaiah, like Moses, had witnessed the glory of God (cf. Exod. 19:18-19; 20:18-19).

The effect of this on Isaiah was devastating. He felt utterly convicted by his sins and cried out: '**Woe to me!... I am ruined! For I am a man of unclean lips, and I live among a people of unclean lips, and my eyes have seen the King, the Lord Almighty**' (6:5). From one point of view this cry seemed out of place. Did not Isaiah have the cleanest lips in Jerusalem? Had he not spoken the Word of God? In comparison with his fellow citizens, Isaiah was a holy man. But as all Christians will know, the more we know of God, the more sinful by comparison we feel ourselves to be. It is a remarkable fact that Paul appeared to grow in his appreciation of his sinfulness, saying to the Corinthians that he was the least of the apostles (1 Cor. 15:9, *c.* 54 A.D.), to the Ephesians that he was the least of all saints (Eph. 3:8, *c.* 61 A.D.) and to Timothy that he was the chief of sinners (1 Tim. 1:15, *c.* 64 A.D.). 'When the corn is nearly ripe,' wrote the Puritan John Flavel, 'it bows the head and stoops lower than it was when green. When the people of God are ripe for heaven, they grow more humble and self-denying...' Isaiah wasn't ripe for heaven just yet, but he was being prepared for a lifetime of service; the more he appreciated his unworthiness of the task, the better he would exalt the Lord who was commissioning him.

If we are to be useful for God we shall need to be humbled like he was. God uses the humble to exalt his name. The proud and arrogant he will humble one day (2:12). Better to be humbled now and receive forgiveness, than to be humbled at the judgement seat and be cast away. If you want to grow in grace, there is no easy, painless way of going about it. There are no short cuts to holiness. God must show us the wretchedness of our hearts and then begin the lifelong process of rebuilding our lives to be what they should be. For Isaiah it was a discovery of something he already knew, but inadequately: the fact that in our hearts, as Robert Murray

M'Cheyne said, lie the seeds of every known sin. Discovering that truth can overwhelm us as it did Isaiah. He was broken up before God, dismayed at the revelation of his depravity. Though he was a prophet of God, he was in essence 'only a sinner saved by grace'.

God is merciful

The fifth strand of God's character disclosed to the prophet is that he is full of mercy to those who repent of their sins. **'Then one of the seraphs flew to me with a live coal in his hand, which he had taken with tongs from the altar. With it he touched my mouth and said, "See, this has touched your lips; your guilt is taken away and your sin atoned for"'** (6:6-7). Coals of fire were taken inside the Most Holy Place on the Day of Atonement (Lev. 16:12), when sacrifice was made to atone for sin.

It is only *after* he has confessed his sins that the seraphs come with God's word of forgiveness. This is always the order of Scripture. It was the burden of Jesus' first recorded sermon (Matt. 4:17). It was a failure to appreciate this that caused the rich young man to walk away from Jesus (Mark 10:22).

The coal is applied to Isaiah's 'lips' — the very part he found sinful and unworthy. Think of the pain. Isaiah was given, in essence, a preview of the cross — the altar of sacrifice. From the perspective of the New Testament, his sins were atoned for by the application of the blood of Jesus Christ to his guilty conscience. God takes the initiative to find a way to forgive our sins. This is the burden of Isaiah's message.

Several things follow which helped Isaiah overcome discouragement in his own ministry.

1. An appreciation of his calling

This encounter with God (cf. Amos' encounter with Amaziah in Amos 7), a fresh reminder of God's love for him which is so thoroughly undeserved, impels him into service. **'Then I heard the voice of the Lord saying, "Whom shall I send? And who will go for us?" And I said, "Here am I. Send me!"'** (6:8). God makes demands on us; that is his right. As I have written elsewhere, 'As

Christians, we are to serve our Master. The Lord has something for
each of us to do for him. Learning what our special task for God is
can be both frustrating and rewarding at the same time. Frustrating,
because the process of learning it is hardly ever as straightforward
as we imagine. Rewarding, because there is nothing in this life more
pleasant than knowing we are doing our Father's will.'⁵ Isaiah knew
all about this and he was about to launch forth on a lifetime of
ministry as a prophet, a mouthpiece of God.

2. An appreciation that, with privilege, comes difficulty

Isaiah learned that with service come difficulties and opposition.
Every young Christian wants success; but often we are made to feel
that any success we have is of God and not of ourselves. The way
God underlines it is to show us that we are bankrupt without his help.
Maybe Isaiah needed to learn this lesson. He was a high-ranking
prophet with access to the royal chambers. Maybe he was dreaming
of a successful ministry. God comes to him with a warning:

'Go and tell this people:

"Be ever hearing, but never understanding;
be ever seeing, but never perceiving."
Make the heart of this people calloused;
make their ears dull
and close their eyes.
Otherwise they might see with their eyes,
hear with their ears,
understand with their hearts,
and turn and be healed'

(6:9-10).

This is not encouraging for a young man! Isaiah was warned that
his message was going to be rejected; men and women would
become hardened to his message, as they do to ours today.

We may ask, what is the cause of unbelief? Isaiah is telling us
here that a part of the answer to this question lies with a judicial sentence brought about by God himself! To underline the point, John
picks up verses 9-10 by way of an explanation of the widespread

disbelief of the Jewish people in Christ's day, who looked for a Messiah, but steadfastly refused to acknowledge Christ as the fulfilment of that hope (John 12:37-43); the people of John's day did not believe because they *could not*! Isaiah will return to this point at the end of the book, begging God to show mercy (cf. 63:15-19). The truth that God hardens the hearts of sinners is taught frequently in the Scriptures (Rom. 9:18; 2 Thess. 2:11). But it is equally important to bear in mind that the hearts that he hardens are not morally neutral, but corrupt and sinful. If the sovereignty of God in these matters troubles us, we should also remember that only a sovereign God can redeem us.

The chapter ends with a warning that Judah's cities will be destroyed (6:11) and the inhabitants taken **'far away'** (6:12). In the distant future there is a glimmer of hope: a 'stump' remains after a tree is cut down. Though it is small, there will be a remnant who will remain faithful and through whom God's promises will continue to unfold (6:13). It is not much, but it is all that Isaiah can expect. We are called, as the old saying goes, 'to be faithful and not fruitful'. Instant success is not something we can count on; it is something only God can give. To be as faithful to God as Isaiah was is something we should pray for right now.

3. A concern for theology in preaching

C. H. Spurgeon was convinced as to the need for a minister to study theology. 'We shall never have great preachers,' he said, 'till we have great divines.'[6] The same thought comes from the hymn writer Isaac Watts, living a hundred years earlier. Samuel Johnson said of him: 'Whatever he took in hand was, by his incessant solicitude for souls, converted to theology.'[7]

4. A sense of the majesty of God in preaching

James Stewart, the famous Scottish preacher, and author of the book *Heralds of God*, wrote that genuine preaching is: 'to quicken the conscience by the holiness of God, to feed the mind with the truth of God, to purge the imagination by the beauty of God, to open the heart to the love of God, to devote the will to the purpose of God'.[8]

What is true of preaching must be equally true of listening to preaching and the effect that must have on our lives.

Summary

We should make it our aim to extol the majesty of God: the freedom of his sovereign will to do as he pleases without question from sinners like ourselves. Are we responding to preaching as Isaiah responded that day in the temple? J. I. Packer tells us how he felt when he first heard Dr Martyn Lloyd-Jones' preaching: he brought to him 'more of a sense of God than any other man'.[9] We, too, need 'a sense of God' as we read and study the Scriptures. Isaiah was never the same again. His message became one dominated by the theme: 'Your God reigns!' (52:7). Learning that our God is sovereign is an altogether transforming experience.

6.
The virgin birth

Please read Isaiah 7

In the years 1562-67, the cause of the Reformation in Scotland was under considerable duress from the opposition of Queen Mary. John Knox was to prove God's prophet during those years. Mary's intention was plain: to restore the nation to Roman Catholic rule. In France, many Protestants had been overcome, and a ball held in Holyrood, at which Mary was said to 'dance until the wee small hours', was interpreted by Knox as a victory celebration and he promptly attacked this unseemly conduct. Knox was duly summoned to Holyrood to meet the queen, but he was to say of the meeting, 'I have looked into the faces of many angry men, and yet have not been afraid above measure.' Isaiah was a man of this sort too. He came before King Ahaz and spoke God's Word; and like Knox, Isaiah was not unduly afraid because the Lord was with him.

The next six chapters belong together and have sometimes been called 'the Book of Immanuel', because of a promise given in 7:14 and repeated in 8:8 of the coming of 'Immanuel'. Further, fuller descriptions are given of him in chapters 9 (9:1-7) and 11 (11:1-10). Their combined effect is to draw our attention to the fulfilment of the promise given to our first parents in Eden: that from them would emerge a Saviour who was to crush Satan and sin.

Chapter 7 relates two contrasting attitudes: the apostasy of Ahaz, and the grace of God to the remnant of Judah who still love him. But before that, we are plunged into some facts of history to remind us that we are not at the beginning of Matthew, but in the eighth century B.C.!

Troubled times (7:1-10)

God had given a warning, at the time he entered into a covenant with
David, that 'When he [any descendant of David] does wrong, I will
punish him with the rod of men, with floggings inflicted by men' (2
Sam. 7:14). That is what Ahaz was suffering in 735 B.C.
Chapter 1 of Isaiah told us that we were going to encounter four
kings of Judah: Uzziah, Jotham, Ahaz and Hezekiah (1:1); chapter
6 informed us that Uzziah has died (6:1). This chapter begins, not
with Jotham as we might have expected, but with his son, Ahaz
(7:1). Jotham, the twelfth king of Judah, reigned with Uzziah whilst
the latter suffered leprosy, but was sole monarch for only eight years
(*c.* 740 - *c*.732 B.C.). The event recorded in Isaiah 7:1, the invasion
of Rezin and Pekah, can be dated precisely as 735 B.C. This causes
some problems if Ahaz did not begin to reign until 732 B.C. The
answer seems to lie in the fact that quite often in Israel and Judah,
two kings would reign at the same time. Thus it is widely believed
that Ahaz began to rule jointly with Jotham in 735 B.C., becoming
sole monarch only when Jotham died in 732 B.C.
The relationship between Israel in the north and Judah in the
south had been fractious since the division of the kingdom in the
time of Jeroboam (some 200 years earlier). Judah's strength had
grown under Uzziah, and her northern neighbours had every reason
to fear a potentially hostile power on the southern borders. Several
attempts had been made by Israel to overthrow Judah, but now Israel
had formed an alliance with Syria (7:1 'Aram'[1]) and together they
marched upon Judah (2 Kings 16:5-18; 2 Chron. 28:16-21; Hosea
5:8 - 6:6). This has become known as the Syro-Ephraimite War.[2]
Briefly, it went something like this: in the east, Assyria was, as
we know, on the rise and threatening. Both Israel and especially
Syria were more or less vassal states to Assyria by this time. In an
attempt to revolt, a kind of NATO alliance was needed to counter the
Assyrian menace. Judah, nestling at it did in the hills, and much
further south, refused to have any part in it — at least during the early
part of Jotham's reign, hoping that this stance would be taken as a
kindly gesture by Assyria. Aram (Syria), led by King Rezin, and
Israel, led by King Pekah, decided this wasn't fair and attempted to
invade Judah and depose the Davidic king in Jerusalem, replacing
him with a puppet figure from Aram. A study of the passages
mentioned above will show that the accounts are difficult to piece

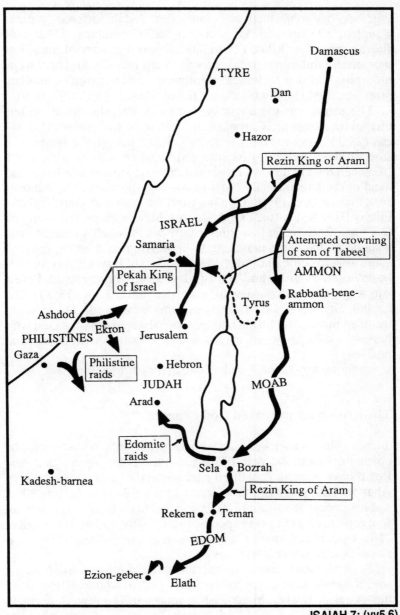

ISAIAH 7: (vv5,6)

together, but some facts are quite clear: Judah suffered 'a great slaughter' (2 Chron. 28:5). According to 2 Chronicles 28, 120,000 Judean men were killed (28:6), and almost a quarter of a million women and children were taken away as captives (28:8). These were promptly returned to Jericho through the intervention of another prophet called Oded who ministered in Samaria (2 Chron. 28:9).

The cause was the apostasy, led by Ahaz, who made molten images for worship (2 Chron. 28:2), worshipped the gods of Damascus (28:23), shut the temple doors (28:24), put out the lamps and stopped the offerings of incense and sacrifices (29:7).[3] Judah had 'forsaken the Lord God of their fathers' and suffered defeat at the hand of the Israelites. The 'last straw' was the attempt by Ahaz to seek assistance not from God but from the Assyrian king, Tiglath-Pileser III (2 Kings 16:7). God, we are told, was 'provoked to anger' (2 Chron. 28:25). Tiglath-Pileser duly noted Judah's request (and weakness) and came marching in upon Aram and Israel, moving south towards Philistia and on to the borders of Egypt. Later, in 733, he devastated Galilee and Transjordan. Meanwhile in Israel, Pekah was murdered by Hoshea, who succeeded him (2 Kings 15:30). The capital city of Aram, Damascus, was destroyed. These were troubled times. And for such times God raises up a man of God who bravely speaks his Word, even to a king who thinks he can do what he likes.

In summary, Isaiah 7 makes two contrasting points.

Their sins have provoked God to anger

Firstly, Ahaz is a wicked king who has provoked God to anger. The chapter opens in the year 735 B.C., at the point when Pekah and Rezin have formed a coalition against the threat of Assyria. Since Ahaz will not join them they decide to teach Judah a lesson. Ahaz and his people are afraid (7:2). Isaiah and his son Shear-Jashub are sent to meet Ahaz in a very specific place: 'at the end of the aqueduct of the Upper Pool, on the road to the Washerman's Field' (7:3). God knew exactly where Ahaz was!

Several matters come to the surface: first, *the mention of Isaiah's son, Shear-Jashub*. Isaiah had two sons, both of whom had symbolic names (cf. 8:1,3,18). Shear-Jashub means in Hebrew 'A remnant will return' (cf. Jer. 40:11,15; Micah 2:12). This is crucial to the whole of Isaiah's message. Ahaz was a covenant-breaker; he, and the people who followed him, would be forsaken. But within the elect nation there was another election: an election of grace. The remnant, a faithful company who survived even in the darkest of days, survived to fulfil God's covenant promise to save a people for himself (see 6:13). It is more than a little interesting that the promise given to Abraham, which included a word about his children, should also be symbolically recalled here also by Isaiah's son standing at his side while he delivered the Word of God!

Second, though the precise location is unknown, *the place at which Isaiah and Ahaz met* is very interesting. Ahaz seems to have been inspecting Jerusalem's water supply. It was, apparently, here that the women of Jerusalem gathered to wash their clothes. The city's water supply was vulnerable to attack and, later, during Hezekiah's reign, this became a crucial factor in holding Assyria at bay (see chs 37-39). The Lord sends Isaiah to the very place where Ahaz thinks the city is vulnerable. At the weakest point, God ensures its strength.

In a message that can only be defined as 'gracious', considering the apostasy of Ahaz, the Lord tells him not to be afraid (7:4). Rezin and Pekah are just **'two smouldering stubs of firewood'**. Ahaz was shaking like a tree blowing in the wind at the thought of these two aggressors (7:2), but they were, as one commentator puts it, 'mere fag-ends'! The mighty are nothing before God.

The plot of Aram and Israel to place a puppet king (the son of Tabeel) in Jerusalem **'will not take place'** (7:6-7). Why not? Because in 732 Aram (Syria) will be crushed; and as for Israel, her northern territories were lost in 734, her national existence came to an end in 722 and by 669 (sixty-five years after this prophecy delivered in 734 B.C., see 7:8) through a series of deportations and repopulating, Israel **'will be too shattered to be a people'** (7:8).

This is precisely what happened. God's promises are sure. When things are at their blackest, God's light still shines for those who wish to see it. Isaiah saw it clearly. God was giving Ahaz an opportunity to see it too. He was not to lose heart and become afraid (7:4). He was being urged to become a good shepherd, and trust in God like David did (Ps. 78:70-72). But he would not. He was to violate the covenant God had made with David (2 Sam. 7:14-17; 23:5). With a typical Hebrew way of repeating things to make a stronger point, Isaiah confronts the king with a warning: **'If you do**

not stand firm in your faith, you will not stand at all' (7:9; cf.
1:19-20). Those who do not persevere in the faith, though they may
entertain hopes of salvation, are deluded: 'We must believe the
promises of God, or it is in vain for us to expect salvation.'[4]
   Ahaz, as we know, did not listen and turned for help to the
Assyrian monarch, Tiglath-Pileser (2 Kings 16:7). This action was
disastrous both politically and spiritually. It revealed Ahaz to be
spiritually bankrupt.

A covenant-breaker

God spoke once more to Ahaz, through Isaiah (7:10), urging him to
ask for a sign by way of proof that what God has promised is true
(7:11). We are led to believe that had Ahaz asked for anything, he
would have been granted it. God is long-suffering with sinners. God
had shown a sign to Moses when he faltered in his faith — a bush
on fire but which was not consumed (Exod. 3:2). A singularly
miraculous sign was granted to Hezekiah, the son of Ahaz, when the
king saw the shadow on the sundial recede (38:8; 2 Kings 20:9-11).
Ahaz refused to have anything to do with it. He would not believe,
even though a miracle was promised him. He is typical of all
unbelievers: defiant, wilful and rebellious. Despite the resurrection
of Christ — which is the best attested fact in the universe — they still
refuse to believe in him. Ahaz even attempts to justify his unbelief
from Scripture, citing Deuteronomy 6:16: 'Do not test the Lord your
God'! (7:12). The sign was something God was prepared to give;
God actually commanded Ahaz to ask for it. It was not therefore a
question of putting God to the test, but a gracious confirmation of his
word. The sacraments of baptism and the Lord's Supper are visual,
tangible aids to help our faith too. To accept them as such is not a sign
of weakness but of obedience. What Ahaz said was breathtaking in
its audacity: he was telling God that he knew better! It is not a mere
coincidence that Jesus too used this text from Deuteronomy to counter the devil (Matt. 4:7). Jesus accused Satan of tempting God; Ahaz
accused God of tempting him! Ahaz and Satan belong together!
   What follows is meant for a wider audience than just Ahaz (the
'you' in verses 13 and 14 is in the plural). Isaiah tells the king that
he is wearying God. God's patience is running out (7:14). He will

give Ahaz a sign which will turn into a threat and not a promise. The coming of the Saviour is a gracious matter for those who have faith, but equally a confirmation of judgement to those who do not.

Ahaz's fear, the people's terror, God's offer of a sign and Ahaz's refusal to be a trusting, worshipping leader have all brought us to the point where David's house is going to be destroyed. It is just here, at the edge of the precipice, that God shows how he will fulfil his promise despite the rejection of God's Word by Ahaz (and most of Judah). What Ahaz has refused to ask for, God will grant.

The king is warned to pay attention (7:14)

The sign: the virgin

The second major point of this chapter is that, although God has been provoked to anger, he nevertheless proposes to show his love to a remnant within Judah. Contrary to what Ahaz deserves, God remains gracious. **'Therefore the Lord himself will give you a sign: The virgin will be with child and will give birth to a son, and will call him Immanuel'** (7:14). Pages have been written on this verse! The facts are these:

1. Isaiah 7:14 cannot be understood apart from the context of the opening verses of the chapter. Though the words spoken are to King Ahaz, it is clear that Ahaz is viewed as a descendant of David and the promise (covenant) made with him (2 Sam. 7:14-17; 23:5). That is the significance of the phrases **'house of David'** (7:2,13) and **'the house of your father'** (7:17). Ahaz was to draw strength from the promises God made to David. Ahaz's sinful ways may well have brought Judah to the brink of disaster; Judah's elimination seemed imminent. But God had not forgotten his promise. When Isaiah took his eldest son with him this was in itself a sign of his confidence in the future. 'A remnant shall return,' says the prophet, underlining the fact that God's covenant remains intact. Ahaz is thus reminded of his responsibilities to God and the covenant of grace (7:4).

Four words underline what he must do: **'Be careful'** — Ahaz is not to act rashly out of terror; he must trust in the Lord. **'Keep calm'** — a word he later uses for the fruit of righteousness in a believer's heart (32:17). **'Don't be afraid'** — a word that God had used in addressing Abraham when he was troubled about his future (Gen.15:1). **'Do not lose heart'** — underlining what God expects of Ahaz: he must be a covenant-keeper.

What follows in verses 10-17 is a continuation of an address to Ahaz. God offers to do for Ahaz what he had offered to do for Moses when he had faltered — to give him a sign (cf. Exod. 3:12).

2. When the Old Testament was translated into Greek (the Septuagint), the translators chose the Greek word *'parthenos'* for the word 'virgin' (*'Alma* in Hebrew). *Parthenos* means very specifically 'virgin'. An examination of the use of *'Alma* in the Old Testament shows that it refers primarily to a virgin, like Rebekah (Gen. 24:43, NIV 'maiden'; NKJV 'virgin') or Miriam (Exod. 2:8, NIV 'girl'; NKJV 'maiden').[5]

3. The New Testament testimony (Matt. 1:23) makes it impossible to believe that Isaiah 7:14 could have meant simply a 'young unmarried woman' without any reference to her virginity. Isaiah meant and said 'virgin'.

4. Isaiah uses a definite article: *the* virgin. This means that he spoke of someone who was well known to both himself and Ahaz. What follows goes something like this: 'Look, a virgin, who at the moment is not pregnant, or even married, but, nevertheless (as a sign to you) in the not too distant future, will be pregnant, and will give birth to a son.'

5. The son will be called **'Immanuel'**, a significant name meaning 'God with us' — the heart of God's covenant relationship with his people, and something which Ahaz was denying.

6. Verses 15-16 speak of the early stages of the child's development. There are two stages: first, he will be eating curds and honey or solid foods; and, second, he will be at the stage of knowing how to differentiate between good and evil, right and wrong behaviour. He will choose the right as opposed to the wrong. The child will not be very old when this is so. This could not be a long time away from the time Isaiah is speaking to Ahaz. In any case it must happen before Israel and Aram (Syria) are destroyed (7:16; something which happened

for Aram in the year 732 B.C., and for Israel in 722 B.C. a maximum of about twelve years from the time Isaiah was speaking).

7. Isaiah continues his address to Ahaz with a warning. Any appeal to Assyria for help is foolish. Israel and Aram (Syria) will be no more, and the very nation from which he seeks help will be used by God as his weapon of destruction upon Judah herself (7:17). Isaiah then paints a few scenes of the future: **'Flies'** from Egypt and **'bees'** from Assyria will invade Judah (7:18) — even the rockiest and barest parts will be infested; then economic poverty, domestic deprecation and agricultural chaos will characterize Judah (7:18-25).

Two matters are worth noting as we close this chapter.

1. Ahaz represents the house of David through whom God had promised to fulfil his promise of a coming mediator (2 Sam. 7:8-16)

The promise that stretched from Adam (Gen. 3:15) had found a line through Abel and followed through Noah to Shem to Abraham. The line continued through Jacob and Judah and was eventually brought to full expression in David and Solomon. Ahaz now represents a danger to this promise. His refusal to serve God was a challenge to the covenant of grace. But God is not about to give up his plan; through Isaiah he speaks directly to Ahaz of his assurance that Aram (Syria) and Israel will be defeated. Nothing can nullify the purposes of God!

2. Who is the virgin, and her son?

This question has been a matter of considerable debate for centuries! Some have inferred that the virgin was Isaiah's wife: the woman spoken of in Isaiah 8:3, when Isaiah takes what is thought to be another wife and gives birth to a son called Maher-Shalal-Hash-Baz — he already has one son called Shear-Jashub (7:3). This is unlikely since the child's name was not called Immanuel as the prophecy indicated.[6] Others have seen it as a reference to the birth of a son to Ahaz, namely Hezekiah. But Hezekiah, apart from *not* being called Immanuel, was already born by this time. E. J. Young thinks that Isaiah was given a vision of the Virgin Mary.[7]

There are those who insist that the sign to Ahaz involved a woman, a contemporary of Ahaz, who was then a virgin but who later got married, conceived and gave birth to a child called Immanuel and that Ahaz actually witnessed this.[8] And in doing so, he saw by way of type, the woman over 700 years later whose birth would be truly miraculous: a conception brought about by the Holy Spirit in fulfilment of a story that goes all the way back to the garden of Eden. This is possible and held by many to be what happened.[9] It has the advantage of making complete sense of the time reference in verses 15-16. The fact that no record exists of such a woman or of a child called 'Immanuel' is not sufficient to discount this view. It must further be recalled that the Virgin Mary's son was called 'Jesus', not 'Immanuel'.

The sign of judgement

Another view sees not just chapter 7, but also the chapters that follow as part of the 'sign' promised to Ahaz. These interpreters reject any idea of a double fulfilment.[10] The sign included not only the promise of Immanuel, but *also* the rejection of Ahaz and those like him (7:13). God's patience was running out. The Warrior of Israel was even now putting on his battle-dress, making ready for war. Ahaz witnessed the revelation of God's wrath in person; the birth of Immanuel, he did not. The promised Immanuel (7:14) lay in the future; when he comes, Isaiah tells us, he will possess the land (8:8), conquer all opponents (8:10), appear in Galilee of the nations (9:1) as a great light to those in the land of the shadow of death (9:2). He is the Child and Son called 'Wonderful Counsellor, Mighty God, Everlasting Father, Prince of Peace' (9:6), whose government and peace will never end as he reigns on David's throne for ever (9:7).[11]

The fact that 7:15-16 sets a time limit between Isaiah's word and the defeat of the two kings (a few years at most) is overcome in this interpretation by drawing attention to the fact that verse 15 can be translated in a non-temporal way: 'He will eat curds and honey *in order that* he may know how to refuse the evil and choose the good.' As William J. Dumbrell points out: 'The announced birth of a child to a young woman could involve a reversal of Israel's fortunes in the far distant future (i.e. beyond the immediate Assyrian crisis) and be a promise which concerns the house of David more than it does Ahaz, the current ruler.'[12]

One thing is clear: in either case, Isaiah had Jesus in mind when he spoke to Ahaz! Isaiah is not finished yet, but already we can see why he is called the 'Evangelical Prophet'.

Summary

Isaiah's message is all about Jesus. Despite Ahaz's rebellion and wickedness, the Lord continues to show mercy. He promised a Deliverer, born in a way no one has been born before or since, to make sure that his word would stand. Jesus came into the world to deliver us from Satan's power. Knowing Christ is to know his presence and power in our lives: God with us! Without him, we have no hope.

7.
'God is with us'

Please read Isaiah 8:1 - 9:1

Isaiah's domestic life

We tend to forget that the prophets were family men. It is not hard to imagine Isaiah in the court of Ahaz or preaching in the temple precincts. That seems to be what we expect of an Old Testament prophet. But Isaiah had a wife and a son called Shear-Jashub (7:3). In chapter 8 we are given a little more insight into Isaiah's personal life; but it soon becomes obvious that we are only told about it because his second son has a name that is important for Judah to know.

When God calls a man to serve him in some special way, it soon becomes apparent that the call affects the entire family. Missionaries agonize over their children's education when far away from home. Some of the greatest sacrifices that have to be made are by the wives and children. I had been a Christian for some time before I discovered that Peter was married! All that time he spent with Jesus — and all the time he had a wife back home in Galilee!

Isaiah's wife isn't even given a name! She is referred to as **'the prophetess'** (8:3).[1] It is a hard calling to be asked to work for the Lord without any recognition whatsoever. She is a bit like those women who provided for Jesus' financial needs during the course of his public ministry. We are told the names of two of them, Joanna and Susanna, but there were also 'many others' (Luke 8:1-3) whose names we do not know.

The fact that Isaiah's wife is called a 'prophetess' reminds us that women exercised the prophetic gift in the Old Testament. Examples are Miriam in the days of Moses (Exod. 15:20), Deborah in the time of the judges (Judg. 4:4) and Huldah during the reign of Josiah (2 Kings 22:14). Here it seems more likely that the expression is a more formal one, meaning 'the wife of a prophet'. If that is the case, her anonymity is even further highlighted. She was perhaps content to be used in the shadows of domestic life so that her husband's usefulness in public be furthered. Hers was a noble and sacrificial calling needing much grace.

'Maher-Shalal-Hash-Baz' is quite a name! Its meaning is even stranger: 'Quick-pickings-easy-prey' (J. B. Phillips). Just as Shear-Jashub was significant (meaning 'A remnant will return'), Maher-Shalal-Hash-Baz was full of meaning too. It was a double-edged name implying that Ahaz's enemies would be plundered, but that Judah was vulnerable and would suffer. The suffering is something Isaiah has been preaching about already (7:18-25). Isaiah had warned of the coming of the Assyrian aggressor. 'But because the wicked,' says Calvin, 'are not terrified by any threatenings, it was therefore necessary that this prediction should be repeated and demonstrated by some outward sign.'[2]

If Isaiah were preaching today, he might have hired a full-page advertisement in one of the daily newspapers. Instead he was told to take a **'large scroll'** (8:1) and write on it **'with an ordinary pen'** the name 'Maher-Shalal-Hash-Baz'. The scroll may well have been a board of some kind; extant examples of such boards dating back to the years 707-5 B.C. have been discovered. The purpose of this 'scroll' was similar to that of a birth certificate. Two trustworthy men, Uriah the priest and Zechariah son of Jeberekiah, were to act as witnesses.

The birth of Isaiah's second son was a sign of God's word of judgement. Before the boy could say 'Mummy' or 'Daddy' (8:4) the kingdoms of Syria and Israel were plundered by Assyria. This was the first stage of the destruction of the northern kingdom; it was completed in 722 B.C. Every parent can tell you the first time their son or daughter says 'Mummy' or 'Daddy'. When Maher-Shalal-Hash-Baz first mumbled those words in Isaiah's home, Jerusalem's inhabitants were trembling with fear at the rise of one of the most brutal empires the world has known.

Local geography

God speaks again to Isaiah (8:5-10). This time it is not Isaiah's sons that are in view, but rivers well known to the inhabitants of Jerusalem. East of Jerusalem was one of the principal sources of water supply to the city: the Gihon spring. From this source, in a southerly direction, flowed a channel of water known as the 'Siloam Channel' emerging in the 'Pool of Siloam'. It is to the 'Siloam Channel' that **'the waters of Shiloah'** (8:6) probably refer. The Old Pool was probably the 'Pool of Siloam' used in New Testament times for sick persons and others to wash in (John 9:7-11). It has also been suggested that the part of the city round the Upper Pool 100 metres above was called 'Siloam'. Later, when the Assyrian threat upon Jerusalem was at its greatest, Hezekiah stopped all the sources of water to Siloam (which would have been an easy source of water for the Assyrians and a means of bringing the city to its knees) and constructed a tunnel through solid rock into the city and onwards to the Upper Pool (a reference to this is found in 22:11).

Jerusalem's water supply was important for obvious reasons. The name given to this supply, 'Siloam', means 'peace' and speaks of God's care and protection. The 'Euphrates', on the other hand, means 'floodwaters' and was the large river flowing through Assyria and Babylon and on to the Persian Gulf. The flooding of the Euphrates caused devastation to crops on its fertile banks and the Lord was saying to Judah what he had said before: that Assyria will sweep down and engulf Judah, **'reaching up to the neck'** (8:8). This is a graphic picture of the distress that will come upon Judah for her sins. Changing the metaphor he speaks of Assyria like the outstretched wings of a bird swooping down upon its prey (8:8).[3]

Renewed strength

In the middle of this calamity, Isaiah turns to the Lord in prayer and seeks his help. He cries out to **'Immanuel'** (8:8). Even though some have thought that 'Immanuel' here is just another name for the land of Judah, this seems unlikely. It is better to see it as an Old Testament believer's cry to Christ. Isaiah has already foretold his birth (7:14); now he pleads with him to come to Judah's help as the bird of prey swoops down to take it away. We see here a sign of Isaiah's

Riblah
HAMATH
Lebo-Hamath
Zedad
SUBITE
Berothah
MANSUATE
GREAT SEA
Damascus
DAMASCUS
KARNAIM
SIDONIANS
MEGIDDO
Karnaim
Dor
Megiddo
Ramoth-Gilead
HAURAN
Bezer
DOR
Way of the Sea
Samaria
GILEAD
'Beyond the Jordan'
Aphek
ISRAEL
Joppa
AMMON
Ekron
Rabbath-bene-ammon
Ashdod
Jerusalem
Ashkelon
MOAB
Gaza
DEAD SEA
PHILISTINES
JUDAH
Kir-moab

Assyrian
Provinces

Subject
Kingdoms

EDOM

ISAIAH 9: 1

**The districts of Assyria in the days of
Tiglath - Pileser III 732 B.C.**

spirituality. He is a man who is walking with God. Faced with sudden destruction he can do only one thing: like Nehemiah, when confronted with a formidable situation, he sends up an arrow-like prayer to God (cf. Neh. 2:4). 'Prayer,' J. C. Ryle once remarked, 'is the very life breath of Christianity.'

Having uttered the name of Immanuel, Isaiah seems to have been immediately strengthened. In a bold cry to Assyria he dares them to sound their battle cry and come. They will not destroy Judah entirely. What powers they have are only such as have been given them. The mystery is this: behind their evil work lies the hand of God. He is using them to chastise Judah; but it is as though he says, 'So far, and no further!'

Joseph could testify to the same truth in connection with the wicked behaviour of his brothers: 'You intended to harm me, but God intended it for good to accomplish what is now being done, the saving of many lives' (Gen. 50:20). And so could Peter about the crucifixion of Jesus in Jerusalem: 'Men of Israel, listen to this: Jesus of Nazareth was a man accredited by God to you by miracles, wonders and signs, which God did among you through him, as you yourselves know. This man was handed over to you by God's set purpose and foreknowledge; and you, with the help of wicked men, put him to death by nailing him to the cross. But God raised him from the dead, freeing him from the agony of death, because it was impossible for death to keep its hold on him' (Acts 2:22-24). God overrules the sinful actions of men and women.

Isaiah's confidence lay in God's covenant. **'It will not stand, for God is with us'** (8:10). The name 'Immanuel' means 'God is with us'. Two things suggest themselves.

1. God remembers his promise

Like a golden thread, the covenant weaves it way through this prophecy to encourage those who knew God to hold on to their faith. God had promised his presence and they could depend on it now.

2. God's presence is a source of power

The presence of God with his people is a theme that runs through the Bible. It is in essence what God meant when he said to Abraham: 'I will ... be your God' (Gen. 17:7). Moses was reassured, when a price lay on his head, that he could safely re-enter Egypt to deliver the Israelites because the Lord was with him (Exod. 3:12). This knowledge proved to be a solace to him, for he could write in Psalm 90, 'Lord, you have been our dwelling-place throughout all generations' (Ps. 90:1). The same promise was given to Joshua when he took over the leadership from Moses (Deut. 31:6). Israel needed to hear this word on the Plains of Moab, on the verge of crossing into the promised land: 'Do not be afraid, the Lord will fight for you' (Deut. 1:17,21,29; 3:2,22; 7:18; 20:1). Isaiah will later apply the same lesson to those who are floundering (43:2). And eventually this promise would be realized in a way that exceeded their every expectation. The eternal Son of God became incarnate and 'made his dwelling among us' (John 1:14). Jesus pitched his tent (a literal translation of 'made his dwelling') among us!

Recommitment

It comes as something of a surprise that Isaiah needs to be warned against following the evil ways of Jerusalem's inhabitants (8:11). We have here a reminder that the best of men are only men at their best.[4] The moment we tend to think any part of Scripture does not apply to ourselves is the time when we are sure to fall. Scripture abounds with the faults of the greatest of men, and Isaiah, like all God's children, is only a 'sinner saved by grace'. He needs to apply to his own heart the words he preaches to others. It is a call to consecration. 'Watch your life,' Paul urged Timothy (1 Tim. 4:16). 'Keep watch over yourselves,' he exhorted the Ephesian elders (Acts 20:28).

What are the leading features of a man of God? We have already seen the prophet's *prayerfulness*. This passage also suggests several other characteristics.

1. Separation from the ways of the world

Usefulness in God's kingdom involves a calling to live and think differently from the world around us. Isaiah is to have nothing to do with the schemes of Ahaz (8:12). He is not to fear what the worldly fear. The person who knows God knows the source of all power. Events in Washington, Moscow, Tehran or Baghdad do not terrify

him. The centre of all power and authority resides with God — the
very same God who is with Isaiah.

2. The fear of God

'He is the one you are to fear' (8:13). Fearing God means holding
him in reverence and awe. It means thinking of him as he truly is.
The fear of the Lord is the soul of godliness (2 Chron.19:9; Job
28:28; Ps. 19:9; 111:10; Prov. 1:7; 2:5; 9:10; 14:27 etc). In this
context, it means to remember God's power and thereby be strengthened. A similar thought occurs in Psalm 34:

> 'I sought the Lord, and he answered me;
>   he delivered me from all my fears.
> Those who look to him are radiant;
>   their faces are never covered with shame.
> This poor man called, and the Lord heard him;
>   he saved him out of all his troubles.
> The angel of the Lord encamps around those who fear him,
>   and he delivers them.
> Taste and see that the Lord is good;
>   blessed is the man who takes refuge in him.
> Fear the Lord, you his saints,
>   for those who fear him lack nothing.
> The lions may grow weak and hungry,
>   but those who seek the Lord lack no good thing.
> Come, my children, listen to me;
>   I will teach you the fear of the Lord'

(Ps. 34:4-11)

3. Looking to Christ

Verse 14 is picked up again in 28:16 and Peter cites it as an allusion
to Christ (1 Peter 2:6-8). Peter is concerned to show the status that
Christians have in order to encourage them to live as they should. In
Christ we are God's people, God's temple, God's kingdom, God's
priesthood (1 Peter 2:9). Our status is founded on who (and what)
Christ is: he is the Rock.

   Using the temple as a figure, both Isaiah and Peter are saying the same thing. You can either trip over a rock (stone) or else you can use it as a foundation upon which to build something solid and permanent. In 28:16 Isaiah emphasizes the positive aspect: Christ is the cornerstone of the lives of his people. Here he is alluding to the apostate life of Ahaz and the majority in Jerusalem for whom Christ would be 'a rock of offence', something to trip over. They are some of the many who will reject Christ (cf. 53:3; 1 Peter 2:4). Isaiah is urged not to do the same. No matter how far along the road of sanctification we are, we are still in need of this exhortation: 'Therefore, since we are surrounded by such a great cloud of witnesses, let us throw off everything that hinders and the sin that so easily entangles, and let us run with perseverance the race marked out for us. Let us fix our eyes on Jesus, the author and perfecter of our faith, who for the joy set before him endured the cross, scorning its shame, and sat down at the right hand of the throne of God' (Heb. 12:1-2).

4. Walking with God

'Wait' and 'trust' are the key words of verses 17-18. But here again is a reference to Christ (Heb. 2:13). At first it might appear that these words are addressed to Isaiah, particularly in view of the fact that his children (Shear-Jashub and Maher-Shalal-Hash-Baz) are spoken of as being at his side (8:18). But this would be to miss the point entirely. Isaiah is a seer. He sees into the future of another who stands in the midst of the worshipping people of God, leading their worship. He too is waiting on God. He too is trusting God. He too is singing, 'Here am I, and the children God has given me.' What a privilege! We are the children of God — Jesus says so!

5. A commitment to God's Word

The inhabitants of Jerusalem were consulting mediums and spiritists. Isaiah has already condemned them (2:6). The only rule of thumb for a Christian is the Word of God: **'To the law and to the testimony! If they do not speak according to this word, they have no light of dawn'** (8:20). The Scriptures are the only safe guide to heaven. To forsake their testimony is to commit one's life to sure perdition (8:22).

As though to impress upon them the danger they face, Isaiah

warns of the Assyrian menace. The Bible warns, and history has shown it to be true, that times of trouble have a twofold effect. Some are brought to a sense of their need and caused to turn to God for help and rescue. But the hearts of others are hardened. It was so in the days of the wilderness wanderings (Exod. 17:1-7; Num. 20:1-13). It appears there was a similar danger in New Testament times (Heb. 3:8,15). During the Assyrian invasions, some in Israel cursed the king, and even cursed God (8:21). Of the two crosses on other side of Jesus at Calvary, one proved a converting experience; the other, just as surely, proved an instrument of hardening. Even in the darkness, the light of Jesus Christ shines for those who will see it. But for the impenitent, there is only darkness — **'utter darkness'** (8:22).

Chapter 8 finishes with a reference to the distress felt in Judah as a result of the coming of the Assyrian aggressor. Chapter 9 begins by referring to this again: **'Nevertheless, there will be no more gloom for those who were in distress'** (9:1).[5]

Summary

It is the year 732 B.C. The events spoken of in chapter 7 have begun to take place. Aram (Syria) has been overthrown entirely. The city of Damascus has been destroyed. Assyria, led by Tiglath-Pileser III, has brought his armies into northern Israel capturing **'the way of the sea'** *(Via Maris)*, **'Galilee of the Gentiles'** and **'along the Jordan'** (Transjordan, 9:1).[6] The warnings of earlier chapters have proved to be true! Will Judah repent, and do so quickly? Isaiah has set a wonderful example of how to live before God, which was meant for Judah to follow. Living this way is the lesson for us also.

8.
Darkness and light

Please read Isaiah 9:2 - 10:4

Chapter 8 closed with a reference to the distress of the days of Assyrian aggression. This chapter begins (in our English Bibles) with a contrast: 'Nevertheless, there will be no more gloom for those who were in distress' (9:1). Another contrast emerges in verse 2: **'The people walking in darkness have seen a great light.'**

The Syro-Ephraimite war led by King Rezin of Aram (Syria) and King Pekah of Israel had led Ahaz to contemplate an alliance with Assyria to the north to restrain their advances. Events moved quickly, and Aram and much of Israel had been swallowed by the bird of prey, Assyria (8:8).

The evangelical prophet has already prophesied concerning the virgin's son (a sign to Ahaz of God's covenant faithfulness, 7:14). The birth of Maher-Shalal-Hash-Baz has also given further testimony to the truthfulness of his warnings regarding Judah's future. The official witness to his birth (8:1-2) added extra weight to it. Twice the prophet has warned that Judah will be overwhelmed, but not overthrown (8:8,10).

Here in verses 2-7 an even clearer depiction of the coming Saviour is given: so clear that some 'scholars' of the Old Testament cannot believe Isaiah could have spoken them! They forget (or cannot accept through unbelief) that Isaiah was a 'mouthpiece of God'. He was being 'carried along by the Holy Spirit' (2 Peter 1:21).

The darkness

The darkness of Israel and Judah was almost complete. Isaiah has already referred to a catalogue of gloom: superstitions (2:6), materialism (2:7; 5:8-9), idolatry (2:8,20), arrogance (2:12-17; 5:15), lack of good leadership (3:1-4), social disintegration (3:5-6,12-14), sensuality (3:16-26), and alcoholism (5:11-13,22). The final years of Israel's monarchy were a period of political uncertainty. Kings like Shallum and Menahem were quickly assassinated. Religion was synchretistic: a mixture of every conceivable practice of the Canaanites, Assyrians and Egyptians. Cultic prostitution was practised at various shrines to please the sexual appetites of the gods. Children were sacrificed to Molech, the god of the Ammonites (2 Kings 23:10; cf. Jer. 7:31; 19:5). Not only did Samaria (Israel) do so (2 Kings 17:17), but Judah also. King Ahaz sacrificed his children this way (2 Chron. 28:3) and Manasseh did the same (2 Kings 21:6).[1]

Zebulun and Naphtali, two of the northernmost tribes of Israel, had already suffered the onslaught of Assyria (9:1). Towns and villages had been destroyed. People had been taken away and resettled hundreds of miles away from home. There was darkness and gloom everywhere.

This is a biblical picture of the darkness of unbelievers. 'So I tell you this, and insist on it in the Lord, that you must no longer live as the Gentiles do, in the futility of their thinking. They are darkened in their understanding and separated from the life of God because of the ignorance that is in them due to the hardening of their hearts. Having lost all sensitivity, they have given themselves over to sensuality so as to indulge in every kind of impurity, with a continual lust for more' (Eph. 4:17-19). Sinners behave as they do because they are blind. Their hearts are darkened. 'This is the verdict: Light has come into the world, but men loved darkness instead of light because their deeds were evil' (John 3:19). It was Paul's mission to preach the gospel to the Gentiles that they might be turned 'from darkness to light' (Acts 26:18). Isaiah himself cries towards the end of his prophecy: 'Arise, shine, for your light has come, and the glory of the Lord rises upon you' (60:1).

William Wilberforce, a member of Parliament and a social reformer for the abolition of slavery, was a good friend of William Pitt the Younger, prime minister of Britain towards the end of the

eighteenth century. He once asked the prime minister to come and
hear a great Anglican preacher called Richard Cecil. Pitt agreed to
come but was unimpressed by what he heard. Wilberforce had felt
'his soul rise to heaven' under the preaching, but Pitt commented
upon leaving: 'I haven't the faintest idea what that man was talking
about.' Light had shone into Wilberforce's heart; Pitt's heart, on the
other hand, was darkened.

The light

Light shines through Isaiah's words in several ways.

1. The people of God

Isaiah refers to **'the people'** (9:2,3) and **'the nation'** (9:3). He
means the people of God, the remnant from within Judah. Though
Assyria is God's rod, the razor that will shave their heads and cause
them to be ashamed (7:20; cf. 2 Sam. 10:4-5), the Lord will not
forsake them entirely. He will gather them again; and through them
bring to pass what he has promised.

2. The light of Jesus

When Jesus was forced to move from Nazareth to Capernaum (in the
region of Naphtali and Zebulun), Matthew says that this was the
fulfilment of Isaiah 9:1-2 (Matt. 4:14-16; cf. Luke 4:14-30). The
point of the quotation in Matthew is to indicate that people who had
been living in darkness now had the light of God's Son in their midst.
Matthew is always keen to point out the missionary implications of
the gospel to his Jewish readers. **'Galilee of the Gentiles'**, so long
despised by the Jews, was earmarked for evangelism by Jesus. And
this was only the beginning, for Matthew will tell us at the end of his
Gospel of Jesus' commission to go 'into all the world' (Matt. 28:19).

3. The impossible is possible with God

Isaiah knew his Bible! He remembers that, in the time of the judges,
God had whittled down Gideon's army from 32,000 to 22,000 to 300
to do battle with the Midianites. He was anxious to demonstrate the

principle of 'Not by might, nor by power, but by my Spirit' (Zech. 4:6; cf. 1 Cor. 2:4). A surprise attack upon the Midianite camp was enough to send them packing (Judg. 7:22-25). This is a message Isaiah will take up again and again (40:10,26; 63:12). 'Acknowledge my power,' God says (33:13).

Three pictures are brought together in verse 4 to remind them that Assyria's oppression is nothing new. They had been this way before in Egypt, 700 years earlier. Judah is compared to an ox. Assyria's yoke is described as a painful burden, a staff (placed across the shoulders and carrying such a heavy burden that it presses down on the flesh and bones of the shoulders) and a rod (a picture of a slave-driver with his whip).

Poor Judah — to be a beast of burden! But things can change. The **'zeal of the Lord Almighty'** can change things. If Judah would only listen!

4. An end to warfare

Assyrian young men are seen lying dead from battle with blood-stained clothes (9:5). Everywhere there is the stench of battle. The enemy has been totally destroyed and disarmed. The refuse of war is burnt, and there is peace. And the cause of all this? The birth of a child to the royal house of David (9:6). Assyria, to which Ahaz now looked for help, would bring only death and darkness. This child, however, would bring peace and light. Peace is the first fruit of our justification (Rom. 5:1).

It seems likely that the child referred to here is the same one who is mentioned in 7:14. Whoever he was — and some think he was Maher-Shalal-Hash-Baz, Isaiah's second son, but that seems unlikely — he was a foreshadowing of Jesus Christ. It is Jesus who is in view here, for there are things said of him that could not be said of anyone else.

'God contracted to a span'

Two contrasting ideas are now highlighted. The first is *the humanity* of the deliverer: **'For to us a child is born, to us a son is given'** (9:6). Mention of the words 'child', 'son', 'born' and 'given' remind us of the incarnation of Christ. There is nothing unreal about the form which Jesus took. He became a little baby! It has sometimes been pointed out that the words 'Counsellor', 'Mighty', 'Father' and 'Prince' are expressions of his humanity.[2]

But the passage also speaks of *the deity and divine authority* of the deliverer: 'And the government will be on his shoulders' (9:6). The power that Gideon saw in the defeat of the Midianites (cf. 9:4) is the same power that will destroy the Assyrians too. It is the power of God's Mediator and Son. He is King. Again it has been pointed out that the words 'Wonderful', 'God', 'Everlasting' and 'Peace' are expressive of the child's deity.[3] Four names explain his regal attributes and identify his sovereign character .

1. Wisdom

Taking the words **'Wonderful Counsellor'** as a single title,[4] we have an expression which means something like: 'He is a wonder of a counsellor.' The word 'wonder' is generally attributed to a work of God.[5] The word is sometimes used of works performed by man (e.g., Deut. 17:8; 2 Sam. 12:6; Dan. 11:36), but it is generally used to describe the miracles and wonders performed by God: the plagues in Egypt (Exod. 3:20), the conquest of Canaan (Exod. 34:10), the crossing of the Jordan (Josh. 3:5) and the miracles in the wilderness (Neh. 9:17). Miriam and Moses sang a song after the crossing of the Red Sea, which included the lines:

> 'Who among the gods is like you, O Lord?
> Who is like you —
>   majestic in holiness,
>   awesome in glory,
>   working wonders?'

(Exod. 15:11).

The psalmist, too, said the same thing:

> 'Many, O Lord my God,
>   are the wonders you have done.
> The things you planned for us
>   no one can recount to you;

were I to speak and tell of them,
  they would be too many to declare.'

(Ps. 40:5).

'Give thanks to the Lord of lords:
  His love endures for ever.
to him who alone does great wonders,
  His love endures for ever'

(Ps. 136:3-4).

'I praise you because I am fearfully and wonderfully made;
  your works are wonderful,
  I know that full well'

(Ps. 139:14).

In case we are in any doubt, Isaiah himself tells us that this is a word he attributes to God: 'All this also comes from the Lord Almighty, wonderful in counsel and magnificent in wisdom' (28:29). His every instruction is wonderful. His opinions are extraordinary. His recommendations are impressive. His advice is phenomenal. He is the only one worth listening to. In the history of the Old Testament, Solomon, David's son, whose name means 'peaceful' (1 Chron. 22:9), had been in possession of this gift too, but it was only a shadow of the wisdom that Christ possessed. Jesus, and not Solomon, is the wisdom of God (1 Cor. 1:24).

2. Deity

The **'Mighty God'** is an expression that is used again in the next chapter (10:21; cf. Deut. 10:17; Neh. 9:32). It refers both to the divinity and the power of the child. This is the One of whom John would say, 'In the beginning was the Word, and the Word was with God, and the Word was God... The Word became flesh and made his dwelling among us. We have seen his glory, the glory of the One and Only, who came from the Father, full of grace and truth' (John 1:1,14). And of himself, Jesus would claim: 'I and the Father are one' (John 10:30).

Again the psalmists make use of this expression and they too are speaking about the Saviour: 'Gird your sword upon your side, O mighty one; clothe yourself with splendour and majesty' (Ps. 45:3; cf. 50:1; 89:8)

3. Fatherhood

'**Everlasting Father**' is literally 'Father of eternity'. The rule of Messiah is enduring and everlasting. It knows no end. And his government will be like that of a father. We are not meant to confuse this with the title 'Father' given to the first person of the Trinity. What this means is again set forth by the psalmist:

'For as high as the heavens are above the earth,
     so great is his love for those who fear him;
as far as the east is from the west,
     so far has he removed our transgressions from us.
As a father has compassion on his children,
     so the Lord has compassion on those who fear him;
for he knows how we are formed,
     he remembers that we are dust'

(Ps. 103:11-14).

4. Peace

'**The Prince of peace**'. He is the 'peaceful prince'. The word 'prince' is the same word translated 'commander' in the account of Joshua's vision beneath the walls of Jericho. In pondering which way to capture the city, Joshua the commander met his Commander: 'Now when Joshua was near Jericho, he looked up and saw a man standing in front of him with a drawn sword in his hand. Joshua went up to him and asked, "Are you for us or for our enemies?" "Neither," he replied, "but as commander of the army of the Lord I have now come." Then Joshua fell face down to the ground in reverence, and asked him, "What message does my Lord have for his servant?"' (Josh. 5:13-14).

Jesus, says Peter, is the Author *(Archegos)* of life (Acts 3:15). He was the first to be resurrected from the dead, and he is also the One whose resurrection causes our resurrection (1 Cor. 15:20-23). Hebrews tells us that Jesus is the Author *(Archegos)* and the Pioneer *(Archegos)* of our faith and salvation (Heb. 2:10; 12:2). He is the great trail-blazer.

It is peace that he brings:

'For this is what the high and lofty One says —
     he who lives for ever, whose name is holy:

"I live in a high and holy place,
  but also with him who is contrite and lowly in spirit,
to revive the spirit of the lowly
  and to revive the heart of the contrite...
creating praise on the lips of the mourners in Israel.
Peace, peace, to those far and near,"
  says the Lord. "And I will heal them"'
                                        (57:15,19).

It is only what Scripture has led us to expect. There was Melchizedek who came from Salem (meaning 'peace', cf. Heb. 7:3). Jacob's prophecy regarding Shiloh pointed in the same direction (Gen. 49:10), as did the naming of David's son 'Solomon' (cf. 1 Chron. 22:9). Isaiah refers several times to this aspect of the Messiah's character and work (32:17; 53:5,7; 54:10,13; 60:17; 66:12). Little wonder that when the angels witnessed the fulfilment of this prophecy, they burst into song: 'Glory to God in the highest, and on earth peace to men on whom his favour rests' (Luke 2:14). As Jesus was leaving his disciples, it was peace that he promised them (John 14:27). When he had risen from the grave, he greeted them with the words: 'Peace be with you!' (John 20:19). The enjoyment of peace is, according to Paul, an essential part of belonging to God's kingdom (Rom. 14:17), the firstfruits of being made right with God through faith in Jesus' atoning death (Rom. 5:1).

This prophecy is enclosed, as between two book-ends, by two references to Jesus' rule (9:6,7). His greatness will never cease. His character is abiding. Aram, Israel, even Assyria, are nothing in comparison. Ahaz is foolish to look to anyone other than God to help him in his difficulty. Besides, Assyria could not be trusted. Only God can be trusted to provide justice and righteousness. And he will do what he says: his **'zeal'** (jealousy) will make sure of that.

This remarkable passage has brought together almost everything that God had been doing since Eden! His promise made then (Gen. 3:15) and repeated to Abraham (Gen. 12:2; cf. 21:1-3), Judah (Gen. 49:8-12), Moses (Exod. 19:6), David (2 Sam. 7:12-16) and Solomon (1 Kings 2:4; 3:11-14; Ps. 72) is summarized here in seven verses. Capture the meaning of this passage and you have a key to the Old Testament!

The darkness again! (9:8-10:4)

Israel, in the north, had already rejected God's covenant. They had travelled further down the road to rebellion. It is not just geography that accounts for Israel's downfall before that of Judah. They had consistently turned away from God's ways. The rest of this chapter takes up a theme hinted at in 5:25: God's hand is ready to strike (9:12,17,21; 10:4).

Four features of their rebellion are singled out for rebuke.

1. The sin of make-believe

Already the Assyrian invasion of Damascus has taken place. Samaria's downfall is imminent (722 B.C.). The bricks have fallen down, but Israel are preparing to build with even more expensive and elaborate materials (9:10). They are pretending that nothing has happened. God's judgements are treated like a child's game of Lego!

2. The sin of bad leadership

Elders and prophets are singled out for rebuke (9:13-17). Those who are at the head and those who are at the tail are alike rebellious (9:14). They have not urged the nation to turn to God (9:13).

3. The sin of disunity

Like a raging forest fire, God's wrath sweeps through Israel, setting fire to everything in its path. And in the confusion, the people turn upon each other (9:21). Disunity, turning against others, is always his plan. When God's people fight each other, the kingdom retreats, hearts grow harder and God is forgotten.

4. The sin of injustice

Legalized wrongs of governments are something God hates (10:1). Ancient Israel is no different from our own modern society, where abortion, homosexuality and other sins against humanity as God meant it to be are given the credibility of positive legislation. Our society too must face the dreadful question:

'What will you do on the day of reckoning,
    when disaster comes from afar?
To whom will you run for help?
    Where will you leave your riches?'

(10:3).

Summary

Israel and much of Judah had forsaken the Lord. Ahead lay the
certainty of judgement. Assyria were already threatening at the
borders. There was no escaping it, and they were unprepared for it.
At the risk of repeating himself, Isaiah cannot help but point out
Jesus — in prophecy, of course. The only hope lay in God's
promised child, Jesus, the light of the world (John 8:12). It is in his
light that we are to walk (cf. Matt. 5:14).

9.
The sin of pride

Please read Isaiah 10:5-34

When I was a boy, I collected birds' eggs. Just as any other 'country boy' could tell you then, birds' eggs were things to boast about. Many a tree I climbed, and fell from, to acquire my booty. Things have changed; I am far more environmentally conscious now than I was then. Still, my conscience is a little eased by the fact that collecting birds' eggs is something Isaiah knew all about (10:14).

Many theologians, from Augustine to Jonathan Edwards, have noted that pride is the essence of sin. Proof, if such were needed, is found in Paul's words in his letter to the Ephesians. Describing their former, unconverted state, the apostle says it was a way of life characterized by 'gratifying the cravings of our sinful nature and following its desires and thoughts' (Eph. 2:3). 'The desires of the mind', pride, are what sin is all about. This is what Isaiah means in this chapter when he threatens to punish the Assyrian aggressor: **'I will punish the king of Assyria for the wilful pride of his heart and the haughty look in his eyes'** (10:12). This is the problem with Israel (9:9) and the entire world:

> 'I will punish the world for its evil,
>   the wicked for their sins.
> I will put an end to the arrogance of the haughty
>   and will humble the pride of the ruthless'

(13:11).

People who do not know their Bibles are surprised, even repulsed, by what they find in the Old Testament. They forget that it was Jesus' Bible. And he found no problems with it but, on the contrary, insisted that he had come to uphold every part of it (Matt. 5:17). What such people find most objectionable are allusions to the anger and wrath of God. The reason is clear enough: folk who have an inadequate impression of *what sin is* will also entertain false notions about *what sin deserves*. Once you have seen God's holy character the way that Isaiah had in the temple, you can only respond by saying that sin is something which deserves to be driven from God's presence.

Assyria is a **'club'** in God's hand to beat his disobedient people (10:5). The terror which Assyria wields is awesome:

> **'I send him against a godless nation,**
> **I dispatch him against a people who anger me,**
> **to seize loot and snatch plunder,**
> **and to trample them down like mud in the streets'**
>
> (10:6).

What follows in verses 8-14 is an account of Assyria's boasting.

A philosophy of war

Assyria can boast of the power of her princes (10:8), and the speed of her conquests (10:9-10). In 717 B.C. city after city fell: Calno, a region in northern Syria; Carchemish, the great fortress of the Euphrates river; Hamath, a city on the Orontes river which marked the northern extent of Solomon's rule (2 Chron. 8:4); Arpad, a city near Hamath and just south of Calno; Samaria, capital of Israel; and Damascus, capital of Syria. The boasting is not over. Jerusalem too, is in Assyria's sights (10:11). One is reminded of the words of Rabshakeh (NIV, 'the field commander') which were later addressed to Judah (2 Kings 18:33-35). And on it goes: all that Assyria has accomplished is by her own power and wisdom (10:13); it was as easy as stealing eggs from a nest (10:14). We are meant to catch the inflated pride of Assyria by the use of such words as **'pride'** (10:12), **'pomp'** (10:16), **'haughty'** (10:12) and **'by the strength of my hand'** (10:13). In particular, the use of the first person in verse 13 highlights it:

'By the strength of *my* hand *I* have done this,
     and by *my* wisdom, because *I* have
     understanding.
I removed the boundaries of nations,
     I plundered their treasures;
     like a mighty one *I* subdued their kings.'

A series of questions reveals the problem with Assyria: does an axe, or a rod, or a club boast of power in and of itself? (10:15). Any prominence given to Assyria for a moment in world history was by the Lord's permission. Assyria did not recognize this; she flattered herself, and she will pay the penalty.

Days of empire

God sent Assyria to punish a godless, disobedient people. She was to be 'the sword of the Lord' in their midst. But like all great powers before and since, Assyria credited herself with autonomy. Her motivation was greed and ambition.

'Assyria' denotes the country and empire which grew up around the city of Asshur on the northern Tigris, one of the oldest cities in ancient Mesopotamia. 130 years previously, Israel had first paid tribute to Assyria in the time of Jehu, but in the next century civil war had weakened her powers. Assyrian fortunes were restored by the accession in 745 B.C. of one of her greatest kings, Tiglath-Pileser III. During his reign Assyria became an empire again. Under him, Assyrian power stretched through Syria (which fell in 732 B.C.) and into northern Israel. In 729 B.C. he took control of Babylon. The events recorded in this chapter cover the period of Tiglath-Pileser III's successors, Shalmaneser V (726-722 B.C.) and Sargon II (722-705 B.C.). Samaria (10:9) fell in 722 B.C. at the point when Sargon II took over the leadership. The years of his reign were full of trouble. Many battles were fought: Egypt on the south-west and Elam on the east raised as much trouble as they could. Control of Babylon was lost for some twelve years when a Chaldean named Merodach-Baladan captured the throne.

What general principles are suggested by all of this? Four suggest themselves.

1. Evil has a tendency to claim too much for itself

Later, Assyria would collapse to Babylon without so much as a struggle. Her energies were spent. Her boasting came to nothing. Sin in individuals and nations persists in stretching itself only to fall into God's judgement. Every kingdom built on such shaky foundations will eventually topple. Nebuchadnezzar and Belshazzar of Babylon would also have to learn this same lesson (Dan. 4; 5).

Sometimes the wicked prosper for a while. When they do, the pious may be mystified, even angered, that God should allow it. Asaph envied the wicked in their boasting (Ps. 73). But he came to his senses in the end. God will not let them prosper for ever:

'...I entered the sanctuary of God;
    then I understood their final destiny.
Surely you place them on slippery ground;
    you cast them down to ruin'

(Ps. 73:17-18).

The same lesson is taught in the pages of the New Testament. The promised child of Isaiah's vision in the previous chapter will be slain. Satan seems for a moment to be victorious. Certainly he lies behind it (Matt. 16:23; Luke 22:3; John 13:27). But Satan boasted too much. Jesus had, in fact, destroyed his power (Heb. 2:14-15). Assyria, too, has overreached herself. She is terminally ill (10:18). Visualizing Assyria's armies as a forest, God threatens to fell them down so that their number will be so small that a child can count them (10:19; cf. chs 33-34).

2. God uses the unregenerate to accomplish his overall plan and purpose

We often limit God's ability to work in certain situations. When things seem at their worst we conjecture that his power is somehow curtailed. But not only did God use Assyria to teach his people a lesson, he had also used Egypt in the past; and he would in the future use Babylon in a similar way.

This lesson is taught in Peter's sermon on the Day of Pentecost (Acts 2:14-47). The death of Jesus had been the result of the deliberate, premeditated scheming of the Pharisees, together with the hysterical outbursts of the Passover crowds in Jerusalem. Nevertheless, Peter tells us, it took place by 'God's set purpose and foreknowledge' (Acts 2:23). God can, and does, use those who do not love him to carry out his purpose. Nothing can ultimately frustrate what he has determined to do.

3. Without God, even the mightiest are nothing

Tiglath-Pileser III, Shalmaneser V and Sargon II were among the greatest leaders the world has ever seen. Yet their power diminished quickly. The reason is clear from this passage. They believed that their strength was their own.

When men believe in their own power they are inevitably heading for a fall. Uzziah had learned this lesson when he attempted to burn incense in the temple. His leprosy was God's judgement for his arrogant behaviour: 'But after Uzziah became powerful, his pride led to his downfall. He was unfaithful to the Lord his God, and entered the temple of the Lord to burn incense on the altar of incense' (2 Chron. 26:16). His consequent fury at being discovered cost him dearly (2 Chron. 26:19). What such men lack is humility: 'When pride comes, then comes disgrace, but with humility comes wisdom' (Prov. 11:2).

4. Pride is a failure to acknowledge God

Assyria's boasting is similar to that of Nebuchadnezzar at a later period when he said,'Is not this the great Babylon I have built as the royal residence, by my mighty power and for the glory of my majesty?' (Dan. 4:30). This arrogant stance is a failure to reckon with God. Many of the problems we face derive from a failure to submit to God's ultimate sovereignty over us. The God who reveals himself in this chapter as 'Almighty' (10:16), 'the Holy One' (10:17) and the Judge (see references to his 'anger' (10:5,6) and 'wrath'(10:5), is a God to reckoned with! He has power over life and death (cf. Rev.1:18). Assyria never reckoned with it and thereby revealed her spiritual bankruptcy.

The remnant

Isaiah's firstborn son was named Shear-Jashub because the name means in Hebrew 'A remnant will return'. This is the theme of the remainder of this chapter. Assyria has overreached herself and her eventual doom is certain. Israel will cease to exist as a political entity. Even Judah will be brought to the brink of disaster—but only to the brink! God has not forgotten his promises and from Judah a child must come to establish the promise made to David's house regarding God's everlasting kingdom. To secure this, a remnant must be saved from the destruction.

The idea of **'the remnant'** is important in Isaiah (10:20-22; 11:11,16; 17:3; 28:5; 37:4; 37:31-32; see 'The covenant of grace and the doctrine of the remnant'). Behind it lies the idea of election, both of Israel as a nation through which God accomplishes his purpose with regard to the coming of his Son, and of individuals, through whom he accomplishes his purpose to save a people for himself. When the world was in ruins, God saved a remnant of eight people: Noah's household (Gen. 6-8). From Abraham's family, it was Isaac alone who received the promise (Gen. 17:19-21). Isaac's twin boys were similarly divided: Jacob was the son who carried forward the promise (Rom. 9:13). Out of Jacob's family, God chose Judah. The period of the wilderness underlined the idea that though many were outwardly called, only a few (the remnant) were chosen (Deut. 30:1-5; Ps. 95:10-11). At the time of Ahab's apostasy, a remnant of 7,000 prophets kept the faith (1 Kings 19:18). In the days of Jehu's reform, a group known as the Rechabites emerged who were faithful (2 Kings 10:15-23). In every age, God secures a few who are prepared to serve him. It is this thought that Isaiah takes up here. Elsewhere he uses other expressions to convey the idea: one man left for every seven women (4:1); a tenth (6:13); the gleanings left on a harvested olive tree (17:6; cf. 30:17)

Paul takes up this passage (10:20-22) in Romans 9:27-8, together with one of the very first things the prophet had said in chapter 1:

'Unless the Lord Almighty
    had left us some survivors,
we would have become like Sodom,
    we would have been like Gomorrah'

(1:9).

Paul is arguing that this forms a key to unlock everything that God was doing, and all that he will yet do, for Israel.

It is important to recall that Isaiah is speaking about a time in the very near future (701 B.C. to be exact) when the Assyrian threat will be at the very gates of Jerusalem. All the places mentioned in verses 28-30 are towns and cities of Judah.[1] Aiath is about thirty miles north-east of Jerusalem, but Michmash is only just over seven miles away! (This is something we shall have to consider in more detail when we look at chapters 37 and 38.) Sennacherib has invaded Judah, but God has put both a godly king (Hezekiah) and a fearless prophet (Isaiah) to comfort the hearts of his people. The promise Hezekiah held on to then was this one here in chapter 10:20-22! (cf. 37:30-35). Sennacherib's army was smitten with a terrible illness and was compelled to withdraw. The lesson is double-edged: God saves his people through judgement. In one sense it is *only* (see Rom. 9:27, NIV) a remnant that is saved. That implies that a work of judgement has been necessary. The dross has first to be removed, but, equally, a remnant *is saved.*

What lies behind all of this is grace. The fact that any at all have been saved from destruction is due to the grace of God. There is no room for boasting anywhere. Judah may have had secret thoughts that Assyria, after all, deserved what they got. Perhaps they were encouraging the Lord to spare nothing when he came to judge them. Immediately God turns round and tells them: 'You are just as bad! No, you are even worse. You should have known better!' It this lesson we so desperately need to hear ourselves. We have nothing to boast about except this: that God has been gracious to us.

'This is what the Lord says:

"Let not the wise man boast of his wisdom
    or the strong man boast of his strength
    or the rich man boast of his riches,
but let him who boasts boast about this:
    that he understands and knows me,
that I am the Lord, who exercises kindness,
    justice and righteousness on earth,
    for in these I delight,"
           declares the Lord'

                    (Jer. 9:23-24; cf. 1 Cor. 1:31).

Naught have I gotten but what I received;
Grace hath bestowed it and I have believed;
Boasting excluded, pride I abase;
I'm only a sinner saved by grace!

(James M. Gray).

Summary

God hates pride. It was pride, especially in the later years of King Uzziah, that caused judgement to fall upon him. Judah, too, were filled with arrogance, thinking they knew better than God's prophet. Disgrace was sure to follow (Prov. 11:2). But once more Isaiah brings into focus the mercy of God. A remnant will return. The clouds of God's anger against sin are lined with the silver thread of his covenant commitment to his people.

10.
War and peace

Please read Isaiah 11:1 - 12:6

Wolves, lambs, leopards, goats, calves, lions, cows, bears, cobras, vipers — all these creatures are mentioned in Isaiah 11. I have always been fascinated by animals; it stems from having been raised on a farm! Perhaps that's why I find Walt Disney's animation of *Jungle Book* so appealing. It partly explains why this chapter is one that makes me smile when I read it. But first there are serious matters, things to make us tremble.

Ever since chapter 7 our attention has been focused on the response of Ahaz, King of Judah, to the northern threat of Israel and Syria led by Pekah and Rezin. The response of Ahaz has been to call upon Assyria for help. Isaiah has warned him how disastrous this policy is — both politically and spiritually. Assyria is God's rod of chastisement, but she too will be chastised. There is no future in this course; that is not what God intends for Judah. Ahaz is deaf to what God is saying, but the faithful prophet makes one more attempt to warn him.

Three metaphors are employed in this chapter, all of which are symbols of Jesus. The first is one we have seen before in chapter 4 (4:2-6): Jesus is the Branch that grows out of David's family tree. Here he is the **'shoot'** that grows from the stump of a felled tree. The second is that of a banner unfurled and carried at the head of an advancing army. Third is a picture of Jesus, the mighty warrior of God.

The mighty Warrior

Folk whose awareness of Jesus goes little further than the line of the hymn, 'Gentle Jesus, meek and mild...' have never thought of him as a warrior going into battle. Perhaps before we examine this chapter closely we should remember that this is precisely how the apostle Paul saw him. When Jesus was nailed to the cross of Calvary he was waging war against the powers of darkness. 'And having disarmed the powers and authorities, he made a public spectacle of them, triumphing over them by the cross' (Col. 2:15). Similarly the writer of Hebrews sees him as the Captain of our salvation (Heb. 2:10; 12:2; NIV has 'Author'). He leads his men through every conceivable obstacle, destroying all his enemies, and emerging with the crown of victory on the other side. We need fear nothing if we have Jesus as our Leader.

The figure of a warrior emerges from the description of the shoot from Jesse in verses 4-5:

> **'But with righteousness he will judge the needy,**
> **with justice he will give decisions for the poor of**
> **the earth.**
> **He will strike the earth with the rod of his mouth;**
> **with the breath of his lips he will slay the wicked.**
> **Righteousness will be his belt**
> **and faithfulness the sash around his waist'**
>
> (11:4-5).

A belt was worn by one ready to engage in a bout of wrestling, the object being to try to wrest this belt from the opponent's waist. In verse 11 it becomes more specific still: **'In that day the Lord will reach out his hand a second time to reclaim the remnant that is left of his people from Assyria, from Lower Egypt, from Upper Egypt, from Cush, from Elam, from Babylonia, from Hamath and from the islands of the sea.'** Just as God had gone to war against Egypt and reclaimed his people in Moses' time, so now he will go to war against the proud Assyrians and bring back his prisoners of war a second time.

The Lord is Commander. That was what Joshua, a commander too of sorts, had to learn at Jericho. The humiliating way he and his men walked around the city, only to destroy it with the sound of trumpets, was a lesson that this was God's battle. It was a holy war, a *jihad*! Jericho, and the Amalekites in Saul's time, had violated God's law and suffered God's chastisement. We must understand this carefully. Men like Joshua, Saul and Isaiah were proclaiming God's *jihad* with God's authority.

Today Jesus sends his servants into the world swordless — at least in the sense that is meant in the Old Testament. Jesus bade Peter put away his sword (Matt. 26:52). The state may use one (Rom. 13:4); but the church may not. But one day the sword will fall — on the day of the Lord. What we see in these Old Testament accounts of real events are only pictures of what all the nations will experience on that day (2 Thess. 1:7-10).

The Lord has come for battle. The figure is enhanced by reference to a flag. In the part of the world where I live, flags are somewhat emotive things. They are symbols of deep-seated convictions and fears. Many lives have been lost defending the political (and religious) issues that lie behind them. Another flag flutters in the breeze of Isaiah 11: it is the banner of the Lord (11:10,12). It has flown once before (5:20), and it will do so again (13:2; 18:3; 30:17; 49:22; 62:10). Three images highlight the significance of the prophet's words.

But where does this Commander come from? This question is answered in the opening verse. Think of a large tree which has had all its branches cut off, together with the main part of its trunk. All that remains is the base of the tree, the stump (11:1). The roots of this tree are firmly embedded in the ground and very much alive. The stump will sprout eventually, as any gardener will tell you.

1. His origin

The stump here is Jesse, David's father. Jesse is mentioned and not David because David's house has become so corrupt. The promise made to David's house (2 Sam. 7:7-16) will continue. We have heard this before many times already; and we shall hear it again. The deaf will not hear it, but those who have ears will, and will take courage from it.

2. His gifts

The shoot that emerges from this stump is now depicted in this way:

> 'The Spirit of the Lord will rest on him—
> the Spirit of wisdom and of understanding,
> the Spirit of counsel and of power,
> the Spirit of knowledge and of the fear of the
>   Lord'

(11:2).

It has been suggested that John the Baptist may have had these words in mind when he explained what happened the day Jesus came for baptism in the river Jordan. After John had baptized him, he saw what looked like a dove come down from heaven and rest upon him (John 1:32-33; NIV has 'remain' for 'rest'). The Holy Spirit who filled Jesus' heart was to 'remain' with him all his life. The presence of the Holy Spirit in Jesus' life is crucial.[1] In every aspect of Jesus' life he was dependent upon the Holy Spirit. This accounts for his wisdom, power, dependability and faithfulness (11:3-4).

It was a characteristic of Daniel that he was a man 'in whom is the Spirit of the Holy God' (Dan. 5:11, NKJV). That was what accounted for his wisdom and bravery. Others, too, are said to have received the Spirit in a similar way: Eldad and Medad (Num. 11:26), Othniel (Judg. 3:10), Gideon (Judg. 6:34), Jephthah (Judg. 11:29), Samson (Judg. 13:25; 14:6) and Elijah (2 Kings 2:15). We too share that same Spirit in our lives; we too taste of the powers of the world to come (Heb. 6:5).

3. His equipment

His weapons are words! Little children are told a proverb which goes like this: 'Sticks and stones may break my bones, but words will never hurt me.' It hasn't proved to be the most effective one-liner in my own life! Words most certainly can hurt. The book of Proverbs tells us, 'Reckless words pierce like a sword, but the tongue of the wise brings healing' (Prov. 12:18). The apostle James teaches the same message: 'The tongue also is a fire, a world of evil among the parts of the body. It corrupts the whole person, sets the whole course of his life on fire, and is itself set on fire by hell' (James 3:6).

Here it is God's words that are in view. His words can heal. They can also condemn. '**He will strike the earth with the rod of his**

mouth; with the breath of his lips he will slay the wicked' (11:4).
God has spoken, and men and women will be accountable for their
responses. Those, like the Assyrians (and many in Israel and even
Judah), who despised his Word will be condemned.

The Warrior's conquests

If the Lord is unremitting in his warfare upon his enemies, he is
equally unremitting in his desire to save his people: **'In that day the
Lord will reach out his hand a second time to reclaim the
remnant that is left of his people from Assyria, from Lower
Egypt, from Upper Egypt, from Cush, from Elam, from
Babylonia, from Hamath and from the islands of the sea'**
(11:11). This is, of course, still future, but Isaiah can see a time when
a 'remnant' of Israel and Judah will be brought back again, just as
in the days of Moses.

Several points come to the surface. Firstly, the salvation promised can only be accomplished *by the Lord's sovereign intervention.*
Salvation, as Isaiah's own name reminds us, is of the Lord. Secondly, once more (cf. 10:20-22) it is *a remnant* that is rescued.
Nowhere does the Bible lead us to expect a universal salvation.
Thirdly, the remnant is *one.* The hostility between Israel (Ephraim)
and Judah is broken down (11:13). Most interesting of all is Isaiah's
missionary vision. The remnant will include Assyrians (to the north)
and Egyptians (to the south). The covenant relationship will include
Assyrians as 'his people' (cf. 19:23-25). This is a theme which will
occupy chapters 13-23. And what is seen only in a shadow here is
seen in its full light when Jesus commissioned the church to take the
gospel throughout the world (Matt. 28:19; Acts 1:9).

We must pause and take note of an interpretation of this passage,
and others like it, which is widely believed in some quarters. It is the
view that verses 11-12 refer, in part, to the restoration of the Jews to
Palestine and the creation of the state of Israel on 14 May 1948.
What happened in 1948 is just a signal for what will happen in the
future, at Christ's second coming.

Literal interpretations of this kind fall down due to the selective
nature of what is taken literally. Verse 14 mentions the subjugation
of the Philistines, Edomites, Moabites and the Ammonites. That this
did indeed take place during the time of the Maccabees is clear from

history, but any belief that this has any reference to the twentieth century is ill-informed for the simple reason that the Philistines, Edomites, Moabites and Ammonites do not exist any more.

It is true that many passages in the prophets refer to a restoration of Israel (e.g. Jer. 23:3-6; Amos 9:11-15; Micah 4:1-4; Zech. 14:1-9,16-21). All these passages seem to predict that Israel will once again be gathered in the land of Canaan and enjoy a time of blessing and prosperity. Since these have not yet been fulfilled, some (dispensationalists) expect their fulfilment during the millennium. This all seems unlikely. It is true that Isaiah 11:11 refers to a second recovery, but the context makes clear that here the first refers to the exodus in the time of Moses. The second therefore refers to the return from Babylonian exile in the time of Ezra and Nehemiah.

As we have already noted in connection with Isaiah 2:1-4 (and we shall see again in dealing with a similar passage later in 65:18-25) this vision of a restored Israel fits in better with a picture of heaven than a literal restoration to Canaan. Here, in Isaiah 11, the reference is to the return of the exiles from Assyrian (and later Babylonian) exile in the days of Ezra and Nehemiah. When that happens, it will be like a foretaste of heaven. It is as though Isaiah were looking through a telescope and events which were separated by great intervals are brought close together. In the immediate future is the restoration from captivity, but just beyond it he sees heaven itself, where Messiah will settle down and **'his place of rest will be glorious'** (11:10).

Literal fulfilments of this passage involve absurd notions: the banner on the comparatively low hill of Zion, if it is to be seen by the surrounding nations, would require the mountain to rise. Some have suggested that Isaiah 2:1-4 suggests as much, but that is to misunderstand the nature of images in prophecy. Prophets, like good preachers, liked to use pictures to illustrate what they were saying.

The response

Isaiah does not tell us how Ahaz responded to this message. We were told earlier that he refused the offer of a sign as a confirmation of what Isaiah was saying (7:12). The Chronicler, however, informs us that Ahaz ignored Isaiah and asked Assyria for help (2 Chron. 28:16). Things then grew worse: 'In his time of trouble King Ahaz became even more unfaithful to the Lord' (2 Chron. 28:22).

One point is worthy of stress. It is something that Ahaz refused to see, and his failure to do so cost him dearly. The battle is the Lord's. It is the Lord himself who plants this banner as a symbol of his conquests. There is another reference in Scripture to something similar. Early in the days of the wilderness wanderings, the Israelites found themselves in a place called Rephidim on the way to Mount Sinai (Exod. 17:1-7). Since there was no water in the camp and since dehydration was a real threat, they quarrelled and complained to Moses. Technically, they 'lodged a complaint' against Moses.[2] It is the same word that is used in Isaiah 3:13 to describe God's covenant lawsuit against his own people for their sins. As far as the Israelites in the desert were concerned, Moses was guilty and deserved to die. Moses saw it differently: their accusation was not against him, but against God. They were putting the Lord on trial (Exod. 17:7). God had brought them into the desert to make a covenant with them. The fact that they were being tested was part of God's training programme. They had failed.

The miraculous provision of water from the rock (a symbol of Christ, cf. 1 Cor. 10:4) led to another test — the attack of the Amalekites. Joshua was asked to gather an army of men together and Moses climbed a nearby hill. With God's staff in his hands, he lifted up his arms, Aaron and Hur helping him. So long as his arms were held upwards, the Amalekites were defeated. Afterwards, Moses built an altar and called it 'The Lord is my banner'. It marked a place where Moses and the people of God had witnessed God fighting on their behalf. When God's banner is planted in the ground, God's people have no cause to worry. As King Jehoshaphat was told later, 'This is what the Lord says to you: "Do not be afraid or discouraged because of this vast army. For the battle is not yours, but God's"' (2 Chron. 20:15).

When the people of God find themselves in any trouble they are urged to glance at the banner which flutters in the breeze. The very sight of it tells them that their strength comes from 'his mighty power' (Eph. 6:10).

Songs of praise

It seems most appropriate that after so many allusions to the coming
of Christ in chapters 1-11, the prophet now bursts into song (ch. 12).
According to Calvin, the thought behind this chapter is that God,
though justly offended at his people, is satisfied with inflicting a
moderate chastisement. 'We ought, therefore, to be fortified by this
doctrine, that, though we feel the anger of the Lord, we may know
that it is of short duration, (Ps. 30:5) and that we shall be comforted
as soon as he has chastened us.'³

The chapter consists of two short psalms, or hymns (12:1-3, 4-
6). Both are expressions of thanks for God's deliverance.

Some see an allusion in these two songs to the deliverance
experienced by Jerusalem in the days of Hezekiah when
Sennacherib of Assyria was suddenly forced to retreat (chs 36-39).
But the scope of these words goes beyond that: Isaiah has been
speaking of the coming of a child who will prefigure the virgin birth
of Christ (7:14), whose names reflect his divine qualities (9:6). He
will emerge like a shoot from the stump of Jesse (11:1) and will save
his people, the remnant (10:20-22; 11:11). Isaiah has telescoped his
vision of the future to take in not just the deliverance of Jerusalem
in Hezekiah's day, or even the return of the people of God from
Babylon, or even the birth of Jesus Christ himself. He has brought
the very end of time itself into the foreground and seen the entire
scope of God's plan and purpose. He can see a time when sin and its
effects have been eradicated entirely. The Lord is going to bring
about a new earth (11:6-9).

What we have here is similar to what happens when the apostle
Paul views the work of God in Romans 9-11. After seeing a day
when 'all Israel shall be saved' he too bursts into acclamation:

'Oh, the depth of the riches of the wisdom and knowledge
        of God!
    How unsearchable his judgements,
    and his paths beyond tracing out!
"Who has known the mind of the Lord?
    Or who has been his counsellor?"
"Who has ever given to God,
    that God should repay him?"

For from him and through him and to him are all things.
To him be the glory for ever! Amen'

(Rom. 11:33-36).

A recognition of our real need

'Salvation' (12:2,3) is what we are most in need of. In order to describe it, Isaiah makes use of a widely used biblical symbol, water: **'With joy you will draw water from the wells of salvation'** (12:3).

Water is a symbol which Isaiah is fond of using, expressing as it does the blessings of salvation:

'The poor and needy search for water,
    but there is none;
    their tongues are parched with thirst.
But I the Lord will answer them;
    I, the God of Israel, will not forsake them.
I will make rivers flow on barren heights,
    and springs within the valleys.
I will turn the desert into pools of water,
    and the parched ground into springs'

(41:17-18).

'Come, all you who are thirsty,
    come to the waters;
and you who have no money,
    come, buy and eat!
Come, buy wine and milk
    without money and without cost'

(55:1).

'As the rain and the snow
    come down from heaven,
and do not return to it
    without watering the earth
and making it bud and flourish,
    so that it yields seed for the sower and bread for the eater'

(55:10).

Possibly the most well-known use of this imagery is found in the words of Jesus himself to the Samaritan woman at the well: 'Everyone who drinks this water will be thirsty again, but whoever drinks the water I give him will never thirst. Indeed, the water I give him will become in him a spring of water welling up to eternal life' (John 4:13-14). What the Samaritan woman needed most of all was the water of salvation to relieve the spiritual thirst in her soul. This has always been what sinners need in every age. Isaiah's first hymn gives clear expression to it.

God's provision

The opening line of the first hymn gives expression to the sovereign provision of God for the total relief of our need:

'In that day you will say:

"I will praise you, O Lord.
    Although you were angry with me,
your anger has turned away
    and you have comforted me"'

(12:1).

God is angry with sinners! Isaiah has made the point perfectly clear already. Though he had promised that his anger would soon be turned away (10:25), Assyria was coming as 'the rod' of his anger (10:5-6). For now, Ahaz is assured that his anger is not turned away; his hand is still raised against him and the people of Israel and Judah (9:12,17,21; 10:4).

'Therefore the Lord's anger burns against his people;
    his hand is raised and he strikes them down.
The mountains shake,
    and the dead bodies are like refuse in the streets.
Yet for all this, his anger is not turned away,
    his hand is still upraised'

(5:25).

Those who violate God's law can expect God's wrath: it is

revealed against all ungodliness (Rom. 1:18). God's holy nature had shaken even the righteous prophet into saying he was 'unclean' (6:5). And just as Isaiah felt the burning sensation of a live coal from off the altar touching his lips, a symbol of his sins being purged away by means of the sacrifice offered on the altar in his place, so too can other sinners experience God's forgiveness. Though God is angry, his anger is turned away. But how? How can God's righteous anger against sin be appeased? The answer lies in the provision of One who stands in the sinner's place and takes upon himself the punishment that sin deserves.

God's provision of a shoot from Jesse's family line culminates in a portrayal of his substitutionary sacrifice on behalf of sinners (52:13 - 53:12). Those who have received God's provision for their salvation have known that even their 'scarlet' sins can be washed away (1:18). However great their sins, God is greater still (12:6). His power assures that even the most wretched can find forgiveness by trusting in his promise of salvation through his Son. Such people can do nothing else but sing the praises of God's grace and clemency.

The church, the **'people of Zion'** (12:6), is spoken of in the feminine. The church is the bride of Christ (Rev. 19:7; 21:2,9; cf. Eph. 5:23). Three specific responses are solicited in the two hymns.

1. The response of trust

'I will trust and not be afraid' (12:2) 'Trust' is an Old Testament way of describing what we might more usually express as 'faith'. It is related to the idea of leaning on, or having confidence in someone or something (Ps. 4:5; 9:10; 22:4; 25:2, etc.). It is a trust in the character of God as he has revealed himself. In contrast to the apostasy which currently surrounds him, Isaiah can see a day when multitudes will trust in the Lord.

They will trust him with their *past*. Their sins which mount up as a great barrier between God and themselves will be taken away through the atoning work of God's promised Son. They will trust in him and be assured that their sins really have been atoned for.

They will also trust him for the *present*. Faith in the Bible is much more than just the initial response to Christ which secures our justification. Faith is also the controlling principle of our entire lives. We are to walk by faith (Eph. 4:1,17; 5:2,15, AV).[4] Hebrews 11 informs us that Old Testament saints not only believed in 'the

Jesus of promise', but they also lived their entire lives leaning upon God for strength and courage. All kinds of troubles surround Christians in every era. It is through many difficulties that we enter God's kingdom (Acts 14:22). It is confidence, in the face of opposition, that we find in Psalm 56:

> 'Be merciful to me, O God, for men hotly pursue me;
>   all day long they press their attack.
> My slanderers pursue me all day long;
>   many are attacking me in their pride.
> When I am afraid,
>   I will trust in you.
> In God, whose word I praise,
>   in God I trust;
> I will not be afraid.
>   What can mortal man do to me?'
>
> (Ps. 56:1-4).

They will trust him with their *future* also. It is especially **'in that day'** (12:1,4) that their confidence will find expression. Ahead lay such events as captivity in Babylon, but we are to understand something much more universal that lies ahead of us all. What salvation delivers us from in particular is the sting of death (1 Cor. 15:55), and the threat of eternal punishment (Matt. 25:46; John 3:16).

2. The response of thanks

'Give thanks to the Lord...' (12:4). We are always to be thankful: 'always giving thanks to God the Father for everything, in the name of our Lord Jesus Christ' (Eph. 5:20; cf. Col. 3:17). It is God's will for us (1 Thess. 5:18). When we do so, we are reflecting heaven itself (Rev. 11:17). To say 'Thank you' is something we teach children from the moment they can speak; it is what we expect of children. God expects it from his children too.

3. The response of joy

Closely related to thanksgiving is joy. Begrudging praise is not praise at all. Both hymns speak of 'joy' (12:3,6). John Trapp once said, 'No duty is more pressed in both Testaments than this, of rejoicing in the Lord. It is no less a sin not to rejoice than not to repent.' It is what the Westminster divines saw as the hallmark of our responsibility, giving as a reply to the question, 'What is the chief end of man?' the familiar statement: 'Man's chief end is to glorify God and enjoy him for ever.' It was part of God's plan from the beginning that we should know joy. Sin spoiled it; salvation restores it. Nowhere is this seen to greater effect than in Jesus' high priestly prayer in John 17. Interwoven with Jesus' intimate conversation with his Father is the request 'that they may have the full measure of my joy within them' (John 17:13). It is, according to the apostle Paul, an essential quality of the Christian life (Rom. 14:17). What Isaiah speaks of here is a reflection of what Paul wrote to the Philippian church when he called his converts his joy (4:1), prayed for them with joy (1:4), assured them that his joy was brimful as he saw their unity (2:2), and urged them, not once but twice, to be joyful — always! (3:1; 4:4).

Summary

The sight of the mighty Warrior is awesome. The effect of God's judging activity cuts Judah down to a mere stump. There are times when the church has almost been extinguished. But the roots remain and from them grow once more fresh signs of life. We are part of this new growth. Those who know the salvation of which Isaiah speaks know, too — how thankful they should be, and how full of joy it makes them!

Focus

Eschatology in the Old Testament prophets

Isaiah 13 introduces us to an important biblical expression: 'the day of the Lord' (13:6,9). The first occurrence refers to a not-too-distant horizon: the invasion of Babylon, some 150 years away. But the second instance is quite different. Here we are in the far distant future:

> 'See, the day of the Lord is coming
>   — a cruel day, with wrath and fierce anger —
> to make the land desolate
>   and destroy the sinners within it.
> The stars of heaven and their constellations
>   will not show their light.
> The rising sun will be darkened
>   and the moon will not give its light.
> I will punish the world for its evil,
>   the wicked for their sins.
> I will put an end to the arrogance of the haughty
>   and will humble the pride of the ruthless'
>
> (13:9-11).

It is vital to understand that events actually separated by long periods of time are seen from an Old Testament perspective as following close after each other. The perspective is similar to what we experience when looking at two objects from a long distance away: they *appear* close together when in fact they are not.

The prophecy in Joel regarding the Day of Pentecost is an

example of this. Immediately after the prophecy of the outpouring of the Spirit (Joel 2:28-29) Joel gives an apocalyptic account of the coming of 'the day of the Lord':

> 'I will show wonders in the heavens
>   and on the earth,
>   blood and fire and billows of smoke.
> The sun will be turned to darkness
>   and the moon to blood
>   before the coming of the great and dreadful day of the
>   Lord'
>
> (Joel 2:30-31).

'The day of the Lord' can sometimes refer to a day that is in the near future, but usually it is a phrase used by the prophets to describe the final day of consummation when the wicked will be punished and this world destroyed. Isaiah makes full use of this phrase (13:6,9; cf. 'that day' in 2:11,17,20; 3:7,18; 4:1,2; 5:30; 7:18,20,21,23; 10:20; 11:10,11; 12:1,4; 17:4,7,9, etc.).

In Isaiah's day it was common to think that the day of the Lord would bring nothing but blessing and prosperity for Israel. Then as now, good news was appreciated. But Isaiah, like so many of the prophets, disturbed this naive view by reminding his listeners that for those who are not in fellowship with God it will be a day of judgement:

> 'The Lord Almighty has a day in store
>   for all the proud and lofty,
>   for all that is exalted
>   (and they will be humbled)...
> the arrogance of man will be brought low
>   and the pride of men humbled;
> the Lord alone will be exalted in that day'
>
> (2:12,17).

It is a day of 'darkness, and not light' (Amos 5:18; cf. 8:9). It is:

> '... a day of wrath,
>   a day of distress and anguish,
> a day of trouble and ruin,

> a day of darkness and gloom,
> a day of clouds and blackness'
>
> (Zeph. 1:14-15).

But the 'day of the Lord' is associated with brighter things, too. The eschatological hope of Old Testament prophets like Isaiah included the formation of a new heavens and a new earth (Isa. 65:17; 66:22). It is this final state that lies behind such pictures as the wilderness becoming a fruitful field (32:15), the desert blossoming as the rose (or 'crocus' 35:1), the dry places turning into springs of water (35:7), peace among carnivorous animals (11:6-8), and a world in which the gospel seems to have captivated the entire population (11:9). Isaiah will have nothing to do with a future existence that is not material and physical! Not for him the idea of 'floating on clouds in glory'. As George Eldon Ladd has written, 'The Old Testament nowhere holds forth the hope of a bodiless, non-material, purely "spiritual" redemption as did Greek thought. The earth is the divinely ordained scene of human existence. Furthermore, the earth has been involved in the evils which sin has incurred. There is an interrelation of nature with the moral life of man; therefore the earth must also share in God's final redemption'.[1] This is, of course, Paul's point of view also. Christ's death was 'to reconcile to himself all things, whether things on earth or things in heaven' (Col. 1:20).

This is the vision that preoccupies the prophet as he sees a new Israel emerging in the future, glorious and redeemed:

> 'Behold, I will create
>   new heavens and a new earth.
> The former things will not be remembered,
>   nor will they come to mind'
>
> (65:17).

This is theology which should warm our hearts!

11.
The origin of evil

Please read Isaiah 13:1-14:23

Chapter 13 begins a new section in Isaiah's prophecy. The first twelve chapters have dealt largely with the crisis caused by the invasion by King Pekah of Israel and King Rezin of Aram (ch. 7).[1]

Isaiah has, so far, been concerned to urge Judah not to place any confidence in Assyria as a means of warding off the northern threat. Assyria was not the only problem for Judah and the next eleven chapters comprise a series of pronouncements upon Judah's territorial neighbours (13:1 - 23:18).

Chapter 13 introduces another aggressor: Babylon (13:1). Powerful as Assyria was, Babylon was greater still. Though the threat of Assyria amounted to nothing, Babylon's menace was to prove successful.[2] This time Judah would be taken into captivity. Before we look at this chapter in any detail, however, we shall need to consider a problem: how could Isaiah speak of things that had not yet occurred?

The chapter is quite specific as to what is going to happen. There is mention of Babylon as **'the jewel of the kingdoms'** (13:19). At this point in time Assyria was the dominant empire and the city of Nineveh far and away outranked Babylon. Nineveh did not fall until 612 B.C., which was still possibly a century in the future. Then there were the Medes, who were going to be God's instrument in the destruction of Babylon's power (13:17); yet they did not come into prominence until after the fall of Babylon in 538 B.C. — at least 150 years in the future for Isaiah's first readers (cf. Dan. 5:31 and the rise of Darius the Mede after Belshazzar's death).

It is not surprising that some have argued that Isaiah could not have written these words! The root of the problem is not all that difficult to spell out. It is unbelief. It is of the nature of prophets that they, as opposed to the idols, could predict the future (cf. 41:21-29). There is nothing to warrant the view that this is impossible for the Holy Spirit to accomplish. Sometimes the prophets were merely stating what the Holy Spirit told them. Failure to credit this reflects a predisposition to state what God can and cannot do. That is always a mistake.

The Babylonians rose to prominence towards the end of the seventh century and the beginning of the sixth century B.C. Jerusalem was attacked as part of an expansionist policy, and the city's fall happened in three stages in the period spanning the years 605, 597 and 587 B.C. The story is recorded in 2 Kings 24:1 - 25:1, and is summarized in the statement: 'He sent them to destroy Judah, in accordance with the word of the Lord proclaimed by his servants the prophets' (2 Kings 24:2). As we have seen before, the pride of Assyria became its downfall (10:12); the same was true of Babylon. Evil has this tendency to overreach itself. Chapter 13 brings us as spectators in a battle scene:

'Listen, a noise on the mountains,
    like that of a great multitude!
Listen, an uproar among the kingdoms,
    like nations massing together!
The Lord Almighty is mustering
    an army for war.
They come from faraway lands,
    from the ends of the heavens—
the Lord and the weapons of his wrath—
    to destroy the whole country'

(13:4-5).

The tension here is dramatic: we are meant to capture something of the very sights and sounds of fear: wailing (13:6), failing courage (13:7) and absolute terror (13:8). War is something horrible and those who glory in it have their perspectives twisted. War is about the killing and slaughter of young soldiers and little children (13:14-18); about rape and enforced prostitution (13:16; cf. Amos 7:17). There is nothing remotely sentimental about it.

War is a consequence of sin. James asks, and answers, the question as to the origin of war: 'What causes fights and quarrels among you? Don't they come from your desires that battle within you?' (James 4:1). This section in Isaiah goes further than that.

God brings war

It seems that God not only allows war, but brings it about (13:4) — in this case upon the Babylonians — to show that we must bear the consequences of our actions. There were times when Israel sinned and God withdrew his protective shield and allowed the nations to ravage them. This had been the cause of the rise to power of both Assyria and Babylon. This appears to be the lesson of verse 3. Just as Assyria had been called 'the rod of my anger' (10:5), so now the Medes are referred as his **'warriors'** and **'holy ones'**. 'Holy' here means 'separated for a particular task'.

Though the Medes are called God's 'warriors', they themselves would not have acknowledged it to be so. They were simply seeking to give expression to their hatred of the Babylonians, and take revenge for what they had done. The conquests of Israel and Judah in the seventh century B.C. were part of expansionist policies by emerging empires. Behind all of this, however, lies an age-old conflict. We have in these events a kind of snap-shot of what we see happening throughout all of history: the continuing conflict against what Augustine of Hippo called 'the city of God'. We see an early example of it in the building on the plains of Shinar of a city whose towers reached right up into the skies in defiance against God (Gen. 11:1-4) Ultimately it can be traced back to the Garden of Eden and the enmity which exists between sinful man and God (Gen. 3:15). More precisely, it finds its origin in the tyranny of the king of evil himself, who lies behind the Fall. His shadow lies behind the statement in 14:12 by way of explanation of the historical process. Some commentators have seen 14:12 as a reference to the fall of Satan from heaven, though Calvin does not agree. He says of this interpretation: 'The exposition of this passage which some have given, as if it referred to Satan, has arisen from ignorance, for the context shows that these statements must be understood in reference to the King of the Babylonians.'[3] The problem seems to lie in the fact that what is pictured here is the end of a reign. The fall of Satan was not, however, the end of his reign. He continues to this day to deceive (Gen. 3:13; 1 Tim. 2:14), to hinder (1 Thess. 2:18) and to accuse the people of God (Rev. 12:10). It is also common to find Satan referred to as 'Lucifer' (14:12, AV). This arises from the Latin word *Lucifer* meaning 'morning star'. Some Church Fathers, such as Tertullian, regarded Luke 10:18, 'I saw Satan fall like lightning from heaven,' as being an explanation of Isaiah 14:12, but this, too, is mistaken.

This conflict that we see in these Old Testament times will emerge again in Bethlehem when Herod seeks the death of the promised Saviour of sinners (Matt. 2:16). It is graphically portrayed in the book of Revelation: 'The dragon stood in front of the woman who was about to give birth, so that he might devour her child the moment it was born. She gave birth to a son, a male child, who will rule all the nations with an iron sceptre. And her child was snatched up to God and to his throne' (Rev. 12:4-5).

The origin of evil

Despite the fact that Satan is not referred to specifically in 14:12, his shadow lies behind this passage. The actual reference is to the King of Babylon and his self-deification, but in this he proves to be a type of Satan, who is by nature anti-Christ (Dan. 11:36; 2 Thess. 2:4). Several features of his tyranny are highlighted for us in this chapter.

The most basic is the spirit of *self-aggrandizement:*

**'You said in your heart,
    "I will ascend to heaven;
I will raise my throne
    above the stars of God;
I will sit enthroned on the mount of assembly,
    on the utmost heights of the sacred mountain.
I will ascend above the tops of the clouds;
    I will make myself like the Most High."
But you are brought down to the grave,
    to the depths of the pit'**

(14:13-15).

Self-deification was a characteristic of Babylonian kings (cf. Dan. 3:15; 4:30; 8:25; 11:3,12,16) and of Roman emperors. What emerges as a whisper in Eve's ears at the beginning, 'Listen to me!' becomes a shout at the end: 'He will oppose and will exalt himself over everything that is called God or is worshipped, so that he sets himself up in God's temple, proclaiming himself to be God' (2 Thess. 2:4).

Coupled with self-aggrandizement is pr*ide* (13:19; **'pomp'**, 14:11). This is what lies behind the adoption of the title 'O morning star', a title which rightly belongs to Christ (Rev. 22:16). The devil is always taking what belongs to Christ. That is his nature. It is also the characteristic of those who are held in his power, like these Babylonian kings. To take such a title is arrogant in the extreme. Pride, according to Augustine of Hippo, is the very essence of sin. What Nebuchadnezzar, Belshazzar and others like them have personified is the very spirit of Satan himself: to think too highly about oneself.

The Babylonian kings believed that 'might is right'. Their rule was characterized by *tyranny and oppression* (14:2,4). They were known for their **'relentless aggression'** (14:6). They knew nothing of mercy.

There seems little doubt about the fact that during the Old Testament times, *Satan deceived the nations*. This is what lies behind his power over such tyrannical regimes as Babylon. We find it too in the expression 'prince of Persia' in Daniel 10:13. Behind the scenes lies a conflict of cosmic proportions: a battle 'against the rulers, against the authorities, against the powers of this dark world and against the spiritual forces of evil in the heavenly realms' (Eph. 6:12).

These are the symptoms of every tyrant. They are still present today, but we need to be careful, for the seeds of these sins are in our own hearts too.

Every tyrannical rule comes to an end. The downfall of Babylon was swift and complete. After the Medes came the Persians, and after them the Greeks. They built a new city, Seleucia, nearby, and before long Babylon was completely deserted. By the time of Christ, it was no more than a village (13:20-22). Other empires of evil have come and gone. Satan's empire remains for the present, but his reign too, will end (Rev. 20:10).

Wars are a foretaste of what is coming

Twice in chapter 13 Isaiah makes use of the expression 'the day of
the Lord (13:6,9; cf. 13:13). It is important to note that these verses
refer to two quite different things. In the first instance (13:6) Isaiah
is speaking of a 'day' in the not too distant future (150 years or so
later). In the second instance (13:9-13) he is referring to something
much further away and with far greater consequences:

> **'See, the day of the Lord is coming**
> **— a cruel day, with wrath and fierce anger —**
> **to make the land desolate**
> **and destroy the sinners within it.**
> **The stars of heaven and their constellations**
> **will not show their light.**
> **The rising sun will be darkened**
> **and the moon will not give its light.**
> **I will punish the world for its evil,**
> **the wicked for their sins.**
> **I will put an end to the arrogance of the haughty**
> **and will humble the pride of the ruthless'**
>
>   (13:9-11).

There are images here which are reminiscent of passages in Joel
(Joel 2:10,30-31) and the book of Revelation (Rev. 6:12-13). It is a
feature of Bible prophecy to bring together side by side two events
that are actually separated by lengthy time intervals. This prophetic
foreshortening is rather like what happens when someone looks into
a telescope, and distant objects appear as though it were possible
simply to reach out and touch them.

The principle which lies behind this phenomenon is an important
one: namely, that the Day of Judgement is symbolized in history by
wars such as this one. Speaking of the destruction of the temple and
the overthrow of Jerusalem in A. D. 70, Jesus warned his disciples
that these events would only be the 'beginning of birth pains': 'You
will hear of wars and rumours of wars, but see to it that you are not
alarmed. Such things must happen, but the end is still to come.
Nation will rise against nation, and kingdom against kingdom.
There will be famines and earthquakes in various places. All these
are the beginning of birth pains' (Matt. 24:6-8). The expression

'Nation will rise against nation' is taken from Isaiah 19:2 and is meant to be a warning that the Judge is standing at the door (James 5:9). If we think wars are terrible — and they are — the Day of Judgement will be on a different scale altogether. 'Let men who delight in the cruelties of war', said William Plummer, 'remember that their day is coming.'

Summary

Tucked away in this section of the prophecy is a striking allusion to the future of God's church. In the midst of this battle scene, where we can almost hear the command to attack in 13:4-5, leading to the overthrow of Babylon (13:17-22), is a word of promise to God's faithful people:

> **'The Lord will have compassion on Jacob;**
> **   once again he will choose Israel**
> **   and will settle them in their own land.**
> **Aliens will join them**
> **   and unite with the house of Jacob.**
> **Nations will take them**
> **   and bring them to their own place.**
> **And the house of Israel will possess the nations**
> **   as menservants and maidservants in the Lord's**
> **   land.**
> **They will make captives of their captors**
> **   and rule over their oppressors'**

(14:1-2).

What amounts to a wholesale judgement on God's enemies (represented by Babylon) turns out to be a blessing and deliverance for God's people (Jacob). God uses Babylon to purge his church of sin and purify to himself a people who will serve him. Once Babylon has served its purpose of purging it will be destroyed, making way for the Saviour to come. This little section is a cameo sketch of a theme which will occupy twenty-seven chapters (40-66) of Isaiah's prophecy. Even now, in the midst of words of terrible doom, God wants his own children to take refuge: he has not forgotten his promise. What a glorious future lies in store for the church of God!

12.
Can anyone escape God's judgements?

Please read Isaiah 14:24 - 16:14

Jeremiah lived almost a hundred years after Isaiah. He prophesied during the fulfilment of Isaiah's words in 13:19 when Babylon had become great and Jerusalem was finally overthrown in 597 B.C. He lived through the days of the decisive battle of Carchemish in 605 B.C. against the rising Egyptians. Some in Jerusalem were beginning to wonder whether it was only they who would suffer the judgements of God. The answer was sobering: 'See, I am beginning to bring disaster on the city that bears my Name, and will you indeed go unpunished? You will not go unpunished, for I am calling down a sword upon all who live on the earth, declares the Lord Almighty' (Jer. 25:29). Not only Jerusalem, but the nations too are to experience the judgements of God.

The judgements against the nations are what the lengthy section from chapter 13 to the end of chapter 23 is all about. So far, we have seen Babylon brought to trial. In the passage under consideration (14:24-16:14) we shall see Assyria, Philistia, Moab and Damascus in the dock. Others, including Cush, Egypt and Edom are to come.

Assyria (14:24-27)

We have already noted that there is no break between verses 23 and 24 in this chapter. This has led some to think that the reference to Babylon in 14:3-23 really relates to Assyria during the Assyrian empire. Assyrian kings did sometimes refer to themselves as 'Kings of Babylon'. Nevertheless, others have suggested that 14:24-27 forms a distinct prophecy against Assyria. Twice, Isaiah mentions God's **'plan'** (14:24,26). Four times he refers to God as **'Almighty'** (14:22,23,24,27). Together, these facts serve as a reminder to the Assyrians that the ultimate power behind everything belongs to God. He owns all things (Ps. 50:10). He can impose his will on all things, and nobody can stop him (40:10-31).

International affairs may not figure largely in church prayer meetings, but they appear on God's agenda. Assyria will be crushed, and it is the Lord who will do it (14:25). God's people may suffer for a while, to teach them some essential lessons, but eventually God will say to Assyria, 'Enough!'(14:25).

Philistia (14:28-32)

This section introduces the Philistines[1] and a possible alliance with Judah against a preoccupied Assyria, currently engaged in wars elsewhere. The timing is precise: **'This oracle came in the year King Ahaz died'** (14:28). This was in 715 B.C.

King Ahaz, despite Isaiah's warnings, had sought an alliance with Assyria to ward off the threat of incursion by hostile Israeli and Syrian forces. When the combined forces of Pekah and Rezin stormed into Judah, inflicting many casualties and taking thousands as hostages, Ahaz caved in. He sought, not the help of God, as Isaiah had urged (ch. 7), but the aid of Assyria to the north-east.

The price of such an alliance was high. Political and religious compromise followed. Judah became a vassal state, at considerable cost to the exchequer. Ahaz sacrificed his own son to the fire, introduced an Assyrian-type altar in the temple court, used the bronze altar made in Solomon's time for purposes of divination and closed the temple doors (2 Kings 16:3-4,10-16; 2 Chron. 28:2-4,23-25). When Ahaz died, Judah was in a weakened condition and Philistia and the Edomites, noting that Assyria was preoccupied elsewhere, took advantage of the situation.

The death of Ahaz occurred in 715 B.C. and marked a possible turning-point in Judah's affairs. For Judah's new king, Hezekiah, the thought of freedom from Assyria must have been very tempting indeed. The alliance had, after all, been contrary to God's will. Surely, Jerusalem's famous prophet would sanction breaking it, even if this did mean an alliance with the Philistines. But such thinking is ethically bankrupt. What Isaiah had warned against in the time of Ahaz could not become right under Hezekiah. God's people in Old Testament times lived in a theocracy. That meant having to depend upon him for everything. Political compromise may be commonplace in international affairs today, but it was not an option for Judah, and Isaiah said so in clear terms. The prophet's reply is threefold.

1. There is worse yet to come for Assyria

'Do not rejoice, all you Philistines,
    that the rod that struck you is broken;
from the root of that snake will spring up a viper,
    its fruit will be a darting, venomous serpent'

(14:29).

The broken rod appears to be King Sargon II, who had suffered a revolt in Babylon. But even after his demise a little later, others like him would follow, including Sennacherib, Esarhaddon and Ashurbanipal — all equally formidable. (We see from 20:1-6 and the so-called 'Ashdod crisis' in 713 B.C. just three years later, that Ashdod, one of the Philistine cities, did not listen to this message. An abortive attempt at rebellion from Assyrian rule ended in the sacking of the city and the overthrow of its king.)

2. The destruction of the Philistines

More shocking still was Isaiah's warning that the Philistines had no future:

'But your root I will destroy by famine;
    it will slay your survivors.
Wail, O gate! Howl, O city!
Melt away, all you Philistines!'

(14:30-31).

In 715 B.C., the year of the death of King Ahaz, and possibly just months after this prophecy, Sargon II attacked the Philistine cities of Gath and Ashdod (20:1). Within only a few years all the major

Philistine cities (Ashdod, Gath, Ekron, Gaza) had accepted Assyrian domination. By the middle of the next century, Babylonian dealings with the cities were merciless. In 604 B.C. Nebuchadnezzar's scorched earth policy wiped Philistia off the map entirely. Such is the accuracy of God's Word!

3. A call to trust the Lord

Most importantly of all, Judah was meant to trust in the Lord for her welfare.

> **'The poorest of the poor will find pasture,**
> **and the needy will lie down in safety...**
> **What answer shall be given**
> **to the envoys of that nation?**
> **"The Lord has established Zion,**
> **and in her his afflicted people will find refuge"'**
>
> (14:30,32).

God has always promised to take care of his people, no matter what threats may be made against them. 'For I am convinced that neither death nor life, neither angels nor demons, neither the present nor the future, nor any powers, neither height nor depth, nor anything else in all creation, will be able to separate us from the love of God that is in Christ Jesus our Lord' (Rom. 8:38-39).

This message is as timely for the church today as it was in Hezekiah's day. Alliances with unbelief are sure to fail. Only in leaning upon God can we be sure of safety. This is a lesson that some ecumenical enterprises have consistently failed to learn. Amos' question remains pertinent: 'Do two walk together unless they have agreed to do so?' (Amos 3:3). Outward apprearances of unity and co-operation based on uncertain foundations are sure to come to nothing.

Moab (15:1 - 16:13)

Isaiah's prophecy concerning the Moabites cover two chapters (15-16).²The first (ch. 15) gives a picture of total destruction; the second (ch. 16) gives some of the causes of Moab's downfall.

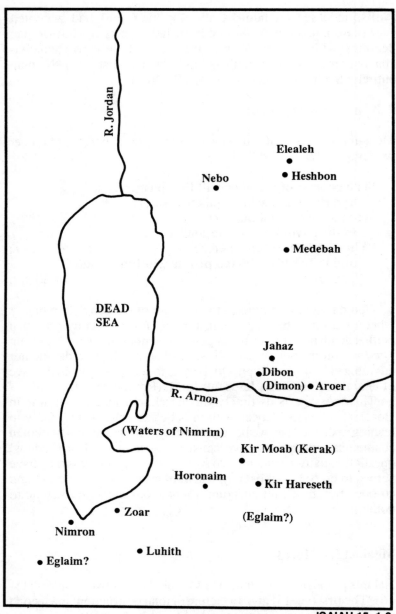

R. Jordan

Elealeh
●
Nebo   ● Heshbon
●

● Medebah

DEAD
SEA

Jahaz
●
●Dibon   ● Aroer
(Dimon)
R. Arnon

(Waters of Nimrim)

Kir Moab (Kerak)
●
Horonaim
●   ● Kir Hareseth

(Eglaim?)

● Zoar
Nimron
●   ● Luhith
● Eglaim?

ISAIAH 15: 1-9

The devastation is complete and the story receives even fuller treatment in Jeremiah 48. Within a short period, Isaiah's words were fulfilled. Assyria came into Moab, marching southwards and driving those that escaped the sword (cf. **'waters ... full of blood'**, 15:9) or capture into the territory of Edom (**'Sela'** in 16:1 is the capital of Edom and situated on a 1000-foot plateau). City after city has fallen and most of the places mentioned can be located, but not all.

The picture of Moab that builds up is one of *arrogance*:

> **'We have heard of Moab's pride—**
> > **her overweening pride and conceit,**
> **her pride and her insolence—**
> > **but her boasts are empty'**

> (16:6).

Jeremiah repeats the charge (Jer. 48:29), adding for further clarity that God's patience had run out:

> 'Make her drunk,
> > for she has defied the Lord.
> Let Moab wallow in her vomit;
> > let her be an object of ridicule'

> (Jer. 48:26).

For defence, Moab had wealth in terms of sheep. Joram, Ahab's son and successor in Samaria, had dealings with Moab. By way of a tribute, Moab paid heavily with huge numbers of sheep: 'Now Mesha king of Moab raised sheep, and he had to supply the king of Israel with a hundred thousand lambs and with the wool of a hundred thousand rams' (2 Kings 3:4). Here, Moab is asked to send tribute to Jerusalem instead (16:1). The picture of the Moabites crossing the border into Edom with their family treasures (15:7) is a graphic portrayal of the insecurity of riches. The river sources have been stopped up and the land upon which Moab depended, for sheep grazing and for growing grapes, provided nothing (15:6; 16:8,10). Hysterical women are running southwards away from the aggressor; they are like young birds shaken out of their nests and fluttering about on the floor below (16:2).

Those who defy God turn to religion for justification. Man's religions are his greatest crimes. Moab is no different: but even as she presents herself at the high places, it is only to wear herself out. Her praying **'is to no avail'** (16:12). Jesus said the same thing about pagan religion: 'Do not keep on babbling like pagans, for they think they will be heard because of their many words' (Matt. 6:7).

Nothing but grief comes to those who defy God. The scene depicted here is a wretched one: a city destroyed in a night (15:1); public humiliation (15:2-3); starvation and loss of exports (15:6; 16:8-10); bloodshed (15:9) weeping and wailing (15:2-3,5,8; 16:7,9-11). And this is only a picture of what awaits all who ultimately defy him (Matt. 8:12).

But not all is dark. In a display of divine pity, God cries out for Moab (15:5; 16:7,9,11). Calvin is of the impression that Isaiah was merely putting himself in the position of the Moabites, as an actor would. The feelings he relates are not his own, but those of the Moabites.[3] This is unlikely. Isaiah is an evangelist. He longs that his enemies turn to God and find salvation. He takes no delight in the death of the wicked (Ezek. 18:23; 33:11). As Jeremiah puts it so movingly,

> 'Oh, my anguish, my anguish!
>   I writhe in pain.
> Oh, the agony of my heart!
>   My heart pounds within me,
>   I cannot keep silent.
> For I have heard the sound of the trumpet;
>   I have heard the battle cry'
>
> (Jer. 4:19).

God is patient with sinners. We have seen several times that there comes a point when his patience runs out, but we need to note, too, that this only occurs after a prolonged period of long-suffering. Amos, who preached in the northern kingdom of Israel during Isaiah's early ministry, reminded his listeners that God was coming like a roaring lion (Amos 1:2). His word of judgement was 'for three sins ... even for four' (1:3,6,9,11,13; 2:1,4,6). To be sure, after the third and fourth sins God holds out no longer, but he has not come after the first or second! God is slow to anger (Ps. 103:8). He has no pleasure in the death of the wicked (Ezek. 18:23). He is not like the pagan Canaanite deities — malicious, irascible and petty. They could 'see red' at a moment's notice. Ill-temper may be one of their characteristics, as it is of some parents when they discipline their children (Heb. 12:10), but Israel's God is never like that. When the disciples wanted to bring down fire upon a Samaritan village for the way it had spurned Jesus, he turned and rebuked them (Luke 9:52-56).

Thus the nations and their inhabitants who spurn the offer of mercy can expect no mercy. They will become Christ's footstool and be trodden upon (Ps. 110:1); he will dash them to pieces like broken pottery (cf. Ps. 2:9). But, standing like an oasis in the desert is a word of undeserved grace (16:5). Moab is urged to seek for refuge in Judah (16:1). The picture is that of lambs being sent as a tribute. As King Mesha had sent 100,000 lambs to King Ahab of Israel each year (2 Kings 3:4), so now proud Moab is urged to yield to the King of Jerusalem.

Specifically, there is the promise of Judah's Saviour, the seed from David's house that will eventually be born as the Messiah. An enemy though Moab had been, and devastated as she now is, there is still hope. Ruth, a Moabitess, had said to Naomi, 'Don't urge me to leave you or to turn back from you. Where you go I will go, and where you stay I will stay. Your people will be my people and your God my God' (Ruth 1:16). Now there is a plea for more from the land of Moab to do the same; if they seek the refuge of Christ they will not be disappointed.

This is a message that remains valid today. When all is confusion around us, Jesus Christ remains the Rock (Matt. 7:24-27). And what is the cause that lies behind this unexpected offer? **'Love'** (16:5; Hebrew, *chesed*). This is the word repeated twenty-six times in Psalm 136: 'His love endures for ever.' Behind it lies the idea of loyalty, as in the following passage: 'Know therefore that the Lord your God is God; he is the faithful God, keeping his covenant of love to a thousand generations of those who love him and keep his commands' (Deut. 7:9).

Summary

God keeps the power of the nations in check. Though they may wreak havoc, it is only for a season, and is all part of God's mysterious purposes. Eventually they will overstep themselves. God's people are to keep themselves free from entanglements which might compromise the truth of God's Word, for nothing but grief awaits those who defy the Lord. The source of the church's strength lies in God's promise. Having entered into a covenant to save sinners who deserve no mercy whatsoever, God's love shows itself in his loyalty to his word. Having said that he will show us his lovingkindness, he will be as good as his word. What a wonderful truth that is to repentant sinners who come to him for mercy!

Can anyone escape the judgements of God? Yes, by turning to Christ for mercy!

13.
Trophies of grace from unlikely sources

Please read Isaiah 17:1-19:25

All of us who are involved in doing the Lord's work have experienced the trial of labouring in difficult conditions, with little, or no fruit. Sometimes we convince ourselves that the area in which we labour can bring forth nothing of any value, but we are often wrong. God, in his sovereignty, can produce trophies of grace from the most unpromising of conditions. This is what these next chapters (17-19) are all about. They may, initially, seem difficult reading: the concentration on judgement is only to remind us just how abhorrent sin is to Almighty God. He detests it and will not pass it by as though it were not there: 'He does not leave the guilty unpunished' (Exod. 34:7). The fact that we may find this out of balance only shows how far we have strayed. Sin does not offend us as much as it should and if we find the sustained emphasis on judgement in these chapters irritating that says more about us than it does about Scripture. Perhaps it is just in this area that we need to re-evaluate ourselves as God sees us.

Isaiah continues to pronounce judgements on surrounding nations; three more states are taken up here in chapters 17-19. They are Damascus (Syria), Cush (Ethiopia) and Egypt.

Damascus and Ephraim

This oracle comes from Isaiah's early days. In 14:28 we were told that King Ahaz had died. That was the year 715 B.C., but this section refers to the fall of Damascus (17:1), something which occurred in

732 B.C. (cf. ch. 7). Perhaps it was given about the same time as the early chapters of Isaiah (*c*. 734 B.C.). If that is the case, as seems most likely, this prophecy concerns an event which was two years in the future. The former British prime minister, Harold Wilson (now Lord Wilson) once said during his days of office, 'A week in politics is a long time.' Two years must have seemed even longer. Who, apart from a prophet of God, would claim to know the outcome of events in a distant city, two years ahead?

Damascus was Syria's capital city.[1] Syria's future is one of *ruination* (17:1) and *loneliness* (17:2). The picture is of flocks grazing with no one to look after them. It is a vivid portrait of what life is like for those who do not know God. When Eli the priest's daughter-in-law knew that her husband, brother-in-law, and father-in-law were all dead, and that the ark of the covenant had been taken by the Philistines, she named the child that was born at this time Ichabod, meaning 'The glory has departed' (1 Sam. 4:21). Whatever is left of Aram, after the Assyrians have raided it, will be like Israel's so-called 'glory' once God had departed (17:3-4). It will be no more than the few gleanings left in a field after harvest (17:5), or the few olives on an olive tree once it has been shaken (17:6).

Ephraim was the name given to Israel,[2] and she too would suffer the same fate (17:3). Their alliances in the eighth century B.C. meant that Israel and Syria shared a common destiny. It must be seen as a singular rebuke for Israel to be classed by the prophet in the same category with pagan Syria, but that is what happens when people disregard God's warnings and invitations. Despite all the teaching and religious advantages Israel had known, in the end she was no better than the heathen![3] Her strong cities will be like those deserted towns in old Western films with the wind howling and bits of bracken blowing along the streets (17:9). The picture is one of *abandonment* (17:9), *fruitlessness* (17:11), and seemingly, *unstoppable power* (17:13).

What is the cause of this rebuke? Why has judgement come upon Syria and Israel? The answer is clear: idolatry (17:8). They have forgotten God, their Maker (17:10; cf. 17:7). Mention of 'Asherah poles' (17:8) is a reminder of how far they had sunk into godlessness. Asherah was the Canaanite mother-god. Poles or 'trees' were used to depict her and were centres of cultic prostitution. Israel had been told to destroy them (Exod. 34:13). When we contemplate the idolatry of sexuality in our modern society, these judgements are particularly relevant. Western society cannot expect a different future from what happened to Syria or Ephraim. Like them, today's society has 'forgotten God' (17:10). Judah was to take note of what happened to Damascus (cf. 10:9-11), but did not.

The account of the visit made by King Ahaz to Damascus shortly afterwards makes chilling reading: 'Then King Ahaz went to Damascus to meet Tiglath-Pileser king of Assyria. He saw an altar in Damascus and sent to Uriah the priest a sketch of the altar, with detailed plans for its construction. So Uriah the priest built an altar in accordance with all the plans that King Ahaz had sent from Damascus and finished it before King Ahaz returned. When the king came back from Damascus and saw the altar, he approached it and presented offerings on it' (2 Kings 16:10-12). Instead of forsaking idolatry, King Ahaz introduced a pagan altar into the central point of the temple, having copied a design which had caught his eye in Damascus! Ahaz was the consummate compromiser. He was prepared to use anything, no matter what the source, so long as it 'helped along' his own brand of religion. The more lurid the better, he reasoned. He displayed an attitude which is abroad in our own day; the latest fashion in church worship is too often a case of the church trying to ape the world.[4]

Intertwined in this oracle of judgement we find two strands of hope. The first is that, as we have seen many times before, Assyria's power, awesome and terrifying though it may be, will come to an end (17:14; cf. 10:28-34). Its dominance is 'only for a night' — but what a night! Secondly, even in the most unlikely place, God has his people. They may only be a few (17:6-7, **'gleanings'**), but they are his! We read of them in 2 Chronicles 30:11: 'Nevertheless, some men of Asher, Manasseh and Zebulun humbled themselves and went to Jerusalem.' They had been snatched 'like burning sticks from the fire' (Amos 4:11).

Cush (18:1-7)

Tsetse flies are buzzing beside the river Nile. We are in the heat of a Sudanese summer (18:1). From Syria in the north Isaiah has taken us south-west and almost to the equator. We might be tempted to think that a country so far away from Jerusalem would not come into God's reckoning, but we would be mistaken. Nothing escapes his

notice, no matter how far away it is. Cush,[5] too, is called to account.
Cush is in trouble. A flurry of ambassadors are bent on achieving
diplomatic solutions to the oncoming Assyrian aggressor, but to no
avail (18:2). The region **'beyond** (NIV, 'along') **the rivers'** would
appear to be the Atbara and Blue Nile (modern Ethiopia). The
reference to a **'tall and smooth-skinned'** people (not 'scattered and
peeled' AV) appears to be an allusion to the Egyptian practice of
shaving their entire bodies every third day.

Isaiah's message to the Cushites is on the face of it encouraging.
It brings out the truth that *God is in absolute control of events*. The
Cushites have no need to be concerned about war: God will allow
the Assyrians to come as far as Egypt (it was conquered in 670 B.C.
by Esarhaddon) and no further. A trumpet will sound from the
mountains of Judah proclaiming the limits of Assyria's power
(18:3).

The exact picture here is difficult to put together, but the point
appears to be that in contrast to all their agitation, God is not the least
bit moved. He is in total control: **'I will remain quiet'** (18:4). If
there is any movement on God's part at all, it is only the shimmering
that one can see on a hot day. God is never taken by surprise. Nothing
can outwit him. He has no need to be worried or frenzied. Before the
harvest arrives, God will act. The Assyrians will not march one
centimetre further than he allows. His pruning knife is ready (18:5)
and evil will grow no larger than he decrees. Isaiah depicts the
Assyrian end with graphic imagery: wild birds and animals will
devour them. This teaching is repeated by the apostle Paul in his
sermon in Athens: 'From one man he made every nation of men, that
they should inhabit the whole earth; and he determined the times set
for them and the exact places where they should live' (Acts 17:26).

We find the same message in the book of Job. Satan is allowed
to bring so much devastation into Job's life. He is permitted to have
Job's possessions, his children and even his health. But there is a
limit. Initially God says, 'Very well, then, everything he has is in
your hands, but on the man himself do not lay a finger' (Job 1:12).
Later he tells Satan: 'Very well, then, he is in your hands; but you
must spare his life' (Job 2:6). It is the same lesson that lies behind
the 'chain' that currently binds Satan (Rev. 20:1-2).

Just as a remnant of Damascus and Ephraim will turn to the Lord
as a result of his chastisements, so too there will be Cushites who

will come and present him with gifts (18:7). This prospect is what
gave the psalmist such obvious joy when he testified:

> 'Envoys will come from Egypt;
>   Cush will submit herself to God.
> Sing to God, O kingdoms of the earth,
>   sing praise to the Lord,
> to him who rides the ancient skies above,
>   who thunders with mighty voice.
> Proclaim the power of God,
>   whose majesty is over Israel,
>   whose power is in the skies.
> You are awesome, O God, in your sanctuary;
>   the God of Israel gives power and strength to his people.
> Praise be to God!'

(Ps. 68:31-35).

We cannot help but be reminded of the story in Acts 8 of the
conversion of the servant of Queen Candace of Ethiopia. Making his
way home from attending a festival in Jerusalem, he pauses to read
a portion of Isaiah's prophecy. The veil over his eyes has made him
unable to see the Saviour of whom Isaiah speaks. But Philip is at
hand, full of the Holy Spirit and burning with desire to witness to
him of the Saviour he has come to know and love. 'Do you
understand what you are reading?' Philip asks, and then proceeds to
give the Ethiopian the best Bible study he ever had. As he read and
listened, the Holy Spirit opened his eyes and enabled him to see the
provision that God had made for his sins. It is folk like this that Isaiah
had in mind when he wrote this chapter around 800 years earlier!

Egypt (19:1-25)

When Isaiah turned his attention upon Egypt her great monuments
were already old. Perhaps some 750 years earlier the ancestors of
some of those to whom this prophecy was addresssed had built the
Sphinx, Karnak and the great Pyramids. The message, like the ones
that have gone before, contains both warnings and encouragements.
    The first fifteen verses of chapter 19 foretell Egypt's downfall.

God shook Damascus like a tree ripe for plucking fruit (17:6). The Cushites were warned that Assyria's power would be cut down as a gardener prunes his crops (18:5). Egypt is told the same story using another picture. God is coming like a cloud that moves quickly across the sky (19:1; cf. Ps. 68:4; 104:3). This figure of an approaching storm soon to appear is the same one that Jesus used to portray the Second Coming and the approach of the final judgement (Matt. 26:64).

When God judges, everything crumbles. Every support is removed. Egypt had many things in which she trusted, including *false religion* (19:1), *unity* (19:2) and *worldly wisdom* (19:3). Disintegration follows in the wake of God's rebuke. Men lose heart and purpose. They consult their sources of wisdom, only to find them empty. That is the message, told with relentless repetition, of the Book of Ecclesiastes. Without God, everything is 'meaningless'! (Eccl. 1:2,14; 2:1 etc.).

Weakness and disintegration are followed by *oppression and subjugation.* A ruthless tyrant will tyrannize Egypt (19:4). This could be a reference to Tirhakah of Cush, a ruler who lived in Isaiah's lifetime, or it could refer to the Assyrian king, Esarhaddon, who conquered Egypt in 670 B.C. Next comes *deprivation.* The Nile is stopped up, causing drought, starvation, industrial decline and economic recession (19:5-10). The scene portrayed could hardly be more contemporary! When a society is suffering God's wrath (cf. Rom. 1:18) these are the symptoms to look out for.

What follows is worse: *the wise are looked upon as fools* (19:11-13), and only anarchy prevails as men stagger about the streets like drunks (19:14). Instead of wisdom, they are given **'a spirit of dizziness'.** **'Zoan'** and **'Memphis'** were the current and ancient capitals of Egypt. When officials lose their way, society has most to fear. When leaders can no longer give direction, society is heading for collapse. We see here a picture of modern civilization. People are dizzy looking for meaning and purpose — anywhere except in Jesus Christ. 'Like men with sore eyes,' wrote Chrysostom, 'they find the light painful, while the darkness, which permits them to see nothing, is restful and agreeable.'[6]

In 19:16-25 we are given another picture of Egypt. That it refers to events in the future is signified by the sixfold repetition of **'in that day...'** (19:16,18,19,21,23,24). We have seen Isaiah's concern for the Gentiles before, but the idea that Egypt, Israel's cruellest oppressor in days gone by, should now be promised a place at their side is breathtaking.

The progression from sin to salvation is worth noting. There appear to be five elements.

1. A state of fear

The Egyptians are likened to hysterical women. Fear has gripped their hearts. Even the mention of 'Judah' will produce fear: **'They will shudder with fear'** (19:16), **'... Judah will bring terror'**, **'Everyone will be terrified'** (19:17). Although Assyria is the aggressor now, and Babylon will be later (under Nebuchadnezzar) the underlying reason for their fear is that the One who lies behind it is the God of Judah.

2. A state of submission

Verse 18 is intriguing. **'Five cities in Egypt'** will **'swear allegiance'** to the Lord and **'speak the language of Canaan'**. One in particular is called the City of Destruction, probably a reference to Heliopolis which was destroyed by Nebuchadnezzar (see Jer. 43:12-13). 'Five' is probably meant to convey a small number in contrast with the vast number of Egyptian cities, along the same lines as earlier references to the remnant that will turn to the Lord from such places as Damascus and Cush (cf. the 'gleanings' in 17:6). Though they may be few in number, they will speak the language of faith and trust in the God of Israel. It is still one of the most moving experiences to listen to the testimony of a man who at one time could only curse and swear, and to hear him now speak with love and reverence the name of 'Jesus'.

3. A state of access into God's presence

'Altar' (19:19) and **'sacrifices and ... offerings'** (19:21) speak of worship directed to God in a way that finds an access into his presence. The 'saviour' (or probably 'Saviour') of verse 20 is no doubt a further reference to the promised son of David's house who would fulfil God's covenant promise to his people (11:1-10).

4. A state of fellowship

The fellowship envisaged is not that of Egyptians with God, but of what follows once sinners have been justified through faith in God's Son. Egyptians and Assyrians, now enemies, will be brothers and sisters in the Lord (19:23). And there is more.

5. A state of full acceptance

God calls Egypt, once Israel's enemies, **'my people'** (19:25). Imagine it: Egypt, Assyria and Israel (here comprising Judah also), once enemies in battle, now united as the children of God. The linking of Egypt, Israel and Assyria is like a motorway: **'In that day there will be a highway from Egypt to Assyria'** (19:23). A highway links Egypt and Jerusalem! The church is being filled with former enemies of Israel.

Summary

Paul describes the calling of the Gentiles and their inclusion in the church as a breaking down of the wall that once separated Jews and Gentiles (Eph. 2:14). What happened when the Berlin Wall was dismantled and a people who had been kept apart for forty years were brought together is an illustration of it, but only a faint one. The fellowship that binds Christians together is much more profound. They share together the promise of heaven (Rom. 8:17; Gal. 3:29) 'This mystery is that through the gospel the Gentiles are heirs together with Israel, members together of one body, and sharers together in the promise in Christ Jesus' (Eph. 3:6). What these chapters have been about is that God can raise up children from the most unlikely sources: a Ruth from Moab, a Naaman from Damascus, a government official under Queen Candace of Ethiopia or an Athanasius from Alexandria in Egypt. In teaching us this, they give us a foretaste of heaven (cf. Rev. 7:9).

14.
Insights into a prophet's life

Please read Isaiah 20:1 - 21:17; 23:1-18

We are a third of the way through the book of Isaiah and so far we know almost nothing about Isaiah himself! We do know that he was married — but again Isaiah's long-suffering wife remains entirely in the background. We know too that he had two sons: Shear-Jashub and Maher-Shalal-Hash-Baz, both of whom have stood at their father's side on occasions as he delivered his prophecies. But what kind of man was Isaiah himself?

We can surmise a few things about him from the nature of the prophecies he delivered: words like 'courageous', 'uncompromising', 'faithful' and 'consecrated' come to mind immediately. We know too that he had a concern, both for the glory of God (impregnated into his soul by the experience in the temple recounted in chapter 6) and the salvation of sinners. No one can preach about the Saviour as much as Isaiah did without a heart for evangelism. The plea for sinners to reason with God about their condition in the opening chapter (1:18) shows us that Isaiah was a true evangelist. In the two chapters before us here (20-21) we glimpse a little more about the prophet's character.

The Ashdod crisis (20:1-6)

This forms a kind of epilogue to chapters 18 and 19. Ashdod was a Philistine city. Previously, Isaiah had prophesied against Philistine euphoria in the wake of Sargon II's downfall at the hands of Babylon in 715 B.C.(14:28-32). Sargon wasn't finished. In three years' time,

713 B.C., Ashdod attempted a rebellion, but failed. Its king, Azuri, was deposed. A successor, Yamani, endeavoured to continue the struggle, trying to make an alliance with Egypt and Ethiopia (hence its inclusion here after chapters 18 and 19). Yamani also approached Judah. But all was to no avail. Egypt failed to fight, Ashdod was subjugated and Yamani was handed over to the Assyrians!

In the middle of all this a lonely voice pleads for a hearing. The speaker is Isaiah, who appears in a somewhat shocking state: '**At that time the Lord spoke through Isaiah son of Amoz. He said to him, "Take off the sackcloth from your body and the sandals from your feet." And he did so, going around stripped and barefoot'** (20:2). For three years[1] Isaiah walked about almost entirely naked.[2]

The cost of obedience to God's will is high, but few have had to pay this price. Have you ever felt that you were called to do something that was just a little beneath your dignity? Many Christians feel just like that: when the church needs cleaning, they insist that God has gifted them with theological insights, not the skill to use a vacuum cleaner. It is along these lines that David once said,

'Better is one day in your courts
    than a thousand elsewhere;
I would rather be a doorkeeper in the house of my God
    than dwell in the tents of the wicked'

(Ps. 84:10).

Paul urged the Philippians not to think too highly of themselves (Phil. 2:3).

The message is not for Philistia but for Judah, and especially for King Hezekiah, who was tempted more than once to look to Cush and Egypt for help against the Assyrian menace. Hezekiah must know that there was no point in doing so. Egypt would surrender to Assyria's king, Esarhaddon, in 670 B.C. and its people be carried away 'stripped and barefoot'; and Cush, though not conquered, would prove a hopeless ally. 'In only a short time,' Isaiah is saying, 'people will point to Egypt and Cush and say, "Look at what's happened to them!"' (20:6).

It is foolish to trust anyone apart from God. Though Hezekiah was essentially a godly king, given to reform, he was also capable of compromise in a crisis. His glances at Egypt for help did not win him favours with Isaiah. This is a message Hezekiah is going to have to hear again (30:1-3). The attraction of Egyptian-Philistine military expertise might bring short-term benefits, but as guardians of the truth, God's people were to be separate from all forms of unbelief. Their cry must be that of the psalmist:

'Some trust in chariots and some in horses,
  but we trust in the name of the Lord our God.
They are brought to their knees and fall,
  but we rise up and stand firm'

(Ps. 20:7-8).

Babylon (21:1-10)

Something of Isaiah's personality can be glimpsed in the following chapter. This time the focus of attention is further away, both geographically and historically. So far, Isaiah has concerned himself with Judah's near neighbours. Babylon, on the other hand, was about as far away as the Bible world knew. Not only that, the events of which he speaks were not to take place until the middle of the sixth century B.C., almost 200 years after Isaiah's time.[3]

We have already glimpsed the coming of Babylon as a great power in the future (13:1-14:23). Babylon will be 'the jewel of kingdoms' (13:19). Assyria, though currently dominant, would fall to Babylon. Assyria's capital city, Nineveh, fell in 612 B.C. The Medes were then to arise as God's instrument in the destruction of Babylon's power (13:17). The Medes are mentioned here too, and so are the Persians, **'Elam'**.[4] The capture of Babylon took place during the reign of Belshazzar in 539 B.C., at a time when its defenders were feasting and unprepared:

'They set the tables,
    they spread the rugs,
    they eat, they drink!
Get up, you officers,
    oil the shields!'

(21:5).

Isaiah calls, as it were, for watchmen to be posted on the city walls of Jerusalem (21:6). They are to look out for messengers coming from Babylon with the news that Babylon is indeed fallen (21:7-10). The event itself is told in greater detail in Daniel 5.

Belshazzar was the man who finally brought the patience of God with the Babylonians to an end. During the great feast (Dan. 5:1) he ordered that the gold and silver vessels confiscated from the temple by Nebuchadnezzar be used for that occasion. What happened next was a fulfilment of the words of Proverbs 6:15: 'Therefore disaster will overtake him in an instant; he will suddenly be destroyed — without remedy.'

Anyone reading Daniel 5 for the first time might not appreciate the full extent of Belshazzar's folly. Not until the end of the chapter are we told that the city was already under siege. Belshazzar is the embodiment of arrogance (cf. 47:10-11). The occasion was not just foolish; it was blasphemous. The appearance of the hand writing on a plaster wall gave eloquent testimony that Belshazzar's days were numbered. He had been weighed in the scales and found to be wanting (Dan. 5:27). It was the truth of these words in Isaiah, together with an apocalyptic vision of a lion suddenly overtaken by a bear, that made Daniel strong in Belshazzar's presence (cf. Dan. 7:4-5).

'The prince of darkness grim...'

The fall of Babylon is of great significance. The Bible seems to use this historical event of the sixth century to symbolize the fall of everything that is evil. Babylon comes to epitomize evil *per se*. The apostle John, in the book of Revelation, represents the destruction of the powers of evil in terms of the fall of Babylon (Rev. 14:8, citing Isa. 21:9; cf. Rev. 17:5; 18:2,10,21).[5]

The kingdom of God cannot ultimately be shaken. Assyria, Babylon, Rome — all these empires come and go. In their wake is a trail of destruction. Judah, too, would suffer at the hands of the Babylonians, **'crushed on the threshing floor'** (21:10). The New American Standard Version makes the meaning clearer: 'O my threshed people, and my afflicted of the threshing-floor!' God will permit Babylon to thresh Judah. The process will not be without its pain, but what emerges will be the true grain. God will not allow his church to be utterly destroyed in the process.

It is this confidence that evil will be destroyed that is so characteristic of Martin Luther in the sixteenth century:

A mighty Fortress is our God,
A Bulwark never failing;
Our Helper he amid the flood
Of mortal ills prevailing.
For still our ancient foe
Doth seek to work us woe;
His craft and power are great;
And, armed with cruel hate,
On earth is not his equal.

Did we in our own strength confide,
Our striving would be losing;
Were not the right man on our side,
The man of God's own choosing.
Dost ask who that may be?
Christ Jesus, it is he,
Lord Sabaoth his name,
From age to age the same,
And he must win the battle.

And though this world, with devils filled,
Should threaten to undo us,
We will not fear, for God hath willed
His truth to triumph through us.
The prince of darkness grim,
We tremble not for him;
His rage we can endure,
For lo! his doom is sure;
One little word shall fell him.

That Word above all earthly powers,
No thanks to them abideth;
The Spirit and the gifts are ours
Through him who with us sideth;
Let goods and kindred go,
This mortal life also;
The body they may kill:
God's truth abideth still;
His kingdom is for ever.[6]

What emerges clearly from this chapter is Isaiah's reaction to
what he sees:

'At this my body is racked with pain,
**   pangs seize me, like those of a woman in labour;**
I am staggered by what I hear,
**   I am bewildered by what I see.**
My heart falters,
**   fear makes me tremble;**
the twilight I longed for
**   has become a horror to me'**

(21:3-4).

Clearly Isaiah was a sensitive man, deeply affected by the
destruction which he saw ahead for the Babylonians. A similar
picture emerges in the next chapter when he asks to be left alone so
that he might weep (22:4).

Isaiah had a share in the spirit of the Messiah who, when
beholding the sinful state of Jerusalem, wept over it (Luke 19:41;
Matt. 23:37). The apostle Paul, too, could experience similar
emotions when he thought about the lost condition of his Jewish
fellow countrymen (Rom. 9:3). Those who labour for God cannot
help but be stirred by their own message. There can hardly be
anything worse in a preacher, or Christian worker, than insincerity.
Jesus condemned the Pharisees because 'They do not practise what
they preach' (Matt. 23:3). It is because of this danger that James
warns, 'Not many of you should presume to be teachers, my
brothers, because you know that we who teach will be judged more
strictly' (James 3:1).

David Hume, the eighteenth-century British deistic philosopher,
rejected Christianity. A friend once met him hurrying along a
London street and asked him where he was going. 'To hear George
Whitefield preach,' he replied. 'But surely,' his friend said with
some astonishment, 'you don't believe what Whitefield preaches,
do you?' 'No I don't,' answered Hume, 'but he does.' Hume would
have gone to hear Isaiah too, I think.

Edom (21:11-12)

Edom, or **'Seir,'** (21:11) was where Jacob's twin brother Esau went, and 'Edomites' is the Bible's name for Esau's descendants (Gen. 32:3). God has many things to say to them. Isaiah addresses Edom again in 34:5-15. Other prophets, too, spoke to them (e.g. Amos 1:11-12). The book of Obadiah is devoted entirely to Edom.

Amos was a prophet who was active during the initial period of Isaiah's ministry. However, he lived and worked in the northern kingdom of Israel, even though he originally came from Tekoa, eleven miles south of Jerusalem (cf. Amos 1:1). According to Amos, the Edomites had treated God's people with brutality (Amos 1:11-12; see also Num. 20:18-21; 1 Sam. 14:47, where they are referred to as the 'enemies' of God's people; 1 Kings 11:14-22; 2 Kings 8:20; 14:7; 2 Chron. 28:17). There will come a time, however, when their pride will be broken and they will be silent (the word **'Dumah'** in 21:10 means 'silent'). They will no longer look down from the mountains of Edom with contempt at God's people.

Such is the terror depicted that the watchman on duty cries out for morning, but when it comes he finds it as dark as the night (21:12). The prophecy seems to indicate either the brief respite from Assyrian domination before the coming of the Babylonians,[7] or more likely, following the previous oracle, the Medo-Persian empire which overthrew the might of Babylon.[8] Either way, there is a way out of the darkness for those who ask God's help: **'... ask, then ask; and come back again'** (21:12). Once more the evangelistic heart of the book of Isaiah comes to the surface. Even for the rebellious sons of Esau, there is a way back to fellowship with God. That they failed to take it is the prevailing message of the book of Obadiah.

Arabia (21:13-17)

Just in case those on the distant periphery thought they had escaped the all-seeing eye of God, Isaiah now turns his attention to Arabia. Deep in the Persian Gulf (modern Saudi Arabia), Arabia was the home of many groups of people well known in the Bible. Descendants of Abraham, through Hagar and Keturah, came from Arabia

(Gen. 25), including the Ishmaelites and Midianites (Gen. 37:25-36). The Queen of Sheba who came to visit Solomon was Arabian. During the reign of Jehoram (in Elisha's time) a raiding party from Arabia carried off his wives and sons (2 Chron. 21:16-17), leaving only Ahaziah, the youngest (2 Chron. 22:1). By Hezekiah's day Arabians served as mercenaries in the defence of Jerusalem against Sennacherib's invasion. But a day will come, Isaiah now warns, when caravans (the Arabians were famous traders) would have to leave the main trade roads for fear of their lives (21:13).

The Assyrians first invaded Arabia in 732 B.C., the same year that Syria was crushed. The simple bows of the Arabs were ineffective against them (21:15).[9] When Isaiah speaks of the fulfilment of this prophecy taking place **'within one year, as a servant bound by contract would count it'** (21:16) it may mean that this prophecy was given in the year 733 B.C., at the same time as many of the early chapters in Isaiah. On the other hand, a later and more successful invasion was made during the reign of King Sargon II in 725 B.C., three years before the fall of Samaria. In that case Isaiah may have been speaking in the year 726 B.C.[10] Later the Babylonians were equally successful under Nebuchadnezzar (Jer. 25:17,23-24).

The conclusion to this section seems necessary after the sequence of judgements given. These are not Isaiah's words; they are God's: **'The Lord, the God of Israel, has spoken'** (21:17). The wise will listen to what God has to say.

Tyre (23:1-18)

We include chapter 23 in our study at this point, leaving chapter 22 for separate treatment. The judgement on Tyre concludes the long line of nations under review which began in chapter 13. Chapter 22 is a word of dire warning to Jerusalem and the people of God. It must be noted, however, that Isaiah has placed it in the middle of similar warnings to the heathen nations. The people of God were meant to be different, but their present condition suggested otherwise. They were no better than their pagan neighbours. It is this sobering fact that guides Isaiah to place this judgement before that of Tyre. However, because chapter 22 includes matters particularly relevant to our own age and condition I have left it for separate treatment in the next chapter of this commentary.

'The Onedin Line'

If Isaiah 23 were to be set to music, the theme of Kachaturian's *Spartacus* would be suitable, famous as it now is as a signature tune for a TV story about sailing ships. Ships are what this chapter is all about — or the lack of them. It is a prophecy about the downfall of Tyre's influence in commercial trading on the high seas.

These prophecies against the nations began with Babylon (ch.13) and end with Tyre. If Babylon stands for power, then Tyre stands for commerce. The connection between them is clear: both represent the attempts of man to live without God. In Revelation 17 and 18 the two nations are combined as representative of the world's seductive and oppressive powers. Tyre is portrayed as a prostitute plying her trade (23:17 cf. Babylon in Rev. 17:1). Many of the prophets had something to say about Tyre (e.g. Ezek. 26-27; Amos 1:9-10).

The marketplace of the nations

Tyre was the capital of Phœnicia,[11] which also included such independent city states as Sidon and Byblos ('Gebal'[12] in the Old Testament). These were all Mediterranean ports and, together with the Philistines, the Phœnicians were the great merchant traders of the ancient Near East. The celebrated mountains and forests of Lebanon formed a natural defence on their eastern side. During the reigns of David and Solomon, Tyre established good relations with Israel. King Hiram I of Tyre provided wood and craftsmen for Solomon's temple (1 Kings 5:18) and sailors for his commercial fleet (1 Kings 9:27).

By Isaiah's time, Tyre's strength had waned. Assyria threatened but never conquered Tyre, but Luli, King of Tyre, was forced to flee to Cyprus in 701 B.C. (the year when Sennacherib besieged Hezekiah's Jerusalem). Where Sennacherib failed, his successor Esarhaddon succeeded. Throughout the century that followed, Tyre (like Judah) looked to Egypt for help against Assyrian aggression, until at last Assyria's decline set in. Tyre regained her independence for a short period until the rise of the Babylonians. A thirteen-year siege under Nebuchadnezzar brought Phœnicia to an end in 572 B.C. An attempt to regain some power during the time of Alexander the Great resulted in the total destruction of both Tyre and Sidon in

332 B.C. (see the prophecy of Ezek. 26:3-5). The cities never recovered from it. Hellenistic culture took over, the language of the Phoenicians was lost and by New Testament times they were known as Syro-Phœnicians, reflecting their Hellenistic identity.[13]

Tyre's greatness was legendary: **'the marketplace of the nations'** (23:3), **'whose merchants are princes, whose traders are renowned in the earth'** (23:8). Her downfall was swift and is graphically portrayed. News of it reaches her ships at Cyprus (23:1). The Mediterranean appears childless for lack of her trading ships (23:4). Egypt is dismayed by the loss (23:5) and the people of Tyre are scattered as far as distant Tarshish (23:6) or nearby Cyprus (23:12).

The hand of God

As for the cause of her downfall, humanly speaking it is the Babylonians (23:13), but as ever in Isaiah we see behind such forces the almighty power of a sovereign God. God **'planned'** it (23:9).

> **'The Lord has stretched out his hand over the sea**
> **and made its kingdoms tremble.**
> **He has given an order concerning Phœnicia**
> **that her fortresses be destroyed.**
> **He said, "No more of your revelling,**
> **O Virgin Daughter of Sidon, now crushed!**
> **Up, cross over to Cyprus;**
> **even there you will find no rest"'**
>
> (23:11-12).

Lessons

Two themes emerge here and deserve closer inspection. The first has to do with the danger of *materialism*. Tyre's commercial activity is compared to that of a prostitute (23:15-17). The figure seems apt: commercialism can easily assume the policy of the highest profit regardless of means. It is this characteristic of ungodliness which is underlined in the book of Revelation:

> 'For all the nations have drunk
> the maddening wine of her adulteries.

The kings of the earth committed adultery with her,
   and the merchants of the earth grew rich from her
      excessive luxuries'

(Rev. 18:3).

Few are the businesses run on principles that seek first the glory of God. A friend of mine, who runs a small business, refuses to do any trade on Sundays. When he was asked to exhibit at a national exhibition in London his exhibit remained closed on the Sunday. Enquirers on Monday morning seeking explanations were incredulous of the reason given!

We need to take heed of our Saviour's warning about the seductiveness of material things: 'Do not store up for yourselves treasures on earth, where moth and rust destroy, and where thieves break in and steal. But store up for yourselves treasures in heaven, where moth and rust do not destroy, and where thieves do not break in and steal' (Matt. 6:19-20).

The second has to do with *God's ownership of all property*. Isaiah gives us a glimpse of things to come. He sees a day when Tyre's earnings will be given to the Lord's treasury (23:18; cf. 18:7; 60:5-11; 61:6). The psalmist has the same vision:

'The kings of Tarshish and of distant shores
   will bring tribute to him;
the kings of Sheba and Seba
   will present him gifts'

(Ps. 72:10).

Once more there is a reflection of this in Revelation: 'The nations will walk by its light, and the kings of the earth will bring their splendour into it' (Rev. 21:24). The law forbade money gained by prostitution being given to the Lord (Deut. 23:18). What appears to have happened here, however, is that Tyre has been converted (cf. Zech. 9:3).[14] As for a fulfilment, we see a glimpse of it in the supply of materials provided for the reconstruction of the temple after the exile in Babylon (Ezra 3:7), and another in the remarkable faith of the Syro-Phœnician woman in Mark 7:24-30. There were also Christians present in the city at a later period (Acts 21:3-6). But there are even greater things in mind here: a day when 'the nations' will have turned to the Lord — in the 'new heavens and the new earth' (60:5-11).

Summary

Isaiah was evidently prepared to do whatever God asked of him. Like C. H. Spurgeon he could say, 'Let my name perish; but let the name of Jesus Christ endure.' He was faithful enough to tell the nations of their eventual ruin, and the church of the affliction that awaited them under the Babylonians. He did not shrink from the difficulty of the task set out for him, even when it caused him such obvious pain.

15.
'Let us eat and drink for tomorrow we die'

Please read Isaiah 22

So far Isaiah has pronounced judgements on Babylon (twice), Assyria, Moab, Damascus, Cush, Egypt, Philistia, Edom and Arabia. It is perhaps useful to recall that Isaiah did not personally visit all these countries to deliver these messages. Much of what he said, though no doubt passed on to various officials in the countries under review, was meant for Judah's ears. In hearing what was in store for the heathen nations, Judah was meant to tremble — for she resembled the heathen more than the covenant people of God. These passages belong to the same order of thought as the solemn warning delivered to the church at Ephesus: 'Remember the height from which you have fallen! Repent and do the things you did at first. If you do not repent, I will come to you and remove your lampstand from its place' (Rev. 2:5).

To come are words to Tyre (23:1-18). Chapter 22 is a word to Jerusalem, Isaiah's base and God's city.[1] The people of God are not going to escape his judgements; indeed, because of their privileged position and superior knowledge and opportunity, they will be judged even more severely. Jesus, speaking similar words of judgement in his day, warned Korazin and Bethsaida, saying, 'If the miracles that were performed in you had been performed in Tyre and Sidon, they would have repented long ago in sackcloth and ashes. But I tell you, it will be more bearable for Tyre and Sidon on the day of judgement than for you' (Matt. 11:22).

The nations, despite their ignorance of some things, were not guiltless. They had a responsibility to live up to the light they possessed. The people of Jerusalem, and indeed Judah as a whole, were entirely different. They had been entrusted with the Word of God (cf. Rom. 3:1-2). But we have already seen that Jerusalem was guilty of apostasy. Chapter 1 introduced us to a catalogue of the sins of God's people (1:10-20). The vine that was Jerusalem had produced only bitter fruit (ch. 5).

King Ahaz led the way: 'The Lord had humbled Judah because of Ahaz king of Israel, for he had promoted wickedness in Judah and had been most unfaithful to the Lord. Tiglath-Pileser king of Assyria came to him, but gave him trouble instead of help. Ahaz took some of the things from the temple of the Lord and from the royal palace and from the princes and presented them to the king of Assyria, but that did not help him. In his time of trouble King Ahaz became even more unfaithful to the Lord' (2 Chron. 28:19-22). He had disclosed the moral and religious bankruptcy of Judah by sacrificing his own son to the sacrificial flames of Molech's altar (2 Kings 16:3-4), as did Hezekiah's successor Manasseh (2 Kings 21:6; cf. Isa. 30:33). Clearly, it was time for God to act.

Hezekiah succeeded Ahaz in 715 B.C. (though he had been co-regent since possibly 729 B.C.). Hezekiah was largely devout and a reformer; though he must share in the blame for the abortive 'Ashdod revolt' in 713 B.C. (recorded in ch. 20).

Hezekiah never attempted rebellion again — at least, not until after Sargon II had died in 705 B.C. Sennacherib picked up where Sargon II left off. He brought his men to the very gates of Jerusalem itself. Isaiah seems to be reporting the event in this chapter.[2]

Escapism

The scene depicts a contrast. On the one hand there is revelry:

> **'O town full of commotion,**
> **O city of tumult and revelry? ...**
> **But see, there is joy and revelry,**
> **slaughtering of cattle and killing of sheep,**
> **eating of meat and drinking of wine!**
> **"Let us eat and drink," you say,**
> **"for tomorrow we die!"'**

(22:2,13).

On the other hand there is the depiction of death and destruction in Jerusalem's downfall: starvation (22:2), fleeing leaders (22:3 — perhaps King Zedekiah and his army who fled Jerusalem but were captured near Jericho, 2 Kings 25:4-6), encroaching armies including mercenaries from Elam and Kir (22:6-7), houses being torn down to strengthen the wall (22:10, perhaps connected with Hezekiah's preparations in 2 Chron. 32:5).

Sennacherib became King of Assyria in 705 B.C. By 701 B.C. he had marched into Palestine to confront Hezekiah and his allies. Elsewhere, he had dealt with the revolt of Merodach-Baladan, who had successfully kept Sargon II at bay in Babylon for twelve years, but in 702 B.C. his revolt collapsed in the face of Sennacherib's troops. In the west Sennacherib dealt Phœnicia a severe blow (this is, in part, the background to the next chapter, ch. 23). He then marched down to Philistine territory, taking effective action against them (the so-called 'Ashdod crisis' of 20:1-6). An Egyptian army put in an appearance, but was routed by the Assyrians at Eltekeh, halfway between Joppa and Ashdod (cf. 19:1-15). Next, Assyria turned its attention upon Judah. 'As for Hezekiah,' Sennacherib recorded, 'forty-six of his strong walled towns and innumerable smaller villages in their neighbourhood I besieged and conquered ... I made to come out from them 200,150 people ... and counted them as spoils of war.' As for Hezekiah himself, he was 'shut up like a caged bird within Jerusalem, his royal city'.

One of the major cities to fall was Lachish, nearly thirty miles south-west of Jerusalem. Since the Assyrians never captured Jerusalem (cf. what Isaiah had already predicted in 10:27-32), Lachish became important to them as a base of operations. It was from Lachish that an armed embassy was dispatched to Jerusalem, which included the commander-in-chief, the chief eunuch and the chief officer. The entire story is recorded in 2 Kings 18 and elaborated upon later in Isaiah (36:2 - 37:8). For now it is important to realize that Sennacherib was caused to retreat due to pressures elsewhere in his empire.

Perhaps Isaiah is thinking of the escapist mentality of Jerusalem's inhabitants after Sennacherib's retreat from Jerusalem. He was unsuccessful in his attempt to sack the city, though the three stages of the siege did inflict many casualties from disease and starvation.[3] In the very first chapter of Isaiah, we are told that

Jerusalem resembled 'a shelter in a vineyard, like a hut in a field of melons, like a city under siege' (1:8). That description was never as apt as it was now.

The philosopher Hegel once said that the only lesson that can be learnt from history is that man learns nothing at all. During Sennacherib's invasion of Judah two-thirds of the population died or were taken captive! Less than a century later Babylon came with even greater strength, destroying Jerusalem and its temple in 586 B.C. In a century that has known two world wars it would seem that the West has learnt virtually nothing from them. People have not turned to God in any great numbers as a consequence; indeed, it would seem that escapism is a characteristic of our age also. Just as in Isaiah's day, so now, there is a lack of repentance evidenced in the face of calamity.

Isaiah suggests that the inhabitants of Jerusalem looked to three sources for protection from the aggressor.

The first was the *weapons* stored **'in the Palace of the Forest'** (22:8). This was an armoury built in the time of King Solomon: 'He also made three hundred small shields of hammered gold, with three minas of gold in each shield. The king put them in the Palace of the Forest of Lebanon' (1 Kings 10:17).

Secondly, the city of Jerusalem was surrounded by *thick walls*, thought to be impregnable. During the three-year siege by Sennacherib, Hezekiah secured these walls further by using material taken from some of the houses within Jerusalem (2 Chron. 32:5).

Thirdly, the *water supply* into Jerusalem was always a crucial factor in the city's defence (see comments on 8:6). When Hezekiah was threatened by Sennacherib he stopped up all the sources of water that led down into the Kedron 'stream that flowed through the land' (2 Chron. 32:4). The upper Gihon waters were then diverted through a 'conduit' or tunnel into an upper cistern or pool on the west side of the city (2 Kings 20:20). The new water source was then defended with a rampart (2 Chron. 32:30). It is this reservoir that is referred to in verse 11.

This remarkable feat of engineering survives to this day and is 540 metres long, twisting to avoid a rock fault or to follow a fissure. It is about two metres high and in parts only fifty centimetres wide. Bathers in the upper pool in 1880 found about five metres inside the tunnel a cursive Hebrew inscription (now in Istanbul) which reads:

'... was being dug out. It was cut in the following manner ... axes, each man towards his fellow, and while there were still three cubits to be cut through, the voice of one man calling to the other was heard, showing that he was deviating to the right. When the tunnel was driven through, the excavators met man to man, axe to axe, and the water flowed for 1,200 cubits from the spring to the reservoir. The height of the rock above the heads of the excavators was 100 cubits.'[4]

Jerusalem's confidence in all of these things reveals her lack of faith. They had no regard for God: **'You did not look to the One who made it, or have regard for the One who planned it long ago'** (22:11). A similar warning will be given again, this time when Jerusalem looked to Egypt for help:

'Woe to those who go down to Egypt for help,
   who rely on horses,
who trust in the multitude of their chariots
   and in the great strength of their horsemen,
but do not look to the Holy One of Israel,
   or seek help from the Lord'

(31:1).

A better confession is that of David: 'Some trust in chariots and some in horses, but we trust in the name of the Lord our God' (Ps. 20:7).

A prophet's tears

Clearly, the trouble that came upon Jerusalem was from the Lord (22:5). God was chastising his own people, as he had said he would if they strayed from his ways. Though Eliphaz was not always right when he spoke, he was only expressing a biblical truth when he urged upon Job the admonition: 'Blessed is the man whom God corrects; so do not despise the discipline of the Almighty' (Job 5:17). This was David's testimony too: 'Blessed is the man you discipline, O Lord, the man you teach from your law' (Ps. 94:12). Discipline involves 'hardship' (Heb.12:7); it is invariably unpleasant and painful (Heb. 12:11). There are times when the Lord 'whips' his children! (Heb. 12:6).

Even so, there is virtually nothing in this passage to indicate that they listened to what God was saying. So impenitent were they, that Isaiah makes it perfectly clear what the consequences would be: **'The Lord Almighty has revealed this in my hearing: "Till your dying day this sin will not be atoned for," says the Lord, the Lord Almighty'** (22:14). Isaiah did not believe in universal atonement. He did not believe that there was a way to heaven for the ungodly. Views currently fashionable which suggest that holiness is an option but not a necessity as a mark of regeneration find no approval with Old Testament prophets. Those who lacked repentance were not assured of heaven. Isaiah only says what later biblical writers would confirm: 'But because of your stubbornness and your unrepentant heart, you are storing up wrath against yourself for the day of God's wrath, when his righteous judgement will be revealed' (Rom. 2:5). 'Make every effort to ... be holy; without holiness no one will see the Lord' (Heb. 12:14).

It is the prophet's own response that is most touching. Confronted by Jerusalem's lack of faith and repentance, Isaiah himself is moved to exclaim:

'Turn away from me;
  let me weep bitterly.
Do not try to console me
  over the destruction of my people'

(22:4).

Calvin comments: 'Thus, when in the present day the church is afflicted by so many and so various calamities, and innumerable souls are perishing, which Christ redeemed with his own blood, we must be barbarous and savage if we are not touched with any grief. And especially the ministers of the Word ought to be moved by this feeling of grief, because, being appointed to keep watch and to look at a distance, they ought also to groan when they perceive the tokens of approaching ruin.'[5]

Only a spirit sensitive to the concerns of God will keep us from the dangers of professionalism and formalism in Christian work. Richard Baxter's maxim, 'to preach as a dying man to dying men,' seems appropriate as the way all Christians should approach work done for the Lord. It was evidently the way Isaiah approached his calling.

How are the mighty fallen! (22:15-25)

We are now introduced to a man called Shebna (22:15; cf. 36:3 - 37:8). His position is variously described as **'steward'**, or treasurer (22:15), minister **'who is in charge of the palace'** (22:15), and 'secretary' (2 Kings 18:18; 19:2; Isa . 36:3).

Shebna was typical of worldly politicians who, in a time of crisis, resort to anything but prayer to Almighty God. It appears he was the leader of a party of men in high office in Jerusalem who believed a treaty with Egypt was in order to counter Assyrian threats (cf. chs 30-31). He was a traitor in Hezekiah's cabinet!

It appears that he was busily engaged in hewing out a tomb for himself.[6] Shebna was not of puritan stock; he was not one of those who believed it right to be ready to die at God's behest and to be 'packed up and ready to go' to be the best attitude to life. Nor was he like Paul, anxious to 'depart and to be with Christ' (Phil. 1:23). Shebna's concern was for recognition and honour after his death. The elaborate tomb among the honoured and rich of Jerusalem was vanity, pure and simple. Isaiah has only one word for him: he is a **'disgrace'** (22:18).

Shebna, like all worldly men, had one plan for his future; God had another. Instead of glory and recognition would come abandonment and dismissal. The language is graphic: God would **'hurl'** him away like a rolled up ball of wool (22:17-18). Perhaps we are meant to understand that the very chariots on which he prided himself would be the means of his transport to Babylon, where he would die —unknown and forgotten (22:18). Shebna is a symbol of the futility of those who think they can carve out glory for themselves and do not reckon upon God.

Before Shebna suffered this fate, however, he appears to have been demoted. In 36:3-22 Eliakim has succeeded him; Shebna appears to hold a lesser office. Perhaps Isaiah's words were listened to in Hezekiah's next cabinet meeting!

If, as I have suggested, Isaiah has so far been reporting the facts about Shebna (i.e. some time around 701 B.C.) what follows with respect to his successor Eliakim, on the other hand, is prophecy (note **'in that day...'** 22:25). His responsibilities will be enormous. He will be given the **'key to the house of David'** (22:22). All the secrets and treasures of David's house were under his safe keeping. His power would be unquestionable: **'What he opens no one can**

shut, and what he shuts no one can open' (22:22); his security sure: **'I will drive him like a peg into a firm place'** (22:23); his dignity majestic: **'He will be a seat of honour for the house of his father'** (22:23).

In a fallen world, power breeds corruption, and absolute power breeds absolute corruption. Eliakim seems to have been guilty of nepotism — giving preferential posts to members of his family. In violent imagery Isaiah predicts that his **'peg ... will give way ... sheared off'** (22:25). It is not clear when this took place, but we may be sure that it did, because **'The Lord has spoken'** (22:25).

Where Eliakim failed, God's Messiah did not. As so often in the Bible, the type must give way to the antitype. Priests, prophets and kings are each one frail and sinful — until God's Son arrives, who alone is sinless and perfect. The ultimate authority belongs to him: he it is who has the key of David, who opens the door that no man can shut (Rev. 3:7-8). Through Christ, his servants in the church possess disciplinary authority too — but only through him (cf. Matt. 16:19; 18:18).

Summary

There is a tendency — even amongst God's people — to escape the reality of God's wrath. Things are never as bad as what the Bible depicts; the need for reformation is never as acute as prophets like Isaiah declared it to be. But this is muddled, even fatal, reasoning. The time to repent is now!

16.
Isaiah's Apocalypse

Please read Isaiah 24

Chapter 24 introduces us to a new section of the prophecy. Following the judgement on the nations (chs. 13-23) the whole world now comes into view. The next four chapters are sometimes known as the 'Isaiah Apocalypse' because they reflect, in part, what John has to say in the book of Revelation. They form a conclusion to the judgements that have already been uttered.

Although set in Isaiah's world, the chapters cover the overthrow of the supernatural (24:21-3; 27:1) and of death (25:8), and the promise of bodily resurrection (26:19)

Initially, Isaiah depicts a 'local' scene, but we are meant to see beyond it a foretaste of another judgement far more awesome.

Devastation (24:1-12)

'If Felix trembled when Paul preached of judgement (Acts 24:25),' exclaimed Thomas Watson, 'how will sinners tremble when they shall see Christ come to judgement!'[1] Few chapters in Scripture underline the seriousness of what Christianity is all about more clearly than this one. Those who bid Christians 'Smile! God loves you,' must also remember that it is a dreadful thing to fall into the hands of the living God (Heb.10:31). Several matters regarding the judgement of God surface in this chapter.

1. The judgement is universal

The first thing to settle is what the prophet means by the word
'earth':

> **'See, the Lord is going to lay waste the earth**
>   **and devastate it;**
> **he will ruin its face**
>   **and scatter its inhabitants'**

(24:1).

Commentators differ widely: some limit verses 1-12 to Judah;[2]
others include in the reference the known inhabited world of Isaiah's
day;[3] but it would seem more appropriate to see in these verses a
reference to the judgement at the end of time.[4] Certainly, there
appear to be things of cosmic proportion in view here. God is
coming to judge the world! But it would seem appropriate to limit
the scope of the prophecy initially to Judah and its forthcoming
exile. The reference to 'breaking the everlasting covenant' (24:5) is
then a clear reference to the covenant made with Israel at Sinai (see
comments below). However, there are intimations of wider things
in the chapter: Judah's future — judgement followed by a restoration of the remnant — is a cameo of what will take place at the
judgement at the end of the age.[5]

2. The judgement is cataclysmic

The language is of devastation, destruction, scattering and plunder-
ing (24:1,3). It is the language of divine displeasure and is of the
same order as other metaphors: 'unquenchable fire' (Matt. 3:12),
'where the fire is not quenched' (Mark 9:48), 'weeping and gnash-
ing of teeth' (Matt. 25:30) and 'shut out from the presence of the
Lord' (2 Thess. 1:9).

3. The judgement affects all classes

In judgement, as in grace, God is no respecter of persons. Social
distinctions provide no means of escape (24:2). All come before him
'uncovered and bare' (cf. Heb. 4:13).

4. The judgement destroys joy

What characterizes the fate of the judged in this chapter is their lack of joy. The contrasts are telling: those who lived for joy and pleasure (7-8; cf. 22:13) have been silenced: **'All joy is turned to gloom'** (24:11). It is a solemn reminder that the pleasures of sin are only 'for a short time' (Heb. 11:25).

5. The breaking of the covenant

The cause of the judgement is sin, here defined as a violation of God's laws (24:5; cf. 'sin is lawlessness', 1 John 3:4). Specifically, they have **'broken the everlasting covenant'** (24:5). This needs some explanation. Since the judgement is universal it might be argued that this is unfair since the Gentiles were not in possession of the law. But, as Paul argues in Romans, 'The requirements of the law are written on their hearts' (Rom. 2:15).

Reference to the 'covenant' raises the question: 'Which covenant?' It may, at first, appear to be the covenant made with Noah, a universal covenant made with every living creature (Gen. 9:9-10; cf. Isa. 24:18-20).[6] God did indeed promise to Noah never again to destroy the earth by a flood in the way that he had done (Gen. 9:11). But since this covenant contained no requirements on man's part (it was an unconditional covenant), how can it be broken? E. J. Young, who takes the view that this is a reference to the covenant with Adam, argues more generally by suggesting that Isaiah has in mind the fact that all mankind was represented in Adam. All mankind are deemed covenant-breakers by virtue of the covenant of works which Adam transgressed as our federal representative.[7]

Others have seen here a reference to the Mosaic covenant.[8] This would seem the most appropriate. God's denunciation of Judah is due to the way she has violated the covenant. Consequently, the curse (24:6) or 'vengeance of the covenant' (Lev. 26:25) has come upon her.

6. The restoration of the remnant

Following the judgement, there is a restoration of a remnant. Isaiah has led us to believe before now that after God has done his judging

work, there will be a remnant who will return in faithfulness to him
(cf. 10:20-22). Here, he speaks of a **'very few'** (24:6) and **'gleanings'** (24:13). Specifically, this is a reference to the 42,360 mentioned in Ezra 2:64 who returned in the initial phase from Babylon.
But a wider scenario is in view: the inheritance, by the meek, of the
land, as Jesus promised: 'Blessed are the meek, for they will inherit
the earth' (Matt. 5:5; cf. Ps. 37:11). Only the new heavens and new
earth inherited by Christians following the return of Christ fulfil
these prophecies adequately.

Give me joy in my heart!

At first glance the **'joy'** of verses 14-16 seems out of place in a
chapter that has depicted such awesome judgement.[9] The explanation for it is twofold: first, it must be remembered that those who
walk closely with God develop a mind-set that is akin to his. Taking
the matter to its limit, we may ask, 'How shall I cope when loved
ones are punished by God in hell?' This outlines the very periphery
of what we can understand about the hereafter. What can be said is
this: the redeemed will rejoice in the destruction of Satan and his
seed as the vindication of his kingdom. Robert Murray M'Cheyne
put it like this: 'As sure as there is a God in heaven, and as there is
a hell for the wicked, so surely will the redeemed rejoice over the
eternal damnation of the wicked. And this is the reason: we will
enter into the same mind with God.'[10] This is evident here by their
desire to exalt the 'righteous' nature of God (24:16).[11] Everything he
does is right and defies questioning on our part.

As Donald Macleod writes, 'What must guide us in this whole
area is, surely, the attitude of God himself and that is described for
us unmistakably in Ezekiel 33:11: "As I live, saith the Lord, I have
no pleasure in the death of the wicked." This makes it perfectly plain
that God Himself is not excited to joyful praises by the destruction
of the impenitent. We have already seen that however resolutely He
condemns the defiant, His condemnation is rooted not in malice but
in equity. He condemns only beacuse it is right and even then we
must believe (on the basis of Hosea 11:8) that He acts with
reluctance, not as one doing something He relishes but as one doing
something he must.'[12]

Secondly, the joy expressed here is a response by the remnant to what God has done for them. Repeatedly, it is to God that the glory is given: **'Therefore ... give glory to the Lord; exalt the name of the Lord'** (24:15). The knowledge that God is in control of our lives is cause for joy. Indeed, joy was God's plan from the beginning. What Eden robbed us of, Christ restores. Joy is our chief end, the Reformers taught. It is something we must cultivate. 'Complete' joy is what we are meant to possess, Jesus said (John 16:24).

'The day of the Lord'

If the remnant are singing with joyful hearts it is because the judgement is over. Isaiah himself is filled with grief and sorrow because, from his perspective, it is still future. The sight of God's people in trouble moves him.

> **'But I said, "I waste away, I waste away!**
> **Woe to me!**
> **The treacherous betray!**
> **With treachery the treacherous betray!"'**

(24:16).

Here is yet another insight into the heart of this preacher. What he warns affects him deeply. 'Preach to yourselves', warned Richard Baxter, 'the sermons which you study, *before* you preach them to others.'[13]

Preachers are taught to construct sermons with clear headings and divisions. Clarity aids understanding. Isaiah knew a thing or two about sermon technique. Using alliteration and assonance he powerfully responds in Hebrew:

> *'Razi li, razi li! 'Oy li!*
> *Bogedim bagadu! Ubeged bogedim bagadu!'*

In the next verse he adds three more words descriptive of the forthcoming judgement: *pahad, pahat, pah* (terror, pit, snare).

Isaiah has moved forward in time to cover not only the coming of the Babylonians, but the Day of Judgement itself. The heavens are opened, the earth shakes (24:18-20); the heavenly powers are deployed against the 'kings of the earth' (24:21); the enemies of God are kept in prison for a while and then punished (24:22); the sun and moon are darkened (24:23); God reigns gloriously (24:23) — all these are intimations of passages elsewhere in the Bible which describe the final judgement. In addition to what Isaiah has already told us in the opening verses of this chapter, he now adds the following points.

1. The final judgement is final!

When the earth is judged, the judgement will be such that it will never rise again (24:20). There is something decisive and irrevocable about this event. Sinners whose sin is not pardoned by faith in God's Son — a promise for Isaiah and his contemporaries, a reality for you and me — will be cast out never to find a way of return. The story of Lazarus and the rich man in Luke 16 emphasizes this point: 'And besides all this, between us and you a great chasm has been fixed, so that those who want to go from here to you cannot, nor can anyone cross over from there to us' (Luke 16:26).

2. The judgement will include Satan and the fallen angels

The fact that angels will be judged is clear from 1 Corinthians 6:2-3: 'Do you not know that the saints will judge the world? And if you are to judge the world, are you not competent to judge trivial cases? Do you not know that we will judge angels? How much more the things of this life!' It is also evident from 2 Peter 2:4: 'For if God did not spare angels when they sinned, but sent them to hell, putting them into gloomy dungeons to be held for judgement...' (cf. Jude 6). The battle that we wage is never as simple as it appears: arrayed against us are 'the powers of this dark world and ... the spiritual forces of evil in the heavenly realms' (Eph. 6:12).

3. The judgement takes place after a period of imprisonment

Clearly, there are similarities here to the famous (and difficult!) passage in Revelation 20:1-3 which refers to the binding and release of Satan, together with his final doom. God's enemies are to be imprisoned, but when? If the judgement does not take place until 'after many days' of imprisonment, and if we take this judgement to be the final judgement, when does the initial imprisonment take place?

It is clear that the demons are aware of their impending doom from their words to Christ: 'Have you come here to torture us before the appointed time?' (Matt. 8:29). But there are also indications in the New Testament that Satan and his hosts were 'bound' at the time of Christ's first coming. When the Pharisees accused Jesus of casting out demons by the power of Satan, Jesus replied, 'Or again, how can anyone enter a strong man's house and carry off his possessions unless he first ties up the strong man? Then he can rob his house' (Matt. 12:29). The word used for 'tying up' here is the same word used in Revelation 20 to describe the binding of Satan (cf. Luke 10:17-18; John 12:31-32). The passage is consistent with a view that sees Satan and his hosts as curtailed in their power during the period between the two advents of Christ.

4. The end is sheer glory

Whatever the precise details of future prophecy, the end is certain: God will reign gloriously. Even the light of the sun and moon pale into insignificance before his light (Rev. 21:22-24). This is a theme to which Isaiah will return again in chapter 60:

> 'The sun will no more be your light by day,
>   nor will the brightness of the moon shine on you,
> for the Lord will be your everlasting light,
>   and your God will be your glory.
> Your sun will never set again,
>   and your moon will wane no more;
> the Lord will be your everlasting light,
>   and your days of sorrow will end'
>
> (60:19-20).

Summary

One thing is clear: no one can be complacent about the future. Isaiah, in his youth, may well have heard Amos preach. Both share certain themes and in this chapter certain verses are identical (compare

24:17-18 with Amos 5:19). Amos warned the northern Israelites about complacency, saying,

> 'Woe to you who long
>   for the day of the Lord!
> Why do you long for the day of the Lord?
>   That day will be darkness, not light'

(Amos 5:18).

History is moving towards its inevitable goal: the day of the Lord. For those who are in fellowship with God, this is a matter of supreme joy (cf. 24:14-16). For those who are not, it is a day of 'darkness, not light'.

17.
The shadow of a mighty rock within a weary land

Please read Isaiah 25-27

Like Mary's Magnificat (Luke 1:46-56), Isaiah 25:1-5 is a song of praise for what God has done. The remnant were pitifully small — like the gleanings left in the corner of a field, or a few olives missed at the top of a tree (24:13; cf. 17:6). Amos compared the remnant to a single coal left glowing after a camp-fire, or to the legs and ears left from a lion's kill (Amos 3:12; 4:11-12).

But after the storm comes a bright rainbow of promise. God will not only deliver his people; he will take away their hearts of stone and give them new ones (Ezek. 36:26-27). He will establish a New Covenant with them (Jer. 31:31-34). He will spread his feast for all kinds of people (25:6-8). Little wonder, after the darkness of chapter 24, that this chapter opens with a song of the redeemed.

Three features of this song are particularly important.

1. God is faithful to a plan made 'long ago'

'Faithfulness' (25:1) is a particularly Old Testament word signifying loyalty and commitment to the covenant God has made with sinners through his Son. At Sinai, with the two tablets of the covenant in his hands, Moses heard the Lord declare about himself that he abounded in faithfulness (Exod. 34:6). Over thirty times, the Psalms rejoice in God's faithfulness (Ps. 36:5; 40:10; 57:3,10; 71:22). It is something the psalmist was to repeat every evening (Ps. 92:2).

Especially interesting is the passage in Psalm 91 which uses a metaphor that is repeated in Isaiah 25:4, that of God as a shelter in the storm: 'He will cover you with his feathers, and under his wings you will find refuge; his faithfulness will be your shield and rampart' (Ps. 91:4). By way of a summary statement Jeremiah caught the mood of Old Testament believers when he said,

'Because of the Lord's great love we are not consumed,
  for his compassions never fail.
They are new every morning;
  great is your faithfulness'

                                                              (Lam. 3:22-23).

God keeps his word. You and I can depend on it.

2. *God helps the helpless*

The 'poor' and 'needy' are promised help from a merciful and gracious God (25:4). This is how Isaiah saw himself, crying out in response to God's majesty,'Woe to me!' (6:5; 24:16).

In the searing heat of a Middle-Eastern summer, the shelter provided by a shadow can be a life-saver. But shadows of this kind are temporary and shifting. As Jonah found, crouching under the gourd vine, such protection is short-lived. There is, however, a source of relief from the heat that is permanent:

**'You have been a refuge for the poor,
  a refuge for the needy in his distress,
a shelter from the storm
  and a shade from the heat.
For the breath of the ruthless
  is like a storm driving against a wall
  and like the heat of the desert.
You silence the uproar of foreigners;
  as heat is reduced by the shadow of a cloud,
  so the song of the ruthless is stilled'**

                                                              (25:4-5).

This is also the theme of Psalm 91:

'He who dwells in the shelter of the Most High
  will rest in the shadow of the Almighty.

I will say of the Lord, "He is my refuge and my fortress,
    my God, in whom I trust."
Surely he will save you from the fowler's snare
    and from the deadly pestilence.
He will cover you with his feathers,
    and under his wings you will find refuge;
    his faithfulness will be your shield and rampart.
You will not fear the terror of night,
    nor the arrow that flies by day,
nor the pestilence that stalks in the darkness,
    nor the plague that destroys at midday.
A thousand may fall at your side,
    ten thousand at your right hand,
    but it will not come near you'

(Ps. 91:1-7).

And again in Psalm 121 we read:

'He who watches over you will not slumber;
indeed, he who watches over Israel
    will neither slumber nor sleep.
The Lord watches over you —
    the Lord is your shade at your right hand;
the sun will not harm you by day,
    nor the moon by night.
The Lord will keep you from all harm —
    he will watch over your life'

(Ps. 121:3-7).

Nor are we to be uncertain as to the means by which protection and shade are offered to needy sinners: the metaphor has been used before in Isaiah in connection with the Branch (4:6). Christ is the only shelter from God's wrath, having taken it upon himself as our substitute (53:5).

3. God is immutable

The implication of verse 4 is that just as God has proved a help in the past, he will continue to do so now and in the future. His faithfulness implies dependability. God's 'shadow' never shifts, because God does not change: 'Every good and perfect gift is from above, coming down from the Father of the heavenly lights, who does not change like shifting shadows' (James 1:17). God is not evolving, or in flux; the Bible is resolute as to the immutability of God. He is 'the same yesterday and today and for ever' (Heb. 13:8).

Here, Isaiah implies that God's *character* does not change. The immutability of God is something Isaiah is fond of emphasizing again and again. God's *life* does not change: 'Listen to me ... I am the first and I am the last' (48:12). God's *truth* does not change: 'All men are like grass ... the grass withers ... but the word of our God stands for ever' (40:7-8). God's *purposes* do not change. He has a 'plan' made in eternity (25:1; cf. 14:24,26-27; 23:8-9). 'One of two things,' wrote A. W. Pink, 'causes a man to change his mind and reverse his plans: want of foresight to anticipate everything, or lack of power to execute them. But as God is both omniscient and omnipotent there is never any need for him to revise his decrees.'[1]

Death is swallowed up in victory (25:6-12)

The Bible often uses the picture of a feast to describe the future state of believers. Jesus foretold of a day when 'Many will come from the east and the west, and will take their places at the feast with Abraham, Isaac and Jacob in the kingdom of heaven' (Matt. 8:11). In the account of the parable of the great banquet, someone says to Jesus, 'Blessed is the man who will eat at the feast in the kingdom of God' (Luke 14:15). A similar figure is deployed in the parable of the Ten Virgins (Matt. 25:1-10). And in Revelation, John sees believers, one day, partaking of a marriage supper (Rev. 19:9).

A remnant will be delivered and the Lord will spread a feast for them:

> **'On this mountain the Lord Almighty will prepare**
> **a feast of rich food for all peoples,**
> **a banquet of aged wine—**
> **the best of meats and the finest of wines.**
> **On this mountain he will destroy**
> **the shroud that enfolds all peoples,**
> **the sheet that covers all nations;**
> **he will swallow up death for ever'**

(25:6-8).

Death, the great swallower of all, will itself be swallowed up. Paul, taking up these words in 1 Corinthians 15:54, sees the destruction of death as the ultimate consequence of the resurrection of Jesus Christ. 'Victory' is what Christ has gained for us. This is what Isaiah was portraying centuries before Christ came. There is a way for sinful men and women to be restored into fellowship with God. It is bound up with the Messiah, God's suffering Servant, of whom Isaiah had so much to say. Verse 9 undoubtedly refers to his triumphant work on our behalf.

The words of verse 9 are capable of a threefold interpretation:

'In that day they will say,

"Surely this is our God;
 we trusted in him, and he saved us.
This is the Lord, we trusted in him;
 let us rejoice and be glad in his salvation"'

(25:9).

First, they could well refer to *the siege of Jerusalem* by Sennacherib. For three years and ten months he attempted to starve the people into submission, but was unsuccessful. Hezekiah ensured that they put their trust in the Lord (see chs 36-39).

Second, this victory is, as we have seen, part of *the victory celebration of the redeemed in heaven*. Having trusted in God's Son, the redeemed will emerge through the judgement to an eternity of paradise: a time of endless praise to him who conquered death and hell (cf. Rev. 7:14-17).

Thirdly, these words depict yet another event: *the appearance of the great Deliverer*. It is as though Isaiah can see the godly remnant in Judea who had long expected Messiah to appear: folk like Anna, Zecharias, Simeon, Elizabeth and John the Baptist. One can almost hear the aged Simeon, as he takes the baby Jesus into his arms, saying, 'This is our God! He will save us!' (Luke 2:29-32). Calvin summarizes the meaning this way: 'Christ will never disappoint the hopes of his people, if they call on him with patience.'[2]

In contrast to the mountain of Zion (25:6), where all is peace and blessedness, Moab's mountain (25:10), which lies across the Jordan, is under God's judgement. Between Zion and Moab is a great gulf. Standing on the mountain range between Jerusalem and Bethlehem, looking eastwards towards Moab, one is impressed by the depth of the valley which separates Judah from Moab. It is a gulf which reminds us of the chasm separating Lazarus from the rich man (Luke 16:19-31). Moab is merely symbolic of all God's enemies. When Messiah comes, he will put down the pride of his enemies. They are treated with the contempt of a dung-pit. Again, as in the previous chapter (24:16), Isaiah uses the literary technique of assonance to get his point across. The Hebrew word for 'dung-pit' (*madmenah*) is similar to the name of a Moabite city called Madmena.[3] There could hardly be a more graphic way of portraying the end of the wicked than to stand in one of Jerusalem's backstreets and point to a pile of dung and say, 'That's what becomes of God's enemies!'

Peace, perfect peace! (26:1-15)

The theme of praise, which began chapter 25 (25:1-5), continues in chapter 26: **'In that day this song will be sung in the land of Judah...'** (26:1). In contrast to what has happened to Moab, 'the city of God' remains **'strong'** (26:1) and **'lofty'** (26:5). When Augustine wrote his book *The City of God* depicting the Christian life, he was merely picking up the Bible's own metaphor. Isaiah depicts pilgrims coming from afar, arriving at the gates of the city and calling out in song for the doors to be opened wide to receive them (26:2). Jerusalem's strength, the peace enjoyed by its inhabitants, comes from the salvation which God has caused to make known within its walls. The song is not only a testimony of what those who sing it have come to know; it is also an exhortation to others to put their trust in the Lord and experience the same transformation in their own lives.

Edward Bickersteth caught the meaning of these words in these lines of his hymn, 'Peace, perfect peace':

Peace, perfect peace, in this dark world of sin?
The blood of Jesus whispers peace within.

Peace, perfect peace, with sorrows surging round?
On Jesus' bosom naught but calm is found.

Peace, perfect peace, our future all unknown?
Jesus we know, and he is on the throne.

Peace, perfect peace, death shadowing us and ours?
Jesus has vanquished death and all its powers.

It is enough: earth's struggles soon shall cease,
And Jesus call us to heaven's perfect peace.

Several points are worth noting which are distinctive features of those who occupy the city of God.

1. They are righteous

Thus those who are **'righteous'** (26:2,7) have received their righteousness from the Lord. As E. J. Young puts it, 'Into the holy city of God there will not enter anything that defileth; the people that was defiled, however, will enter in; for their defilement has been removed and they have received the Lord's righteousness.'[4]

2. They are blessed

The 'way' they traverse is **'level'** and **'smooth'** (26:7), whereas the way of the wicked is crooked and full of obstacles: in the end, fire will consume them (26:11). Isaiah did not believe in universal redemption: in the end everyone will *not* be saved. God, however, will ensure that the righteous will reach heaven. 'But for this,' Calvin remarks, 'they would easily fall or give way through exhaustion, and would hardly ever make way amidst so many thorns and briars, steep roads, intricate windings, and rough places, did not the Lord lead out and deliver them.'[5]

3. They long for God's presence

The song, having spoken of the pilgrim's arrival at the city, now turns into a prayer for God's presence: **'Yes, Lord ... we wait for you; your name and renown are the desire of our hearts'** (26:8). Recalling that this section is of the nature of an apocalypse of the last days, we are reminded that the presence of God is not always gracious. There are times when he comes in judgement, and when he does the righteous will learn repentance. But not so the wicked (26:9-10). They remain in their unbelief despite the providential warnings all around them.

'Though grace is shown to the wicked,
    they do not learn righteousness;
even in a land of uprightness they go on doing evil
    and regard not the majesty of the Lord.
O Lord, your hand is lifted high,
    but they do not see it'

(26:10-11).

The longing for God to come here in order that he might speedily
execute his judgements upon the wicked and ungodly is the same
longing that characterizes the last few verses of the Bible: 'Come,
Lord Jesus' (Rev. 22:20).

4. They enjoy peace

Following on from and intimately related to the three points already
made, Isaiah sees the righteous in a state of peace (26:3,12). In
particular, other rulers who once ruled over them have now died:

'They are now dead, they live no more;
    those departed spirits do not rise.
You punished them and brought them to ruin;
    you wiped out all memory of them'

(26:14).

Isaiah is not denying the resurrection of the dead as such. His
point is merely to give comfort to the Lord's people that the ones
who troubled them so much will trouble them no more.

5. They confess their past failure and frustration

Times of trouble can bring us to our knees. Evidently, Israel had
been in such distress that they were barely able to pray (26:16). But
God hears even our whispers. Eli thought Hannah was drunk when
she mumbled in the outer courts of the temple, but the Lord knew it
to be otherwise (1 Sam. 1:9-20). The trouble was a chastisement, of
course: God was teaching his people to trust him more than they did.
Israel had conceived many ways to free herself from her troubles:
alliances with foreign nations, for example. But they had come to

naught. It was a like a pregnant woman giving birth to nothing but wind! (26:18). Every attempt at self-salvation is doomed to failure. It is the prevailing lesson of Old Testament history that salvation is by grace — sovereign grace!

After the prayer comes the Lord's answer (26:19-27:1). And what an answer!

'But your dead will live;
their bodies will rise.
You who dwell in the dust,
wake up and shout for joy.
Your dew is like the dew of the morning;
the earth will give birth to her dead'

(26:19).

This is Isaiah's description of the resurrection of the body. Not only are the Lord's people delivered from their enemies in this world; they are promised a total deliverance in a new life to come. It is similar to what Daniel saw in his apocalypse: 'Multitudes who sleep in the dust of the earth will awake: some to everlasting life, others to shame and everlasting contempt' (Dan. 12:2). Together, these two Old Testament verses depict a bodily resurrection of the just and the unjust to an eternity of blessedness or condemnation.

6. They wait patiently and quietly for the coming of the Lord

The Lord's wrath is not yet revealed. As Noah was encouraged to hide in the ark (Gen. 7:1), and Israel was told to take refuge from the destroying angel (Exod. 12:22), so now God's people are encouraged to hide behind locked doors from God's wrath (26:20). Salvation will be accomplished by God alone. The immediate reference is the exile in Babylon, but the judgement at the end of time is in view also: **'In that day...'** (27:1).

God's enemies are described by an allusion to a mythical sea monster, **'Leviathan'** (27:1; cf. Ps.74:14; 104:26; Job 3:8; Isa. 51:9). This reminds us of John's description of the devil and his followers as 'the dragon and his angels' in Revelation 12:7 - 13:1. The fact that Isaiah mentions a mythical creature need not imply that the prophet was under an apprehension of its genuine existence. In the same way that we might refer to some dictator today as a 'monster', Isaiah uses a figure of speech that would readily have meaning to his hearers. The point is clear enough: Satan is doomed.

The harvest theme (27:2-13)

Isaiah's Apocalypse (24:1-27:13) has shown the coming judgement of the world (24:17-23), the downfall of God's enemies (24:21-23; 27:1) and of death itself (25:8). It has also spoken of the safety of God's people within his own eternal city (26:1-6), promising complete deliverance from his wrath and eventual bodily resurrection (26:19-21).

The aim of God for his people is not only their salvation from sin and its curse; it is that they might be fruitful. The passage in chapter 27 depicting a vineyard must be read in parallel with chapter 5, where we were shown the picture of Israel as having been unfruitful. The vinedresser had come to his vineyard only to find 'bad fruit' (5:2). All the attention given to the vineyard had been to no effect. The coming exile into Babylon was God's chastisement for their backslidings.

'The gates of hell shall not prevail'

The vineyard of chapter 27 is quite unlike the one in chapter 5. This one is **'fruitful'** (27:2,6). The reason for the difference is that chapter 27 is a picture of a great future day when the Lord's work will have come to a climax. The fruitfulness of the vineyard on that day is due to the loving care and attention given to it by God:

> **'I, the Lord, watch over it;**
> **I water it continually.**
> **I guard it day and night**
> **so that no one may harm it'**

(27:3).

The wrath which once he had threatened against his vineyard (cf. 5:5-6, where God threatens to tear down the walls so that animals may enter and trample it), and revealed in the exile that came upon

Israel soon after Isaiah's ministry, is now removed entirely. 'I am **not angry'** God says (27:4). Verses 4-5 are difficult, but seem to mean that God's wrath is no longer against his vineyard, but only against the **'briers and thorns'** (that is, his enemies) that overran it in 5:6. But even here there is a note of hope: he would rather that his enemies turn in repentance and live (27:5). God would rather reconcile than destroy.

This is God's hymn about the condition of the church at the end of time. 'Sing it,' he tells us! (27:2).

'The Lord disciplines those he loves'

It is not difficult to imagine some of Isaiah's readers, then as now, wondering as to the truthfulness of his vision with regard to the church and the purposes of God in the last days. After all, some of his readers are suffering hardships and trials. How can I be sure of God's love when he seems to send one trial after another? This is a perennial question. The answer is an analysis of the ways of God with his people. God has smitten Israel's oppressors much more severely than he smote his own people (27:7). The point being made here is that discipline is necessary in God's kingdom. God's children suffer for reasons of education and instruction (cf. Heb. 12:3-6).

Indeed, the very presence of such discipline is evidence that he loves us and wants us to mend our ways. The motive behind God's discipline is love. As John Owen says, 'There is nothing properly penal in the chastisements of believers.'[6] And again, 'There is no chastisement in heaven, nor in hell. Not in heaven, because there is no sin; not in hell, because there is no amendment.'[7] The eventual renouncing of idolatry proved the beneficent purpose behind the Lord's chastening (27:9).

Verse 10 pictures the destruction of **'the fortified city'**. Interpretations vary from Samaria, the capital of Israel,[8] to Jerusalem, the capital of Judah.[9] The thought is that even though Jerusalem's inhabitants will not be completely destroyed (the point of verses 7-9), the city itself and even some of its inhabitants will be. At the same time as desiring their salvation, God will show them 'no mercy' when they remain unrepentant (27:11).

Harvest home

The chapter ends with a summons to the dispersed Jewish exiles to come home from Assyria and Egypt. A great trumpet sounds summoning their return (27:13). The words are echoed to this day in synagogue worship in the tenth of the Eighteen Benedictions: 'Sound the great trumpet for our liberation; lift up the ensign to gather our exiles...' The language is picked up by Paul in 1 Thessalonians 4:16 to describe the ushering in of the end: 'For the Lord himself will come down from heaven, with a loud command, with the voice of the archangel and with the trumpet call of God, and the dead in Christ will rise first' (cf. Joel 2:1,15; Zech. 9:14; Matt. 24:31; 1 Cor. 15:52; Rev. 11:15). We find the same picture in Psalm 47:5: 'God has ascended amid shouts of joy, the Lord amid the sounding of trumpets.'

Summary

In fulfilment of his plan and purpose, God is going to spread a feast for all kinds of people; the redeemed church is cosmopolitan. Heaven and glory await God's people. And what will be their occupation? Singing the praises of God!

18.
The Assyrian crisis

Please read Isaiah 28:1 - 29:24

Chapter 28 begins a new section in the prophecy. Following the 'Isaiah Apocalypse' (24:1-27:13) we are now brought back to the details of Judah's impending trouble with Assyria (28:1-35:10). Two changes now need to noted.

Firstly, so far Isaiah's ministry has taken place largely during the reign of King Ahaz. Now a new king, Hezekiah, takes the throne. Although basically a good king, Hezekiah did nevertheless attempt an alliance with Egypt to see Judah out of its impending catastrophe. This was to prove an ill-founded decision and behind the historical narrative which will take us up to the end of chapter 35 lies the spiritual truth that deliverance is to be secured only by the Lord's help.

Hezekiah's attempted revolt against Egypt came in 701 B.C. To prepare us for this period, Isaiah takes us back some twenty years, before the fall of Samaria in the north (722 B.C.). His point is to compare Judah (28:14) with their apostate neighbours and relations in Israel.

Secondly, so far in Isaiah's prophecy, lengthy sections have been taken up with oracles of judgement against the nations (13-27), with only a brief reference to Jerusalem (22). The next eight chapters, however, are sometimes called 'The Book of Zion'. After an initial section on Samaria (28:1-6) the rest of this section is all addressed to Jerusalem.

It may be helpful at this point to note something about the structure of Isaiah's prophecy. Chapter 27:1-6, with its picture of a vineyard, reminded us of chapter 5. There is a further similarity with that chapter, which included a series of six 'woes' (5:8,11,18, 20,21,22). These six 'woes' are now taken up in the following chapters (28:1; 29:1; 29:15; 30:1; 31:1; 33:1)

The first woe:
the marks of a fallen church (28:1-29)

The northern kingdom of Israel had by now fallen to the Assyrians, apart, that is, from its capital, Samaria. King Menahem forestalled a total pillage of the city by paying hefty taxes to the Assyrian aggressor (2 Kings 15:19-20). His ten-year reign is summarized in this way: 'He did evil in the eyes of the Lord. During his entire reign he did not turn away from the sins of Jeroboam son of Nebat, which he had caused Israel to commit' (2 Kings 15:18). The next, and last king of Israel, Pekah, attacked Judah (by now a vassal state of Assyria due to the compromises made by Ahaz). This brought Assyrian armies down on Samaria, resulting in its collapse in 722 B.C. 27,000 captives were taken into exile. But in Isaiah 28:1, this collapse has not yet happened.

A point we need to remember is that God had his people in Samaria also. They are a **'remnant'** (28:5). Eventually (28:14) Isaiah will turn his attention towards Judah. His purpose here is to draw a comparison. Judah has no more to boast about than does Israel. Both are in a moribund, lifeless condition. The church is in a backslidden condition and ripe for judgement. God's patience is running out — fast!

What are the marks of a backslidden church?

1. Their leaders are drunk

Drunkenness was a problem in Isaiah's day, as it is in our own (28:1,3; 5:11; 19:14; 24:20; 29:9). Amos had cause to speak about it, too (Amos 2:12; 4:1; 6:6). Samaria's outward beauty is nothing but a garland set on a drunkard's brow (28:3-4). Her glory is quickly fading. Any minute now Samaria, like a ripe fig, will be swallowed (28:4). A hailstorm is coming (28:2). In verses 7 and 8, where Judah rather than Samaria is in view, Isaiah depicts prophets in the very act of prophesying, reeling from their beer. The picture here is so vivid that it seems likely that Isaiah actually witnessed it himself.

Drunkenness implies a loss of perspective and self-control. One of the effects of alcohol is a distortion of values. People do things under the influence of alcohol that they would be ashamed of doing when sober. Alcohol releases folk from their inhibitions. It is at once pleasure-orientated. We have such leaders in our own day, who encourage us to go with our feelings rather than the law of God.

2. They are cynical of spiritual things

Judah's wickedness expressed itself in personal attacks upon the Lord's spokesmen — in this case Isaiah himself. They mock his words (cf. 5:19). They are not in need of the prophet's wisdom (28:9). In their drunken stupor they babble a jingle: '**Do and do, do and do, rule on rule, rule on rule; a little here, a little there**' (28:10). Contempt for God's law is a characteristic response of the backslidden and unregenerate. They 'make nonsense of God's sense'.[1]

There is an important message here, relevant to our situation today. In response to their babbling, God threatens a curse: '**Very well then, with foreign lips and strange tongues God will speak to this people**' (28:11). Paul picks up this verse in 1 Corinthians 14:21 as a reference to the phenomenon of tongue-speaking in the Corinthian church. The point needs to be examined carefully. Tongues, says Paul, are part of God's covenant curse upon a rebellious people (cf. Deut. 28:49). The infantile response of Judah in insulting Isaiah's message, and in so doing insulting the Lord himself, invites a solemn warning. 'The sign of God's covenantal judgement on Israel will be the sound of babbling in a foreign tongue.'[2] If they persist in their childishness, God will judge them in a similar way. Further support for this interpretation is found in verse 16:

'**So this is what the Sovereign Lord says:**

"**See, I lay a stone in Zion,
    a tested stone,
a precious cornerstone for a sure foundation;
    the one who trusts will never be dismayed.**"'

This verse, too, is important for Paul. He cites it in Romans 9:31-

33 as a way of explaining the stumbling (and eventual rejection) of
Israel.

Corinth's problem, like that of Judah in Isaiah's day, was a
childishness as to the things of God. Israel did indeed receive the
sign of disobedience to the covenant in its day: Jeremiah, speaking
at the time of Israel's exile, could say,

> '"O house of Israel," declares the Lord,
>   "I am bringing a distant nation against you —
> an ancient and enduring nation,
>   a people whose language you do not know,
>   whose speech you do not understand'
>
> (Jer. 5:15).

Tongues, like 'babbling Babylonians in Jerusalem', were proof
that God had come in judgement. Tongues in Paul's day were to
represent the fact that the kingdom had been taken away from Israel
and given instead to all nations.[3] What Isaiah is saying here will be
developed in the later part of his message. Though Israel stumbles,
the nations of the world will benefit.

3. Her confidence lay in her own strength

The boast of Judah is staggering in its proportions. They have made
'a covenant with death' (28:15). This may allude to necromancy
(cf. 8:19) or it may be a metaphorical allusion to their alliance with
Egypt. Their message was plain: 'No one can touch us.' But such
delusions of invincibility are short-sighted. They are a **'lie'** and
'falsehood'. Salvation is found in the 'cornerstone' which God lays
in Zion. Jesus Christ, as the New Testament makes plain, is the One
alluded to here as the only source of hope (Rom. 9:33; 1 Peter 2:6).
All who trust in Jesus will not be dismayed.

The tragedy is that Isaiah's listeners are not prepared to put their
confidence in God's Son. Consequently they will not escape the
coming wrath. The metaphors are many: God will judge according
to a perfect standard of justice, with **'measuring line'** and **'plumb-
line'** (28:17); the judgement will resemble the onset of a hailstorm
or a flood (28:17); like someone lying on a bed that is too short, or
wrapped in a blanket that is too small, they will find no comfort in

their sleep (28:20). Israel's defeat (28:21) will be like the time when God 'broke out' against the Philistines at Baal Perazim (2 Sam. 5:20), or when the hail demolished the Ammorites at Gibeon (Josh. 10:10-12). There is no point in rebellion against God: it will only end in disaster.

The chapter ends on a more promising note. A ploughman doesn't keep on and on ploughing indefinitely. He sows in order to reap (28:23-29). Spiritual discipline is what this has all been about. Those who see the Father's hand in it will profit. It involves hardship (Heb. 12:7); it is unpleasant and painful (Heb. 12:11). God's discipline is revealed in a variety of ways: like a farmer, he ploughs and he sows; he deals differently with particular children in order to produce the appropriate harvest of grace. He may 'rebuke' us as we read his Word (2 Tim. 4:2). He may use sickness (1 Cor. 11:30-32), or pain (1 Cor. 7:20-31; 2 Cor. 12:10), or 'tribulation' (Rom. 5:3-4). Sometimes, he even 'uses' Satan himself! Paul's 'thorn in the flesh' was also 'a messenger of Satan' (2 Cor. 12:7). That is the lesson of the book of Job (Job 1:9-11).

To those who have eyes to see, behind a frowning providence there hides a smiling face. Our lives, even when under discipline, are ordered by a God who is **'wonderful in counsel and magnificent in wisdom'** (28:29; cf. 9:6).

The second woe:
a chapter of quotations (29:1-24)

We noted that chapter 28 was delivered *before* the fall of Samaria in 722 B.C. Chapter 29, however, comes much later; anywhere from 705-701 B.C. has been suggested. The reason for placing it around this period lies in the contents of this chapter: the shadow of Egypt is present (cf. 30:1-5). Despite Isaiah's success in persuading Hezekiah ten years earlier (c.711 B.C.) to avoid calling upon Egypt for help when the Philistines attempted a revolt against Assyria (the so-called 'Ashdod crisis' of Isaiah 20), by now the mood has hardened. The Assyrians have arrived in power and the city of Jerusalem is threatened with extinction. The temptation to call for help from Egypt seems overwhelming. Indeed, diplomatic nego-tiations have made considerable progress (30:1-5). Hezekiah's faith is wavering. It is time for a prophet to do his work: to threaten the consequences of disobedience and encourage, instead, quiet, patient trust in the living God.

Doom and deliverance (29:1-8)

Unbelief must always be challenged. The **'woe'** which opens the chapter signifies Isaiah (and God's) displeasure at Jerusalem's unfaithfulness. The reference to **'Ariel'** (29:1; cf. 29:8 'Mt Zion') and **'altar hearth'** (29:2) is yet another instance of Isaiah's use of two Hebrew words which sound the same. Jerusalem is God's hearth, where he has chosen to make his home. Think of how welcoming a sight a coal fire is on a cold wintry day and you will get the picture. However, the picture changes in verse 2. Instead of a cosy fire Isaiah depicts the altar hearth, dripping with sacrificial blood and surrounded by fire. God is about to shake the foundations of those who are 'at ease in Zion' (Amos 6:1, AV). David's proud city is about to be encircled (29:3). The details of Jerusalem's fate are now given:

> **'Brought low, you will speak from the ground;**
> **your speech will mumble out of the dust.**
> **Your voice will come ghostlike from the earth;**
> **out of the dust your speech will whisper'**

(29:4).

Suddenly, Jerusalem is given a momentary reprieve from the Assyrian threat against the city (29:5-8). The details of this divine intervention are recorded later:

'Therefore this is what the Lord says concerning the king of Assyria:

> "He will not enter this city
>   or shoot an arrow here.
> He will not come before it with shield
>   or build a siege ramp against it.
> By the way that he came he will return;
>   he will not enter this city,"

declares the Lord.

"I will defend this city and save it,
  for my sake and for the sake of David my servant!"

'Then the angel of the Lord went out and put to death a hundred and eighty-five thousand men in the Assyrian camp. When the people got up the next morning — there were all the dead bodies! So Sennacherib king of Assyria broke camp and withdrew. He returned to Nineveh and stayed there'

(37:33-37).

It seems clear enough that this is what Isaiah is alluding to in verses 5-8. Those nations that attempt the destruction of Jerusalem will in turn be destroyed. Isaiah has introduced this theme before (10:5-19). But, as so often happens in prophecy, the picture also relates to wider scenarios. Jerusalem's deliverance in 701 B.C. was a foretaste of many such deliverances: 'There have been already innumerable minor occasions when the world has prematurely licked its lips over the demise of the church.'[4]

This is the theme of Martin Luther's hymn, 'Ein' Feste Burg':

And though this world, with devils filled,
Should threaten to undo us,
We will not fear, for God hath willed
His truth to triumph through us.
The prince of darkness grim,
We tremble not for him;
His rage we can endure,
For lo! his doom is sure;
One little word shall fell him.

Isaiah's message was not received in faith. Unbelief has made them blind; they stagger like drunkards, unable to walk in the Lord's straight paths (29:9).

Isaiah makes a series of points, each of which is taken up in the New Testament as an illustration of God's ways.

1. Judicial hardening

Verse 10 introduces the fact that Judah's blindness was part of God's judicial sentence upon their unbelief: **'The Lord has**

brought over you a deep sleep: he has sealed your eyes (the prophets); he has covered your heads (the seers).' The apostle Paul takes up this idea in Romans 11:8 to argue that it is part of the Lord's prerogative in election to save some and pass by others. What is threatened here is precisely what Scripture tells us happened to Pharaoh, when God 'hardened his heart' (Exod. 4:21). John Calvin comments: 'As it belongs to him to give eyes to see, and to enlighten minds by the spirit of judgement and understanding, so he alone deprives us of all light, when he sees that by a wicked and depraved hatred of the truth we of our own accord wish for darkness.'[5]

John Owen suggests that there are two ways by which God accomplishes this. The first is by withholding from them those supplies of light, wisdom and understanding, without which they cannot understand their condition, see their danger, or avoid their ruin. The second is by withholding the means which would bring them to conviction and repentance.[6] Such a condition, he suggests, is the severest of divine punishments, comes upon those who are 'habitually wicked' and is 'remediless' and 'incurable'.

The hardened show no desire to be affected by Scripture, inward guilt or threatened sentence of eternal doom. 'Those who continually harden their hearts reach a point when they become impervious to God's Word. God hardens their heart, and punishments of warning give way to punishments of destruction.'[7] To such, the Bible is a closed book: **'For you this whole vision is nothing but words sealed in a scroll. And if you give the scroll to someone who can read, and say to him, "Read this, please," he will answer, "I can't; it is sealed." Or if you give the scroll to someone who cannot read, and say, "Read this, please," he will answer, "I don't know how to read"'** (29:11-12). There are things which happen, especially in God's dealings with individuals, that are incomprehensible to us. They are part of his 'sealed book'. And to those unenlightened by the Spirit, they will remain unintelligible.

2. *Men without grace*

Verse 13 is quoted by Jesus to show the hypocrisy of the Pharisees (Matt. 15:8-9; Mark 7:6-7). Jesus was making three points: that the Pharisees were *hypocrites*; that their *hearts were far from God*; and that *they placed tradition above Scripture*. All of this is captured in Isaiah's words:

'The Lord says:

"These people come near to me with their mouth
 and honour me with their lips,
 but their hearts are far from me.
Their worship of me
 is made up only of rules taught by men"'

(29:13).

Sadly, it is possible to have a heart that desires orthodoxy, but at the same time is closed to God's grace. It is a warning we need to take to heart.

3. Disdain for the gospel

In times of trouble they looked for wonders to deliver them. God had showed Israel wonders at the time of the exodus (Exod. 15:11; Ps. 78:12). But the wonders promised this time are wonders of judgement. Paul quotes part of verse 14 in 1 Corinthians 1:19 to make the same point. The Corinthians were proud of all their wisdom and sophistication. But their wisdom was foolishness. It was unable to appreciate the gospel. It spurned the wisdom of God: hence Isaiah's threat: 'I am the Lord ... who overthrows the learning of the wise and turns it into nonsense' (44:24-25).

4. There is no point in quarrelling with God!

The people of Isaiah's day believed that even if God existed, he could be ignored. They believed that they could hide their wicked works from God (29:15). It is as if the clay could rise up and say to the potter, 'I have no need of you! You do not exist!'

God is sovereign. He sees everything. He knows everything. He has the right to do as he pleases. He may elect one and harden another. Objections abound: what right has God to judge in this way? It is Paul's use of these words in Romans 9:20 that has occasioned debate over the doctrine of election and perdition. Why is one elected and another passed over? The answer: God has a right to do as he pleases. The real question is: why should God save anyone at all? The answer lies in his own 'good pleasure, which he purposed in Christ' (Eph.1:9). Those who desire to know more should heed Calvin's advice: 'It will do us no good to proceed farther...'[8]

5. *The turning of tables*

To plan against God, as these people did, is absurd. Once more the prophet glimpses days of great change: when the uncultivated land of Lebanon will become **'a fertile field'** (29:17) and injustices of the present will be made good (29:18-21). A day is coming when the deaf will hear and the blind will see (29:18). That Isaiah is thinking here of the Messianic age, our own day, seems clear from what he says later in 35:5: 'Then will the eyes of the blind be opened and the ears of the deaf unstopped.'

6. *A day of rejoicing*

Jacob now appears, as one who is ashamed of the behaviour of his descendants. As though he were actually present, Isaiah depicts him with head bowed in shame at the condition of Judah (29:22). As Calvin comments, 'Here the Prophet intended to pierce the hearts of the people and wound them to the quick, by holding out to them their own patriarch, on whom God bestowed blessings so numerous and so great, but who is now dishonoured by his posterity; so that if he had been present, he would have been compelled to blush deeply on their account.'[9]

Summary

The prophet has carefully outlined the marks of a fallen, corrupt church. But things are going to change. A new age will dawn, and what rejoicing there will be! What is the cause of his rejoicing? The holiness of God's people, their fear of God and their implicit obedience to God's ways (29:22-24). In the future, the prophet sees a glimpse of a revived church and eventually of heaven itself. God will intervene and halt the decline.

Lying behind this vision is an age-long promise that goes all the way back to Abraham: **'Therefore this is what the Lord, who redeemed Abraham, says to the house of Jacob...'** (29:22). When God redeemed Abraham a promise was held out to his spiritual descendants which holds good to this day: 'If you belong to Christ, then you are Abraham's seed, and heirs according to the promise' (Gal. 3:29). Looking back to Abraham is something which Isaiah urges on his hearers more than once (cf. 41:8-10; 51:2-3; cf. Micah 7:20).[10] At the heart of this emphasis is the promise of Christ himself (Gal. 3:14). It is the coming of Christ which takes away Jacob's shame. Looking to the promises of God — and to *the* promise of the covenant of grace with Abraham in particular — is Isaiah's way of encouraging us in a situation that otherwise would drive us to despair. God has spoken! That is all we need!

19.
'Tell us pleasant things!'

Please read Isaiah 30:1 - 32:20

Sometimes a message needs repeating to get the point across. That appears to be the case with chapters 30 and 31. What was only alluded to in chapter 28:14-22 is now disclosed more fully: **'Woe to the obstinate children ... who go down to Egypt without consulting me'** (30:1; cf. 31:1). They were looking to Pharaoh (30:2) and not looking to the Holy One of Israel (31:1). Judah's misplaced confidence in Egypt to save her from the Assyrian aggressor was an indication that she had not been listening to Isaiah, and therefore to God's Word.

Ten years earlier Hezekiah had heeded Isaiah's warnings when the Ashdod crisis caused a ripple of fear to pass through the land (ch. 20). Now the mood has hardened and the temptation to harness worldly powers in defence of one's survival is too great; Egypt offers a way of out of the impasse. Judah's envoys are on their way: they are in **'Zoan'** (30:4) where Israel were once slaves (cf. 19:11). This is possibly Tanis, in the north-eastern part of the Nile Delta, which had become familiar to Israel during their time in Egypt (Num. 13:22; Ps. 78:12.43). **'Hanes'** (30:4) is possibly Heracleopolis Magna, about fifty miles south of Cairo and close to Zoan.

Misplaced confidence

The journey to Egypt is full of dangers (30:6), and though there are treasures and splendours the enterprise is a waste of time. Isaiah depicts Egypt's help as coming to nothing. Using an allusion to a mythical sea-monster called Rahab (30:7), which literally means 'arrogant' or 'turbulent'and is associated with 'the dragon' in 51:9, he refers to Egypt as 'Dragon Do-nothing'. Prophets could be satirical, too. What Isaiah is doing is something like the modern political newspaper cartoonist does: depicting statesmen and stateswomen in exaggerated, overblown terms. The point would not be lost: the arrogance of Egypt (think of their pyramids) will not come to the aid of little Judah! Judah's confidence is misplaced.

The problem with Judah's thinking was its total lack of faith. Assyria was God's instrument of chastisement. The way to avoid defeat at her hands was to repent and seek the Lord's mercy. Worldly alliances only added to their guilt.

Isaiah's message was thus full of condemnation: there were covenant curses as well as blessings to be reckoned with (Deut. 27-28). As far as Isaiah was concerned, a wayward people needed a message that underlined their sinfulness and their guilt: 'For the Lord is a God of justice' (30:18; cf. 34:2,8).

We tend to think of Scripture as a book 'of precious promises'; and in one sense, of course, it is. But there is a sense, too, in which the Bible is God's written charge against the unrepentant. One of the reasons why Isaiah wrote his prophecy was to provide a witness against the people for ever (30:8; cf. Deut. 31:19,26). In this sense, the book of Isaiah is like a written charge-sheet presented in a court of law, indicating the nature of the charges against the accused.

As I write these words, a fierce storm has been blowing for several days. Tragically, two men, seeking relief from the fierce winds, had been sheltering in a van behind a wall. The news today contained the story that the wall fell down and killed them. To reject a prophet's words is to invite a similar destruction by God:

'Therefore, this is what the Holy One of Israel says:

"Because you have rejected this message,
relied on oppression
and depended on deceit,
this sin will become for you
like a high wall, cracked and bulging,
that collapses suddenly, in an instant.
It will break in pieces like pottery,

shattered so mercilessly
that among its pieces not a fragment will be found
for taking coals from a hearth
or scooping water out of a cistern"'

(30:12-14).

The course of rejection

Isaiah's words, like those of the other Old Testament prophets, are God's words. To reject them was to invite certain destruction by God. When Saul disobeyed Samuel's command to wait seven days at Gilgal 'until I come to you and tell you what you are to do' (1 Sam. 10:8), Samuel rebuked him: "'You acted foolishly," Samuel said. "You have not kept the command the Lord your God gave you ... now your kingdom will not endure ... because you have not kept the Lord's command"' (1 Sam. 13:13-14). Similarly, to disobey a command of one of 'the sons of the prophets' who was speaking 'by the word of the Lord' (1 Kings 20:35) was to disobey 'the Lord,' and could lead to sudden death (1 Kings 20:36). To disbelieve, or disobey, anything a prophet says in God's name is to disbelieve or disobey God.

Preaching like this was as distasteful then as it would be today. **'Tell us us pleasant things'** they cried (30:10). The temptation to conform, to comfort people rather than disturb, must have been enormous. They said to the men like Isaiah,

'Give us no more visions of what is right!
Tell us pleasant things,
    prophesy illusions.
Leave this way,
    get off this path,
and stop confronting us
    with the Holy One of Israel!'

(30:9-11).

Ezekiel likened those who told the people what they wanted to hear to shoddy builders who covered the cracks in their walls with plenty of whitewash! (Ezek. 13:10-16). It was, in fact, a mark of the false prophets that they refused to be curbed by the limits which revelation laid down. They felt free to soothe, to speculate, to imagine whatever they thought desirable. 'They speak visions from their own minds, not from the mouth of the Lord' (Jer. 23:16). Why did they do this? 'The prophets prophesy lies, the priests rule by their own authority, and my people love it this way' (Jer. 5:31).

John Stott cites the case of Alexander Whyte, who came to a crisis towards the end of his ministry in Edinburgh on this very point. Some regarded him as 'little short of a monomaniac about sin', and he was tempted to muffle this note in his preaching. 'But one day while walking in the Highlands — he could ever after remember the exact spot — "What seemed to me to be a Divine Voice spoke with all-commanding power in my conscience, and said to me as clear as clear could be: 'No! Go on, and flinch not! Go back and boldly finish the work that has been given you to do. Speak out and fear not. Make them at any cost to see themselves in God's holy law as in a glass. Do you that, for no one else will do it. No one else will so risk his life and his reputation as to do it. And you have not much of either left to risk. Go home and spend what is left of your life in your appointed task of showing my people their sin and their need of my salvation.'"'[1] We need to pray for such boldness amongst preacahers today.

Two things seem to summarize the apostasy.

1. They desired a message that rewarded self-effort

Their trust was 'in horses' (i.e. in their own strength; 30:16-17; cf. 31:1 which also mentions 'chariots'). The alliance with Egypt, like the policy of Ahaz against Pekah and Rezin (ch. 7), was an attempt to gain deliverance by self-effort. It was symptomatic of their refusal to see their inability, due to sin, to save themselves. Isaiah's message was:

> Cast your deadly 'doing' down,
> Down at Jesus' feet.
> Stand in him, in him alone
> Gloriously complete.[2]

2. Their disobedience to the Lord was total

'You said, "No..."'(30:16). Their disobedience was specifically manifested in a rejection of godliness and the covenant. In contrast, Isaiah demanded **'repentance'** (30:15; cf. 31:6) and faith: a new

trust in the Lord: **'in quietness and trust is your strength'** (30:15).
Without repentance, there can be no heaven (cf. Heb.12:14). 'The
two graces essential to a saint in this life,' wrote Thomas Watson,
'are faith and repentance. These are the two wings by which he flies
to heaven.'[3]

Grace amidst rebellion

Anyone who finds no gospel in the Old Testament — and there are
many who do not — are not reading it correctly. Despite Judah's
sinful condition, God longs to be gracious:

> **'Yet the Lord longs to be gracious to you;**
>   **he rises to show you compassion.**
> **For the Lord is a God of justice.**
> **Blessed are all who wait for him!'**

                                                              (30:18).

The Lord is long-suffering, not desiring that any should perish
(2 Peter 3:9). What we have in the rest of this chapter is a discourse
that anticipates the closing chapters of the prophecy. In view is,
partially, the threat of Assyria and Babylon against the Lord's
disobedient people and their eventual deliverance. But once more,
there are greater things in Isaiah's mind. Days of the New Covenant
are dawning in the prophet's vision. He depicts days when preachers
of the gospel abound (30:20-21). Initially, Isaiah is not thinking of
heaven, for adversity and trials abound (30:20). But as so often with
this prophet, his thought soars beyond our own age to a new order
of things.

Prosperity

Isaiah's description of future blessing (30:23-26) is couched in
terms of Old Testament ideas familiar enough to his first hearers.
Rain, food and abundance of crops were part of what God had
promised to Moses: 'The Lord will grant you abundant prosperity
— in the fruit of your womb, the young of your livestock and the
crops of your ground — in the land he swore to your forefathers to

give you. The Lord will open the heavens, the storehouse of his bounty, to send rain on your land in season and to bless all the work of your hands. You will lend to many nations but will borrow from none' (Deut. 28:11-12).

The images of dazzling light in the place of the sun and moon (30:26) will occur again: 'The city does not need the sun or the moon to shine on it, for the glory of God gives it light, and the Lamb is its lamp' (Rev. 21:23).

Justice

Isaiah insists constantly that salvation cannot be achieved at the expense of justice. Sin has to be dealt with; later on, Isaiah makes very plain that God's own Son will bear the guilt and punishment of the sins of his people (52:13 - 53:12).

Those who are truly the Lord's will experience his protection: like hovering birds he will shield Jerusalem (31:5). In language that reminds us of the exodus from Egypt, he will 'pass over' them (31:5). The same word is used when the Lord 'passed over' every house in Egypt that had the blood of sacrifice sprinkled on the doorposts, thus saving those within from the destroying angel (Exod. 12:13,23). God shielded the Israelites in Egypt like a hovering bird protecting its little ones!

The unrepentant, however, cannot look forward to anything but destruction and woe. As the prophet began his message, by warning that 'Those who forsake the Lord will perish' (1:28), so he now continues:

'See, the Name of the Lord comes from afar,
    with burning anger and dense clouds of smoke;
his lips are full of wrath,
    and his tongue is a consuming fire'

(30:27).

Though the initial context is the destruction of the 'Assyrians' (30:31) — the angel of the Lord struck down 186,000 Assyrian soldiers (31:8; cf. 37:36) and later Nineveh was destroyed by the Medes and Babylonians in 612 B.C. (cf. 31:9) — it is clear that all the godless are in view here. The **'rod'** of God will strike them in judgement (30:32; cf. 31:4 'come down'). He will **'rise up against them'** (31:2). It was a 'rod' that Moses used to turn the Nile waters into a stench of blood (Exod. 17:5). A man found guilty of a crime in Israel could be sentenced to lie down before the judge and be beaten. The law limited the number of strokes to forty (Deut. 25:1-3). The Gentiles will one day be beaten, too:

> **'The Lord will cause men to hear his majestic voice**
> **and will make them see his arm coming down**
> **with raging anger and consuming fire,**
> **with cloudburst, thunderstorm and hail.**
> **The voice of the Lord will shatter Assyria;**
> **with his sceptre he will strike them down.**
> **Every stroke the Lord lays on them**
> **with his punishing rod**
> **will be to the music of tambourines and harps,**
> **as he fights them in battle with the blows of his**
> **arm'**

(30:30-32).

The end of the wicked is now described in graphic terms. Topheth (30:33) was a region outside Jerusalem where children were sacrificed to Molech (2 Kings 23:10; Jer. 7:31-32). It was a place of burning that symbolized the very essence of degradation. Such a place is hell:

> **'Topheth has long been prepared;**
> **it has been made ready for the king.**
> **Its fire pit has been made deep and wide,**
> **with an abundance of fire and wood;**
> **the breath of the Lord,**
> **like a stream of burning sulphur,**
> **sets it ablaze'**

(30:33).

Rejoicing

Where does the music fit in? What place is there for rejoicing at the contemplation of such destruction?

First, there is the sense of wonder and joy that the redeemed experience in their own salvation. The fact that they have been spared the fate of 'Topheth' is due to one thing: the grace of God. Grace is always worth singing about.

Second, and more difficult is the idea of rejoicing in the wrath of God.[4] It must be remembered that in heaven, cleansed of all traces of sin, we will see things as God sees them. We will see sin as he sees it.

Repentance

Judah desired to hear 'pleasant things' (30:10). Isaiah, like all good evangelical preachers, had begun his message by calling for repentance (30:15; 31:6). The people of Isaiah's day were guilty of looking to men and not to God to save them from their troubles: **'Woe to those who go down to Egypt for help...'** (31:1). The power of man is not to be compared to that of God. All Egypt's **'chariots'** and **'horses'** were **'flesh and not spirit'**[5] (31:3). It is inadequate to instruct sinners 'to accept Jesus as your personal Saviour'. Apart from the fact that this is not a biblical expression, it says nothing about repentance. Jesus began his public ministry with this message: '"The time has come," he said. "The kingdom of God is near. Repent and believe the good news!"' (Mark 1:15). As he encountered the woman at the well, he urged her to turn from her adultery (John 4:16-18). Zacchaeus was warned to turn away from stealing (Luke 19:2-9). The rich young ruler was allowed to go away, despite Jesus' great love for him, because he loved his riches more than God (Mark 10:17-22). Paul went from house, declaring 'to both Jews and Greeks that they must turn to God in repentance and have faith in our Lord Jesus' (Acts 20:21). Old and New Testaments concur: 'He who conceals his sins does not prosper, but whoever confesses and renounces them finds mercy' (Prov. 28:13); 'Without holiness no one will see the Lord' (Heb. 12:14)

God looks after his own

Isaiah has already alluded in the previous chapter to the protection God's own people may expect, using images of God as a lion and a

bird of prey (31:4-5). The picture is one of protection: he will be a
'**shield**' to his people and '**pass over**' them. He will fight for his
children. Hardly anything is more comforting than the realization
that the battle is the Lord's (1 Sam. 17:47; 2 Chron. 20:15). The Bible
gives this consolation again and again: 'The angel of the Lord
encamps around those who fear him, and he delivers them' (Ps.
34:7). 'He who dwells in the shelter of the Most High will rest in the
shadow of the Almighty' (Ps. 91:1). 'I give them eternal life, and
they shall never perish; no one can snatch them out of my hand'
(John 10:28). 'For I am convinced that neither death nor life, neither
angels nor demons, neither the present nor the future, nor any
powers, neither height nor depth, nor anything else in all creation,
will be able to separate us from the love of God that is in Christ Jesus
our Lord' (Rom. 8:38-39). There is no happiness to be compared
with taking shelter from the storms of life — and the storm that is
to come on Judgement Day — in Jesus Christ.

A shelter in the time of storm

Having introduced the idea of a new order of things in chapter 31,
Isaiah now launches into a description of the righteous rule of the
king which will characterize it. As to the identity of the '**king**'
(32:1), commentators have been divided. It seems clear enough,
however, that it cannot be Hezekiah (as Calvin thought),[6] for the
king Isaiah has in mind is completely righteous. Isaiah must therefore be speaking about a messianic rule, the righteous government
of Jesus Christ.

Chapter 32 introduces the fourth prediction by Isaiah of the
coming king (cf. 7:14; 9:6-7; 11:1-11). Vernon Charlesworth's
hymn 'A shelter in the time of storm' seems to have been derived
from the opening words of this chapter:

> '**See, a king will reign in righteousness**
> **and rulers will rule with justice.**
> **Each man will be like a shelter from the wind**
> **and a refuge from the storm,**
> **like streams of water in the desert**
> **and the shadow of a great rock in a thirsty land**'
>
> (32:1-2).

The Lord's our Rock, in him we hide,
A shelter in the time of storm;
Secure whatever ill betide,
A shelter in the time of storm.

Oh, Jesus is a Rock in a weary land,
a weary land, a weary land;
Oh, Jesus is a Rock in a weary land,
A shelter from the time of storm.

Wisdom

The unbeliever is a fool (cf. Ps. 14:1; 53:1). The foolish enjoy the company of folly. Their perception is twisted. The folly and confusion which characterized Isaiah's day will change when Messiah comes (32:5-8). Whereas the foolish are crafty and cunning (32:5), dedicated to doing evil things (32:6), using all kinds of tricks and plots to deceive (32:7), the disciples of Messiah will be enlightened and noble (32:8). Salvation changes men's minds and makes them wise. This is something God promised to do in Isaiah 29:

'Therefore once more I will astound these people
    with wonder upon wonder;
the wisdom of the wise will perish,
    the intelligence of the intelligent will vanish'
(29:14; cf. 1 Cor. 1:19).

A warning to the women of Jerusalem

Prophets were not to be afraid of men or women. They were to apply the Word of God without showing any degree of favouritism. Isaiah had spoken to the pampered women of Jerusalem in his opening words (3:16-26). He now attacks their complacency (32:9-11). Like Amos before him, Isaiah sees them having no care for spiritual things (Amos 4:1). They were at ease in Zion (Amos 6:1). Their lives were spent in diversions, escaping the reality of what faced them. This carefree spirit has been mentioned before:

'But see, there is joy and revelry,
    slaughtering of cattle and killing of sheep,
    eating of meat and drinking of wine!
"Let us eat and drink," you say,
    "for tomorrow we die!"'

(22:13).

In just over a year's time things will change drastically (32:10).
Isaiah may be referring to Hezekiah's revolt against Assyria, for
which the invasion of 701 B.C. was the reprisal. But the description
of Jerusalem that follows seems to transcend anything that happened in Isaiah's time. Once again the prophet is using the events of
his day to teach greater truths. Following the judgement of Jerusalem (32:14) comes the outpouring of the Spirit (32:15). Pentecost
naturally comes to mind (cf. references to the 'pouring of the Spirit'
in Joel 2:28-32; Acts 2:17-18,33; 10:45). But there are even greater
things here: a new order of things will be established where there is
fruitfulness, peace, righteousness, quietness, security and rest
(32:16-20). Though these are, in part, the possession of the church
right now, they are descriptive of the new earth, 'the home of
righteousness' (2 Peter 3:3).

Summary

God's people were tempted to look to Egypt instead of trusting in the
Lord. It was a misplaced confidence. Once more Isaiah bids his
listeners to trust in God's promise of deliverance for those who wait
upon him. It is the same lesson as the one Jesus gave his own
troubled, uncertain disciples in the Upper Room when he spoke
about the 'many mansions' that await each one of his own (John
14:1-4, AV). As J. C. Ryle comments on John 14: 'We have ... in this
passage a precious remedy against an old disease. That disease is
trouble of heart. That remedy is faith.'[7]

20.
A psalm for use in a national emergency

Please read Isaiah 33

In 1947, a Bedouin goatherd searching for lost animals entered one of the caves high in the Marly cliffs of the Wadi Qumran, a mile or so west of the north-west corner of the Dead Sea. There he stumbled upon several jars, over two feet high and about ten inches wide, containing leather scrolls wrapped in linen cloth. After their removal from the cave, they were smuggled to an antique dealer in Bethlehem, who bought some of them, while the rest came into the possession of the archbishop of the Syrian Orthodox monastery in Jerusalem. This was, and remains, the most important discovery ever made of Old Testament manuscripts. The scrolls are thought to date from as early as 168 B.C. One of these scrolls contains the words of Isaiah 33:1-24 and can be seen on view at the Hebrew University, Jerusalem.

The Assyrian threat was a considerable one. Having warned Jerusalem of its potency, the prophet now feels the need to turn to God in prayer. His mood changes rapidly from criticism of Assyria (33:1), to entreaty (33:2-4), praise (33:5,6) and lamentation (33:7-9).

The 'emergency psalm' seems to have three clear divisions: a prayer for the promised destruction of Assyria (2-9); God's challenging answer (10-16) and the future Messianic kingdom (17-24).

The prayer

'Those who are in trouble and distressing fear,' wrote Jonathan Edwards in a sermon based on Isaiah 33:2, 'if they come to Jesus

Christ, have this to ease them of their fears, that Christ has promised
them that he will protect them; that they come upon his invitation;
that Christ has plighted his faith for their security if they will close
with him; and that he is engaged by covenant to God the Father that
he will save those afflicted and distressed souls that come to him.'[1]
The peace and security Christians feel in times of trouble comes
from knowing God. When testing comes, Christians desire a deeper
knowledge. Hence the cry of Isaiah:

> **'O Lord, be gracious to us;**
> **we long for you.**
> **Be our strength every morning,**
> **our salvation in time of distress'**
>
> (33:2).

Several points are worth noting.

Firstly, in calling upon the Lord to be gracious when people cry
to him in their need, Isaiah turns a promise already given (30:19)
into a prayer. As one of the Puritans said, 'God's promises are the
cork to keep faith from sinking in prayer.'

Secondly, spiritual strength is something we need at the very
start of the day, hence 'every morning' (33:2). It must be of some
importance since Mark felt it necessary to tell us in the first chapter
of his Gospel that praying early in the morning was part of Jesus'
own practice (Mark 1:35).

Thirdly, Isaiah reminds himself in prayer of God's power: once
he rises up, nations will scatter at the sound of his voice (33:3). This
had been Israel's confidence in the wilderness, as they were reminded each morning when the ark, the symbol of his presence, was
to be moved:

> 'Whenever the ark set out, Moses said,
>
> "Rise up, O Lord!
>   May your enemies be scattered;
> may your foes flee before you"'
>
> (Num. 10:35).

Whatever the enemy's strength may be, our God is stronger still.
The spoils of the enemy are not for keeping (33:4). Thinking perhaps

of the sudden demise of Sennacherib in the near future, Isaiah speaks
of the coming Harvester who will take their spoils from them. God
is exalted (33:5). The Assyrian arrogance will be broken (cf. 10:9-
11,15; 36:18-20; 37:10-13). Ultimate victory is assured. When
everything else is shaking under our feet, the Lord is a sure
foundation (33:6). Trusting him, when all else fails, is what faith is
all about. The **'key'** to the treasure of contentment amidst battle is
in fearing the Lord (33:6).

In contrast, Assyria cannot be trusted. Sennacherib had demanded from Hezekiah three hundred talents of silver and thirty
talents of gold as the price for peace (2 Kings 18:14), but even this
did not satisfy him. Sennacherib broke his word and required the
surrender of the entire city. Assyria's word proved worthless: **'The
treaty is broken'** (33:8). Such is the end of all misplaced confidence
in man. Prayer is an acknowledgement that we need another in
whom to trust.

The answer

'"Now will I arise," says the Lord' (33:10) introduces God's
answer to the prophet's prayer for Assyria's demise (33:1). He
allows evil men and nations to prosper for a time, but only for a time.
The Pharaohs, the Persian kings, the Roman emperors — these all
have their day. Their activity is described as **'pregnant'** —'full of
plans and schemes which it is seeking to carry out'.[2] However, when
God decides to 'arise' they will be destroyed: the sound of them
crackling in the fire will be like that of dry thorns, cut down and set
ablaze (33:11).

Not only will the Assyrians eventually be judged, but the sinners
in Zion too will come under his **'consuming fire'** (33:14). Consideration of God's holiness raises the question: **'Who of us can dwell
with the consuming fire? Who of us can dwell with everlasting
burning?'** (33:14). David asks a similar question in two of his
psalms (Ps. 15:1; 24:3). The idea of God's holiness — purity
unapproachable by the impure without the greatest danger — was
something impressed on Moses. At the time when God gave the law
to Israel, the people were made fully aware of what God's holiness
meant. They were warned to keep off the mountain lest they perish
(Exod. 19:16-22). The same principle applied to the tabernacle and

its contents. When Moses gave instructions for their transportation, he insisted that those involved must be Levites specially consecrated to that service, and even they '... must not touch the holy things or they will die' (Num. 4:15). The same warning is attached to unworthy participation in the Lord's Supper (1 Cor. 11:26-31). This accounts for the question: 'Who then may live on your holy hill?'

A summary of holiness

A fourfold summary of a holy man follows: a righteous walk, total truthfulness, financial honesty and inward integrity (33:15). *A righteous walk* consists of doing what conforms to the standards of God's law. James insists upon this truth when he teaches that it is not the hearers, but the doers of the law who are justified (James 1:22,25). Truthfulness is essential in godliness. *Speaking what is right* is a reflection of God himself, who 'does not lie' (Titus 1:2). Paul felt it necessary to emphasize the importance of this when writing to converted Colossian believers whose former lives were characterized by a sinful habit of telling lies (Col. 3:9). The tongue is a potent weapon in the devil's hands: we are to be careful in using it. Augustine is said to have inscribed over his table, 'He that doth love with bitter speech the absent to defame, must surely know that at this board no place is for the same.'³ Holiness must go deep into our lives and effect changes in thoughts and sense-impressions. It must also have influence on our attitudes to money. The love of it is the root of all kinds of evil (1 Tim. 6:10).

Having described the man who is worthy to dwell with God, Isaiah now tells us what such a man may expect:

**'This is the man who will dwell on the heights,
     whose refuge will be the mountain fortress.
His bread will be supplied,
     and water will not fail him'**

(33:16).

Jesus gave a similar promise after his own exposition of the law in the Sermon on the Mount: 'Therefore everyone who hears these words of mine and puts them into practice is like a wise man who built his house on the rock. The rain came down, the streams rose, and the winds blew and beat against that house; yet it did not fall, because it had its foundation on the rock. But everyone who hears these words of mine and does not put them into practice is like a foolish man who built his house on sand. The rain came down, the streams rose, and the winds blew and beat against that house, and it fell with a great crash' (Matt. 7:24-27).

The future

In contrast to the images of desolation after the siege of Jerusalem depicted in 33:7-9, the future is quite different. The constriction of Jerusalem during those days will give way to wide, open spaces (33:17); instead of Assyrian forces, pilgrims will once more make their way to the city (33:20); in contrast to the indignities of recent days, Messiah's rule will be peaceful (33:18,19). The security and defences of the city are assured (33:21). All confidence lies in what God is and what he promises to do (33:22). The new Jerusalem will know no spiritual or physical suffering: **'No one living in Zion will say, "I am ill"; and the sins of those who dwell there will be forgiven'** (33:24). 'He will wipe every tear from their eyes. There will be no more death or mourning or crying or pain, for the old order of things has passed away' (Rev. 21:4).

Shutting our eyes to evil (33:15) and concentrating upon heaven and the glorious sight of Christ (33:17) is God's answer to trouble. The charge of escapism is never far away, but the true believer knows that this world is not his home: **'Your eyes will see the king in his beauty and view a land that stretches afar'** (33:17). Old Testament believers were as confident as New Testament ones that heaven would mean, quite literally, a sight of the Redeemer (cf. 1 John 3:2). The promises of other sights — golden streets, pearly gates, crystal rivers —are not nearly as important.

The cause of this confident expectation lies in God's power: he is the **'Mighty One'** (33:21; cf. 10:34). The ultimate proof that the Lord's people are safe in his hands is that in his own time he will bring about this final state of peace. Isaiah could as easily echo Peter's words: 'But in keeping with his promise we are looking forward to a new heaven and a new earth, the home of righteousness' (2 Peter 3:13). It is by the Lord's power that this will be brought about. 'My faith,' said Samuel Rutherford, 'has no bed to sleep upon but omnipotency.'

Summary

Isaiah's instinctive response to a crisis is to pray. He pours out his troubles and fears to the Lord. He brings his concerns and lays them at the feet of his Saviour, reminding himself as he does so of the assurances God has given to those who commune with him. This was the secret of Isaiah's holy life.

21.
The waste land and the oasis

Please read Isaiah 34 and 35

Just as the judgements on the nations that occupied chapters 13-23
were followed by the so-called 'Isaiah Apocalypse' in chapters 24-
27, so, too, after concentrating upon the Assyrian threat in chapters
28-31 Isaiah once more turns to matters far removed from the events
of the seventh century B.C. Chapter 33 closed with a glimpse of the
new heavens and the new earth. Chapters 34 and 35 concentrate on
the universal judgement of the wicked surrounding the 'day of the
Lord' (ch. 34) and the endless joy of the redeemed, portrayed in
terms of the 'flowering of the desert' (ch. 35, anticipating chapters
40-66).

The portrayal of the day of the Lord continues, focusing, initially
at least, on the negative side: it is '**... a day of vengeance, a year of
retribution ...**' (34:8). God is angry with the nations whom he has
called before him (34:1-2). He threatens their total destruction
(34:3). The language is apocalyptic:

> '**All the stars of the heavens will be dissolved**
> **and the sky rolled up like a scroll;**
> **all the starry host will fall**
> **like withered leaves from the vine,**
> **like shrivelled figs from the fig tree'**

(34:4).

Confirmation that the Day of Judgement is upon us in Isaiah 34
is found in the fact that the picture drawn by the prophet is taken up
by the apostle John in Revelation 6:12-17. At the opening of the

sixth seal the entire world is gathered for judgement; the mood is awesome: 'For the great day of their wrath has come, and who can stand?' (Rev. 6:17).

'Edom', just like Moab in 25:10-12, is singled out, highlighting the fact that these are God's enemies (34:5; cf. 63:2-3). 'Edom' denotes either the name of Esau, the Edomites collectively, or the land occupied by Esau's descendants, formerly the land of Seir. The Edomites are representative of God's enemies. After the fall of Judah, they rejoiced (Ps. 137:7). For their bitter hatred the prophets warned of judgement (Jer. 49:7-22; Lam. 4:21-22; Ezek. 25:12-14; 35:15; Joel 3:19; Amos 9:12; Obad. 10-18). Historically, the Edomites were driven from their homeland by the Nabatean Arabs some 200 years following this prophecy. The picture of a land possessed only by owls, jackals, desert creatures, hyenas, wild goats and falcons is to underline the ruined nature of Edom (34:11-15).

The sword of the Lord

The language here is strong. The cause for this judgement lies in God's holy anger at their sinful, rebellious condition. The Lord will come down with a sharp sword:

> **'The sword of the Lord is bathed in blood,**
>   **it is covered with fat—**
> **the blood of lambs and goats,**
>   **fat from the kidneys of rams.**
> **For the Lord has a sacrifice in Bozrah**
>   **and a great slaughter in Edom.**
> **And the wild oxen will fall with them,**
>   **the bull calves and the great bulls.**
> **Their land will be drenched with blood,**
>   **and the dust will be soaked with fat.**
> **For the Lord has a day of vengeance,**
>   **a year of retribution, to uphold Zion's cause.**
> **Edom's streams will be turned into pitch,**
>   **her dust into burning sulphur;**
>   **her land will become blazing pitch!**
> **It will not be quenched night and day;**
>   **its smoke will rise for ever.**

> **From generation to generation it will lie desolate;**
> **no one will ever pass through it again'**
>
> (34:6-10).

God is often described in the Scriptures as a Warrior. One such example, where Yahweh is described as riding a storm cloud into battle against his enemies, is Psalm 18:9-15:

> 'He parted the heavens and came down;
>   dark clouds were under his feet.
> He mounted the cherubim and flew;
>   he soared on the wings of the wind.
> He made darkness his covering, his canopy around him—
>   the dark rain-clouds of the sky.
> Out of the brightness of his presence clouds advanced,
>   with hailstones and bolts of lightning.
> The Lord thundered from heaven;
>   the voice of the Most High resounded.
> He shot his arrows and scattered the enemies,
>   great bolts of lightning and routed them.
> The valleys of the sea were exposed
>   and the foundations of the earth laid bare
> at your rebuke, O Lord,
>   at the blast of breath from your nostrils.'

The psalmist calls to his Lord for aid, and the Lord responds by doing battle against his enemies and by saving him. Salvation and judgement are the two halves of the same great warring activity of God (cf. Ps. 104:1-4). Revelation 19:11-16 describes the second coming of Christ, employing military imagery heavily dependent upon Old Testament figures. His robe is dipped in blood (v. 13; cf. Isa. 63:2-3). He leads the heavenly armies into battle (v. 14; an idea which lies behind the term 'Lord of hosts' in the Old Testament). He carries a sharp sword (v. 15; cf. Isa. 34:5). He rules with an iron rod (cf. Ps. 2 :9). He treads the wine press of the fierce wrath of God (cf. Isa. 63:3).

The singing that is so much associated with Isaiah's Servant Songs (cf. Isa. 42:10,13) is to be understood in terms of songs of triumph and praise sung by the victorious after a battle.

The covenant Lord

This is the **'day of vengeance'** (34:8; cf. 35:4; 61:2). Israel had comfortably forgotten 'the vengeance of the covenant', the jealousy of God at work within the confines of his chosen people to punish transgression, to discipline them unto greater holiness and to purge out evil. This vengeance on God's enemies will be devastating and complete. The 'vengeance of the covenant' is foretold in Leviticus 26:25 and expanded upon in verses 14-45, the broad truth being that God's saving work, bringing people into his covenant of grace, is not intended to induce a spirit of moral complacency, but rather one of determined ambition to be holy and to obey God's law. Disobedience can expect punishment. Those who remain unrepentant have no hope in passages like these; the way of salvation is to trust in the Lord and live for him. They are a reminder to us of the need to persevere, yielding our lives as holy offerings to the Lord (cf. Heb. 12:1-14). God loves his people and will never forsake them, but he will chastise them when they fall into sinful ways. Those who abandon the Lord can expect only vengeance.

The certainty of prophecy

With daring assurance, Isaiah is able to tell his listeners that his words will come true. Edom is doomed. She has no future. A generation to come will be able to take a scroll of Isaiah 34 in their hands and read just what God promised (34:16). God keeps his word. He is faithful.

The oasis

Chapter 35 is in complete contrast to chapter 34, which portrayed the Lord as a Warrior coming to engage in battle. Coming as it does before a lengthy account of the folly of Assyrian aggrandizement in chapters 36-39, it serves as a beacon of light. It is as though the Holy Spirit knew that we would need encouragement amidst the sombre descriptions of judgement that predominate in these chapters. The **'crocus'** (35:1, not 'rose' as in AV) is the first flower of the spring; it is the precursor of warmer and more fruitful days. Though Israel will be chastised, a better day is in store when the **'ransomed of the Lord will return. They will enter Zion with singing'** (35:10).

It is a rather common belief among Christians that the return of the Jews to Palestine and the establishment of the independent state of Israel in May 1948 is a fulfilment of prophecy. It is widely believed that the physical and economic restoration of modern Israel, together with the rebuilding of the ancient ruins envisaged in Isaiah 35 (cf. 61:4), is being fulfilled today. The diversion of water from the Negev desert is sometimes used as proof of this belief.

The cause of the blossoming desert is clear: it is the presence of the Lord's glory (35:2). But to what precisely does this refer?

Isaiah conveyed the future in pictures which remind us of the garden of Eden: the wilderness becoming a fruitful field (32:15), the desert blossoming as the crocus (35:1), the dry places turning into springs of water (35:7).[1] What is in view here is cosmic in its effect: the whole world is to be changed. This, Calvin says, can only refer 'to the kingdom of Christ.'[2] He continues, 'By "the kingdom of Christ," I mean not only that which is begun here, but that which shall be completed at the last day, which on that account is called "the day of renovation and restoration" (Acts 3:21) because believers will never find perfect rest till that day arrives.' What we have here in chapter 35 is typical of what happens so often in the prophets. The future, seen as it were through a telescope, is contracted so that events which are actually separated by long intervals of time are seen to occur almost simultaneously. Thus the first coming of Christ, which introduced a glimpse of heaven by works of miracles, restoration of sight for example (35:5; cf. Matt. 9:27-34), is the beginning of a work which will eventually lead to the paradise-like nature of the new heavens and the new earth. The removal of the guilt and power of sin which Christians experience when they place their trust in Jesus Christ is only a foretaste of the sinless nature of their existence in the glory that is to come.

The purpose behind this glimpse of the new heavens and the new earth is to provide encouragement:

**'Strengthen the feeble hands,
    steady the knees that give way;
say to those with fearful hearts,
    "Be strong, do not fear;
your God will come,**

he will come with vengeance;
with divine retribution
he will come to save you'"

(35:3-4; cf. 35:10).

The only hope for the world lies in the coming of Christ to save his people. And when he comes his ministry will be announced by healings and miracles (35:5-6) which will be a glimpse of things to come. It should be remembered that when Christ came some had difficulty recognizing him. This was not only due to unbelief; some, like John the Baptist, had difficulty in seeing how he fulfilled Old Testament predictions. John expected Messiah to come in judgement: to lay the axe at the root of non-fruit-bearing trees and cut them down (Matt. 3:10). But he began to have doubts when he saw what Jesus did, and asked, 'Are you the one who was to come, or should we expect someone else?' (Matt. 11:3). Jesus replied by pointing out that his healing miracles and his preaching of the gospel to the poor were things that prophets like Isaiah had foretold (35:5-6; 61:1). John was expecting Jesus to fulfil at his first coming the judging activities which are to be part of his activities at his second coming.

The Lord will establish a **'highway'** for the redeemed that leads to the kingdom of God (35:8). The figure of a road, a path along which the Lord's people may walk, is a common one in Isaiah (cf. 11:16; 40:3; 62:10). Luke picks it up in his description of early Christians who walk in 'the Way' (Acts 9:2; 18:25,26; 19:9,23; 24:14,22).

'The Way of Holiness' is descriptive of Christ's kingdom (35:8). The redeemed will be characterized by their love of holiness, without which they shall not see the Lord (Heb. 12:14). Heaven is to be entirely free from sin. The unholy will not be saved. Only those whose sin is covered by Christ's blood — and who show it in their lives — can entertain an assurance of the kingdom that is in view here.

Summary

Chapter 34 brought us face to face with God's universal judgement. It has been a sobering reminder of his holiness. Chapter 35 came as a most welcome relief and a complete contrast. The redeemed of the Lord are to experience endless joy and delight. Christians 'share' in Christ's calling (Heb. 3:1). They are to be like him: holy and consecrated to God. The process begins the moment the Holy Spirit takes up residence within our hearts, but this is only the beginning. In view is the eradication of sin and the restoration of paradise. It is a process which culminates in the sight of God, in all his glory, living with his people (35:2).

C. S. Lewis put it this way: 'Imagine yourself as a living house. God comes in to rebuild that house. At first, perhaps, you understand what He is doing. He is getting the drains right, and stopping the leaks in the roof, and so on: you knew that these jobs needed doing and you are not surprised. But presently He starts knocking the house about in a way that hurts abominably, and does not seem to make sense. What on earth is He up to? The explanation is that He is building quite a different house from one you thought of — throwing out a new wing here, putting on an extra floor there, running up towers, making courtyards. You thought you were going to be made into a decent little cottage: but He is building a palace. He intends to come and live in it Himself.'[3]

22.
Hezekiah: a good king

Please read Isaiah 36 and 37

Some of God's servants are raised up for one special task. It seems to have been so with Isaiah. Though his ministry covered a period of forty turbulent years, it would appear that everything that had gone before had been a preparation for his contribution in the year 701 B.C., **'the fourteenth year of King Hezekiah's reign'** (36:1), when Assyrian forces reached the city walls of Jerusalem. The opening verse of Isaiah's prophecy informed us that his ministry covered the reign of four Judean kings: Uzziah, Jotham, Ahaz and Hezekiah (1:1). Here and there in chapters 1-35, Isaiah has spoken prophetically about the events of Hezekiah's reign (e.g. 22:1-13). Chapters 36-39 are, however, not prophecy but history. Isaiah witnessed these events. Scripture corroborates what he saw by repeating it, almost word for word, in 2 Kings 18:13 - 19:37 (written much later than Isaiah and probably copied from the prophet).

A godly king

Hezekiah came to power at the age of twenty-nine, when the northern kingdom of Israel was almost at its last gasp. His reign began as co-regent with Ahaz in 729 B.C. and then he became sole ruler in 716 B.C. Samaria, the capital, of the northern kingdom, fell in 722 B.C. during the sixth year of his joint reign with Ahaz. His counterpart in the north, Hoshea, was taken captive by Assyria's powerful ruler Sargon II, and the entire nation was more or less taken captive and transported to Assyria.

Israel and Judah had been bitter enemies during the reign of Ahaz. During the Syro-Ephraimite war the coalition of Israeli-Syrian forces had invaded Judah, killing 120,000 Judean troops and taking captive a quarter of a million hostages, who were promptly returned through the diplomatic intervention of the prophet Oded (see comments on ch. 7). The entire episode had fostered bitter memories of their northern neighbours and blood-relatives. Their loss was not greatly mourned. Ahaz had sought a defensive posture against Judah by an alliance with Assyria, involving idolatry and payment of financial sweeteners. It was a dangerous period in Judah's history, for which Isaiah was raised up by God.

Now that Israel no longer existed, the threat which Assyria posed for Judah was considerable and painful. The reason for Israel's demise lay in her disobedience to the Lord. When Hezekiah came to the throne as sole ruler, he inherited a situation in which his father, King Ahaz, had adopted a similar compromising foreign policy on behalf of Judah. Ahaz had introduced pagan practices, revealing a willingness to show appeasement towards the Assyrian aggressor. Hezekiah had to move quickly to reverse the trend.

Hezekiah, whose name means 'Yahweh strengthens,' introduced immediate reforms, doing 'what was right in the sight of the Lord' (2 Kings 18:3).

A summary of his reforms in 2 Kings 18:4-6 and 2 Chron. 29-30 includes the following points:

1. He removed the high places, breaking down the sacred pillars and wooden images celebrating the Assyrian deities.
2. He opened the doors of the temple, which his father, Ahaz, had closed.
3. He led the Levites to sanctify themselves and begin again their ministry in God's house.
4. He reintroduced the Passover feast;
5. He invited the remnant of the northern tribes to worship with the people of Judah in Jerusalem.
6. He destroyed the bronze serpent, called 'Nehushtan', that Moses had made in the wilderness (Num. 21:6-9) because it had become an idol.

In all this, Hezekiah's faith is underlined, drawing a parallel with Israel's greatest king, David: 'Hezekiah trusted in the Lord, the God of Israel. There was no one like him among all the kings of Judah, either before him or after him. He held fast to the Lord and did not cease to follow him; he kept the commands the Lord had given Moses' (2 Kings 18:5-6). Four expressions in 2 Kings 18:5-6 mark out Hezekiah's godliness: in contrast to pro-Assyrian parties and pro-Egyptian forces in Jerusalem, Hezekiah wholeheartedly 'trusted in the Lord'; he 'held fast to the Lord'; he followed the Lord and he kept the Lord's commands.

The rise of Sennacherib and the threat to Jerusalem (36:1-22)

Things seemed to have gone well for fourteen years until Sennacherib, King of Assyria, invaded from the north, capturing **'all the fortified cities of Judah'** (36:1). Sennacherib was the son of Sargon II and, in 705 B.C., took up where his father had left off. His rule was to last until his grisly death in 681 B.C. The details of his eight military expeditions, including this one against Judah, are preserved in his royal annals. Lord Byron seems to have misjudged the intense fear Assyria brought into the hearts of the people of Judah when he wrote, in his poem, 'The Destruction of Sennacherib', the lines:

> The Assyrian came down like a wolf on the fold,
> And his cohorts were gleaming in purple and gold;
> And the sheen of their spears was like stars on the sea,
> When the blue wave rolls nightly on deep Galilee.

Behind this sentimental piece of poetry lies the gruesome fact that Assyria's war-machine had a reputation for brutality and ruthlessness, the like of which the world had not seen before.

Hezekiah took steps to prepare for Judah's defence. Partly, and unwisely, he toyed with the idea of help from Egypt, incurring Isaiah's displeasure. We have already seen the references to the defences taken by Hezekiah in the construction of the Siloam tunnel, ensuring constant supplies of fresh water for a besieged Jerusalem (22:9; cf. 2 Kings 20:20).[1] The entire project was seen as a signal of rebellion and Sennacherib decided to advance.

Sennacherib's annals claim the capture of forty-six major cities of Judah and an unspecified number of villages. The British

Museum contains a wall relief excavated from Sennacherib's royal palace in Nineveh, depicting the king on a portable throne in his camp outside the Judean city of Lachish. Prisoners are marching by on foot, and all the booty from the city is displayed on ox-wagons on their way to Nineveh. The inscription reads, 'Sennacherib, king of all, king of Assyria, sitting on his "nimedu-throne" while the spoil of the city of Lachish passes before him.'

The climax of the account in Sennacherib's annals comes when he claims to have trapped Hezekiah in Jerusalem 'like a bird within its cage'. The attack was, apparently, in reprisal for Hezekiah's refusal to pay the taxes so willingly given by his father, King Ahaz. What Isaiah's account does not tell us is Hezekiah's immediate response.

Surprised by the suddenness of Sennacherib's attack, Hezekiah offered to pay his dues, surrendering all the silver in the temple and royal treasury, together with the gold overlaying the temple doors and pillars (2 Kings 18:14-15). It has been estimated that the amount comes to over two million pounds. In addition, the Assyrian records reveal that Hezekiah gave 'precious stones, antimony, large cuts of red stone, couches inlaid with ivory, nimedu-chairs inlaid with ivory, elephant hides, ebony wood, boxwood, and all kinds of valuable treasures'. It is widely believed that this is not to be seen as an act of compromise on Hezekiah's part; rather, it was a judicious ploy to purchase time to prepare for Jerusalem's defence.

The tribute did not work. Assyrian forces remained stubbornly outside the walls of Jerusalem. Sennacherib sent his 'field commander'[2] with a detachment of soldiers to Jerusalem to demand Judah's complete surrender (36:2; the account in 2 Kings mentions that two others, a 'supreme commander' and a 'chief officer' were also present (2 Kings 18:17). They met with a delegation of Jerusalem's government at the Upper Pool, the place where Isaiah and his son had met with Ahaz several years earlier (7:3). Included in the Judean delegation were Hezekiah's court officials Eliakim, Shebna and Joah (36:3).

The boastful claims of unbelief

Sennacherib's arrogance is immediately apparent in the commander's address, where he uses the term **'the great king'**, which was probably Sennacherib's own invention. He referred to Egypt's power as a **'splintered reed'**, literally 'a crushed and broken stalk' (36:6). Isaiah also refers to Egypt as a 'bruised reed' in 42:3, and some have suggested that Sennacherib may well have known Isaiah's prophecies, quoting him here to show that he believed he was carrying out the Lord's will. What needs to be remembered is that Hezekiah was facing temptations to form a coalition with Egypt against Assyria, something which Isaiah had consistently warned against in the past (30:1-3). Further support for this idea is found in verse 10, where Sennacherib seemed to be aware of Isaiah's statement that Assyria was a rod which the Lord would use to punish Judah (10:5).[3]

Isaiah, in reporting all of this, wants us to catch the contrast: **'This is what the great king, the king of Assyria, says...'** (36:4) is set against Isaiah's statement in the next chapter: **'This is what the Lord says...'** (37:5). Prophets like Isaiah claimed to speak in God's name, having royal authority. Whereas Sennacherib's use of the formula, 'This is what the king says...' is a case of arrogance, Isaiah's use of it points to the reliability, the self-attestation that Scripture claims with regard to its infallible, inerrant nature.[4]

For Sennacherib, the fact that Hezekiah had destroyed the pagan shrines in Judah meant that God was now angry with him (36:7). The Assyrian king was contemptuous of Judah's army, taunting Hezekiah (literally **'bargain'** means 'a wager' or 'bet') that even if he were given two thousand horses he couldn't find enough soldiers to ride them (36:8).

Behind this speech lies pride. There is no sin so deeply rooted in our hearts.

The temptation to defect to an easier way of life

Obviously this dialogue was conducted by 'megaphone diplomacy'. The population of Jerusalem could overhear it all from the city walls. Hezekiah's civil servants became alarmed that panic might spread and suggested that the language of diplomatic exchanges, Aramaic, be used (36:11). The Assyrian delegation refused; their intent all along was to foster rebellion on the part of Jerusalem's inhabitants. To reinforce their message, they warned of the hardships that the people would endure if they remained, including having to eat their own dung and drink their own urine during the siege (36:12,16-17). The Assyrians went further and

warned that Assyria had been victorious in every battle so far
(36:19; cf. 2 Kings 17:24,31). To their credit, and as a sign of their
faith, Jerusalem's inhabitants refused to yield to the Assyrians'
taunt: **'How then can the Lord deliver Jerusalem from my
hand?'** (36:20,21). Seemingly, Hezekiah had encouraged them to
trust in the Lord to deliver them (36:15,18). The temptation to
submit to this great power was overwhelming.

Battles like these in the Old Testament, whereby the Lord's
people are faced with colossal forces, are meant to encourage us to
persevere in faithfulness in our own trials. The 'odds' may be
stacked against us from a human point of view. The enemy may
appear to be the size of a Goliath. Everything from a worldly point
of view may dictate a policy of appeasement and compromise. But
faith will always inform us of a better way. A 'cloud of witnesses'
from the Old Testament Scriptures will encourage us to stand our
ground and trust in the 'God of battles' to help us in the hour of trial
(Heb. 12:1). We may feel like Paul did,when he confessed to being
'pressed on every side...' But at the same time, he could say that 'We
do not lose heart. Though outwardly we are wasting away, yet
inwardly we are being renewed day by day. For our light and
momentary troubles are achieving for us an eternal glory that far
outweighs them all. So we fix our eyes not on what is seen, but on
what is unseen. For what is seen is temporary, but what is unseen is
eternal' (2 Cor. 4:16-18). Elisha's pastoral word to his servant in
Dothan when surrounded by Syrian forces would be appropriate
here. 'Don't be afraid,' the prophet answered. 'Those who are with
us are more than those who are with them' (2 Kings 6:16).

Jerusalem's deliverance (37:1-13)

The solution of prayer

Hezekiah's response, upon hearing the arrogant and blasphemous
claims of the Assyrian king through his spokesman, is a wonderful
example of what Christians should do when threatened. He humbled
himself, tearing his royal robes and exchanging them for sackcloth
— a signal demonstration of his repentance. More importantly, he
went to the temple to pray (37:1). Though he was king, Hezekiah's
trust in the Lord forced him to acknowledge that he was essentially

powerless in himself. The fact that Eliakim, Shebna and the leading
priests also put on sackcloth before going to see Isaiah suggests that
the king may well have called for a public fast. It is possible that
Hezekiah had urged the population to join him in prayer as he
himself withdrew privately to intercede in the quiet confines of the
temple (37:2). All his earthly resources were no match against
Sennacherib. We know the words well enough, but they bear
constant repetition:

> Have we trials and temptations?
> Is there trouble anywhere?
> We should never be discouraged:
> Take it to the Lord in prayer!
>
> (Joseph Scriven).

Hezekiah's purpose is not just to tell the Lord his troubles; he
wants the Lord to speak to him. J. I. Packer reminds us of the
Methodist saint Billy Bray who often said, 'I must talk to my Father
about this.' 'It was of praying that he spoke,' Packer says.[5] He goes
on to remind us of the two-way character of prayer. 'Does God, then,
really tell us things when we pray? Yes. We shall probably not hear
voices, nor feel sudden strong impressions of a message coming
through (and we shall be wise to suspect such experiences should
they come our way); but as we analyse and verbalize our problems
before God's throne and tell him what we want and why we want it
and think our way through passages and principles of God's written
word bearing on the matter in hand, we shall find many certainties
crystallizing in our hearts as to God's view of us and our prayers and
his will for us and others. If you ask, "Why is this or that happening?" no light may come, for "the secret things belong to the Lord
our God" (Deut. 29:29); but if you ask, "How am I to serve and
glorify God here and now, where I am?" there will always be an
answer.'

Before going to pray he sent his officials to Isaiah, God's
spokesman, to ask him to pray for the **'remnant that still survives'**
(37:4). 'Remnant' is used here in two senses. Jerusalem was the only
Judean city left uncaptured. Archaeological evidence reveals that
many Israelites fled the northern kingdom during the Assyrian
assaults and settled in Judah, and finally Jerusalem (cf. 2 Chron.
30:1). Hezekiah turned to God's Word and prayer in his trial. The

word for prayer, *tepilla,* is used for intercessory prayer, something which the prophets were often called upon to offer on behalf of the people (e.g., Exod. 32:31-34; 33:12-17; Num.14:13-19; 1 Sam. 7:8-9; Jer. 15:1). There is an abiding lesson for us in Hezekiah's action, too.

The Lord who delivers from trouble

Verse 6 of chapter 37 gives the impression that Isaiah knew that Hezekiah's officials were coming and had an answer for them as soon as they arrived. As soon as his children had been threatened, God had begun to intervene. This was something that Daniel discovered in his own devotions in his time of trouble: 'While I was speaking and praying, confessing my sin and the sin of my people Israel and making my request to the Lord my God for his holy hill — while I was still in prayer, Gabriel, the man I had seen in the earlier vision, came to me in swift flight about the time of the evening sacrifice' (Dan. 9:20-21).

God's response is to dismiss Sennacherib's officials as **'under-lings'** (37:6). The **'spirit'** referred to in verse 7 was a 'general impulsion placed in the human mind by God, compelling to action'.[6] It involved a rumour that the King of Ethiopia, Tirhakah, was approaching with warlike intentions against Assyria (37:9). Tirhakah was currently king of Ethiopia only, but later he was to become the ruler of all the Nile nations, including Egypt. Sennacherib had no choice but to leave Jerusalem alone and return to Assyria to defend his own country. This retreat, as we shall soon see, was only temporary. Jerusalem's troubles were not over yet, not by a long way.

Hezekiah's prayer (37:14-20)

The prayer of a righteous man

Sennacherib's envoys returned from the outskirts of Jerusalem to find that the Assyrian army had left Lachish to attack the nearby city of Libnah, a military fortress in the lowland between the Mediterranean and the hills of Judah (2 Kings 19:8). The threat from King Tirhakah forced Sennacherib to retreat; but not before firing a final projectile at Hezekiah (37:10-13). It came in the form of a letter (or letters, cf. 2 Chron. 32:17), probably very lengthy, taking up several leather or papyrus scrolls. Sennacherib had nothing new to say, apart from the all-important fact that initially he had accused Hezekiah of deceiving the people of Jerusalem (36:14); now it was the Lord who was deceiving Hezekiah (37:10).

Hezekiah's response was to return to the temple, to engage once more in prayer to the Lord (37:15). By spreading out the letter, Hezekiah was making a gesture, as if to say, 'Lord, look at this!'

Hezekiah's prayer is a model, containing both adoration and petition (37:16-20). Hezekiah weaves what he knows about God's character into worship. In contrast to the boastful claims of the Assyrian king, God alone is **'Almighty'**: he is enthroned above the cherubim, in control of all the nations, the Maker of everything that is (37:16). Prayer should begin with worship, as Jesus himself taught in the Lord's Prayer (Luke 11:2-4; Matt. 6:9-13). Even when we are pressed into a corner, worship should come first when we approach the Lord in prayer. The petition contains a list of imperatives: **'Give ear ... hear ... open your eyes ... see ... listen...'** (37:17). Two features are particularly noteworthy.

Firstly, *Hezekiah's concern for the glory of God* can be seen from his initial outrage at Sennacherib's blasphemy (37:4), which forms part of his reasoning as to why the Lord should be motivated to respond (37:20). Far from being concerned about his own ego and sense of honour for being publicly humiliated by Sennacherib's officials, Hezekiah is concerned for the name of God. It is the same motivation that impels us to end our prayers with the expression 'for Jesus' sake'.

Secondly, the request for God to **'deliver'** the people of Jerusalem is *a confession of utter helplessness* on Hezekiah's part. Without God's help we are defenceless. Left to ourselves we can do nothing. 'The greatest of men,' as Matthew Henry said, 'must turn beggars when they have to do with Christ.'

Sennacherib's fall (37:21-38)

It seems that Isaiah was not directly consulted this time by Hezekiah, but in answer to the king's prayer, God spoke his answer to the prophet (37:20-21). It comes in the form of a song, similar in form to 10:5-29, which depicts Jerusalem mocking in derision the pitiful threats of Sennacherib. The description of Jerusalem as a **'virgin'** emphasizes the fact that no one had 'violated' her since the time of David (37:21-22). The Lord takes up Sennacherib's boastful claims, beginning with the references to Israel's trees (cedars, pines, the finest of the forests; these had been used for royal palaces, 1 Kings 5:8-10).

To get a flavour of Sennacherib's boasts, we may note that verse 25 mentions the folklore that the Assyrian king commanded so many soldiers that when they marched across river-beds in Egypt, they literally dried up the rivers! It is doubtful if in fact Sennacherib ever visited Egypt.

Sennacherib's success had been possible only because God allowed it: he was simply carrying out the eternal purpose of God (37:26; cf. Acts 4:28). Assyria, as Isaiah had said earlier, was a 'club' in God's hand to chastise his people (10:5-19). Even the defenceless state of the conquered cities had been **'ordained long ago'** (37:27). Every step Sennacherib took was seen and heard by God (37:28). But just as his rise had been foreseen, so was his downfall. God promises to turn back the Assyrian king with **'a hook in [his] nose'** (37:29). The British Museum contains tablets and pottery depicting Assyrians taking prisoners, putting rings through their noses or upper lips in much the same way as animals are sometimes treated today.

In verse 30 God addresses Hezekiah himself. In it, he promises that Jerusalem's siege will not last long and that prosperity will once more flourish in Jerusalem. But the news is also sombre. During the first year of their siege the people would have no opportunity to plant crops. They would have to eat **'what grows by itself'** (37:30). The next year they would have to eat what **'springs from that'**, things which grow from uncultivated crops. In the third year they would be able to **'sow and reap'** because the siege would be over. In summary, the siege was to last for less than three years. But they were to be three years of severe deprivation and trial. Deliverance, when it comes, will not be due to any sense of worthiness on Judah's part; it is the **'zeal of the Lord Almighty'** which **'will accomplish this'** (37:32; cf. 37:35: **'for my sake'**).

As for Sennacherib, God sets boundaries to his aggrandizement:

> **'He will not enter this city**
> **or shoot an arrow here.**
> **He will not come before it with shield**
> **or build a siege ramp against it.**
> **By the way that he came he will return;**
> **he will not enter this city...'**
>
>   (37:33-34).

A promise can easily be turned into a boast, as the people of Jerusalem showed in Jeremiah's day (cf. Jer. 7:1-15). They used what God had promised as an indication that God would turn a blind eye to the way they lived; they believed his promise bore no relationship to their own responsibilities, in terms of the covenant, to live holy lives. They were wrong and Jerusalem fell.

With astonishing simplicity, Isaiah records what happened. The **'angel of the Lord'** destroyed Sennacherib's army of 185,000 men in one night (37:36). It is possible that this is the story referred to by the fifth-century Greek historian, Herodotus. The Assyrian army, having heard of the threat from Tirhakah, had moved from Libnah further south towards Egypt. A plague of mice ate their way through the leather thongs of the soldiers' shields and bowstrings, making Sennacherib's army defenceless against their enemies.[7] Others, citing a third-century Babylonian writer, Berossus, refer to a 'pestilential sickness'.[8] A combination of these two sources may further indicate a case of bubonic plague.[9]

Sennacherib's speedy retreat is underlined by the use of the verbs **'broke camp', 'withdrew,' 'returned,'** and **'stayed'** (37:7). His demise came later in Nineveh, when two of his sons, Adrammelech and Sharezer, murdered him (37:38).

'A man who remains stiff-necked after many rebukes will suddenly be destroyed — without remedy' (Prov. 29:1).

> 'How long will mockers delight in mockery
>   and fools hate knowledge?
> If you had responded to my rebuke,
>   I would have poured out my heart to you
>   and made my thoughts known to you.
> But since you rejected me when I called
>   and no one gave heed when I stretched out my hand,

since you ignored all my advice
and would not accept my rebuke,
I in turn will laugh at your disaster;
I will mock when calamity overtakes you'

(Prov. 1:22-26)

So it was with Sennacherib. He learnt the hard way, as Belshazzar was later to do in Babylon, that God alone is sovereign (cf. Dan. 5:30). Lest we find the same spirit of pride in our hearts, we should pray with the psalmist: 'Teach us to number our days aright, that we may gain a heart of wisdom' (Ps. 90:12).

Summary

The year 701 B.C. was the most crucial in Isaiah's life. In many ways God raised him specially up for the ministry he performed that year. The Assyrian threat was considerable, and it was Isaiah's friend-ship and ministry to King Hezekiah, urging prayer as the way of deliverance, that won the day. God gave Judah a godly leader at its most crucial time. This was a singular act of blessing. We need such leaders today!

23.
Hezekiah's sickness and God's cure

Please read Isaiah 38 and 39

What a remarkable life Hezekiah had! He was twenty-five years old when he became king and he ruled for a period of twenty-nine years. During his lifetime he had turned back the nation of Judah to the ways of the Lord, reversing the godlessness of his father Ahaz. He was a man who had experienced revival. He had had personal dealings with Isaiah the prophet, through whom God spoke directly. He had also known answers to prayer. He had learned to expect great things from God. Then, suddenly, he fell seriously ill, **'and was at the point of death'** (38:1).[1] It was the kind of news we all secretly dread: a terminal illness.[2]

Hezekiah was probably in his mid-thirties; the news was reinforced not with fallible predictions of expert medical opinion, but by the infallible word of God delivered through his mouthpiece, Isaiah. **'Hezekiah turned his face to the wall and prayed to the Lord'** (38:2).

Sir Norman Anderson, former Director of the Institute of Advanced Legal Studies in London, tells in a moving way his reaction to the news of his son's terminal illness. 'We lunched together, carefully avoiding the subject; but afterwards he asked if he could come back to my office for some prayer. To this I gladly agreed, and asked him if he would start; but he preferred to leave that to me. I don't remember what words came to me in those traumatic moments, but I heard Hugh's voice saying, "O God, you know how difficult it sometimes is to say 'Your will be done'. Help me to say that now."'[3]

Christians become ill

Hezekiah's illness is recorded in the context of his godliness (38:3). Firstly, he had walked before God in truth, a description which the Bible reserves for men like Enoch, Noah, Abraham, Isaac, David and Solomon (Gen. 5:22,24; 6:9; 17:1; 48:15; 1 Kings 3:3,14). Secondly, he possessed a loyal heart, wholeheartedly devoted to the Lord (cf. Num. 14:24; 32:12; Deut. 1:36; Josh. 14:8,9; 1 Kings 11:4; 1 Chron. 28:9 etc). Thirdly, he did what was right in the Lord's sight. Chronicles makes much of Hezekiah's godliness, celebrating him as the first of twelve kings since the division of the kingdom of whom it could be said that 'He did what was right in the eyes of the Lord, just as his father David had done' (2 Chron. 29:1-2).

It is just here that a problem arises. Uzziah's leprosy was a result of his disobedience (2 Chron. 26:16-21). But Hezekiah's illness was not attributable to any specific transgression on his part. His godliness is underlined. His gifts were necessary; his wisdom and counsel were sought after and, generally, he was loved and respected by his people. So why did the Lord allow sickness to overtake him?

The Bible devotes an entire book to attempting an answer to this question. The book of Job focuses on a righteous man whose life is ravaged by pain (Job 1:1,8). The lesson that emerges from the lives of both Job and Hezekiah is that not all sickness is the result of sin. It is not part of God's plan that believers, even those whose lives demonstrate an eminent degree of consecration, should be free from deprivation (material or health-related). Arguments that run along the lines that 'Jesus came to make us whole, and that includes being free from sickness,' are at best misguided, and at worst, positively harmful and dangerous. Some have asserted that 'The Israelites were never sick,' conveniently ignoring the fact that both David and Daniel, who walked with God, became ill (Ps. 22, Dan. 8:27), and Jacob died of his sickness (Gen. 48; 49:33), as did Elisha (2 Kings 13:14). It is more than likely that Paul himself, who possessed the gift of healing, suffered some kind of eye-trouble (2 Cor. 12:7-9; Gal. 6:11). Of greater certainty is the fact that he had to leave Epaphroditus at Miletus because of his illness (2 Tim. 4:20); and he prescribed a little wine for Timothy's delicate stomach and 'frequent illnesses' (1 Tim. 5:23). The Bible is quite clear: even the righteous fall sick. Anyone who says anything to the contrary is not facing the facts.

Hezekiah did not want to die

Hezekiah turned once again to prayer. The content of his prayer begins with a detailed account of his godliness (38:3). We must not judge Hezekiah harshly for this. He is not pleading his works as the basis of his salvation. He wants God to spare his earthly life. There appears to be no particular sin that accounts for this providence. That is not to say that Hezekiah feels it to be unjust. Had he been taken, Hezekiah would have blessed the Lord nevertheless. But, like Job, he finds this providence strange and asks that he might be spared.

Just how close to death Hezekiah came is revealed in the song he later wrote about this experience (38:10-20).

> **'I said, "In the prime of my life**
> **must I go through the gates of death**
> **and be robbed of the rest of my years?"**
> **I said, "I will not again see the Lord,**
> **the Lord, in the land of the living;**
> **no longer will I look on mankind,**
> **or be with those who now dwell in this world"'**
>
> (38:10-11).

His life was about to be pulled down in a fashion that reminded of what a shepherd would do to his tent each morning; or to be cut up and rolled away like the way a weaver would roll up his cloth when the garment was finished (38:12). Pain, sleeplessness and an emaciated body were all part of Hezekiah's experience of illness (38:13-14). And Hezekiah did not want to die just yet; upon hearing the news he had wept bitterly and then prayed that what had been revealed to him might not come to pass.

Of some importance is the fact that Hezekiah had no heir. Manasseh, Hezekiah's son, was born some three years after this incident, being only twelve when he came to the throne (2 Chron. 33:1). Had Hezekiah died at this point, there would have been a fatal interruption in the promised line of Messiah's birth (Matt. 1:9-10). Seen from this point of view, Hezekiah's concern for his life is not simply a selfish one. But we must also take note of the fact that he was a relatively young man (in his mid-thirties). His prayer was what any believer might request in such circumstances. The fact that divine revelation had indicated the illness as terminal posed no problem to his willingness to pray about it (38:1; cf. 38:15). What God has revealed is one thing; what he has secretly planned is another (Deut. 29:29).

God answers prayer

Following Hezekiah's intercessory prayer, Isaiah is dispatched with the news that his life is to be extended by fifteen years (38:4-5). He is also promised that the Assyrian forces will not overtake Jerusalem (38:6). David had experienced a similar deliverance from near-death (Ps. 30:3). God does not always heal in answer to prayer. Paul discovered it and tells us so (2 Cor. 12:7-9). God knows best.

Hezekiah's recovery was as the result of a cure. Miraculous healing and the use of medicinal skill are not opposing forces. Isaiah asked Hezekiah's entourage to prepare a poultice of figs for the infection — a remedy used in that day for both humans and animals to draw the poison from a boil or wound (38:21).

As a sign (38:22), which Hezekiah asked for (cf. 2 Kings 20:8), Isaiah allowed him to choose whether to have the shadow on a sundial go miraculously ten degrees backward or ten degrees forward. Since it normally went forward, he asked for the seemingly more difficult display of the shadow going backwards. '**The stairway of Ahaz**' (38:8) may well have been a sundial, invented by the Babylonians, which Ahaz had brought to Jerusalem. Behind it lies the suspicion of astral worship. However, the Septuagint supposes the phrase to refer, not to a sundial as such, but to a flight of steps arranged in such a fashion that the shadow on them could reveal the time of day.[4] A typical Babylonian sundial was divided into twenty-four degrees, so that ten degrees would represent five hours. The miracle does not necessarily require a backward movement of the earth, which would be experienced around the world. It may have been a supernatural bending of the shadow itself.[5]

Miracles are frequently called 'signs' in Scripture (e.g. John 2:18; 4:54; 6:14,30; Acts 2:22). The miracle involved the displacement of time. God is in control of time. Hezekiah's life, like yours and mine, was of a finite duration. How long we have is not for us to determine. Today we may be healthy and expect to live a while yet. Tomorrow it may be different. The matter is in God's hands.

Two other features of Hezekiah's song are worth noting.

Firstly, he mentions in verse 17 something of the underlying purpose behind suffering. **'Surely it was for my benefit that I suffered such anguish...'** There is always a reason for the existence of sorrow. The presence of pain and suffering in our lives is not a matter of mere sovereignty. 'For he does not willingly bring affliction or grief to the children of men' (Lam. 3:33). God corrects us for our profit (Heb. 12:10). Should we find ourselves 'suffer[ing] grief in all kinds of trials' (1 Peter 1:6) it is because there is a necessity for it. There is always a purpose behind the providences of God.

Secondly, praise is always the correct response to the blessings of God. This experience was something Hezekiah would tell Manasseh all about (38:19). But whilst this was Hezekiah's initial response, it did not remain for long. Chapter 39 contains the sad truth that God's answers to our prayers are not always a blessing, a truth that is underlined in Psalm 106:

'In the desert they gave in to their craving;
   in the wasteland they put God to the test.
So he gave them what they asked for,
   but sent a wasting disease upon them'

(Ps. 106:14-15).

Sadly, Hezekiah's greatness is clouded by the sin of pride that developed in his closing years. Merodach-Baladan (39:1), the King of Babylon, wanted, according to Josephus, aid for a rebellion against Assyria. He is identified with Mardukhabaliddina, who seized the Babylonian throne in 721 B.C., was deposed by Sargon of Assyria, and then came back to rule again for a short time about 704 B.C. He sent letters and a present to Hezekiah because he had heard about his illness. Having recovered so wonderfully, Hezekiah was congratulated by the Babylonian king. The flattery was too much for Hezekiah. He fell for it, and in a moment of incredible stupidity, he showed the foreign ruler's envoys all the treasure in his storehouses (39:2). It was an act of folly for which Isaiah gave him a severe reprimand (39:3-7). There is a strong hint of boasting in verse 3, as though Hezekiah wanted to underline just how important he was if such great leaders should show him so much honour.

There is only one explanation for this folly: that pride had grown in his heart. 'But Hezekiah's heart was proud and he did not respond to the kindness shown him; therefore the Lord's wrath was on him and on Judah and Jerusalem' (2 Chron. 32:25). 'Pride is a vice,' said Thomas Hooker, 'which cleaves so fast unto the hearts of men, that if we were to strip ourselves of all faults, one by one, we should undoubtedly find it the very last and hardest to put off.'[6] It would have been better had Hezekiah died, than to live and spoil his testimony in this way. He made no opportunity to witness to these visitors. Instead, he boasted and this was to lead eventually to Judah's overthrow by Babylon (39:6-7; cf. Dan. 1:1-2). The judgement, Hezekiah concurs, is no more than he deserves: it is **'good'** ('just', or 'right', 39:8).

Summary

Illness is part of the curse brought about by the Fall. So long as we live in this sin-cursed world, we cannot realistically expect to escape the ravages of disease and old age. God can, and does, heal in answer to prayer (James 5:14). But such healings are not always the best for us. There are more important matters than bodily healing. Maintaining a good testimony is one, remembering that, sooner or later, heaven is where all Christians belong is another.

24.
Comfort

Please read Isaiah 40:1-11

(Note: Since this chapter is both well known and rich in allusions to aspects of Isaiah's prophecy that will occupy the remainder of the book, I have taken the liberty to include three chapters by way of comment. This may appear disproportionate to the rest of Isaiah; I have a great deal of sympathy with those readers who find it so. However, there are issues of fundamental importance in this chapter—issues which are repeated throughout chapters 40-66. To take time in enumerating some of them here will, I trust, open up the rest of the book with greater clarity.)

'When one turns from the thirty-ninth to the fortieth chapter it is as though he steps out of the darkness of judgement into the light of salvation.'[1] After the clouds of judgement that have overshadowed the entirety of the first thirty-nine chapters comes the sunshine of God's grace that will occupy the final twenty-six chapters.

The chapter begins with a word of comfort: **'Comfort, comfort my people, says your God'** (40:1). The people of Judah are 'my people', God says. They belong to him; they have been chosen by him. They are in covenant with him. Though he had found it necessary for Assyria to punish them and he would eventually send them into exile in Babylon, he will not abandon them. Christians are always to remember that God's chastisements, though sore at the time, are always from our Father who loves us. We are not to lose heart. 'His banner over me is love' (Song of Songs 2:4).

When you think of the word 'comfort', what is it that you think about? Probably a cosy sofa, a cup of tea and a warm log fire at the end of a busy day wouldn't be far off the mark. But suppose we were to use the word 'console' instead, what would come into your mind?[2] Listening intensely to someone as they pour out their troubles to you? An arm around a friend's shoulder in a moment of distress? Writing a sympathy card to someone who has just lost a marriage partner?

Perhaps you imagine yourself to be a fairly good 'comforter'. But can you imagine trying to comfort someone who has just learnt he or she has terminal cancer? Or distressed parents who have learnt their son is homosexual? Or a close friend whose husband you know well is abusing her? Modern society talks about 'comfort zones', by which it means areas in which you feel comfortable and at ease. Are any of the above within your 'comfort zones'?

'Speak tenderly' God says (40:2) The Hebrew for this phrase is used in 2 Chronicles 32:6 to describe the way Hezekiah 'encouraged' Judah to trust in God in spite of the Assyrian invasion. Like Barnabas, whose name means 'son of encouragement', we too are to be encouragers, speaking tender, comforting words.

Isaiah 40:1-11 is a prologue to the rest of the book. The major themes to be discussed are touched upon briefly in these verses. The content of God's comfortable message to his people, which he speaks and to which we are to give witness, is both negative (40:2) and positive (40:3-11). Just as another prophet, Jeremiah, saw his message as one which both tore down and built up (Jer. 1:10), so too Isaiah sees the need to begin by applying the surgical knife to Judah's condition.[3]

Grace abounding

The prophet's message is both negative and positive. Negatively, it has to do with sin, and has three features.

1. Sin is a burden

Isaiah is to proclaim the ending of the burden of sin. The prophet is to speak **'to her that her hard service has been completed'**. When John Bunyan wanted to describe the way a person feels when under conviction of the guilt of sin, he described it as a heavy burden which Christian only managed to get rid of at the cross. There is coming a day when the hardship of Babylonian captivity will be over. When they went into exile there was no song in their hearts (Ps. 137:2-4); when they returned they were ecstatic (Ezra 3:12,13; 6:16,22; Neh. 8:10,12,17). This picture of the exodus from Babylon, just like the former exodus from Egypt some 800 years previously, is a picture of salvation. 'Burdens are lifted at Calvary' is part of their message and it is something Isaiah is going to elaborate upon in detail in the following chapters.

2. Sin incurs a penalty

Isaiah is to proclaim that **'that her sin has been paid for'**. If sin is to be forgiven it must be atoned for. The penalty that is its due must first be met. God had been at pains to teach that lesson from the earliest times. The only way Israel had been spared in the first exodus from Egypt was through the sacrificial blood of the Passover lamb (Exod. 12). Similarly the rituals of the Levitical sacrifices had underlined that 'The law requires that nearly everything be cleansed with blood, and without the shedding of blood there is no forgiveness' (Heb. 9:22). What the prophet is alluding to here is something which he will describe in full in chapter 53: the guilt of sin can only be satisfied through the substitution of another. 'There is no one,' reasoned the meticulous logic of the godly Anselm of Canterbury in the eleventh century, 'who *can* make this satisfaction except God himself... But no one *ought* to make it except man; otherwise man does not make satisfaction.' Therefore, he continued, 'It is necessary that one who is God-man should make it.'[4] This is the logic of Calvary that will occupy this prophet's message through to the end.

3. Sin's punishment is great, but never as great as it deserves

The words, **'She has received from the Lord's hand double for all her sins'** (40:2) are capable of several interpretations. They may be taken to mean that despite the punishment, she has now received from the same hand a double blessing. Another, more coherent, interpretation is to understand 'double' as referring to the severity of the chastisement. Though it was not as much as she deserved, Jerusalem suffered terribly under Babylon's tyranny. The sense, according to this view, is that she has now suffered enough and that Jerusalem's sins are pardoned, having received an abundant punishment from the Lord. This view is fraught with difficulties, militating as it does aginst the whole idea in Isaiah of God's provision of the Servant who takes the sinner's place. Rather, the provision for sin and guilt, received from the Lord's hand, should be seen as standing in close relationship to the satisfaction provided by the Servant of the Lord. In that case the perfect tenses employed here should be regarded as prophetical.[5] It is Jesus, according to this view, that received the double (severe) punishment.

Isaiah's second call

In response to this opening message we are introduced to **'a voice'** (40:3). In fact, three voices are mentioned (40:3,6,9), each showing how the comfort of verse 1 will come about. The voice of verse 3 is not identified immediately — though the New Testament links it with John the Baptist (Matt. 3:3; Mark 1:3; Luke 3:4; John 1:23). It is not unreasonable to see Isaiah, too, fulfilling this role, at least in part. In a mysterious dialogue God addresses the prophet: **'A voice says, "Cry out." And I said, "What shall I cry?"'** (40:6). In verse 9, **'your voice'** is certainly Isaiah's. Isaiah is receiving as it were a second call from God (cf. 6:8).

Thus we are led to expect that though Isaiah will be the bearer of the good news (cf. 41:27 where the prophet is called **'a messenger of good tidings'**), responding to the 'voice' of verse 3, another (John the Baptist) will come in the future to herald this comforting message. The messenger who responds to John the Baptist is, of course, Jesus Christ. In other words 'What the voice is for Isaiah, John the Baptist is for the greatest prophet, Jesus Christ. So, as Isaiah functioned as a predecessor and type of Christ, so the voice functioned in regard to John the Baptist.'[6]

The positive aspect of the message follows, and also falls into three sections.

1. Preparation

The Lord is going to make preparation for the coming of his Son, **'the glory of the Lord'** (40:5). When the apostle John came to write his Gospel he began, unlike the other Gospel writers, with Jesus' deity. John makes no mention of Jesus' birth. Instead he proclaims at the outset that Jesus is God. John knew it to be so for many reasons, but most of all because on the Mount of Transfiguration he had 'seen his glory' (John 1:14). Peter, too, had been there on the mountain and the effect upon him had been just as transforming (2 Peter 1:17-18). Paul also spoke of Christ as the 'Lord of glory' (1 Cor. 2:8; cf. 2 Cor. 4:6).

All kinds of obstacles are in the way, and these will need to be removed before Jesus Christ comes. Have you, I wonder, ever watched a construction company changing the landscape when building a motorway? Motorways are constructed in such a way as not to have sharp bends or steep inclines. They should be as flat and straight as possible. That means levelling mountains, filling in valleys and even boring tunnels through granite. Nothing can stand in the way of the new road. This is how the prophet puts it:

'Every valley shall be raised up,
    every mountain and hill made low;
the rough ground shall become level,
    the rugged places a plain'

(40:4).

This 'preparation' would culminate in the birth of Jesus Christ, but before that a herald would proclaim his coming **'in the desert'** (40:3). This, of course, is a reference to John the Baptist whose preaching ministry took place in the desert (Matt. 3:1). The desert was to remind them of how God had saved his people from the desert (wilderness) after forty long years in Moses' time (cf. Deut. 8:2; Ps. 68:7), and the spiritual desert in their hearts that had led God to drive them into Babylon. In Isaiah's day, just as in Moses' day before him and John's day after him, the need to remove the obstacles that bar the way to fellowship with God is clear. John's word for it was *repentance*, 'a saving grace whereby a sinner, out of a true sense of his sin, and apprehension of the mercy of God in Christ, doth, with grief and hatred of his sin, turn from it unto God, with full purpose of, and endeavour after, new obedience'.[7]

The Old Testament is the story of this preparation. It is the unfolding of the mystery which culminates in the birth of Jesus. If you begin reading the Gospel of Luke, you will find that the story does not begin with Jesus. Its starting-point is a full year before his birth.

An old priest, Zechariah, is standing by the altar of incense in the temple at Jerusalem. Suddenly an angel appears and says to him, 'Do not be afraid, Zechariah; your prayer has been heard' (Luke 1:13). The miracle of Abraham and Sarah, at the beginning of our Bibles, which culminated in the birth of their son Isaac, was to be repeated in the lives of Zechariah and Elizabeth in the birth of John the Baptist. Just as Isaac had been used to prefigure Christ, so too John the Baptist was to be a forerunner and witness to the Messiah. Centuries had passed since God had spoken as he did in Zechariah's time.[8] In fact, the last word he had given was to the prophet Malachi, when he had promised: 'See, I will send you the prophet Elijah before that great and dreadful day of the Lord comes' (Mal. 4:5). John the Baptist, at the dawn of the New Testament, is linked to Elijah at the close of the Old Testament. But the preparation is longer than that. Just a glance at the genealogy of Jesus shows that the royal line stretches back through such characters as Zerubbabel, Nathan, David, the tribe of Judah (to whom Isaiah was preaching), to Abraham, Shem, Noah, Seth and Adam. And you cannot go further back than Adam!

The 'preparation' is the story of the Old Testament. This is in part what Paul means when he speaks of the birth of Jesus Christ as taking place 'when the time had fully come' (Gal. 4:4).

2. A word you can trust

The second aspect of Isaiah's message has to do with the trustworthiness of God's Word. God's Word is sure! In contrast to flowers and grass which wither when they are cut down, there is a durability about the Word of God.

God has spoken, and the words he has caused to be written down in the Scripture are his words. He has bound himself to them. For both Christ and the apostles, what Scripture says, God says. When prophets preached they spoke for God. When biblical writers wrote, they wrote for God. In Christ all his promises are 'Yes' and 'Amen' (2 Cor. 1:20). He cannot lie or deny himself (2 Tim. 2:13; Titus 1:2; Heb. 6:18). That is why his Word abides for ever. There are two mutually corresponding truths here: in contrast to the frailty and fickleness of man, God's Word is both durable and dependable. God is never going to change his mind. 'Scripture,' Jesus assured us, 'cannot be broken' (John 10:35).

3. Good news

It is amazing just how often one still finds people who think that the
gospel is to be found only in the New Testament. They have never
read Isaiah! In fact the first gospel promise is found in Genesis 3,
immediately after the Fall, when God promises Eve that her seed
will be the means of conquering Satan and his kingdom for ever
(Gen. 3:15).

Isaiah is asked to proclaim the same message in effect. It is
'tidings', or news that is to be proclaimed from the 'high mountain'
and 'with a shout'. This is a message worth getting excited about.
And what is the message? Quite simply, 'Behold your God!' Old
Testament believers were to be witnesses to the gospel. 'You who
bring good tidings' (40:9) is one word in the Hebrew. Its Greek
equivalent is 'evangelist'. Evangelism is speaking to others about
God: what he is like, what he threatens to do, what he promises to
those who love his Son.

The Bible never proves the existence of God. You can search
from Genesis to Revelation and what you find on every page is the
assumption that God exists, and that men know that he exists. When
Paul preaches to the philosophers at Athens he takes it for granted
that they believe in God. 'God has endued all men with some sense
of his godhead', with the result that 'a sense of deity is inscribed on
every heart.'[9] What the Athenians needed to know was the nature of
God. What Paul did on the Areopagus was to expound on the
attributes of God: elaborating in turn upon God as Creator, Sustainer, Ruler, Father and Judge. That is exactly what Isaiah is going
to do: preach to the people of Judah about the character of God. He
is going to describe God's attributes in detail. He is going to confront
them with the only God there is and call upon them to make peace
with him.

It is interesting to note that after emphasizing the severity of God
in the opening chapters, he now concentrates upon his goodness (cf.
Rom. 11:22). Isaiah 40 is a chapter which describes both the power
and the tenderness of God:

'See, the Sovereign Lord comes with power,
    and his arm rules for him.
See, his reward is with him,

and his recompense accompanies him'

(40:10).

'Surely the nations are like a drop in a bucket;
    they are regarded as dust on the scales;
he weighs the islands as though they were fine dust'

(40:15)

'"To whom will you compare me?
    Or who is my equal?" says the Holy One.
Lift your eyes and look to the heavens:
    Who created all these?
He who brings out the starry host one by one,
    and calls them each by name.
Because of his great power and mighty strength,
    not one of them is missing'

(40:25-26).

In the middle of this declaration of God's power we find these
words:

'He tends his flock like a shepherd:
    He gathers the lambs in his arms
and carries them close to his heart;
    he gently leads those that have young'

(40:11).

The same passage which stresses the infiniteness of God's power
also portrays his gentleness. And what better way of illustrating
gentleness than by a shepherd carrying his lambs close to his heart?
Gentleness is one of the marks of Jesus (Matt. 11:28-29). It is also
something that we should pray for in our own lives (Gal. 5:22-23;
Col. 3:12). When did you last pray that God would make you gentle?

Summary

Isaiah has introduced a summary of a 'comforting' (strengthening)
message that will dominate the rest of the book. He has received a

second call from God to be his ambassador (40:6,9; cf. 6:8),
proclaiming a message from the covenant God of Judah to his
people ('**my people...your God**', 40:11). At the heart of the message was to be the truth that, no matter what changes may take place
in the world, God's Word stands for ever. God can be trusted to keep
his word, come what may.

25.
God has no equal

Please read Isaiah 40:12-31

During the turmoil of the 1640s that witnessed a violent civil war in England, the trial and execution of King Charles I, the massacre of an Irish city under the leadership of Oliver Cromwell and the covenanting of Scotland to the Protestant and Reformed faith, a group of over 400 ministers met at Westminster Abbey on the banks of the River Thames. Presbyterians, Episcopalians and Independents were summoned together by order of Parliament to write a confession of faith, accurately summarizing the essentials of the Christian faith. Later, in an attempt to crystallize their discussions they came up with a catechism designed for easy memorization by children.

The fourth question was particularly crucial: 'What is God?' The answer, according to Charles Hodge, is 'probably the best definition of God ever penned by man' and reads as follows: 'God is a Spirit, infinite, eternal and unchangeable, in his being, wisdom, power, holiness, justice, goodness and truth.' In unfolding the character of God, Isaiah will attest to many of these attributes.

Theology, as we find it presented in the Bible, is always practical. This section is probably the finest example in the Scriptures of a study of the attributes of God. But there is a very practical reason for it: some of God's children were suffering from depression and loss of assurance due to the onset of trials and difficulties. They were complaining that God either did not know about their condition; or worse, that he did not care:

> **'Why do you say, O Jacob,**
> **and complain, O Israel,**

"My way is hidden from the Lord;
   my cause is disregarded by my God"?'

(40:27).

Some were growing weary (40:30); others were fainting (40:31).
Despondent and despairing people need to have their eyes opened
to behold God's greatness and majesty (40:26).

Two things need to be noted as we study this section of Isaiah's
prophecy. First, God wants us to study his Word (theology) to help
us overcome our spiritual problems; and second, the more we know
and understand of God, the stronger we will be: **'The people that
do know their God shall be strong, and do exploits'** (Dan. 11:32,
AV).[2]

The Creator (40:12-17,26,28)

The Bible begins with an attestation of God's creative power. The
very first thing we read in the Scriptures is of One who is infinitely
more powerful than we are: 'In the beginning God created the
heavens and the earth' (Gen. 1:1). Isaiah 40:12-20 is a creation
hymn extolling God's power. He is the One who has made matter
(40:12), mind (40:13-14) and every living creature (15-17). Many
Christians have lost sight of this truth. The veneration of Charles
Darwin and the idolatry that is given to the theory of evolution have
partially eroded one of the most powerful and practical truths of the
Bible.

The Creator is described using three ideas.

1. Omnipotence: how great thou art!

The argument of the opening section (40:12) is quite clear: 'You
have seen how vast the oceans are, and the sky, and the mountains.
It's really awesome, isn't it? Now meet the One who made them all.'
'Take a look at your hands,' he says in effect. 'Now imagine trying
to measure the oceans with the palms of your hands, or try measuring the sky at night with the distance from the thumb to the tip of the
little finger in an outstretched hand, or even trying to use one of your

measuring devices to weigh all the dust particles on the earth. It is impossible.' But it is *not* impossible to God! He made the world and he is all-powerful.

2. Omniscience

If the creation of the universe involves infinite power, it also involves infinite knowledge. God is both omnipotent and omniscient: **'Who has understood the mind of the Lord, or instructed him as his counsellor?'** (40:13).[3] God did not need to consult with anyone but himself within the Trinity of his being when he made this universe. He knows everything. That's why it is foolish to think that our **'way is hidden from the Lord'** (40:27).

3. Independence

God does not need our help. The God who revealed himself to Moses, encouraging him to return to Egypt and face the powerful Pharaoh, called himself 'I am that I am' (Exod. 3:14). The God disclosed to Moses is self-sufficient and completely independent. 'Aseity' is the word theologians use to describe this quality in God. And the way Moses was helped to see it was by a bush that caught fire but was not itself consumed (Exod. 3:2).

God is totally self-sufficient. It is a very humbling thing, but he can accomplish all his desire without the help of any one of us:

> **'Whom did the Lord consult to enlighten him,**
> **and who taught him the right way?**
> **Who was it that taught him knowledge**
> **or showed him the path of understanding?'**
>
> (40:14).

Indeed there are many things about God that are a mystery to us. That's one of the reasons why Paul quotes this verse at the end of his discourse concerning the future of Israel in Romans 11:34. Just go on remembering that God managed fine before you were born! But all the same he speaks to us, confides in us, uses us in the outworking of his purposes. He takes us, poor broken vessels that we are, and allows us to hear some of his great thoughts and secrets. **'The Lord**

confides in those who fear him; he makes his covenant known to
them' (Ps. 25:14). Doesn't that overwhelm you to think that he has
confided in you?

Three conclusions follow a consideration of God as the Creator.

1. God is greater than his own creation

Think of the ease with which God made the galaxies. Awesome in
their magnitude, God 'stretched' them over the earth in the same
way as many of Isaiah's readers had spread a canvas over the frame
of a tent (40:22).

> **'Lift up your eyes and look to the heavens:**
> **Who created all these?**
> **He who brings out the starry host one by one,**
> **and calls them each by name.**
> **Because of his great power and mighty strength,**
> **not one of them is missing'**
>
> (40:26).

It is absurd to imagine that God's energy can be exhausted in any
way:

> **'Do you not know?**
> **Have you not heard?**
> **The Lord is the everlasting God,**
> **the Creator of the ends of the earth.**
> **He will not grow tired or weary,**
> **and his understanding no one can fathom'**
>
> (40:28).

This is what it means to be God according the psalmist: 'Know
that the Lord, he is God; it is he who has made us, and not we
ourselves' (Ps. 100:3, NKJV).

2. Nothing is a threat to God

The forces in opposition to God ultimately amount to nothing. This
truth should inspire in us great confidence. We have this powerful
God on our side: 'My help comes from the Lord, the Maker of

heaven and earth' (Ps. 121:2). Nothing can be a threat to God — not even the great nations of the world, which are in effect

> ' ... **like a drop in a bucket;**
> **they are regarded as dust on the scales;**
> **he weighs the islands as though they were fine dust...**
> **Before him all the nations are as nothing;**
> **they are regarded by him as worthless**
> **and less than nothing'**

$$(40:15,17).$$

Drop a small amount of flour on the kitchen scales and it will not register: place a drop of water in a large bucket and it will make little effect. The might of Assyria and Babylon may appear awesome, but they are as nothing before God. And individuals, what are they but mere grasshoppers ? (40:22).

Consider for a moment your very worst fears, or your biggest and strongest enemy. They do not begin to compare with the might and power of God. You are 'safe in the arms of Jesus': 'For I am convinced that neither death nor life, neither angels nor demons, neither the present nor the future, nor any powers, neither height nor depth, nor anything else in all creation, will be able to separate us from the love of God that is in Christ Jesus our Lord' (Rom. 8:38-39).

3. No sacrifice on man's part would do justice to the greatness of God

God does not need our worship. The best wood from Lebanon and all the animals that teemed in its forests would be insufficient as a sacrifice to him (40:16).

The Upholder (40:21-26)

God's power and greatness are not limited to the work of creation. They appear equally in his providence. He did not simply bring the world into being; he maintains it in being, 'preserving and governing all his creatures and all their actions'.[4] By a series of four questions (40:21) Isaiah asks whether or not they have sufficiently

understood the greatness of God: he is not only the Creator; he is the
Upholder:

> **'He sits enthroned above the circle of the earth,**
> **and its people are like grasshoppers.**
> **He stretches out the heavens like a canopy,**
> **and spreads them out like a tent to live in'**
>
> (40:22).

E. J. Young comments that the phrase, 'sits enthroned above the
circle of the earth', is 'a figurative expression for God's providential
upholding and maintaining of creation'.[5]

God has not abandoned his control of the universe. He is not the
God of the deists, who believed that God had made the world in the
same way as a watch, once having been wound, could be allowed to
tick away without interference. According to them, if God exists at
all, he is like some benign grandfather asleep in an armchair in some
distant part of the universe. How different is the God of the Bible!
He is constantly interrupting the course of events: politicians and
judges (40:23-24) have their power from him. Even before some of
them have had time to put down roots, God has swept them away.
The same thought is expressed by Daniel, who lived during the
exile:

> 'He changes times and seasons;
>   he sets up kings and deposes them.
> He gives wisdom to the wise
>   and knowledge to the discerning'
>
> (Dan. 2:21).

As I write these lines, the 'two Germanies' have been united.
Yesterday there were two countries and two governments. Just a few
years ago East Germany was in the grip of Communism. What has
brought about the collapse of this god of Marxism? God has done it!
He can destroy the gods of capitalism and materialism too!

What has this passage been saying? In a word: 'Open your eyes
and behold the majesty of God.' Look at the things which God does:
could you do them? Look at the nations: but God is more powerful
than any of them! Look at the world: it is tiny in comparison with

God. Look at the great men, like Sennacherib and Nebuchadnezzar. Where are they now? Behold your God!

A study of the greatness of God in creation and providence focuses in two directions: it serves as a warning as to the folly of idolatry, and it provides frightened Christians with a source of encouragement in that he knows our most intimate of needs.

1. The folly of idolatry

Everything has been leading up to a great proclamation: God — this God of the Old Testament — is the only God there is. We shall consider this matter again when we come to 44:6-23 and 46:1-13. The idols are nothing. God is too big, too great, to be compared to bits of wood or stone. **'"To whom will you compare me? Or who is my equal?" says the Holy One'** (40:25).

The very suggestion that God can be likened in any way to something created is blasphemous. 'Man made God in his own image,' was Voltaire's crack, and he was right! Fallen man is for ever trying to lower God to his standards. When Martin Luther told the humanist Erasmus that his thoughts of God were too human, he was passing sentence upon all rationalistic religion that has infected the church through the ages.[6]

Idolatry is not only wrong, it is stupid. Behind the second commandment, 'You shall not make for yourself an idol in the form of anything in heaven above or on the earth beneath or in the waters below' (Exod. 20:4), lies the thought that to imagine God other than the way he is makes no sense. The infinite, all-powerful, all-knowing God cannot be likened to anything made or fashioned by man. Whenever someone says, 'I like to think of God this way...', what follows is sure to be idolatrous. The gods of our imagination are too small, too frail, too human.

2. God of the little things

God is not only involved in the big things, such as the governments of the world (40:24); he is intimately concerned about the little things too. Idolatry comes from thinking wrong thoughts about God. Depression arises when we think wrong thoughts about ourselves — that we are too insignificant for God to be concerned about.

Think of the stars. To be sure they are big when you are close to one of them, but from your standpoint and mine what possible difference would it make to our lives if tonight, as you looked out of the bedroom window, one of them was missing? Apart from Patrick Moore, who would even notice? It makes no difference at all to that bill that needs to be paid, or the mysterious pains you have noticed in your left side, or that difficult person in the office who seems to be picking on you. But that is just the point. God knows all the stars. **'Not one of them is missing'** (40:26).

God's power lies behind the most trivial of things, like a sparrow that falls in one of Jerusalem's side-streets (Matt. 6:26), or the growth of a lily (Matt. 6:28). If God can remove mountains and command the sun to stop shining (Job 9:5-7) he can also sustain the lion, the mountain goat, the wild ass and ox, the ostrich, horse, hawk and eagle (Job 38:39 - 39:30). And he can take care of all your needs, however small. One small tear can move the great God of the universe to overflow with the most tender compassion. God is not so preoccupied with running this great universe that somehow you escape his notice. Jesus assured those who loved him that 'Every hair of your head is numbered.' Take Peter's advice: 'Cast all your anxiety upon him, because he cares for you' (1 Peter 5:7). Trust God's majesty and you will not go far astray. Taking this thought into our hearts is the theme of the next chapter.

Summary

Certain folk in Jerusalem were complaining that God either did not know, or worse, did not care about their condition. They were, of course, profoundly wrong. To counter this counsel of despair, Isaiah confronts them with supreme theological facts about God: he is the all-knowing, all-powerful Creator to whom nothing is a threat. It is time that his people learn this truth, and learn it well. 'The knowledge of God,' writes Sinclair Ferguson, 'is the heart of salvation and of all true spiritual experience. Knowing him is what we were created for. It will occupy us throughout eternity.'[7] Isaiah would heartily concur!

26.
The mighty eagle's wings

Please read Isaiah 40:27-31

Be honest! Have you ever felt that God doesn't care about you, or else he would not have treated you the way he has? Trials can make us lose sight of God's majesty and cause us to feel sorry for ourselves. Some of God's people in Isaiah's time could not square suffering with his love. If God loves us, they thought, there should be no problems in our lives.

Coping with spiritual depression can be difficult, especially when, as it appears in this chapter, almost the entire church is in the doldrums. 'God either does not know what we are passing through; or else he does not care,' they reasoned (40:27).

The Bible has quite a lot to tell us about depression. It speaks candidly about it in the lives of some of the greatest saints: for example, David (Ps. 42; 43), Elijah (1 Kings 19), Jonah (Jonah 4) and Jeremiah (Jer. 20:14-18). And here in Isaiah 40, even the young and seemingly healthy can suddenly grow weak and sick (40:30).

Though there can be purely medical reasons for depression (and Elijah's case notes would speak of such matters as exhaustion and low energy levels), more often than not the cause is spiritual. Distrust, anger, resentment, disappointment — these and a host of other unmortified sins often lie behind depression. Ask any competent doctor, who deals with this issue every day, and he will invariably tell you that the cause is often other than purely medical. The way God dealt with depressed believers in Isaiah's day was to talk about eagles! 'You may feel like a bedraggled sparrow, but if you pay attention to what I'm saying, you will mount up with wings like eagles' (40:31).

Spiritual depression

What are some of the causes of spiritual depression? The answer, as we noted in the previous chapter, seems to lie in something Luther once said to the humanist Erasmus: 'Your thoughts of God are too human.' Echoes of this charge are found here, too.

> **"To whom will you compare me?**
>   **Or who is my equal?" says the Holy One...**
> **Why do you say, O Jacob,**
>   **and complain, O Israel,**
> **"My way is hidden from the Lord;**
>   **my cause is disregarded by my God"?**
> **Do you not know?**
>   **Have you not heard?**
> **The Lord is the everlasting God,**
>   **the Creator of the ends of the earth.**
> **He will not grow tired or weary,**
>   **and his understanding no one can fathom"'**
>
> (40:25,27-28).

God rebukes the despondent for wrong thoughts about *him* and wrong thoughts about *ourselves*. God is great, and we are not to forget it. But that means that he has not abandoned us any more than he abandoned Jacob, his Old Testament church. Christians who think that God has left them high and dry have cause to be ashamed of themselves, for such a thought deeply dishonours God.

This chapter seems to allude to four such 'dishonouring thoughts'.

1. We fail to remember that God is 'everlasting'

'Do you not know? Have you not heard? The Lord is the everlasting God...' (40:28). God is not subject to the changes that condition living in time: he is, to cite John Wesley's favourite text, 'the same yesterday and today and for ever' (Heb. 13:8). In other words, God is immutable, above and beyond the stresses and strains that too often cause such ravages within ourselves. Consequently God's love is everlasting (54:8); his covenant is everlasting (55:3; 61:8); he makes Zion an everlasting splendour (60:15), a new Zion robed with everlasting light (60:19-20), causing her to rejoice with everlasting joy (61:7). When pressures are threatening to bend us out of shape we are to recall that they are of no consequence to God. He is beyond their reach.

2. We fail to remember God's majesty

All that we have seen in the previous two chapters has been leading up to this conclusion that since God is all-powerful, there is nothing that can stand in his way. There is no situation too difficult or complex for the Lord. There is no need for us to think that somehow certain situations are going to make him weary:

> 'Do you not know?
>   Have you not heard?
> The Lord is the everlasting God,
>   the Creator of the ends of the earth.
> He will not grow tired or weary,
>   and his understanding no one can fathom'
>
> (40:28).

God does not grow weary. His energies are never spent. We on the other hand are often weary. That is why Jesus calls us to rest in himself: 'Come to me, all you who are weary and burdened, and I will give you rest. Take my yoke upon you and learn from me, for I am gentle and humble in heart, and you will find rest for your souls. For my yoke is easy and my burden is light' (Matt. 11:28-30). I have always been struck by these words because of what they *do not* say. Jesus does not say, 'Look at how strong I am. See the way I could just lift you in my arms and carry you with no bother at all.' No, instead he talks about being gentle. No one wants gentle people any more. The world is looking for strong, assertive, macho people. Jesus sees it differently. When you are depressed and needing a shoulder to cry on, it is to the gentle, caring, understanding people that you go for help. Jesus *is* strong. He holds the world in his hands. All power belongs to him (Matt. 28:18). But at the same time he is approachable. He is like a shepherd who 'gently leads those that have young' (40:11). He is anxious to carry our load. He bids weary travellers rest in his house.

3. We forget that God knows all about us

Some were tempted to reason that God did not understand (or care?) about their condition: 'My way is hidden from the Lord; my cause is disregarded by my God' (40:27). That is not true, of course, and the prophet directly refutes the idea: 'His understanding no one can fathom' (40:28).

In our previous chapter we noted that one of the attributes of God alluded to in Isaiah 40 is his omniscience: 'Who has understood the mind of the Lord, or instructed him as his counsellor?' (40:13). God knows all things. That means he knows all about me.

Just think of the circumstances in Jerusalem as Isaiah delivered this message for the first time. Sennacherib was threatening to overthrow the city. We must not underestimate the conditions being complained of here. Isaiah's ministry in Jerusalem lasted down to the city's darkest hour in 701 B.C., when Sennacherib marched into Palestine to confront Hezekiah and his allies. At one point in the campaign, Sennacherib recorded: 'As for Hezekiah, the Jew, forty-six strong walled towns and innumerable smaller villages in their neighbourhood I besieged and conquered ... I made to come out from them 200,150 people ... and counted them as the spoils of war.' He went on to say that Hezekiah was 'shut up like a caged bird within Jerusalem, his royal city'.

Little wonder that God's people began to think God was unaware of their condition. It was to be a lasting memory for God's children that Jerusalem never did fall to the hands of the Assyrian invader. As quickly as they had arrived at Jerusalem's walls, so they retreated. Only a few years later, Sennacherib was assassinated (2 Kings 19:36-37).

It is tempting to think when we are in pain that God has forgotten us. He is too busy with the governing of the universe to be bothered about tiny little me! Why should the mighty God be concerned about the problems that keep me awake at night? But God is concerned — intimately so.

4. We forget that we are only pilgrims

Isaiah's pessimistic pilgrims were anxious to make a point: God was disregarding their 'cause' (40:27). They are making a legal case (cf.

1:23). They are talking about their rights! They have analysed their position and come to the conclusion that God is not dealing with them fairly. They are being trodden upon and they are angry with God.

Elisabeth Elliot writes of an incident in her life when a Christian began to tell her something along the same lines as these joyless believers in Isaiah's day. A woman had just discovered that she was suffering from a progressive illness which would lead to paralysis. She was annoyed and angry. It wasn't fair. On the other end of the telephone Elisabeth Elliot was thinking about how modern Christians think it a matter of their right to be happy and free from trial. How wrong this was, she thought.

Composing herself, she began to respond: 'I didn't weigh in with all of this to the troubled girl on the phone, but I did try to help her see that as a Christian she might look at things from a different angle. She needed to start from the love of God and understand that love, revealed on the cross, does not exclude but must always *include* suffering.

'"But what good will I be flat on my back?" came the plaintive question. So we had to talk about God's idea of "good" — very different from mere utilitarianism. He wanted her to trust and obey ("for there's no other way to be happy in Jesus," as the old gospel song says). The only way she could learn trust and obedience was to have things happen which she could not understand. That is where faith begins — in the wilderness, when you are alone and afraid, when things don't make sense... She must hang onto the message of the cross: God loves you. He loved you enough to die for you. Will you trust him?

'...There was a pause. Then I heard the timid little voice say, "Oh." I'm sure she felt she was about to enter a waste, howling wilderness and she was afraid. I prayed that God would go with her every step of the way and let her know that everything was under control.'[1]

Learning to differentiate between our rights and our calling is what growing in grace is all about. As Christians we are called upon to deny ourselves (Matt. 16:24) and follow the example of Jesus Christ (1 Peter 2:21). We are not to stand upon our rights but must be willing to subject ourselves to the will of God (Phil. 2:5).

Waiting on God

God's prescription for depression and loss of assurance as to his purposes and ways with us is to **'hope in the Lord'** (40:31). Other translations use the word 'wait' for 'hope' at this point. What does the Bible mean by 'waiting' or 'hoping'?

Several answers are forthcoming if we take into consideration the use of this word elsewhere in the Scriptures.

1. We should be patient

The Hebrew word can mean 'to stretch, to hold in tension'.[2] There is another Hebrew word which is also translated 'to hope' or 'to wait'[3] and both of these words occur in Lamentations 3:24-26 where they seem to be used quite interchangeably:

> 'I say to myself, "The Lord is my portion;
>   therefore I will wait for him."
> The Lord is good to those whose hope is in him,
>   to the one who seeks him;
> it is good to wait quietly
>   for the salvation of the Lord'
>
>   (Lam. 3:24-26).

Of interest is the translation 'to wait quietly' in the last verse. The book of Lamentations is talking about suffering. It is dealing with the problem of why it is that we so often have to wait for God's blessing. When difficulties arise, we often question whether or not God still cares for us. But we must remember that 'He does not willingly bring affliction or grief to the children of men' (Lam. 3:33). We must wait patiently. We are not to become impatient with God's ways with us. We must not start to accuse him of any mismanagement. There are times when it is the best policy to shut our mouths (cf. Rom. 3:19).

2. We should be trusting

This is what Psalm 37:7 teaches us: 'Be still before the Lord and wait patiently for him; do not fret when men succeed in their ways, when they carry out their wicked schemes.'

Psalm 37 is talking about the problem of seeing evil men prospering. 'Don't fret about it,' the psalmist exhorts, 'for evil men will be cut off, but those who hope in the Lord will inherit the land.' Sinclair Ferguson comments about this psalm: 'The word which is translated "wait" in Psalm 37:7 originally seems to have carried the idea of twisting or writhing. It conveys a sense of the intensity which can be involved in this waiting on God. It is not a passive tranquillity, by any manner of means. It means *to be on the stretch.* Waiting on God, being silent before him, may involve a protracted battle with the world, the flesh and the devil!'[4]

3. We are to be expectant

We noted earlier that the word used in Isaiah 40:31 (translated 'hope' in the NIV) has to do with holding something in tension. Think of a rope with you at one end and God at the other. If you let go you will probably fall over. Yet another Hebrew word is used in Isaiah 30:18 which is also translated 'to wait'. There the idea is very much the thought of expecting God to bless us:

'Yet the Lord longs to be gracious to you;
    he rises to show you compassion.
For the Lord is a God of justice.
    Blessed are all who wait for him!'

God wants to show us his secret purposes, but only in his own time. Isaiah's Old Testament believers could look back and think of how patient, trusting and expectant Joseph had been under trial, knowing all along that God was working in his life ordering it for his good. Just ahead of them was another great figure: Daniel. He too would learn to wait on God through adversity.

Pulling all this together, we find that what Isaiah is encouraging his depressed disciples to do is to persevere in faith. Isaiah is seeing a future day when God's people will be in captivity in Babylon. The time will pass slowly. It will seem as though God has forgotten them. Their strength will be gone. Running and walking are metaphors chosen to counter weariness and fainting (40:31). These two natural weaknesses can be overcome by waiting on the Lord. But more than this, Isaiah puts forward an even greater possibility. Soaring into the sky seems an effortless task for an eagle. Anyone who has watched the buzzard soaring with ease in the Welsh mountains, as I have done, can only be encouraged to think that no matter how low we may feel, God can enable us to soar on high when we draw near to him.

It may appear as though there is no hope. This is a dangerous time. There is a temptation to give up. Maybe you are at this point right now. The beginning of your Christian life was exciting. Everything seemed to go well for you. Blessing abounded. But lately it seems as though you have been punished. At first you may have thought to yourself, 'Well, I deserved it!' But as the days and weeks passed the problems got worse and worse. Now it seems you are caught up in the middle of something and you don't understand what is happening. You find your resolve is weakening. You know exactly what the writer to the Hebrews meant when he talked about 'feeble arms and weak knees' (Heb. 12:12). You are in the middle of a race and up against what long-distance runners refer to as 'the wall' — the point in the middle of the race when every cell in your body tells you to stop. This is the worst moment of all when you have to resolve to keep going. That's what the Scriptures encourage us to do: 'Let us throw off everything that hinders and the sin that so easily entangles, and let us run with perseverance the race marked out for us. Let us fix our eyes on Jesus, the author and perfecter of our faith' (Heb. 12:1-2). The finishing tape is just ahead: **'Lift your eyes and look to the heavens...'** (40:26) 'Let us fix our eyes on Jesus, the author and perfecter of our faith...' (Heb. 12:1). Do it now, and you will fly high above your troubles like a mighty eagle!

Summary

Wrong thoughts of God twist our perspective on life. Everything gets out of shape and we do great harm to the Lord's cause. Isaiah has sought in this section of his prophecy to lift up our eyes towards heaven and behold God in all his glory. If things are not working out as we would like, it is precisely because what life is all about is not what *we* like, but what God intends for us. Waiting on God — his ways, his thoughts, his timing — this is the key to spiritual growth and maturity.

27.
The sovereignty of God

Please read Isaiah 41

In the ancient Near East whenever a vassal failed to satisfy the obligations of a sworn treaty, the suzerain (usually the king) would take out legal proceedings against him by means of a covenant lawsuit. The legal process was conducted by means of messengers. In the first of its two distinct phases messengers delivered one or more warnings. These were worded in such a way as to reflect the original treaty. The vassal would be reminded of what he had promised and an explanation for the offence would be asked for. The vassal would be told to mend his ways. Just in case he did not take the point, the consequences of continued offence would be stated. The curses of the covenant would have formed part of the original document that had been signed. Such a procedure as this was an ultimatum. Unless they hoped for help to fight the ensuing battle resulting from a treaty with a third party (a neighbouring state), wise vassals would quickly mend their ways.

Sometimes the messenger sent to deliver this ultimatum was rejected, imprisoned or even killed! The matter would then move on to the next and final phase. This would take the form of an official declaration of war. When Jesus told the parable of the vineyard, seeing himself as the last in a succession of messengers, some of whom had been stoned and killed, he had this judicial process in mind (Matt. 21:33-44). Israel had rejected the prophets and they were about to reject the Son of God. They in turn would also be rejected.

Many Old Testament passages, including Isaiah 41, are written in this style. Isaiah is God's messenger sent to deliver a word of ultimatum, not on this occasion to Israel, but to the surrounding nations (**'you islands ... the nations'**, 41:1).

The chapter opens with an astonishing echo of the final verse of the previous one, only this time the meaning is quite different. Chapter 40:31 had encouraged the Lord's people to wait patiently and submissively upon the Lord; in so doing they would renew their strength. Now, the Lord bids the heathen nations stop talking, gather what strength they can so that they may enter into a war against the Lord:

> **'Be silent before me, you islands!**
> **Let the nations renew their strength!**
> **Let them come forward and speak;**
> **let us meet together at the place of judgement'**

> (41:1).

They will need all the strength they can muster; to encounter God in his wrath is formidable. Isaiah 41 begins in a courtroom.

The case for the prosecution (41:2-7)

Someone has appeared on the stage of history who will eventually topple the world order. As yet his identity is unknown; later (in 44:28) it will be made clear. We are being introduced to the historical figure of King Cyrus of Persia, who rises **'from the east'** (and from **'the north'**, 40:25, indicating the direction he will enter Palestine).[1]

Cyrus conquered Babylon in 539 B.C. (see 13:17) and issued the decree allowing the Jews to return to Jerusalem (Ezra 1:1-4). In so doing he was carrying out the righteous purposes of God, **'calling him in righteousness'**. At his coming he would subdue kings (41:3). The reference to the **'bow'** in verse 2 is interesting because the Persians were noted for their skills in archery. This is only an introduction to Cyrus; more will be said of him in 44:28 - 45:5; 45:13; 46:11.

Cyrus the Great was the founder of the Persian empire. Formerly king of the small state of Anshan near the Persian Gulf, he displaced his overlord Astyages in 549 B.C., thereby inheriting the vast Median empire which overarched, to the north and east, that of

Babylon. He extended far into the west into Asia Minor by defeating Crœsus of Lydia in 547, to the growing alarm of Babylon and Egypt, the allies of his victim. In 539 Babylon fell to him without a struggle, and he began unwittingly to fulfil the prophecies of this chapter and of 44:28 and 45:1-13, by repatriating the captive peoples of the Babylonian empire, rebuilding their temples and asking for their intercessions. All this was still future for Isaiah's first readers! They were too preoccupied with their trials to see that history itself is in the hands of God.

The point which this chapter makes is not primarily the coming of Cyrus, but to answer the question: 'Who brought Cyrus onto the stage of history?'

> **'Who has done this and carried it through,**
> **calling forth the generations from the beginning?**
> **I, the Lord — with the first of them**
> **and with the last — I am he'**
>
> (41:4).

God alone is sovereign. The nations are only a 'drop in a bucket' (40:15). God has a plan that stretches right back into eternity. 'God, from all eternity, did, by the most wise and holy counsel of his own will, freely, and unchangeably ordain whatsoever comes to pass,' says the *Westminster Confession of Faith* (III:i). That is what verse 4 is telling us. Oliver Cromwell once said that if one maverick grain of sand could behave without God's permission it would frustrate the course of history. And he was right. If God is not in control, then he is not God!

The case against the nations is being tabled: they pretend to have power and they use it in defiance against the God of Israel. But ultimately they are powerless. They boast of their power, but it does not last. Babylon was one of the greatest empires the world has known, but it fell to Persia without a fight. The ultimate authority does not reside in Babylon, Persia, Greece or Rome, but in the God of Israel! It is with this truth that Isaiah had strengthened his people earlier:

> 'You will keep in perfect peace
> him whose mind is steadfast,
> because he trusts in you.
> Trust in the Lord for ever,

for the Lord, the Lord, is the Rock eternal.
He humbles those who dwell on high,
    he lays the lofty city low;
he levels it to the ground
    and casts it down to the dust'

                                                        (26:3-5).

Strong men like Nebuchadnezzar, Sennacherib, Alexander the
Great or Antiochus Epiphanes are nothing before God. They are not
in control of their fate. This is God's warning: we are never so
vulnerable as when we believe ourselves to be strong by our own
strength. Uzziah, the eleventh king of Judah, had to learn this truth:
'But after Uzziah became powerful, his pride led to his downfall. He
was unfaithful to the Lord his God, and entered the temple of the
Lord to burn incense on the altar of incense' (2 Chron. 26:16). When
he was discovered, 'Uzziah ... became angry' (2 Chron. 26:19), and
was smitten with leprosy. Sin does that to us. Ultimate power does
not reside in man, or his centre of power: not in Washington or
London or Moscow. It lies in the hands of God.

The case is not yet complete. What did the nations do when they
saw King Crœsus fall and Cyrus march across Eastern Europe?
They were afraid and trembled. But did they turn to the Lord? No!
They turned to idolatry (41:5-7; cf. 40:19-20; 44:6 - 45:25).

The nub of the argument (41:21-24)

The case continues in verses 21-29. The drama is now at fever pitch.
God challenges the nations to produce their gods in court for a
contest. And remember, Israel too had bowed down to these gods!
Can they foretell the future? **'Bring in your idols to tell us what is
going to happen'** (41:22).

We shall see later how the modern god of astrology attempts to
do this in our comments on 47:13-15. For now let us just keep in
mind the fact that in the United States there are some 175,000 part-
time and 10,000 full-time astrologers. In Britain there are colleges
which issue diplomas in astrology, and almost every glossy maga-
zine and daily newspaper has its horoscope. Predicting the future is
big business.[2]

Babylon was especially noted for its astrologers. The Bible

mentions them in the story of Nebuchadnezzar in Daniel 2. Nebuchadnezzar was a man who suffered from bad dreams. But all the magicians and astrologers of Babylon were unable to interpret his dreams: They could not see into the future. Their predictions failed. God alone can see into the future and make it known through his prophets. Only Daniel possessed the spirit of wisdom to interpret clearly what lay ahead for Nebuchadnezzar.

In Isaiah's courtroom the gods are challenged to say, or 'do something' (41:23). But they fail. The gods of wood and stone and gold and silver are powerless. After what was possibly a long silence, God says to them, '**But you are less than nothing and your works are utterly worthless; he who chooses you is detestable**' (41:24).

The barrister's summation (41:25-29)

As in all legal cases, the barrister makes a concluding summary of the case against the accused. All the evidence has been cited; the witnesses have been cross-examined. The entire proceedings have been leading to one conclusion: the nations are guilty. Their gods have failed them. They are utterly powerless. When Cyrus comes he will trample them underfoot like a potter smashes his misshapen pots under his feet (41:25). Not one of their gods had predicted their future accurately (41:26); there is only a shocked silence on their part (41:28). The nations are therefore nothing. Their gods are nothing. There can only be one verdict: guilty! The case is closed.

Reassurance (41:8-20)

Suddenly, the proceedings in the courtroom come to a temporary halt and God speaks to his people. They, too, are afraid at the terror of his wrath against the nations. Will they survive? They too are sinners; how can they escape his judgements? It is just here that we are introduced to a concept that we will enlarge upon in the next chapter, when he calls Israel '**my servant**' (41:9).

You may like to take a moment and just glance through the next few chapters at the amazing frequency with which this term appears: 42:1; 44:1,2,21; 45:4; 48:20 etc. It really is a most important word for Isaiah! Its meaning is not always clear and some antisupernatural commentators, who cannot believe that prophets could really see into the future, have been at pains to make sure that Isaiah is never speaking about Jesus Christ — which sometimes he very definitely is! For now, all we need to see is that here in chapter 41 he is talking about Israel — not every single Jew, of course, but those who still loved him and had faith in his promises (cf. Rom. 9:11).

Several things appear very quickly in this section to comfort and strengthen the hearts of the Lord's people who might just be feeling a little terrified as they listen to God challenging the nations and their gods.

1. The doctrine of election

Isaiah believed in the doctrine of election: **'Jacob, whom I have chosen...'** (41:8). This is something he mentions a great deal in these closing chapters (cf. 43:1-4; 44:1-2,21,24; 45:11; 48:12; 49:7,13; 55:5). Obviously, election was important to him.

The doctrine is built up in the pages of the Old Testament by the choosing of Abraham and his family (**'Abraham my friend'**, 41:8). There was nothing special about the Israelites, though they often thought there was (Deut. 7:7). Abraham had no prior claim on God's grace. Salvation, and a calling to a life of usefulness in God's kingdom, is always a matter of grace.

Questions of the order: 'Why did God choose Jacob and not Esau?' (cf. Rom. 9:13) are, for us, unanswerable. God does not disclose his mind to us on everything. We catch only a glimpse of his great purpose. If he does one thing and not another, it is his right to do so, just as it is the right of the potter to decide to keep one clay pot he has made and destroy another. What is astonishing is that God should choose any at all!

Of greater importance is the effect of this truth on the lives of those who will take it to their hearts. Here it is to bring assurance and encouragement: **'Do not fear ... I will strengthen you and help you; I will uphold you'** (41:10), **'Do not fear; I will help you. Do not be afraid ... I myself will help you'** (41:13-14). This is what the apostle Paul saw as one of its main points: to strengthen weak and trembling Christians: 'Who will bring any charge against those whom God has chosen? It is God who justifies' (Rom. 8:33). It is this kind of encouragement that election brings about. It is what Isaiah is keen to underline to trembling believers in his day too.

2. The covenant of grace

The apostle Peter, preaching some time after Pentecost, cited a text from Genesis which he saw as having a connection with Isaiah's Servant, Jesus. Quoting Genesis 22:18, 'Through your offspring all peoples on earth will be blessed', he then went on to say, 'When God raised up his servant he sent him first to you to bless you by turning each of you from your wicked ways' (Acts 3:25-26). Jesus was, for Peter, the fulfilment of the promise to Abraham and also the promise made through Isaiah. Isaiah's reference to Abraham in Isaiah 41:8 tells us that he too saw the same connection. God's promise runs right through the Bible. The appearance of Jesus Christ was something which godly people had been expecting. It explains the response of folk like Simeon and Anna (Luke 2:25,38), who were waiting for the redemption and comforting of Israel. God had kept his promise through 2,000 years of history!

3. The presence of God

'So do not fear, for I am with you' (41:10, cf. 41:17). Later Israel will be reassured again along these lines:

> 'When you pass through the waters,
>   I will be with you;
> and when you pass through the rivers,
>   they will not sweep over you.
> When you walk through the fire,
>   you will not be burned;
>   the flames will not set you ablaze'
>
> (43:2).

Being in God's presence brings with it a sense of awe and is at the heart of what God promises, that is, covenants, to his people. So we read, 'The Lord was with Joseph and he prospered' (Gen . 39:2). Moses was told, when about to panic at the thought of returning to Egypt with a price on his head: 'I will be with you' (Exod. 3:12).

Joshua was told the same thing when he was given the leadership after Moses: 'As I was with Moses, so I will be with you; I will never leave you nor forsake you' (Josh. 1:5,9). The same promise formed the parting words of Jesus before his ascension: 'And surely I am with you always to the very end of the age' (Matt. 28:20). The Bible's covenant language of God's presence is very rich indeed: God is with us (Matt. 28:20), around us (Ps. 34:7), in us (John 14:17), in the midst of us (Ps. 46:5), behind us (Ps. 139:5), underneath us (Deut. 33:27), near us (Ps. 148:14) and before us (John 10:4). Perhaps the most intimate of all biblical metaphors is that of God being like a broody hen with outstretched wings and motherly concern and jealousy (Ps. 17:8; 36:7; Matt. 23:37).

4. The power of God

We have already noticed several occasions in the previous chapter when God's power was mentioned. In this section we have a reference to God's **'right hand'** (41:10,13,20), which will deal with all of his enemies (41:11-12). God's enemies will be as nothing. Though the condition of God's people is likened to that of a **'worm'** (41:14), and they are said to be **'poor and needy'** and **'parched'** (41:17), God's power will ensure their victory. He will ensure that they prevail against all their enemies. Using agricultural images, Isaiah describes them threshing and winnowing (41:15-16). Israel's enemies will blow away like chaff on a windy day!

Instead of a desert, God is going to make a garden (41:17-20). Salvation is often compared to Eden in the Bible. E. J. Young comments: 'In picturing the future age of blessing, the eschatological period when the restoration will occur, Isaiah uses the combined figures of water and trees. It is as though a bit of heaven had come down to earth; and indeed, those who one day will be blessed of these rivers and these trees are in the heavenlies in Christ Jesus.'[3]

5. The redemption of God

God is Israel's **'Redeemer'** (41:14). This is the first of thirteen places where this title occurs (cf. 43:14; 44:6,24; 47:4; 48:17; 49:7,26; 54:5,8; 59:20; 60:16; 63:16). This term uses the language of the market-place and business transactions. It has to do with deliverance from bondage by means of the payment of a price. In the Old Testament property, animals, persons and the nation were all 'redeemed' by the payment of a price. Both Boaz and Jeremiah illustrated how one could play the part of a kinsman-redeemer, buying back a piece of land that had been lost, thus keeping it in the family (Ruth 3; 4; Jer. 32:6-8). The firstborn of all livestock belonged to God, but could on certain conditions be redeemed (Exod. 13:13; 34:20; Num. 18:14-17). Every individual in Israel had to pay a 'ransom for his life' at the time of national census, and since the first Passover, every firstborn son had to be redeemed (Exod. 30:12-16; Num. 3:40-51).

As for the nation of Israel, two historical episodes entailed their release from bondage — the exodus from Egypt and the release from Babylon — and thereby typified the work of the coming Messiah who would redeem them from their sins. The connection between God's power and his redeeming work is clear: he redeemed Israel 'with an outstretched arm' and with a 'mighty hand' (41:10,13; cf. Exod. 6:6; Deut. 9:26; Neh. 1:10; Ps. 77:15). B. B. Warfield has observed that 'The idea that the redemption from Egypt was the effect of a great expenditure of divine power and in that sense cost much, is prominent in the allusions to it, and seems to constitute the central idea sought to be conveyed.'[4] It is this imagery that Jesus took up with regard to his own work: he saw himself fulfilling all that the Old Testament had been illustrating. Our salvation involves the payment of a ransom — his own life: 'For even the Son of Man did not come to be served, but to serve, and to give his life as a ransom for many' (Mark 10:45).

Be encouraged!

Summary

God has brought a prosecution case before his people. They have been guilty of idolatry: they have been worshipping a god of their own imagination. In a climactic moment he bids the idols speak for themselves, but they have remained dumb and lifeless. The people are surely guilty. Yet there is hope for them. It lies deeply embedded in the covenant of grace and the Saviour who is the essence of it.

Focus

The 'Servant of the Lord'

Before we proceed further, we need to stop and take a look at where we are going. As we progress through the last twenty-six chapters we are going to come across an idea that, at first, can be a little confusing. It concerns the 'Servant of the Lord' who appears in these latter chapters of Isaiah. Focusing on this key concept in Isaiah will help us through the chapters that follow.

On the seven-mile journey from Jerusalem to Emmaus, Jesus opened up the Old Testament to two confused and discouraged disciples, showing them as never before that these sometimes dry and often confusing pages were in fact full of himself (Luke 24:13-35). In one sense all the Old Testament finds its focus in Jesus — a particularly important point for an evangelical prophet like Isaiah. He was anxious to encourage weary believers, recently harassed by Assyria and soon to be captive in Babylon, that God had not forgotten them. They may have to be chastised for their apostasy and backsliding. But he will not abandon his own.

God's promises are sure. That is something Isaiah is keen to underline: 'My word ... will not return to me empty' (55:11). The grace of God cannot be frustrated. That is, in part, what is meant by the expression 'irresistible grace'. The future was going to be very stormy indeed for God's people. They had sinned and they were going to suffer for it. The captivity in Babylon was the chastisement of God for their sinful ways. When God comes in judgement, it is a fearful thing. 'But who can endure the day of his coming? Who can stand when he appears?' (Mal. 3:2).

It is one of the abiding lessons of the Old Testament that not one of the great men that God had sent could keep the covenant on behalf of covenant-breaking Israel. All of them — Abraham, Isaac, Jacob, Joseph, Moses, Joshua, Samson, Samuel, David, Solomon, Elijah, Elisha, Jonah, even Isaiah himself — all had fallen short. What Israel needed was a Saviour. Though God had cause to reveal his wrath against their apostasy, the destruction would not be total. He would preserve a remnant of people who still trusted him. The purposes of God to save a people for himself continue.

The Saviour would come as promised. He would be a servant: a prophet like Moses, but a far better mediator; a priest like Aaron, but one of the royal order of Melchizedek; a king like David, but one who is seated on an eternal throne. The new Israel could only be established in the person of the Lord's Servant.

Isaiah 41 introduces us to this promised Servant who will occupy our attention through the rest of the book. This is one of the most important themes in the prophecy. Four 'Servant Songs' refer to him: 42:1-7; 49:1-6; 50:4-9; 52:13 - 53:12.[1] But it needs to be remembered that not every Bible commentator sees these many references to the Servant in Isaiah as speaking of Jesus Christ. Liberals cannot believe that a prophet in the seventh century B.C. could speak of the future with such accuracy. That is one of the reasons why some have believed that Isaiah 40-66, speaking as it does about the coming of Cyrus the Great, must have been written *after* the exile by someone else. And as for the identity of the Servant, several suggestions have been made, including Job, Moses, Uzziah, Hezekiah, Zerubbabel, Jeremiah, Ezekiel and even Isaiah himself! This is a sad reflection upon the unbelief that exists in the hearts of certain theologians!

The theme of the Servant is introduced early in the Bible. Moses was referred to as 'my servant Moses' (Num. 12:7,8; Josh. 1:7; 2 Kings 21:8; Mal. 4:4). To rebel against him was to reject God who had sent him. As a prophet, Moses was the type of another like himself, but far greater: 'I will raise up for them a prophet like you from among their brothers; I will put my words in his mouth, and he will tell them everything I command him' (Deut. 18:18). Moses had been preparing Old Testament saints for the coming of God's Servant, the theme of several songs that Isaiah wrote in praise of the Christ to come (42:1-7; 49:1-6; 50:4-9; 52:13 - 53:12).

The latter chapters of Isaiah reveal a God who calls and commissions an agent or 'servant' to accomplish his purpose. In all, Isaiah speaks of five agents whom God calls and commissions, though not all are referred to by the word 'servant': Isaiah himself; the voice (John the Baptist); the nation of Israel; Cyrus, the Assyrian king; and Jesus. Only Israel (considered collectively as God's Old Testament church, or individually as the 'remnant', 48:20) and Jesus are specifically given the title of 'servant'.

Sometimes Isaiah talks about a 'servant' in the singular and sometimes 'servants' in the plural (compare 42:1 and 43:10 with 54:17 and 63:17). Sometimes when he uses the term in the singular, he means Israel and at other times he quite clearly means Christ (e.g. 42:1-4; 49:1-7; and especially 52:13 - 53:12).[2] Learning to appreciate these points will help us find a surer grip as we climb the peaks of Isaiah 40-66.

There are times when the 'Servant' of God is identified with Israel, and called by the name of Israel (or Jacob, e.g., 41:8; 42:18-19; 43:9-10; 44:1-3; 44:21; 45:4; 48:20; 49:3). Back in the time of the exodus from Egypt, God had commanded that Pharaoh release Israel, his son, 'that he may *serve* me' (Exod. 4:23, NKJV).[3] How can the 'Servant' be identified with the descendants of Abraham and Jacob? 'The answer must be seen in the close relationship that existed, and was to be even more so later, between the speaker named Servant and the people of Israel; he came forth from the people, that is, he was the seed coming forth from the seed of the patriarchs. He was to labour on their behalf, as their representative and head so that the many could and would become as he was. The Speaker or Servant represented ideal Israel in a real sense and as One of Israel, labouring on behalf of Israel, he was to make the transformation of sinful Israel into ideal Israel.'[4]

28.
'Behold my servant!'

Please read Isaiah 42:1-17

Matthew, in writing his Gospel story, cites Isaiah 42:1-4 as a prophecy that had been fulfilled in the ministry of Jesus Christ (Matt. 12:18-21). At a time when the Pharisees were seeking an opportunity to have him destroyed, Jesus departed from them. Crowds of sick people followed him and he healed them. Then follows one of many instances where Jesus warns those who have been healed to keep his identity a secret. He was not to become known chiefly as a miracle-worker, but rather as the Saviour of sinners. Too much publicity about his miraculous powers could cause some folk to think of him as a potential deliverer from the political yoke of Roman occupation and thus bring his ministry to an untimely end.[1] He was to be seen instead as a humble 'Servant of the Lord'. Hence Matthew's allusion to Isaiah 42:1-4. This passage forms the first of four songs (Old Testament hymns, if you like) that the prophet sings, alluding very definitely to Jesus Christ (the other three are in chapters 49-53).

In the midst of threats from Assyria and eventually from Babylon, Isaiah comforts God's people by pointing them to Christ. In the previous chapter (41:8-10) Isaiah had comforted Israel, who was also God's servant (41:8), with the truth that he will uphold his covenant promises to them. Looking 200 years into the future, Isaiah speaks of the coming of King Cyrus, who will defeat Babylon and restore Israel to their land. Still looking ahead, the prophet goes further still, some 700 years, and urges Israel to see another Servant: God's Son. This Servant is God's 'chosen one'. Everything that will

happen to him will show God's plan and purpose to save a people
for himself (Acts 2:23; 4:28).

The Bible pictures the atoning work of Christ as involving, first
of all, an act of incarnation whereby the Second Person of the Trinity
became flesh and blood. In his incarnate state, Jesus was both God
and man at the same time. We are often defensive about safeguard-
ing the divine nature of Jesus Christ — sometimes at the expense of
giving full testimony to his human nature. Scripture testifies to the
reality and completeness of his human nature also. Paul, writing to
the Philippians, put it this way:

'Your attitude should be the same as that of Christ Jesus:

Who, being in very nature God,
    did not consider equality with God something to be grasped,
but made himself nothing,
    taking the very nature of a servant,
    being made in human likeness.
And being found in appearance as a man,
    he humbled himself
    and became obedient to death — even death on a cross!'
                                                    (Phil. 2:5-8).

Paul was familiar with Isaiah's servant!

Jesus and the Holy Spirit (42:1)

Just as Israel, God's servant, was strengthened (41:9-10), so too,
God would uphold his Servant Jesus (42:1) He will **'take hold of
[his] hand'** (42:6).[2] In his incarnation, Jesus became totally dependent upon God. As a servant he was placed in a position where duties
were expected of him. At the threshold of his crucifixion he gave
eloquent testimony to this: 'I have brought you glory on earth by
completing the work you gave me to do' (John 17:4; cf. 4:34). At
every point of his ministry Jesus was dependent upon the strengthening power of his heavenly Father, ministered to him by the Holy
Spirit. His work as the Redeemer — every aspect of it — was carried
out in utter acquiescence to the will of Almighty God.

All of Jesus' ministry was performed by the aid of the Holy Spirit: **'I will put my Spirit on him and he will bring justice to the nations'** (42:1). Isaiah has mentioned this before:

'The Spirit of the Lord will rest on him—
   the Spirit of wisdom and of understanding,
   the Spirit of counsel and of power,
   the Spirit of knowledge and of the fear of the Lord'

(11:2).

Later, he will refer to this again: 'And now the Sovereign Lord has sent me, with his Spirit' (48:16).

'The Spirit of the Sovereign Lord is on me,
   because the Lord has anointed me
   to preach good news to the poor.
He has sent me to bind up the brokenhearted...'

(61:1).

It might be helpful at this point to summarize the testimony of the Gospels to the ministry of the Holy Spirit in the life of Jesus.

1. His conception

At his conception, there was a superintendence of the Holy Spirit (Luke 1:35). The conception itself had been unique: the Holy Spirit supernaturally creating an embryo within the virgin's womb. There was an exercise of creative power upon the human nature; it was the Spirit who was there supplying the foetus of Jesus with all the potential endowments, gifts, graces and capacities — physical, mental, moral and spiritual — which would be required for the accomplishment of his mission.

2. His childhood and youth

During the years of Jesus' growth into manhood, the Holy Spirit superintended his development at every point (Luke 2:40). The fact that the 'grace of God was upon him' is itself eloquent testimony to the fact that Jesus' life bore to the full the marks of the fruit of the

Spirit. The Spirit-given wisdom which he possessed was something which to the folk of Nazareth, who had seen him grow up amongst them, was thoroughly remarkable (Mark 6:2).

3. His baptism

Jesus was filled with the Spirit at his baptism (Matt. 3:16-17). The ministry of the Holy Spirit here was twofold: 'to confirm and encourage the Lord Jesus before entering on his arduous work';[3] and to give eloquent testimony as to his identity to those who heard the voice from heaven saying with obvious approval: 'This is my Son'! Both of these features of Jesus' baptism were designed to encourage him: they assured him of his unique identity and therefore of the Father's love for him. God assured him at the outset of his public ministry that his love for his own Son would never be in question, whatever providences might suggest to the contrary. He was also assured of the Holy Spirit's constant presence and ministry to uphold him and abide with him always.

4. His temptation

In the temptation of Jesus in the wilderness, it was the Holy Spirit who initiated the sequence of events! (Matt. 4:1). Jesus was there, not at the behest of Satan, but at the invitation of the Holy Spirit. The point being made is clear: that whereas Adam in the garden had failed the test which would have confirmed his sonship, Jesus' 'trial by ordeal' in the wilderness was to confirm, in Adam's place, his true sonship. He would take on Satan's claims to power and destroy them one by one. He would defeat Satan's claim upon us by a representative battle from which, by the Holy Spirit's invitation and help, he would emerge as Victor. Of particular importance are the words of Matthew 4:11: 'Then the devil left him, and angels came and attended him.'

5. His public ministry

His preaching, the miracles which he performed and his prayer were all caried out by the help of the Holy Spirit (Matt.12:28; Luke 4:14). When Peter described Christ's ministry during the course of a sermon in Caesarea, he testified to the crucial fact of Jesus' anointing by the Holy Spirit as a testimony to his greatness and uniqueness, saying, 'how God anointed Jesus of Nazareth with the Holy Spirit and power, and how he went around doing good and healing all who were under the power of the devil, because God was with him' (Acts 10:38).

6. His death, resurrection and ascension

Jesus' death, resurrection and ascension were also the work of the Holy Spirit. It was through the eternal Spirit that he offered himself without spot to God (Heb. 9:14; 1 Peter 3:18; Acts 2:33).[4] Just as in the wilderness, so too in Gethsemane (Luke 22:39-46), once the ordeal had been faced an angel appeared and strengthened Christ (Luke 22:43). Alexander Whyte, the famous Scottish preacher, once remarked that after Christ, he wanted, most of all, to meet this angel when he got to heaven! Once Jesus had received this ministry, being filled with the Holy Spirit to face the ordeal ahead of him, his entire disposition changed. He was ready to die the accursed death of the cross in the knowledge that his Father would bring him to glory again.

The character of the Servant (42:2-4)

Four characteristics are mentioned by way of a description of the Servant.

1. Quietness

'He will not shout or cry out, or raise his voice in the streets' (42:2). The word 'shout' is used in other Semitic languages to describe a thunderbolt or a raging bull. Have you ever listened to a sergeant major drilling his men? Jesus never dealt with his disciples that way. There was no screaming or shouting of orders. He did not assume the role of a military commander. People who have to shout have, generally, either a poor case to make or are insecure about the respect they can expect. That goes for preachers too!

2. Gentleness

'**A bruised reed he will not break, and a smouldering wick he will not snuff out**' (42:3). When the Pharisees were conspiring together to destroy Jesus, thereby revealing the wickedness of their hearts, Matthew reveals the gentleness that lay in Jesus' heart by quoting this verse from Isaiah about a bruised reed and a smouldering wick. Hardly anything could be more tender and fragile than a bruised reed or a smouldering wick. Imagine trying to salvage a burnt piece of paper from the fire and how easily it breaks into a thousand pieces in your hand. If you have ever tried to restart a fire that has almost gone out, you will know how tenderly you must deal with it. If you disturb it too much, or blow on it too hard, it is sure to go out. Some of the Lord's people were just like this: bruised and battered and feeling as though they were about to be extinguished. They were discouraged and lacking assurance. Isaiah comforts them by telling them of God's Servant whose dealings with them will be gentle. 'Cast all your anxiety on him,' Peter says, 'because he cares for you' (1 Peter 5:7).

3. Faithfulness

'**In faithfulness he will bring forth justice**' (42:3). God abounds in faithfulness (Exod. 34:6), and his Servant will be like him in this. Previously, the Servant has been described as David's descendant who has faithfulness as a sash around his waist (11:5). In a world of injustice, Jesus is someone who can always be relied upon to be fair and just.

4. Strength

'**He will not falter or be discouraged till he establishes justice on earth. In his law the islands will put their hope**' (42:4). God's Servant will not grow dim, or give poor light like a flickering wick. He will not be crushed like a bruised reed. He will be a Saviour of strength and power, of stamina and courage. Though he will be a servant, he will also be a king.

A new Moses (42:4)

Isaiah makes it clear from the very beginning of his book that God's plan includes much more than the salvation of certain Jews in Palestine. The Redeemer will be the Saviour of the nations (2:2-4). Here too he has the nations in mind: **'In his law the islands will put their hope'** (42:4).

The mention of 'law' reminds us of Moses. It also brings with it problems. Discussions about 'law' usually generate more heat than light. Christians are anxious to safeguard the doctrine of justification by faith alone and not by obeying the law (cf. Gal. 2:16,21). But some Christians want to go further and insist that we are not obliged to keep the law at all! Only the other day I heard of an earnest Sunday School teacher who told her class that the only law God wants us to keep is the one relating to the Sabbath! Clearly, Christians are very confused here.

Isaiah is talking about the gospel which the Servant brings and he does by using the word 'law'! The gospel, at least in one sense, is itself a law. John Calvin puts it this way: 'Here he employs the word "law" to mean "doctrine", as the Hebrew word for "law" is derived from a verb which signifies to teach; and thus the prophets are accustomed to speak of the gospel, in order to show that it will not be new or contrary to what was taught by Moses.'[5] Think of Paul's exhortation to Timothy: 'I charge you to keep this command without spot or blame' (1 Tim. 6:13-14).

The fullest state of blessing comes by keeping God's law out of love for what he has done for us in saving us from our sins through the atoning work of Jesus Christ. We could not have saved ourselves by keeping the law. But having been justified, we ought now to want to obey everything God says. According to Paul, Christian children should obey their parents for this 'is the first commandment with a promise' (Eph. 6:2). Jesus explicitly stated that he had not come to destroy the law or the prophets but to fulfil their requirements. He went on to add that anyone who breaks one of the least of the commandments of the law would be called least in the kingdom of God (Matt. 5:17-19). Chastening will come to those who violate God's law. Just as Israel were going to experience the chastening of God by exile in Babylon, the same is true for New Testament Christians. He disciplines those he loves (Heb.12:6).

The covenant made with Moses did not set aside the promise that God had made to Abraham 430 years earlier (Gal. 3:17). The same promise runs right through the period of Moses too. The law did show up sin more clearly than in the past, but that did not make the law sin or imply that it was meant only for a certain period of time. Part of the law involved ceremonial aspects (which were typical of the coming Saviour and fulfilled in him); and part of the law, too, had to do with the nature of Israel as a theocracy. But the moral law is as abiding today as it was in the time of Moses and Isaiah.

At the heart of the prophet's vision is a picture of Christ as a new Moses (Deut. 18:15-18; Acts 3:21-23,26). Like Moses, the Servant will be the Deliverer. On the Mount of Transfiguration Moses is there talking with Jesus about the coming exodus (Luke 9:30).[6]

Reinforcement (42:5-9)

Two more themes are mentioned in 42:5-9 to add weight to what has already been said about the Servant. One relates to the character of God and the other to the mission of the Servant.

God is the sovereign Creator of heaven and earth, and the giver of all life (42:5). His name is Yahweh, the covenant Lord; he is jealous of his glory, which he refuses to share with any idol (42:8). He is in control of the present and, through his prophets, reveals the future (42:9). In particular, God speaks directly to Jesus Christ, his Servant, commissioning him to become the Saviour of sinners. The commission which took place 'before the foundation of the world' is highlighted through the unfolding centuries of the Old Testament period. Jesus is to be God's covenant for the people, a **'light for the Gentiles'** (42:8; cf. 9:2). The promise of God, revealed in the Garden of Eden, and then through Abraham, Moses and David, was of a Saviour, one who says, 'I am the light of the world' (John 8:12). In fact, this promise extends further back than the Garden of Eden. In 42:6 the commission by God to the Servant seems to take place before the world began:

'I, the Lord, have called you in righteousness;
    I will take hold of your hand.
I will keep you and will make you

> **to be a covenant for the people
> and a light for the Gentiles.'**

Louis Berkhof sees in this verse a reference to the covenant of redemption, the promise made between the Father and the Son in the counsels of eternity.[7]

In our comments on Isaiah 41:8 mention was made of the covenant of grace. Here we have a reference to the covenant of redemption. In the words of Thomas Boston, 'The Covenant of Redemption and Covenant of Grace are not two distinct covenants, but one and the same covenant... Only, in respect of Christ, it is called the Covenant of Redemption, forasmuch as in it he engaged to pay the price of our redemption; but in respect of us the Covenant of Grace, forasmuch as the whole of it is of free grace to us.'[8]

Response: the new song (42:10-17)

The only fitting response to such news as this is to burst into a song of praise to God! That is the meaning of verse 10:

> **'Sing to the Lord a new song,
> his praise from the ends of the earth,
> you who go down to the sea, and all that is in it,
> you islands, and all who live in them.'**

There are saints in heaven who are already singing this new song to Jesus Christ (Rev. 5:9; 14:3). David, too, had anticipated it in six of his psalms (Ps. 33:3; 40:3; 96:1; 98:1; 144:9; 149:1). And literally everyone should see what grace God has shown to sinners and join in the singing of this song (42:10-12).

Salvation has two sides to it: there are those who are saved and also those who are lost. There are those who experience forgiveness and those who do not. When Paul talked about the salvation of Israel he referred to both the goodness and the severity of God (Rom. 11:22, AV)[9] Isaiah uses both ideas here too. Describing the severity of God against unrepentant sinners (42:17) he uses the language of violence: **'warrior', 'zeal', 'battle', 'woman in childbirth', 'gasp', 'pant', 'lay waste', 'dry up'** (42:13-15). On the other hand,

God is tender to the needy who seek his salvation, leading **'the blind'** by the hand.

> I will sing the wondrous story
> Of the Christ who died for me,
> How he left his home in glory
> For the cross on Calvary.
>
> I was lost: but Jesus found me —
> Found the sheep that went astray,
> Threw his loving arms around me
> Drew me back into his way.
>
> I was bruised: but Jesus healed me —
> Faint was I from many a fall;
> Sight was gone, and fears possessed me:
> But he freed me from them all.

(Francis H. Rawley)

Summary

The first of the so-called Servant Songs has introduced us more clearly than anything that has come before to Jesus Christ. He will be a deliverer of the same order as Moses. God's people can expect another exodus. When Moses and Elijah appeared on the Mount of Transfiguration their conversation was about Jesus' 'departure' (Luke 9:31, Greek *'exodus'*). The cross of Christ is something which brings great joy to the hearts of God's people.

29.
Grace abounding and grace despised

Please read Isaiah 42:18 - 43:28

Deafness is a particularly distressing and common problem, especially among the elderly. For those who have loved the sound of a symphony orchestra, a string quartet or a bass baritone, deafness can mean the loss of the singular pleasure that music can bring into one's life. But there is another kind of deafness: one that springs from a stubborn heart!

As I write these comments, a picture of a collie dog hangs on the wall in front of me. Her name was Floss. She was a sheep-dog and quite a character in her own right. But she had a problem: she did not like to be shouted at! She was a nervous creature, unsure with strangers. I can remember her response when shouted at for doing something wrong; she would disappear for days! Sometimes, when sent up a steep mountainside to collect some sheep, she would pause halfway and put her head to one side. My father would get cross and shout at her! She would pretend for a while not to hear (I'm convinced that she heard every word!). When the decibels reached a certain point she would run away and not appear again for several days. Deafness can sometimes mean an unwillingness to hear what we don't want to hear. That is what God accuses Israel of here (42:18), as he has previously in this book (29:18; 35:5).

God's people are not only deaf; they are also blind (42:18). God accuses Israel of the same disabilities as the idols that they worship (44:17-18). Not even the terrible things that are going to happen will change them (42:23). There is none so deaf as those who will not hear; there is none so blind as those who will not see.

God's Servant has been mentioned twice so far (41:8-10; 42:1-9). In the first instance the reference was to Israel as God's covenant people. In the second, it was to an individual, God's Servant Jesus. In Isaiah 42:19 the word 'servant' appears twice . As in the first instance, it is once more a reference to God's covenant people.

Failure in evangelism (42:18-25)

God's covenant people are not only referred to as God's servant, but God's **'messenger'** (42:18). In the next chapter, Israel are called God's **'witnesses'** (43:10). The agents that God had dispatched into the nations with his message had themselves refused to listen, to see, to learn and to speak. They had refused to be obedient messengers: **'For they would not follow his ways; they did not obey his law'** (42:24). That is why Israel has become **'plunder'**, and been cast into **'pits or hidden away in prisons'** (42:22). The exile they were to experience was a result of their disobedience to the call of God to be his witnesses amongst the nations.

Speaking in the next chapter as though the exile had already occurred (using a prophetic perfect tense), and as though God's people were already returned (43:8), God challenges the gods of the nations to foretell events like this.

J. H. Bavinck once observed that 'At first sight the Old Testament appears to offer little basis for the idea of missions,' adding that 'That entire pagan world is portrayed more as a constant threat and temptation to Israel than as an area in which God will reveal his salvation.'[1] Evangelism is sometimes thought to be something which only the New Testament knows anything about. That is a mistake, as Bavinck goes on to point out. Abraham had been called to be an agent of blessing to the nations (Gen. 12:1-3). And remember, Abraham himself, as the rabbis were fond of saying, was the first proselyte! Deuteronomy 26:5 is still quoted in Jewish synagogues today to remind the Jews that 'The religion of Israel was born with and born by converts.'

Just think of the consequences if Naomi hadn't given such eloquent testimony to her faith before Ruth in the midst of her sadness. When Matthew writes the genealogy of Jesus, he makes sure we get the point: he includes Ruth — a Gentile from Moab! Evangelism was essential in the coming of God's Servant Jesus!

The church of the Old Testament had failed to live up to its calling. She was to be a holy nation (Exod. 19:6; cf. 1 Peter 2:9), but she failed miserably. Despite her enormous privileges, she failed to give testimony to the Lord's goodness. Paul reflected on this theme (Rom. 11:13). Why had God called him to be an apostle to the Gentiles? So distorted had the vision for evangelism and mission become amongst the Jews in Paul's day that they accused him of being a renegade, of betraying his own people to curry favour with the heathen. Israel had been called to worship God. Through Abraham's seed the nations would come to worship him too. But Israel failed in her mission. God rejected Israel. Instead of blessing had come judgement. Like Isaiah, Paul too can see Jerusalem being destroyed and the smoke of incense being exchanged for the smoke of burning. The tragedy was that the remnant who returned from exile, and who took up the law with a fresh zeal, went about establishing their own righteousness instead of pointing to the grace of God. They became nationalistic instead of evangelistic. Was there nothing left but the wrath of God against the wicked husbandmen who killed the son that the inheritance might be theirs? (Matt. 21:33-43). In contrast to this dreadful scene Paul takes refuge in his own conversion, and his calling to take the gospel to all the nations (Acts 9:15-16).

A failure to evangelize will always incur God's severest displeasure (Ezek. 3:18). 'Therefore go and make disciples of all nations,' Jesus said (Matt. 28:19) and the early disciples did so assiduously (Acts 8:4).

Multifaceted grace (43:1-7)

God is slow to anger (Exod. 34:6). And when he chastises his children it is always less than they deserve! How extraordinarily beautiful are the opening words of Isaiah 43:

> **'But now, this is what the Lord says —**
> **he who created you, O Jacob,**
> **he who formed you, O Israel:**
> **"Fear not, for I have redeemed you;**
> **I have summoned you by name; you are mine"'**

(43:1).

God will bring a remnant back from captivity (i.e. from **'Babylon'**, 43:14). Having begun a good work, he is not about to let them go despite their obvious failures (cf. Phil. 1:6). God is building his church, and even from the ashes of Babylon he will enable her to rise like Phœnix in the Greek legend.

God's grace is revealed in several ways in this section.

1. God has redeemed Israel

As we have seen before (e.g. 41:14), the language of redemption is never far away from God's thoughts in these latter chapters. God has delivered them by the payment of a price. Israel, God's servant, had been purchased. God has paid the ransom price. He is even willing to let other nations (like Egypt, Cush and Seba) become substitutes for judgement so that his people might go free! (43:3-4).

2. God's children belong to him

God had chosen Israel (Jacob), calling her by name and saying to her, **'You are mine'** (43:1). This is the language both of affection and possession. God loves his adopted children extensively and jealously. At the heart of the covenant relationship is the expression: 'I am your God; you are my people.' This has been called the 'Immanuel principle'[2] of the covenant. The heart of God's dealings with us is the declaration: 'God with us' (cf. Gen. 17:7; Exod. 6:6-7; 19:4-5; Lev. 11:45; Deut. 4:20; 29:13; 2 Kings 11:17; Ezek. 34:24; Zech. 8:8; 2 Cor. 6:16; Heb. 8:10).

3. The trials will not overcome you

That is why God's people have nothing to fear from the trials, described in terms of **'water'** and **'fire'** (43:2). Just as Noah and his family emerged from the flood, and Israel passed through the Red Sea, so God's children will survive the judgements that will come to pass. Think of the words of Psalm 93:

> The floods, O Lord, have lifted up,
> Have lifted up their voice;
> The floods have lifted up their waves,

> And made a mighty noise.
> But yet the Lord, who is on high,
> Is more of might by far
> Than noise of many waters is,
> Than great sea-billows are.[3]

We are reminded here, too, of the climax of Romans 8: 'If God is for us, who can be against us? He who did not spare his own Son, but gave him up for us all — how will he not also, along with him, graciously give us all things? Who will bring any charge against those whom God has chosen? It is God who justifies. Who is he that condemns? Christ Jesus, who died — more than that, who was raised to life — is at the right hand of God and is also interceding for us. Who shall separate us from the love of Christ? Shall trouble or hardship or persecution or famine or nakedness or danger or sword? As it is written: "For your sake we face death all day long; we are considered as sheep to be slaughtered." No, in all these things we are more than conquerors through him who loved us. For I am convinced that neither death nor life, neither angels nor demons, neither the present nor the future, nor any powers, neither height nor depth, nor anything else in all creation, will be able to separate us from the love of God that is in Christ Jesus our Lord' (Rom. 8:31-39).

4. God calls his children by name

Think of the names God calls his redeemed ones. There is the term 'Israelite'. The *'el'* in the name Israel is a reference to God. Christians are the 'Israel of God' (Gal. 6:16). The term 'Israel' means 'he who struggles with God'. The name reminds us of the prayer life Christians enjoy with the Lord. Then there is the term 'Christian' first deployed at Antioch (Acts 11:26). We are not as conscious as we should be that as Christians we are carrying about the very name of our Saviour.

Yahweh — the only God there is (43:8-13)

Polytheism, the belief that there exist many gods, was and remains a problem. In fact much of the background of the history of Israel and of the early New Testament church lies in the world of polytheism. Scripture denounces it as something which debases God. Israel had always shown a tendency to worship other gods (e.g. Judg. 2:12-13). The Bible consistently condemns this by insisting on the absolute uniqueness of the Judeo-Christian God, Yahweh.

In Athens Paul found the inhabitants worshipping all kinds of idols (Acts 17). One commentator says of Athens, 'It was easier to find a god there than a man.' In the Parthenon stood a huge gold and ivory statue of Athena. Elsewhere there were images of Apollo, the city's patron, of Jupiter, Venus, Mercury, Bacchus, Neptune, Diana and Aesculapius. All this made Paul distressed (Acts 17:16). Starting from the point where they confessed themselves to be ignorant, Paul preached to them the only God there is.

In a courtroom scene reminiscent of chapter 41, the God of Israel challenges the idols. They are quickly eliminated as having nothing to say (43:9). God, on the other hand, is true and powerful and Israel is witness to it:

> **"'You are my witnesses," declares the Lord,**
> **"and my servant whom I have chosen,**
> **so that you may know and believe me**
> **and understand that I am he.**
> **Before me no god was formed,**
> **nor will there be one after me.**
> **I, even I, am the Lord,**
> **and apart from me there is no saviour"'**

(43:10-11).

Several features are worth noting.

1. The eternity of God

God will share his glory with no one — least of all with an idol! The message will bear repeating (44:6,8; 45:5-6,18,21-22; 46:9). The passage brings to mind the truth given to Moses when he saw the bush that burned without being consumed. The 'I AM' is. He has no beginning nor end. He is eternal.

2. The uniqueness of the Mediator

There is no other Saviour apart from the Servant whom God will send. When he comes he too will insist upon his uniqueness and that of the salvation he promises to those who trust him (John 14:6; Acts 4:12; 1 Tim. 2:5-6).

3. The faithfulness of God's ways

God had called Israel by name. Israel is his (43:12). And that which he sovereignly brings about (**'I have revealed and saved and proclaimed...'**, 43:12) he will maintain. Israel, to whom God gave his staggering word of promise, could rely upon him to do as he had said. Because he is almighty, his word is invincible: **'When I act, who can reverse it?'** (43:13).

A new thing (43:14-28)

The chapter closes with a promise of something new:

> **'Forget the former things;**
> **do not dwell on the past.**
> **See, I am doing a new thing!**
> **Now it springs up; do you not perceive it?**
> **I am making a way in the desert**
> **and streams in the wasteland'**
>
> (43:18-19).

What God is about to accomplish is on a different level from what he had done in the past when he saved Israel from Egypt (43:16-17). The salvation which his Servant Jesus will perform at Calvary is something which the Old Testament has been preparing for, but Israel had missed the point again and again. They are to think along very different lines. God is going to establish a new covenant (Jer. 31:31-34). The covenant had been breached. God's people had broken it and abandoned his promise. God brought about exile as a punishment. But he would restore them again and make everything new. The coming of Jesus Christ as a little baby in Bethlehem was in one sense something entirely new. No one else had been born quite like this before. The old ways, centred as they were around Palestine and the temple and the sacrifices, were going to be set aside.

But we must be careful not to think that there was no continuity at all between what God had done in the Old Testament and what he promises under the New Testament, or Covenant. There were, for example, aspects of the law which belonged to the nation of Israel and to the sacrificial rituals. These would be set aside. But the moral law, far from being set aside, would be brought closer: God would write it on the hearts of those who love him (Jer. 31:33).

Israel's response to all this is a big yawn! (43:22-24). It is almost as though all that God had said was of no consequence. In comparison to the lavish way God had shown his love to them, they could hardly stir themselves to acknowledge his existence! God spells out their problem:

> **'...you have not called upon me...**
> **you have not wearied yourselves for me...**
> **you have not brought me sheep for burnt offerings,**
> **nor honoured me with your sacrifices...**
> **You have not bought any fragrant calamus for me,**
> **or lavished on me the fat of your sacrifices'**

> (43:22-24).

The church has been redeemed in order to be what man was intended to be: a praising community. By God's grace, those who were no people, whether covenant-breaking Jews or Gentiles outside the covenant, are made the people of God and receive mercy. This is the way it should be: **'The people I formed for myself ... proclaim my praise'** (43:21). It is partly to this verse that Peter alludes when he says, 'You are a chosen people, a holy nation, a people belonging to God, that you may declare the praises of him who called you out of darkness into his wonderful light' (1 Peter 2:9-10).

The Lord desires our worship to be wholehearted: think of the way the psalmist could say, 'I am worn out calling for help; my throat is parched. My eyes fail, looking for my God' (Ps. 69:3).

When did you last worship God that way? Instead of wholehearted-ness, Israel had been a burden to God: **'But you have burdened me with your sins and wearied me with your offences.'** True worship is the bringing of sacrifices to the Lord; false worship is that which is seen as a burden from start to finish (43:23).

If they continue this way (as collectively they did) God will give them over to destruction: **'So I will disgrace the dignitaries of your temple, and I will consign Jacob to destruction and Israel to scorn'** (43:28). The word for destruction *(charem)* is a very distinc-tive Hebrew word. It means 'to ban, devote to destruction, to exterminate, to anathematize'.[4] When Israel entered Canaan, certain cities were to be totally destroyed. Nothing was to be taken. The city was under the 'ban' (Josh. 6:21; 8:26; 10:1). It was a failure to comply with this edict that resulted in Achan's destruction (Josh. 7). Nor is this an Old Testament concept only. Paul could use the same idea when he thought about preachers in Galatia who were insisting upon the necessity of circumcision in order to be saved (Gal.1:8). And he was equally blunt when he thought of those who did not love Christ in Corinth: 'If anyone does not love the Lord — a curse be on him' (1 Cor. 16:22).

Summary

God has been addressing his covenant people who appear to be both deaf and blind! They had failed to be witnesses to his love and mercy. It accounts for their eventual captivity in Babylon: God has chastised them for their failure to evangelize. Nevertheless, a remnant will return, revealing God's continued faithfulness to his covenant word. Isaiah never tires of saying it: God is faithful!

30.
Impotent idols!

Please read Isaiah 44

Chapter 43 ended with a rebuke: Jacob will be consigned to destruction (43:28). But even though this word was solemn in its effects, it was not all that God said. Just a few verses earlier he had promised: 'I, even I, am he who blots out your transgressions, for my own sake, and remembers your sins no more' (43:25). It is precisely this note that Isaiah now develops in chapter 44.

The chapter can be divided into two sections: first, a promise of revival to God's true church (44:1-5); and, second, a contrast between the true God who alone can promise salvation and revival (44:6-8,21-28) and the dumb, worthless idols of men (44:9-20).

A promise of revival (44:1-5)

'This is what the Lord says—
    he who made you, who formed you in the womb,
    and who will help you:
Do not be afraid, O Jacob, my servant,
    Jeshurun, whom I have chosen.
For I will pour water on the thirsty land,
    and streams on the dry ground;
I will pour out my Spirit on your offspring,
    and my blessing on your descendants'

(44:2-3).

Promises like this one abound in Isaiah's prophecy. We shall see later, in chapters 63 and 64, just how fond Isaiah was of speaking about the possibility of revival in the church. Such passages are all the more welcome after the darkness of so much of what Isaiah has said so far.

Relieving thirst is the Bible's favourite description of the experience of God's blessings (see 12:3; 55:1; Ps. 42:1; Jer. 2:13; John 4:14; 7:37; Rev. 7:17). The blessing Isaiah now speaks of is the revival of God's church from its current moribund condition; God discloses in the Scriptures and in history that he intends to advance his church by intermittent revivals. Such times are periods of great blessing, underlined by the use of the name **'Jeshurun'**[1] to describe God's church (44:2). The term had been used by Moses when describing the blessedness the redeemed people could expect from their God (Deut. 33:5,26). Several features come into sharp focus in this passage.

1. Revival follows a period of spiritual desolation and barrenness

'Thirsty' brings to mind something which is dry and shrivelled up.

> 'The poor and needy search for water,
>   but there is none;
>   their tongues are parched with thirst.
> But I the Lord will answer them;
>   I, the God of Israel, will not forsake them.
> I will make rivers flow on barren heights,
>   and springs within the valleys.
> I will turn the desert into pools of water,
>   and the parched ground into springs'
>
> (41:17-18).

Dr Increase Mather, writing in 1721, could say of New England, 'Conversions are rare in these days.' Comparing his own day to what he had experienced initially as a young man in the 1660s under the ministry of men like Thomas Cotton and John Shepherd, he went on to say, 'Having been sixty-five years a preacher of the gospel, I feel as did the ancient men who had seen the former temple and wept when they saw the latter.' Some fifteen years later, during the Great Awakening, he was to witness a revival, and it is estimated that some 300,000 conversions took place in the thirteen colonies.

2. Revival is a sovereign work of God

The emphasis in the passage is upon God's activity: 'I will pour...' (44:3). It is repeated at the end of the chapter with even greater force:

'I am the Lord ...
who says of Jerusalem, "It shall be inhabited,"
of the towns of Judah, "They shall be built,"
and of their ruins,"I will restore them..."'

(44:24,26).

Just as the conversion of one soul is God's work (John 1:13), so revival — which is in essence the same as what God does ordinarily but on a grander scale and all at once (44:5) — is also God's work. When John Livingstone preached on Ezekiel 36 at the Monday evening Thanksgiving Service at the Kirk of Shotts in 1630, he witnessed the conversion of some 500 people. But as far as he knew, not one was converted when he preached on the same text the following Sunday at Irvine. There is a mystery about God's blessings which underlines the fact that they cannot be produced to order.

3. When God comes to renew his church, it is invariably accompanied by a conviction of sin

Isaiah 43:24 had expressed the problem clearly:

'You have not bought any fragrant calamus for me,
    or lavished on me the fat of your sacrifices.
But you have burdened me with your sins
    and wearied me with your offences.'

The nature of their offences is elaborated upon in this chapter in verses 6-20 — a lengthy monologue on the evils and folly of idolatry. The purpose of it all is to underline the sinfulness of Judah's inhabitants. The blessing which God brings focuses upon their sin:

'I have swept away your offences like a cloud,
    your sins like the morning mist.

Return to me,
   for I have redeemed you'

(44:22).

Bad habits, worldliness, a compromised lifestyle — these were things Judah had to recognize and remove.

4. Revival is a work of the Holy Spirit

'I will pour out my Spirit...' (44:3). This is a glimpse of the new covenant promised by later prophets (Jer. 31:31-34; Ezek. 36:26-32; Joel 2:28-32). The effect of the Spirit's ministry is to bring about the addition of many to the church:

'They will spring up like grass in a meadow,
   like poplar trees by flowing streams.
One will say, "I belong to the Lord";
   another will call himself by the name of Jacob;
still another will write on his hand, "The Lord's",
   and will take the name Israel'

(44:4-5).

The picture in verse 5 is similar to the vision of Psalm 87:

'He has set his foundation on the holy mountain;
   the Lord loves the gates of Zion
   more than all the dwellings of Jacob.
Glorious things are said of you,
   O city of God:
"I will record Rahab and Babylon
   among those who acknowledge me —
Philistia too, and Tyre, along with Cush —
   and will say, 'This one was born in Zion.'"
Indeed, of Zion it will be said,
   "This one and that one were born in her,
   and the Most High himself will establish her."
The Lord will write in the register of the peoples:
   "This one was born in Zion."
As they make music they will sing,
   "All my fountains are in you."'

Glimpses of Pentecost, and the thousands from various nations converted under Peter's preaching, seem to be in mind. But the passage is a promise that holds good for every age. One of the effects of the Holy Spirit's work is to mediate the presence of Christ to God's children. The way in which earlier promises in Isaiah of God's presence (such as 41:10,13-14,17; 43:2,5) are accomplished is now made clear: the ministry of the Holy Spirit, although active in Old Testament times, will be intensified in these days of blessing. The same Spirit who fills Christ (11:2) will be given to God's children.

The Holy One of Israel versus dumb idols

Before revival can come, Judah must forsake her idols. A lengthy section on idolatry follows (44:6-20), a theme which will be repeated again in succeeding chapters (e.g. 46:1-13). Assyria had many idols, including, Ashur (or Asshur), the Assyrian national god and the name of Assyria's capital city; Sin, the moon-god; Ishtar, the goddess of lust (women gave themselves to temple prostitution as a kind of vocation); Ninurta, the god of storm; and Nebo, the god of trade and commerce. Assyria brought idolatry into parts of Judah on a grand scale and forced Isaiah from the very start to speak about it (cf. 2:8).

Babylon, too, had its gods, including Bel, sometimes called Marduk, patron of Babylon, and Nebo, son of Marduk, the god of learning and writing. In addition, the native Canaanites had worshipped Baal, a form of idolatry that was still prevalent in Israel in Elijah's time.

Two sad periods of Israel's history showed how prone they were to idolatry. After his momentous encounter with the Lord on Mount Sinai, Moses came down to earth with the discovery that his brother Aaron had been a willing accomplice in the worship of a Canaanite golden calf (Exod. 32). In King Jeroboam's time, Israel, in the north, set up shrines at Dan and Bethel which included the worship of a bull. The prophet Ahijah prophesied the demise of Israel because of this very sin (1 Kings 14:16).

John Wesley once said, 'In his natural state, every man born into the world is a rank idolater.'

1. Idolatry dishonours God

The essence of idolatry is the entertainment of thoughts about God that are unworthy of him. And God is jealous of his glory. **'I am the first and I am the last...'** (44:6; cf. 40:18; 46:5,9). There is no one like him (44:7). God insists upon the uniqueness of his identity. The idols are nothing; they are not gods: **'Is there any God besides me? No, there is no other Rock; I know not one'** (44:8). God is sovereign, the idols (and their makers) are nothing (44:9) — just chunks of metal (44:12) or, more commonly, wood (44:13-20).

Isaiah's considerable knowledge of trees (44:13-14) has led to the intriguing speculation that he may have been a carpenter prior to his calling as a prophet.[2] The folly of idolatry could hardly be more apparent: the same piece of tree that is made into an idol is cast on the fire and burnt to provide heat with which to cook the carpenter's dinner! (44:16-17). **'They know nothing, they understand nothing; their eyes are plastered over so that they cannot see, and their minds closed so they cannot understand'** (44:18). This description fits both idol and idolater!

Behind this ingenuity at making images is an attempt to fashion God in our own image. As Calvin comments, 'Thus their thoughts concerning him are excessively wicked, and they cast aside and stain his glory, by making it like earthly and fading things. Nothing is so inconsistent with the majesty of God as images; and he who worships them endeavours to shut up God in them, and to treat him according to his own fancy. Justly, therefore, does the prophet attack such corruptions, and sharply censure the mad zeal of superstitious persons, since nothing more detestable can be uttered or imagined.'[3]

2. Idolatry misleads man

Isaiah turns the appeal of idolatry into an embarrassment, sparing nothing as he does so. He mocks it, asking such ludicrous questions as, what is the identity of the one who makes a god? (44:10). The notion is both absurd and blasphemous (cf. Rom. 1:25). Chapter 46 takes the mockery a stage further:

'They lift it to their shoulders and carry it;
    they set it up in its place, and there it stands.

From that spot it cannot move.
Though one cries out to it, it does not answer;
  it cannot save him from his troubles'

                                                    (46:7).

Far from helping people in worship, idolatry hinders it. Misguided people who argue that such items as crucifixes are 'aids' to worship should take heed of Isaiah's forthright condemnations here.

3. Idolatry is wrong

Idols are called **'detestable'** (44:19), as indeed are those who worship them (41:24). God abhors idols (Deut 16:21 - 17:7). The second commandment underlined this point (Exod. 20:4-5).

'**Remember**' and '**return**' convey God's desire that his covenant people forsake their sin and turn to him (44:21-22). The basis for this call lies in God's redemptive work: '**I have redeemed you**' (44:22,23). The shadow of the cross falls deep across the Old Testament; more than seven centuries before the coming of Jesus Christ, God could proclaim prophetically through Isaiah that the price of forgiveness, which would necessitate the death of God's Son, had been paid in full. Little wonder that creation itself is urged to burst into a song of thanksgiving (44:23).

Veiled allusions to the coming of Christ as a liberator of God's people have already emerged (e.g. 41:2,25-29). This now leads to the mention of '**Cyrus**' 44:28), and his command to rebuild Jerusalem and its temple in the time of Ezra (cf. Ezra 1:1-8). The poem (44:24-28) falls into three quite definite chronological div-isions: the past (44:24-25), the present (44:.26-27) and the future (44:28). This is a matter which we shall look at in the next chapter.

Summary

Following the devastating warning of 43:28, whereby Jacob was threatened with destruction, Isaiah 44 has developed a parallel theme: God is going to do a purging work. Out of the fire of judgement will emerge his true church, a purified people.

31.
Cyrus: the Lord's anointed

Please read Isaiah 45

Isaiah 44:28 introduces us once more to Cyrus (cf. 41:2-3,25). 'It would be difficult to overestimate the importance of Cyrus the Great in Old Testament history,' writes John C.Whitcomb, Jr.[1]

Cyrus in history

Cyrus was born in about 590-585 B.C., of royal parents, in a small Persian kingdom called Anshan in the territory of Eastern Elam, which was at that time subject to the mighty kingdom of the Medes. Cyrus' mother, who was a daughter of Astyages, the last king of the Medes, gave him an understanding of their ways. Cyrus was evidently ambitious; after the death of his father, he unified the Persian nation and attacked the weak and corrupt Astyages. Welding the Medes and Persians into a single force, he went on to gain Lydia (modern Turkey) in 547 B.C., and later Babylon in 539 B.C. All this had been prophesied in even greater detail by Daniel (2:39; 7:5).

These successive victories of Cyrus against the Medes, Lydians and Babylonians, ratified in sources of secular history, bring into focus the astonishing accuracy of Isaiah's prophecies given 150 years earlier. It was the Lord who called him and gave him these victories:

'Who has stirred up one from the east,
    calling him in righteousness to his service ?
He hands nations over to him

and subdues kings before him.
He turns them to dust with his sword,
    to wind-blown chaff with his bow.
He pursues them and moves on unscathed,
    by a path his feet have not travelled before'

                                                                (41:2-3).

'I have stirred up one from the north, and he comes —
    one from the rising sun who calls on my name.
He treads on rulers as if they were mortar,
    as if he were a potter treading the clay'

                                                                (41:25).

'...whose right hand I take hold of
to subdue nations before him
    and to strip kings of their armour,
to open doors before him
    so that gates will not be shut:
I will go before you
    and will level the mountains;
I will break down gates of bronze
    and cut through bars of iron.
I will give you the treasures of darkness,
    riches stored in secret places'

                                                                (45:1-3).

'From the east I summon a bird of prey;
    from a far-off land, a man to fulfil my purpose'

                                                                (46:11).

'The Lord's chosen ally
    will carry out his purpose against Babylon;
    his arm will be against the Babylonians'

                                                                (48:14).

Prophecy fulfilled (45:1-8)

Isaiah 44:28 indicates that Cyrus would issue a decree concerning
the rebuilding of the temple in Jerusalem: 'Cyrus ...will accomplish

all that I please; he will say of Jerusalem, "Let it be rebuilt," and of the temple, "Let its foundations be laid."'' This is a remarkable prophecy, bearing in mind that the destruction of the temple was still a hundred years away. The fulfilment is set forth in the opening chapters of the book of Ezra.

With respect to the rebuilding of Jerusalem, ('Let it be rebuilt', 'He will rebuild my city', 44:28, 45:13), we know from history that Cyrus made no provision for the fortification of the city. These prophecies are to be understood indirectly. 'When Cyrus gave permission to the Jews to return from Babylon (Ezra 1:1-4) he was indirectly responsible for the rebuilding of Jerusalem.'[2] The books of Ezra and Nehemiah make it clear that, though Cyrus had given permission to the Jews to return to Jerusalem, permission to rebuild the city walls was given by his successor, Artaxerxes I (Ezra 4:12,13,16,21; Neh. 2:3,8).

Cyrus had been concerned about the temple. As a polytheist, he seems to have believed that any help from the Jewish deity would only be to his advantage. A similar desire was expressed by Darius Hystaspes, twenty years later (Ezra 6:10).

The fear of Jerusalem's strength, if the walls were to be rebuilt and fortified, was made clear to Cyrus by Rehum and Shimshei (Ezr i 4:16). Artaxerxes' concession allowing the rebuilding work to b..gin only further underlines that 'The king's heart is in the hand of the Lord; he directs it like a watercourse wherever he pleases' (Prov. 21:1).

Cyrus was not the only foreign ruler whom the Lord was to raise up 'from the east' (41:2), the north (41:25), or 'from a far country' (46:11), nor the only one of whom it could be said, 'whose right hand I take hold of to subdue nations...' (45:1). Nebuchadnezzar is described as God's 'servant' (Jer. 25:9), and Hazael, the cruel militarist of Damascus, is said to have been 'anointed' by Elisha to perform a special work on God's behalf (1 Kings 19:15). God's control over the nations is total.

The fact that Cyrus is referred to in 44:28 as a 'shepherd' poses the question whether he was a true believer. Other references give weight to this suggestion: he would be called 'in righteousness' by God (41:2); he was 'raised up in righteousness' (45:13); he was to 'carry out [God's] purpose against Babylon' (48:14). Of even more significance is the expression in 45:1 that he would be 'anointed' *(messiah)*. This identifies him with Messiah (cf. Ps. 2:2; Dan. 9:25).

However, Cyrus' polytheism seems to be confirmed by what is said in 45:4-5:

'I summon you by name
and bestow on you a title of honour,
though you do not acknowledge me...
I will strengthen you,
though you have not acknowledged me.'

The eloquent language of Ezra 1:2-4, Cyrus' decree to the Jews in Babylon, is best explained by the suggestion that Cyrus commissioned Daniel to word the decree for him. And there is ample evidence in secular history that Cyrus was not a believer. The Cyrus Cylinder found in the nineteenth century — a cylinder of baked clay, some twenty-five centimetres long and inscribed with historical details of Cyrus' capture of Babylon — makes it clear that Cyrus worshipped Bel, Nebo and especially Marduk, the Babylonian gods, and that his treatment of the Jews was along similar lines to the way other transplanted peoples were treated. Josephus adds the intriguing suggestion that Cyrus had read these passages in Isaiah and was eager to fulfil them, the passages being so complimentary about him.[3] The fact that he appointed the godly Daniel as his chief sub-governor makes this suggestion all the more plausible.

All these details confirm the theory that Cyrus is to be looked upon as a type of Messiah.[4] He is God's agent, raised up to deliver God's people and lead them into times of peace and security.

When Isaiah wrote these words, the birth of Cyrus was still over a hundred years away! It is not hard to see why some Bible commentators, whose minds preclude the possibility of miracle and prophecy, deny that passages like these could have been written by Isaiah. The New Testament writers, however, were convinced of Isaiah's authorship of these latter chapters of the prophecy (Matt. 3:1; 8:17; 12:17-21; Acts 8:30-35; Rom. 10:16,20).

As we have already seen in our comments on Isaiah 41:2 and 25, Cyrus is mentioned in the context of God's sovereignty. The same is true of chapters 44 and 45. By way of emphasis, God's sovereignty is underlined: **'I, the Lord, do all these things'** (45:7). Chapter 44 insists, in opposition to the dumb idols, that God alone can foretell events (44:25-26). No intelligent reader of Isaiah would have been impressed by such claims if the document were known to have been written *after* the predicted events were fulfilled! It is difficult to see how Isaiah's prophecy would be of comfort to the Jews in exile if these words regarding Cyrus had just been written *after* Cyrus had given his decree.

Of greater significance is how all this ought to have strengthened Israel's faith. Everything that happens, even in international affairs, is according to the Lord's plan. When everything seems to shaking all around, that thought is of enormous encouragement.

Israel's lack of faith (45:9-15)

But such encouragement is not yet apparent. Far from seeing God in control of history, Israel believes things are in chaos. Isaiah brings a sharp rebuke:

> **'Woe to him who quarrels with his Maker,**
> **to him who is but a potsherd among the**
> **potsherds on the ground.**
> **Does the clay say to the potter,**
> **"What are you making?"**
> **Does your work say,**
> **"He has no hands"?'**

(45:9).

This is the arrogance of unbelief: to question what God is doing (45:11, rightly in the form of a question in the NIV). The Lord who made the stars in the universe is able to order the course of history (45:12). What is this foolishness that questions God's ability to raise up a Cyrus, some 150 years later? It is nothing less than unbelief. This lesson has already been underlined in chapter 40 (40:26-31).

A glorious future (45:14-25)

God's ability to order the course of history goes far beyond 150 years. The fulfilment of the promise of Christ's coming was still over 700 years away! But beyond that, too, lay the promise of the influx of the Gentiles into the church, a theme opened up here and elaborated upon in chapters 60-62. The passage divides into two sections: an address to Israel (45:14-19), and then to the world itself, appealing to everyone to acknowledge the Lord, as one day it must (45:20-25).

Egyptians, Cushites and Sabeans are depicted, coming to Israel weighed down with chains as prisoners of war, and saying, 'Surely God is with you...' (45:14; see earlier comments on 44:6). This is a vivid way of describing what is said later: 'Before me every knee will bow; by me every tongue will swear' (45:23).

The staggering change to the nations envisaged in this passage leads Israel to exclaim that God's ways are incomprehensible: **'Truly you are a God who hides himself...'** (45:15).

The free offer of the gospel

The chapter ends with a glorious and comprehensive call to everyone to come, **'turn'** to the Lord **'and be saved'** (45:22). The universal call to all men is based upon two considerations: God alone is God (**'I am the Lord and there is none other'**, 45:18; cf. 45:22), and God alone can save (**'There is none but me'**, 45:21). There can be no question but that Isaiah has in mind salvation in its fullest sense. Earlier in the chapter he had promised that **'Israel will be saved'** (45:17). This was followed by the title **'Saviour'** appropriated by God himself (45:21). 'Israel', once confined and restricted in scope, now takes on a much wider connotation. The appeal is universal: **'all the ends of the earth'** are invited to come to the Lord and be saved (45:22). God's relationship to *all* men had been underlined by the fact that he is the Creator of all things (45:12,18). Moreover, he is the only God there is (45:14,18,21). In addition, **'Every knee shall bow ... every tongue shall swear'** (45:23) is taken by the apostle Paul as an indication that, one day, the entire universe will acknowledge Christ as Lord, whether they are redeemed or not (Phil. 2:10-11; cf. Rom. 14:11).

This appeal is to every *individual* and not just to nationalities. As John Murray has written, 'This text expresses then the will of God in the matter of the call, invitation, appeal, and command of the gospel, namely, the will that all should turn to him and be saved... Obviously, however, it is not his decretive will that all repent and be saved. While, on the one hand, he has not decretively willed that all be saved, yet he declares unequivocally that it is his will and, impliedly, his pleasure that all turn and be saved. We are again faced with the mystery and adorable richness of the divine will. It might seem to us that the one rules out the other. But it is not so. There is a multiformity to the divine will that is consonant with the fulness and richness of his divine character, and it is no wonder that we are constrained to bow in humble yet exultant amazement before his ineffable greatness and unsearchable judgements.'[5]

Summary

Isaiah has seen into the future; it is a terrible one. The experience of captivity took away the song from the hearts of God's people (Ps. 137). But judgement was tempered with grace, and God raised up a ruler by the name of Cyrus to issue the decree for their return to Jerusalem. Such control over history is only an example of the truth that God 'works out everything in conformity with the purpose of his will' (Eph. 1:11). This truth provides the best incentive to make sure that we are the Lord's.

32.
The fall of Babylon

Please read Isaiah 46 - 48

Having been introduced to the figure of Cyrus, in chapters 46 and 47 we are taken a little beyond that horizon to the eventual downfall of Babylon itself. Behind Babylon's collapse (chapter 47) lies her idolatry (chapter 46). Idolatry and collapse are intimately bound together. For this reason it will be helpful to consider these two chapters together. Chapter 47 ends with a word of encouragement to Israel that despite the judgements that befall Babylon, Israel will be saved. This is the continuing theme of chapter 48.

The instability of nations

In earlier chapters (13-23), Isaiah established the principle of the perennial instability of nations. The fall of Babylon in particular has been alluded to already in chapters 14 and 21. The prophet had warned that God scatters the proud in the imagination of their hearts, and puts down the mighty from their thrones (cf. Luke 1:51-52). The King of Babylon had been depicted as boasting:

'You said in your heart,
    "I will ascend to heaven;
I will raise my throne
    above the stars of God;
I will sit enthroned on the mount of assembly,
    on the utmost heights of the sacred mountain.

I will ascend above the tops of the clouds;
   I will make myself like the Most High'"

(14:13-14).

To which had come the warning: 'But you are brought down to
the grave, to the depths of the pit' (14:15).

Now the point is made even clearer. God will not only bring his
own people back to their own land; he will also vindicate his own
name.

The kingdoms of the world are notoriously unstable. Babylon's
power was awesome, but it disappeared in a moment. 'Man proposes, God disposes,' said Thomas à Kempis.[1] In other words, man's
empires exist only so long as God allows. In a sermon entitled
'God's providence,' C. H. Spurgeon said, 'Napoleon once heard it
said, that man proposes and God disposes. "Ah" said Napoleon, "but
I propose and dispose too." How do you think he proposed and
disposed? He proposed to go and take Russia; he proposed to make
all Europe his. He proposed to destroy that power, and how did he
come back again? How had he disposed it? He came back solitary
and alone, his mighty army perished and wasted, having well-nigh
eaten and devoured one another through hunger. Man proposes and
God disposes.'[2]

Babylon, the queen of nations (47:5) will grovel in the dust; all
her luxury is to be taken away (47:1). Dust, toil, nakedness, shame,
silence and darkness are all symbols of Babylon's eventual damnation (47:1-3).

It is true that Babylon was given power over Israel for a time. God
was angry with his people and he wished to teach them a lesson. But
Babylon showed no mercy; and she will receive none (47:6).
Babylon's arrogance is captured by the striking similarity of her
boast to that of God himself: **'I am and there is none besides me'**!
(47:8,10; cf. 46:9). The fall of the arrogant will be swift and sudden
(47:11).

The nothingness of idols

Everything to which this world's kingdoms are devoted is transi-
tory. This applies not just to idols in the sense that we normally think

of them, but also to such things as ambition, power, fame and
materialism. The same truth is taught in the apocalyptic vision of
Daniel 11. Kingdoms which have no ultimate foundation are bound
to crumble. Success is only guaranteed to the kingdom of God.

The reason for Babylon's instability is that her gods are also
unstable — indeed, they are no gods at all. Isaiah depicts Babylon's
idols being borne into captivity:

> **'Bel bows down, Nebo stoops low;**
> **their idols are borne by beasts of burden.**
> **The images that are carried about are burdensome,**
> **a burden for the weary.**
> **They stoop and bow down together;**
> **unable to rescue the burden,**
> **they themselves go off into captivity'**
>
> (46:1-2).

Man's idolatry is always a result of too small a view of the true
God: **'To whom will you compare me or count me equal? To
whom will you liken me that we may be compared?'** (46:5; cf.
40:18-20,25; 44:7). Images, whether those of Babylonian idol-
worship (44:9-20; 46:1-7), or paganism in the Graeco-Roman world
(Rom. 1:23,25), always dishonour God. That is why idolatry is the
first thing to be condemned in the Ten Commandments (Exod.
20:4). The supreme folly of idolatry is that it involves worshipping
something which man has made (46:6-7; 40:19; 41:7; 44:9-20).
Idols are inherently dumb (46:7). The gods are dead!

Idols obscure God's glory: **'Remember the former things,
those of long ago; I am God, and there is no other; I am God, and
there is none like me'** (46:9). Idolatry is a failure to acknowledge
that God is the sole Creator (40:28; 43:15).

'Bel' ('lord' cf. the Canaanite 'Baal') was a title used for
Babylon's principal deity, Marduk, whose son **'Nebo'** was the god
of learning. Their names appear in those of Belshazzar and
Nebuchadnezzar, kings of Babylon. Both of these gods were transported in processions, but here they are depicted as refugees,
suffering exile just as their worshippers do. It was widely believed
that the loss of these gods meant the end of the nation itself. The gods
who had been their hope of salvation now weary the very animals
who carry them (46:1).

Astrology was one aspect of Babylonian idolatry (47:13-15). Babylon was especially noted for astrologers. Nebuchadnezzar called for astrologers to interpret his dreams (Dan. 2:2). It is sometimes suggested that the tower of Babel was a platform built for the very purpose of viewing, and worshipping, the astral bodies (Gen. 11:4). Astrology receives a robust condemnation in Deuteronomy 18. It plays a significant part in the lives of millions today. There is nothing new under the sun!

The ultimate control of God

Astrology raises the question: 'What can I know about my future?' Isaiah is anxious to give us an answer to this very question. Those who worship idols can expect to be judged. Their future is filled with gloom. But there is an encouraging message for those who are the Lord's people. God is working out his purpose in every circumstance of life. Using the figure of a pregnant mother, Isaiah speaks of God having carried his people from the beginning of their existence (46:3-5; cf. 44:2). 'When man carries his god the end is destruction; when the true God carries man, the end is salvation.'[3] Ultimately, nothing can hinder God from working out his purposes; the emergence of Cyrus **'from the east'** as Israel's deliverer is proof that **'What I have planned, that will I do'** (46:11).

It is matter of enormous encouragement, in this sin-ravaged world, that God is control, that he has purposed to work out everything for the ultimate good of his people (Rom. 8:28-39). That is why chapter 46 ends with yet another appeal to those who are **'far from righteousness'** (i.e. unconverted) to pay heed to what God is doing: he has brought his own righteousness near (46:12-13). Sinners cannot obtain the necessary righteousness by their own works; it is to be received by faith alone in God's promised Messiah. Isaiah once more looks forward to the coming of Messiah and the salvation he brings:

> **'I am bringing my righteousness near,
> it is not far away;
> and my salvation will not be delayed.
> I will grant salvation to Zion,
> my splendour to Israel'**

> (46:13).

It is no wonder that, when Babylon's doom is foretold, God's people exclaim: **'Our Redeemer — the Lord Almighty is his name — is the Holy One of Israel'** (47:4).Worship is the only response a believer can make.

Israel's stubbornness

Not everyone in Israel was a believer. They may have all belonged to God's Old Testament church (48:1-2), but their hearts were far from the Lord. The call of the prophets often fell upon deaf ears. There was, as Paul would have put it, an 'Israel within Israel' (Rom. 9:6). Some were **'stubborn'**: their necks were reinforced with iron bars (48:4). Pride was not only a trait of Babylonian kings (14:13-15). Israel, too, were guilty of idolatry (48:5; 44:12-20). They were in essence no better than the Babylonians.

It is this truth, that *all* are equally sinners before God and undeserving of his mercy, that the Bible is anxious to get across (Rom. 3:23). There were many in Israel who were intent on serving sin, and even the gracious invitations of God would not change that. Already Isaiah has mentioned Israel's faithlessness (40:27) and coldness (43:22). Israel had been guilty of sinning against the light (42:18-25). Now, it seems, they had become hardened by their sin:

'You have neither heard nor understood;
    from of old your ear has not been open.
Well do I know how treacherous you are;
    you were called a rebel from birth'

(48:8).

This is a most dangerous condition. It is all too possible to resist the overtures of God. What does God do with stubborn people? The answer is that he disciplines them!

The refiner's fire

Not for the first time had Israel been tried 'in the fire'. The experience of Egyptian bondage had been to refine: 'But as for you, the Lord took you and brought you out of the iron-smelting furnace,

out of Egypt, to be the people of his inheritance, as you now are'
(Deut. 4:20; cf. 1 Kings 8:51; Jer. 11:4). Isaiah has used this figure
before (1:25; 4:4). Now he makes the point again: **'See, I have
refined you, though not as silver; I have tested you in the furnace
of affliction'** (48:10). The psalmist had also experienced something
similar: 'For you, O God, tested us; you refined us like silver' (Ps.
66:10; cf. Jer. 9:7; Dan. 11:35; 12:10; 1 Peter 1:15).

God disciplines his children (Heb.12:5-11). Being tested is a
sign that we are God's children. There are times when only discipline will bring us to our senses.

> 'Before I was afflicted I went astray,
>> but now I obey your word...
> It was good for me to be afflicted
>> so that I might learn your decrees...
> I know, O Lord, that your laws are righteous,
>> and in faithfulness you have afflicted me'
>> (Ps. 119:67,71,75).

Earlier in his prophecy, Isaiah had outlined the various ways God
deals with different children in order to produce the appropriate
harvest of grace (28:24-29).

Those who know God will be purified through trials such as
these, whereas those who are unbelievers will be hardened —
something which the letter to the Hebrews warns us against (Heb.
12:15). Despite all that may appear to be confusing and alarming,
the wise — those who know that the fear of the Lord is the beginning
of wisdom — will understand and take comfort (Prov. 9:10). They
know that God is working for them; nothing can finally overthrow
their relationship with him. What these trials do is merely remove
the dross that has come in the way of their relationship with the Lord.
Its removal is to be welcomed.

Summing it all up

Verses 12-16 of chapter 48 provide a summary of chapters 40-48.

1. God's people are **'called'** (48:12; cf. 42:6).
2. The one who calls is Creator (48:13; cf. 40:21-22; 42:5); the idols,

on the other hand, are created and powerless (48:14; cf. 41:21-23,26; 43:9).

3. Though captivity is threatened, God will raise up a deliverer, Cyrus, as promised (48:15; cf. 41:2,25-27; 45:1-7).

4. This captivity, like that in Egypt, is only a symbol of the captivity to sin from which the Redeemer, the Servant of the Lord filled with the Holy Spirit, can save (48:16; cf. 42:1).

5. This prophecy comes from the Redeemer, the Holy One of Israel (48:17; cf. 41:14).

6. God's blessing includes peace and righteousness (48:18; cf. 45:8).

7. The experience of deliverance from Babylon (compared to the deliverance from Egypt in 48:21; cf. 43:19) is a joyful one (48:20; cf. 44:23).

The last verse, **'"There is no peace," says the Lord, "for the wicked"'** (48:22) is a reminder of how the last verse of chapter 39 ended. Some have suggested that 'peace' recurs in a refrain in 48:22 and 57:21, dividing the last twenty-seven chapters into three sections of nine chapters each (40-48; 49-57; 58-66). This refrain is a salutary reminder of what awaits unbelievers, but sadly it is too often used lightly as an everyday expression having no more significance than that of some minor inconvenience. Its meaning is far more sombre than that, warning, as it does, 'that hypocrites might not, according to their custom, cherish false confidence in these promises'.[4] The fact that they are excluded from this 'peace' calls forth from God a lamentation: **'If only you had paid attention to my commands...'** (48:18).

Summary

Isaiah has been anxious to tell his listeners that Babylon will fall. Threatening and imposing as she was, she had no lasting future. Her arrogant pretensions to deity (cf. 47:8: 'I am and there is none beside me') mirror the claim of Satan and his subjects from the beginning (Gen. 3:13; 1 Tim. 2:14; Rev. 12:9). Indeed, Scripture sometimes uses the term 'Babylon' to convey everything that is evil and hostile towards God and his people (e.g. Rev. 17:5). But evil will one day be destroyed (Rev. 14:8; 18:2). It has no lasting power. Christ will build his church and the gates of hell will not be able to stand against it.

The divine decree does not prevent Satan launching his attacks against God's people again and again throughout the ages. The last days will be punctuated by times of stress (2 Tim. 3:1). There will be those who reject the crucified Christ, seek to destroy the church, and resist the truth (2 Tim. 3:2-8).

These things will reach their climax in the days of the man of sin, or lawlessness (2 Thess. 2:3-10). But even he will be destroyed (2 Thess. 2:8). The only kingdom with a future is the kingdom of God: 'The seventh angel sounded his trumpet, and there were loud voices in heaven, which said: "The kingdom of the world has become the kingdom of our Lord and of his Christ, and he will reign for ever and ever"' (Rev. 11:15).

33.
The second and third Servant Songs

Please read Isaiah 49 and 50

Isaiah 49 begins a new section of the prophecy. Whereas chapters
40-48 focused, more or less, on Cyrus as the deliverer of Israel from
Babylon, chapters 49-55 look beyond him and take the thought of
Christ's coming — already alluded to in the first 'Servant Song'
(42:1-7) — a step further.

The first 'Servant Song' (42:1-7) had introduced the Servant
(Jesus) as one chosen by God and filled with the Spirit (42:1), who
is humble (42:2) and who introduces the kingdom of God (42:4),
establishing a covenant between himself and God's people, which
will include the Gentiles (42:6). The second 'Servant Song' adds to
this revelation. The Spirit-filled Servant of Isaiah 42:1-7 has a
mission to perform.

The Lord's Servant (49:1-7)

A call goes out to the distant places to pay heed: Jesus, the Servant
of the Lord (49:3), is giving his testimony. His origin is spoken of
in terms of a normal birth: **'Before I was born the Lord called me;
from my birth he has made mention of my name'** (49:1). We have
here an echo of an earlier revelation: 'The virgin will be with child
and will give birth to a son, and will call him Immanuel' (7:14). But
the emphasis falls upon the calling and naming of the Servant. He
is expected. Even before he arrives, his mission has been desig-
nated: he is to be a preacher. Sword and arrow speak of the
opposition he can expect (49:2).

The Servant is also identified closely with Israel (49:3). It is not difficult to see why. Jesus, when he comes, will act as Israel's representative. He will labour on behalf of his covenant people. His mission involves transforming sinful Israel into the ideal Israel. 'The righteous *one* carries the sins of the *many*, and what he accomplishes belongs to them because of the bond between the Servant and the "many".'¹ Jesus came from Israel, identified himself with Israel and acted as Israel's substitute.

Just as Isaiah himself had been warned that his message would be rejected by many (6:9-10), so, too, Jesus' message will be rejected. Speaking in the first person, the Servant says, '**I have laboured to no purpose; I have spent my strength in vain and for nothing...**' (49:4). Yet he is assured that his God will reward him for his efforts. His task is neatly summarized in verse 5: '**to bring Jacob back to him and gather Israel to himself**'. Jesus' coming will be to convert sinners and bring them into a right relationship with God, and in that task — despite the opposition — God will not forsake him: he will be glorified. It is this glory which Isaiah glimpsed the day he went to the temple to worship and was overwhelmed (6:1-13; cf. John 12:41). Eventually the Servant's accomplishments will include the submission of kings: former oppressors will bow down in a restored Jerusalem (49:7).

The Saviour of the Gentiles

The Servant's task continues to be described in verse 6, a verse which contains the refrain: '**I will also make you a light for the Gentiles.**' The gospel of the kingdom which Jesus makes possible is meant for Israel, but not simply ethnic Israel. It is for both Jew and Gentile. Though Jesus restricted himself almost entirely to the Jews during his lifetime, there was a constant outward thrust to his ministry — something which Matthew's Gospel, written to converted Jews, is anxious to underline.

It is Matthew who takes up this prophecy in Isaiah 49:6 to make the point that Jesus will proclaim good news to the Gentiles, and in his name the Gentiles will put their trust (Matt. 12:17-21). Gentile women, Rahab and Ruth, are among Jesus' forebears (Matt. 1:5). Gentile astronomers are the first to offer worship at his birth (Matt. 2:1-12). Jesus' initial ministry is in 'Galilee of the Gentiles' (Matt.

4:15). A Gentile centurion is commended for his faith above those in Israel (Matt. 8:10). Many Gentiles will come, we are told, from east and west and will sit down with the patriarchs while the sons of the kingdom will be ejected (Matt. 8:12). A Canaanite woman is commended for her faith in the Son of David, in contrast to the Jewish leaders (Matt. 15:1-28). The headstone of the corner, rejected by the Jewish builders, will be the foundation of the Gentile mission (Matt. 21:42), and 'He will rent the vineyard to other tenants, who will give him his share of the crop at harvest time... The kingdom of God will be taken away from you and given to a people who will produce its fruit' (Matt. 21:41-43). Finally, the Great Commission is worded in such a way as to lay emphasis on the need to go 'and make disciples of all nations' (28:19).

It is interesting that Paul, as the servant of the Servant of the Lord, justified his missionary expansion to the Gentiles to the folk in Pisidian Antioch with a quotation of Isaiah 49:6! (Acts 13:47).

'Jerusalem above' (49:8-26)

Isaiah is fond of using the Bible (what he had of it) to paint graphic pictures. Thus Jesus, when he comes, will be like Moses or Joshua, delivering the people of Israel out of bondage and into a promised land. Verses 9-10 especially use such images as a **'land'**, **'captives'**, a call to **'come out'** (exodus), **'barren hill'**, **'thirst'** and **'hunger'** — all of which remind us of Israel's wilderness experiences. The church of the New Testament is on its way to the 'promised land'. That is why the book of Hebrews so often uses imagery taken from the period of the exodus to exhort Christians to persevere (e.g. Heb. 3:8-10; 4:1-2, 8-11).

Four promises are given in verses 8-9 to God's Servant. Firstly, in reply to the Servant's questioning about the lack of results, God assures him of an answer. Secondly, God will supply him with whatever he needs to fulfil his mission. Thirdly, God will be with him, watching over him every step of the way; and, finally, the Servant is to be a **'covenant'** for the people.

This last idea has been stated before (42:6). The covenant made with Israel's forebears, including the promise of a Saviour and a renewed, right relationship with God, finds its fulfilment in the

Servant. The New Covenant, established by his death, will guarantee their salvation (Jer. 31:31-34; Heb. 8:6-13; 9:15). The liberated ones will be supplied with food (49:9-10), protection, guidance and water (49:10). The return envisaged here, though reminiscent of the exodus from Egypt and the restoration from Babylon in 586 B.C., transcends both. **'Aswan'** (49:12) is located in southern Egypt. This reading is supported by the Qumran Isaiah Scroll, but other manuscripts have *'Sinim'* — which could be a reference to the Chinese (the Chinese are *Sinai* in Greek).

The return includes the 'prisoners' dispersed throughout the world:

**'They will neither hunger nor thirst,
nor will the desert heat or the sun beat upon them.
He who has compassion on them will guide them
and lead them beside springs of water'**

(49:10).

The quotation of this verse in Revelation 7:16-17 demonstrates that heaven is in view here. The Jerusalem portrayed here is the 'Jerusalem above' (Gal. 4:25-27; cf. Isa. 54:1-3).

Reassurance in face of doubts (49:14-50:3)

But can all this be true? Doubt seems to creep into the mind of Isaiah's hearers. Several misgivings are voiced by the Lord's people to this message.

1. 'The Lord has abandoned us '

The deserted ruins of Zion are personified as a woman destitute of husband or children (49:14). God's reply is swift: she is not deserted, God cannot forget her (49:15-18). This is a promise that holds good for every Christian in trouble: God never forgets his own. The moving ceremony at cenotaphs around Britain on Remembrance Sunday commemorating the fallen from various wars, includes the line: 'Lest we forget...' We all too often forget, but God does not.

2. The church is so small and helpless

Again, the answer is wonderfully encouraging: the best is yet to come! In heaven she will be surrounded by a new family (49:19-20). The vision is of a great number, so many that there is not enough room to move: **'This place is too small for us; give us more space to live in'** (49:20). Zechariah painted a similar picture of a 'Jerusalem ... without walls because of the great number of men and livestock in it' (Zech. 2:4).

3. The enemy is so strong

Babylon is a 'tyrant' (49:24). But her future is grim: they shall be given over to internecine strife, civil war and cannibalism (cf. 9:20). Satan, our most powerful enemy, will suffer the same doom (Rev. 20:7-10). Behind this passage lies the truth that God is in control of history. God is the Creator (50:2-3). The importance of this truth is self-evident:

> **'Was my arm too short to ransom you?**
> **Do I lack the strength to rescue you?**
> **By a mere rebuke I dry up the sea,**
> **I turn rivers into a desert;**
> **their fish rot for lack of water**
> **and die of thirst'**
>
> (50:2).

Nothing is too great for God!

4. Is God willing to save his covenant people?

In contrast to Israel's character, there is no fickleness in God. The Lord asks the question: **'Where is your mother's certificate of divorce with which I sent her away?'** (50:1). A husband who divorced his wife was required to give his wife a certificate of divorce (Deut. 24:1,3; Matt. 19:7; Mark 10:4). No such document had been forthcoming from the Lord. It is true that Judah was living in a state of separation from God, but the blame for that lay with her, not with God. According to Jeremiah 3:8, the northern kingdom of Israel had indeed been given a certificate of divorce.

Nor has the Lord sold his own into slavery:

'Or to which of my creditors
did I sell you?
Because of your sins you were sold;
because of your transgressions your mother was
sent away'

(50:1).

The Babylonian captivity might suggest that God had given his children over to the Babylonians to pay off a long-standing debt (cf. Exod. 21:7; 2 Kings 4:1; Neh. 5:5). The fault for their captivity lay with themselves. They had brought it all upon themselves by their disobedience. 'Without holiness no one will see the Lord' (Heb. 12:14).

The third Servant Song (50:4-9)

Almost as a reflection on what he has been called upon to do, the Servant speaks once more (50:4-9). There are similarities in this passage to Psalms 22 and 69, two psalms which Jesus quoted on the cross. For this reason, some have referred to this third song as 'the Servant's Gethsemane'.

The first song displayed a patient acceptance by the Servant of his calling (42:1-7); the second song focused on the toil and frustration associated with it (49:4,7). Here, in the third song, the Servant faces the fury and acrimony of evil towards him.

Glimpses of Calvary

It is only a short step away from Calvary, and despite the difficulty and hostility, the Servant 'resolutely set[s] out for Jerusalem' (Luke 9:51; cf. Matt. 16:21). He is given **'an instructed tongue'** of wisdom to teach and preach (50:4). 'No one ever spoke the way this man does' (John 7:46). His truth **'sustains the weary'**. 'Come to me, all you who are weary and burdened, and I will give you rest' (Matt. 11:28). All his teaching is **'taught'** him by the Lord. 'The words I say to you are not just my own. Rather, it is the Father, living in me, who is doing his work' (John 14:10). His commitment is total;

he has **'not drawn back'**. 'Father, if you are willing, take this cup from me; yet not my will, but yours be done' (Luke 22:42). He refuses to retaliate:

'I offered my back to those who beat me,
my cheeks to those who pulled out my beard;
I did not hide my face
from mocking and spitting'

(50:6).

To Pilate, 'Jesus made no reply, not even to a single charge...' (Matt. 27:14). He protests his sinlessness: **'Who then will bring charges against me?'** Pilate would say of him: 'I have examined him in your presence and have found no basis for your charges against him' (Luke 23:14). Throughout it all, the Servant is conscious that

'It is the Sovereign Lord who helps me.
Who is he that will condemn me?
They will all wear out like a garment;
the moths will eat them up'

(50:9).

It is amazing just how clearly Isaiah portrays Jesus' suffering and humiliation as he approached the cross. This confidence in God's help which ends this third Servant Song is a confidence which Christians — those who are united to Jesus — sing of too (Rom. 8:31-39). Truly, nothing can sever the relationship God establishes with his children.

Gospel invitations and warnings

Having proclaimed this song, Isaiah now calls upon his audience to obey and fear God, by placing their trust in himself as God's servant:

'Who among you fears the Lord
and obeys the word of his servant?
Let him who walks in the dark,

> **who has no light,**
> **trust in the name of the Lord**
> **and rely on his God'**
>
> (50:10).

Jesus is the light of the world (John 8:12). It is important to see that Isaiah is speaking here to believers, those who 'fear the Lord', but who lack assurance. There are times when believers walk in the dark.

> 'Why do you say, O Jacob,
> and complain, O Israel,
> "My way is hidden from the Lord;
> my cause is disregarded by my God"?'
>
> (40:27).

They had been tried in the fire (48:10). 'Where is God?' they cried. It is a state which the Westminster divines predicted: 'True believers may have the assurance of their salvation divers ways shaken, diminished and intermitted ... by falling into some special sin which woundeth the conscience and grieveth the spirit; by sudden or vehement temptation; by God's withdrawing the light of his countenance, and suffering even such as fear him to walk in darkness and to have no light...'[2] Many of God's children in Babylon would testify that a combination of these factors had caused doubt to cloud their relationship with God.

Curing a loss in assurance of salvation comes by way of a prolonged gaze on the person and work of Christ, his teaching (50:4), his willing service (50:5) and his suffering (50:6). The inclusion of two 'Servant Songs' in chapters 49 and 50 is directed to that end, to encouraging faith in what he does on the sinner's behalf. Those who refuse to exercise faith in God's Servant will be punished for their sins. They who light fires (an ironic reference to those who have lit their own fires as sources of light) will **'lie down in torment'** (50:11). The warning is a fearful one and it will return with great force in the closing verse of the prophecy (66:24).

Isaiah tells us that he set himself to learn from this truth (50:4).

Summary

Chapter 49 began a new section in the prophecy, one which focused once more upon God's Servant, Jesus Christ. He is the Saviour, not just of the Jews, but also of the Gentiles. He pictures the returning exiles making their way back to Jerusalem, reliving the wilderness experiences of their forefathers. God has not abandoned them. But who is to be the new Moses? It is God's Servant, Jesus. Those who follow him are assured of a land in which to dwell; those who do not are doomed.

34.
Roots

Please read Isaiah 51:1 - 52:12

The previous chapter (50:10-11) ended by expressing concern for the spiritually depressed. Chapter 51 continues the application of a remedy. The two 'Servant Songs' (49:1-6; 50:4-9) are undoubtedly meant to encourage true believers, captive in Babylon, to 'turn their eyes upon Jesus'. Chapter 51 elaborates by a threefold use of either **'listen'** (51:1,4), or **'hear'** (51:7), all of which urge tired believers to exercise faith. The three sections of this passage (51:1-3,4-6,7-8) advocate in turn that believers look backwards, forwards and to the present, taking careful stock of the promises of God surrounding each perspective.

Looking back (51:1-3)

God encourages us first to remember what he has done in our past, rescuing us from our sin and assuring us of his covenant love and persevering presence.

Isaiah uses the figure of a piece of rock, shapeless and black, and the quarry from which it is taken — dirty, dark and dismal. The sculptor has fashioned it into a work of great beauty and design (51:1). 'Look back at your roots,' God urges. 'Think of what I have done for you.'

Taking Abraham, the father of the faithful, and his wife Sarah, as examples (51:2), Isaiah reminds his hearers how God took these two people and multiplied them. God blessed Abraham and his descendants. Out of one couple, God formed a great nation. No matter how small and difficult things may be, God can transform the situation beyond recognition. Nothing is too difficult for God. Faith does not operate in the realm of the possible. It begins where man's power ends.

In place of gloom and despair, God promises **'comfort'**, **'compassion'**, paradise (**'he will make her deserts like Eden'**) and **'joy'** (51:3). The desert-like experience of Babylon will give way to restored paradise. The use of a garden ('Eden') as a symbol of what God intends for his church is something which we have seen already in 35:1-2. When the dying thief asked to be remembered by Jesus, he was promised the experience of 'paradise' that day (Luke 23:43). The word Jesus used was originally a Persian word, taken over into Greek, and symbolizing a place of beauty and delight. The Greek Old Testament (the Septuagint) used the word to translate the Garden of Eden in Genesis 2:8. Paul momentarily experienced it (2 Cor. 12:4), and the last book of the Bible takes up the word again, holding out the prospect of heaven (Rev. 2:7).

Looking forwards (51:4-6)

Secondly, God urges us to look forward to the consummation. For Isaiah's hearers the prospect of Christ's coming lay ahead: **'My righteousness draws near speedily, my salvation is on the way...'** (51:5). The injustices and strife, which are part of a fallen world, will then be removed. The focus goes far beyond Jesus' first coming to the consummation of the world, when **'The heavens will vanish like smoke, the earth will wear out like a garment and its inhabitants die like flies...'** (51:6; cf. 24:4; 34:4). What God has begun in the work of salvation, which finds its fulfilment in Jesus Christ, cannot be undone: **'My salvation will last for ever.'**

Looking at the present (51:7-8)

Having looked backwards and forwards, God then urges us to look at the present, reassessing the difficulties in the light of past and future (51:7-8). However hostile present circumstances may be, there will come a day when they will come to nothing.

It is interesting to note that drawing comfort from looking backwards, forwards and to the present is what the Lord's Supper is all about: looking back to the cross ('This do in remembrance of me'), looking forwards to the Second Coming ('till he comes'), and drawing fresh supplies of grace from present communion with Christ (1 Cor. 11:26).

Wake up! (51:9-11)

Verses 9-11 form a conclusion to this first section of the chapter. Isaiah now calls upon God to **'awake!'** (51:9). The call will come again (51:17, where it is a call to Jerusalem, and 52:1, which is a call to Zion). Isaiah is not implying that God is asleep; rather, his call is for God's strength to show itself. The call is quickly answered in verse 12: **'I, even I, am he...'** The call is for another exodus, on a grander scale than the first deliverance of God's children from Egypt, here symbolized by the word **'Rahab'** (cf. 30:7).

When God judged Egypt, he also humbled her gods (Exod. 12:12; Num. 33:4). To describe this deliverance, Scripture resorts to the figure of slaying a dragon: **'Was it not you who ... pierced that monster through?'** (51:9; cf. the use of 'Leviathan' and imagery of sea-monsters in 27:1; Ps. 74:12-14; 104:25; Ezek. 29:3-6; 32:2-10). Water-beasts figured largely in the Babylonian mythology of creation. Obviously, Bible writers were not averse to using mythological figures to underline their message. Their use in this way does not imply that Isaiah believed in their actual existence. It is simply a graphic way of saying, 'It is the Lord alone who can destroy the chaos-powers you believe in. He alone is the God of creation.'[1]

The present reality includes the fact that the God who made this world (51:12) is a God who has entered into a covenant relationship with his people: **'I am the Lord your God ... You are my people'** (51:15,16). The formation of Zion — by which he means his church eventually to triumph in heaven — is God's greatest triumph. This is why those who have placed their trust in Jesus Christ can feel secure; they are covered with the shadow of God's hand (51:16). The thought is captured by Fanny Crosby in her hymn, 'A Wonderful Saviour':

A wonderful Saviour is Jesus my Lord,
A wonderful Saviour to me,
He hideth my soul in the cleft of the rock,
Where rivers of pleasure I see.

He hideth my soul in the cleft of the rock
That shadows a dry, thirsty land;
He hideth my life in the depths of his love,
And covers me there with his hand.

A wonderful Saviour is Jesus my Lord,
He taketh my burden away
He holdeth me up, and I shall not be moved,
He giveth me strength as my day.

With numberless blessings each moment he crowns
And filled with a fulness divine,
I sing in my rapture, Oh, glory to God
For such a Redeemer as mine!

When clothed in his brightness, transported I rise
To meet him in clouds of the sky,
His perfect salvation, his wonderful love,
I'll shout with the millions on high.

Wake up, Jerusalem! (51:17-23)

The call to **'awake'** is this time directed to Jerusalem. She is in
danger, having **'drunk from the hand of the Lord the cup of his
wrath'** (51:17). Experiencing God's anger is often compared to
being drunk (29:9; 63:6; Jer. 25:15-16; Ezek. 23:32-34; Zech. 12:2).
Jerusalem has grown old with no relatives to take care of her; her
own children have forsaken her (51:18). The streets of Jerusalem are
littered with the bodies of the dying (51:20). There is no one to offer
a word of comfort in her time of trouble. 'Who will have pity on you,
O Jerusalem? Who will mourn for you? Who will stop to ask how
you are?' (Jer. 15:5). Her future is terrible; handed over to her

tormentors, she will be walked over like one of the side streets (51:23). This last picture is something Jeremiah would take up (Lam. 2:11,12,19,21).

The church in Isaiah's time was as close to death as possible, but nevertheless God could, and would, revive her. Revival is, after all, a resurrection of the church from a state of death. Calvin remarks that 'The church, though afflicted and tossed in various ways, will nevertheless be set up again, so as to regain her full vigour. By the word "Awake" he recalls her, as it were, from death and the grave; as if he had said, that no ruins shall be so dismal, no desolations shall be so horrible, as to be capable of hindering God effecting this restoration.'[2]

Another call to wake up (52:1-6)

Chapter 52 begins with a repetition of the cry to awake. God throws back at Israel her own cry (cf. 51:9), repeating the same words. Zion, God's church, is in danger. She is drunk with her sins. Foreigners (the **'uncircumcised'**) are at present occupying the streets of Jerusalem. But all of this will change (52:1). She is to arise and sit up in a dignified and royal manner (52:2). Zion will be redeemed; God has promised it (52:3). They had not been sold for money; Babylon had taken Jerusalem. God owes no one anything in Zion's redemption (52:3). He is a debtor to no one (cf. 50:1). God's saving work is to glorify his own name:

> **'Therefore my people will know my name;**
> **therefore in that day they will know**
> **that it is I who foretold it.**
> **Yes, it is I'**

(52:6).

Peter uses the same analogy: 'For you know that it was not with perishable things such as silver or gold that you were redeemed from the empty way of life handed down to you from your forefathers, but with the precious blood of Christ, a lamb without blemish or defect' (1 Peter 1:18-19; cf. Rom. 3:24).

Mounting excitement (52:7-12)

We are moving inexorably towards the fourth 'Servant Song' (52:13 - 53:12) and the most vivid of all the portrayals of Christ in Isaiah. This is the good news which makes possible Jerusalem's redemption and glorious future. The excitement mounts as Isaiah depicts the coming of the messenger (52:7), the watchmen who see him coming (52:8) and the coming of the Lord himself (52:8-10).

As I write these lines, television reporters in Baghdad city are conveying a tragic event of war that occurred only a few hours ago. The messenger in Isaiah's prophecy too is depicted as coming from a battle. In his day, messengers ran — at great peril to their lives — from the scene of battle to convey the news (cf. 2 Sam. 18:26). If they brought bad news, they were sometimes killed! In this case, the messenger is bringing news of a famous victory, the downfall of Babylon and the deliverance of Zion. The very feet of these messengers are regarded as beautiful (52:7), a figure which Paul uses in Romans 10:15.

The good tidings of the preacher, the peace and salvation which he publishes, are summarized in this way: 'Your God reigns!' (52:7; cf. Ps. 96:10). Cotton Mather, who ministered in New England 300 years ago, said, 'The great design...of a Christian preacher [is] to restore the throne and dominion of God in the souls of men.' God's sovereign rule is something that had impressed itself upon Isaiah the day he visited the temple so many years ago (ch. 6).

The watchmen (52:8) are those in Jerusalem who see the messengers coming from a distance, and excitedly begin to call the inhabitants to expect their coming. The very fabric of the city is urged to rejoice and sing. They are to leave Babylon with dignity, taking with them nothing that is sinful (52:11). The reason is because the Lord himself is returning to the city with his people. He goes before them (52:12). Perhaps Ezra's dignified leadership is in mind when he led a procession of God's people back to Jerusalem (Ezra 7:1-10). But the picture is once more of heaven, rather than the sixth century B.C. 'Then I heard another voice from heaven say: "Come out of her, my people, so that you will not share in her sins, so that you will not receive any of her plagues..."' (Rev. 18:4).

Summary

By way of a threefold use of either **'listen'** or **'hear'** Isaiah has urged tired, weary pilgrims to pay attention to what he has to say. These are words of 'comfort', after all (40:1). The way of salvation is being made clear and believers should take note of it. 'Therefore ... let us throw off everything that hinders and the sin that so easily entangles, and let us run with perseverance the race marked out for us. Let us fix our eyes on Jesus, the author and perfecter of our faith, who for the joy set before him endured the cross, scorning its shame, and sat down at the right hand of the throne of God' (Heb. 12:1-2). It is that 'cross' that now comes sharply into focus in the next section.

35.
Calvary

Please read Isaiah 52:13-53:12

In the preceding chapters, Isaiah has spoken of Cyrus as Israel's deliverer from Babylonian captivity. But the three Servant Songs so far considered (42:1-7; 49:1-6; 50:4-9), interspersed as they have been with the prophecies of Cyrus (41:2-3,25-29; 44:24-28; 45:3,13; 46:11; 48:14-15), have reminded us that Isaiah has a greater Deliverer in mind. The work which Cyrus is raised up to do is a shadow of the work which Christ will do. The fourth Servant Song (52:13 - 53:12) now engages in the longest and most specific representation of the Deliverer to come. There is nothing specifically new in this song: it elaborates upon what has already been stated in the earlier songs.

There are certain passages in the Bible, particularly in Isaiah, that were of great importance to Jesus. One writer has said, 'No other passage from the Old Testament was as important to the church as Isaiah 53.'[1] Jesus himself quoted one particular verse (53:12) and applied it to himself. 'It is written: "And he was numbered with the transgressors." And I tell you that this must be fulfilled in me,' he said (Luke 22:37). On other occasions, when he declared that he 'must suffer many things' and that he had 'not come to be served, but to serve, and to give his life as a ransom for many' (Mark 8:31; 10:45), he also seems to have been alluding to Isaiah 53.

Of great significance too, is the fact that the major contributors to the New Testament refer to at least eight different verses from Isaiah 53. Verse 1 is quoted by John and applied to Jesus (John 12:38); verse 4 is cited by Matthew in relation to Jesus' healing

ministry (Matt. 8:17); and verses 5,6,9 and 11 are picked up by Peter
(1 Peter 2:22-25). Of special interest is the use that Philip made of
this passage in his evangelistic ministry to the Ethiopian eunuch.
Reading this very passage in his chariot, Philip was prompted to
share with him 'the good news about Jesus' (Acts 8:30-35). Others
have suggested that the various statements in the New Testament to
the effect that Jesus would be 'rejected', and 'taken away' are taken
from Isaiah 53.[2] Also, his being 'buried' like a criminal without any
preparatory anointing, the parable of the stronger man who 'divides
up the spoils', his silence before the judges, his intercession for the
transgressors and his laying down his life for others — all these are
rooted in Isaiah 53.[3]

According to John Stott, 'Every verse of the chapter except verse
2 ... is applied to Jesus in the New Testament, some verses several
times. Indeed, there is good evidence that [Jesus'] whole public
career, from his baptism through his ministry, sufferings and death
to his resurrection and ascension, is seen as a fulfilment of the
pattern foretold in Isaiah 53.'[4]

So clear is Isaiah 53 that current Jewish reactions to this passage
are most interesting. A missionary, working for Christian Witness
to Israel in Manchester, distributed a tract which was in effect no
more than a direct quotation of Isaiah 53 printed in Hebrew, Yiddish
and English. Local Jewish authorities were incensed by it; letters
written to the local paper suggested its author was mentally ill!

There are several ways of looking at this song. For example, the
song can be seen as elucidating the *threefold office* of Christ:
Prophet (52:15), Priest (53:1-9) and King (53:10-12). Again, the
song can be seen as giving evidence for the *active and passive
obedience* of God's servant: his obedience to every facet of the law
and his willingness to become a guilt offering. Another interesting
possibility is to divide the song around the *three states* of Christ: his
pre-existence (52:13), his humiliation (52:14 -53:10) and his exaltation (53:11-12).

We may also note the careful construction of the song: five
stanzas of three verses each, beginning and ending with the Servant's exaltation; set within this is a detailed description of the
Saviour's rejection (stanzas two and four). At the very centre is a
stanza which focuses specifically upon the atoning work of Christ.

Stanza 1: A stumbling-block (52:13-15)

Isaiah first lays stress on the *exaltation* of the Servant. He is to rise, be lifted up and elevated to a very high position (52:13). Some have suggested that this implies three separate stages in Jesus' exaltation, but this is unlikely. All three verbs, **'raised'**, **'lifted up'** and **'exalted'** emphasize the degree of his exaltation.[5] It is not that he will *become* exalted; he is already exalted (cf. 6:1-5; 9:2-7; 11:1; 42:1-7; 49:3). We have here an assertion of the pre-existent glory of the Saviour, prior to his incarnation.

The Servant's *humiliation* is now set forth in verses 14-15. The translation of these verses is difficult, but the point seems to be a stress on the contrast between the **'many'** who are ranged against him (52:14), and the **'many'** who will eventually be convicted and enlightened (52:15).

The suggestion that the Saviour should suffer in the way Jesus did was appalling to the Jews (cf. 1 Cor. 1:23). The use of the word **'disfigured'** (52:15), the same one which describes a 'blemished animal' that may not be used in sacrifice (cf. Mal. 1:14), underlines the horror. They treated Christ as they treated no other man. He was disfigured and marred to such an extent that he hardly seemed human, let alone a deliverer, or 'cleanser'.

'Sprinkling' (52:15) has Old Testament roots relating to cleansing rituals (Lev. 14:7; Num. 8:7; 19:18-19). There may also be allusions here to the fact that Old Testament prophecies of the Messiah included the expectation that baptism would be part of his ministry. The question put to John the Baptist by the Pharisees as to his identity was due to the fact that they expected Jesus to come baptizing (John 1:25). Baptism is a symbolic cleansing, a matter which seems out of keeping with such a person as the disfigured Servant.

They are appalled by three things: first, the disfigured nature of the Servant; second, the fact that he should provide cleansing; and thirdly, that many nations would be cleansed. Even the kings are dumbfounded because of what they see and perceive.[6] Once more, the worldwide scope of Jesus' work is underlined. The apostle Paul, describing his ambition to preach in unknown regions of the world, took verse 15 as his motivation (Rom. 15:21).

Stanza 2: Rejected (53:1-3)

When we think of the sufferings of Christ (he was **'familiar with suffering'**, 53:3), we tend to think immediately of his physical sufferings: the crown of thorns forced into his scalp, or the nails hammered into his hands and feet. But he suffered in other ways also: rejection, disappointment, loneliness. These are painful too. This second stanza makes plain that when Jesus comes, he will identify with these painful experiences, too. He was 'tempted in every way' (Heb. 4:15).

As far as his human nature was concerned, Jesus came from humble origins. Most regarded him as simply the son of a carpenter from Nazareth, a place from which they did not expect anything to emerge of any significance (John 1:46). Nor was he, necessarily, the most attractive man on earth.

> **'He had no beauty or majesty to attract us to him,**
> **nothing in his appearance that we should desire him.**
> **He was despised and rejected by men,**
> **a man of sorrows, and familiar with suffering'**
>
> (53:2-3).

To look at, he appeared to be an ordinary Jewish young man. The people of Palestine did not immediately see in him anything different from anyone else. He looked to most people very ordinary.

'Suffering' was an important part of Jesus' ministry (53:3). The figure who emerges from these Servant Songs is sometimes referred to as 'the suffering Servant of God'. But a deliverer who would free the Jewish people from oppression and tyranny seemed incompatible with an ordinary man given over to suffering. This 'Messiah' seemed more of a victim than a conqueror; the cross was, after all, a symbol of rejection and curse (cf. Gal. 3:13; Deut. 21:23). Consequently, he was 'despised and rejected'.

Stanza 3: The heart of the song (53:4-6)

Verses 4-6 form the very centre-piece of this song. They also speak most clearly of the atoning work of the Servant on behalf of sinners.

Here, as perhaps nowhere else in the Old Testament, we see Calvary most plainly disclosed.

The pain and rejection experienced by the Servant are not his own but *ours*. The entire cause of his suffering lies in the ideas of substitution and satisfaction:

> 'He took up *our* infirmities[7]
>   and carried *our* sorrows,
> ... he was pierced for *our* transgressions,
>   he was crushed for *our* iniquities;
> the punishment that brought *us* peace was upon
>   him,
>   and by his wounds *we* are healed.
> *We* all, like sheep, have gone astray,
>   each of *us* has turned to his own way;
> and the Lord has laid on him the iniquity of *us* all'
>
> (53:4-6).

The notion of substitution is that one person takes the place of another, especially in order to bear pain and so to save the other from it. The idea finds early approval in the Bible. Abraham 'sacrificed ... instead of his son' the ram which God provided (Gen. 22:13). Moses laid down that, in the case of an unsolved murder, the town's elders should first declare their own innocence and then sacrifice a heifer in place of the unknown murderer (Deut. 21:1-9). The daily, weekly, monthly and annual offerings of biblical Old Testament worship were all based on this principle (cf. **'guilt offering'**, 53:10). Although there were variations, depending upon the sacrifice, the basic ceremony was identical. The worshipper brought the offering, laid his hands on it and killed it. The priest then applied the blood, burnt some of the flesh, and arranged for the consumption of what was left of it. The laying of hands on the victim's head was 'a symbolic transferral of the sins of the worshipper to the animal'.[8] Most clearly of all, the Old Testament sacrifices of the Passover (Exod. 11-13) and the scapegoat (Lev. 16) underlined the principle of substitution by the shedding of blood (Lev. 17:11). Thus, Isaiah's depiction of the Saviour-Servant in substitutionary terms, involving the shedding of blood (cf. **'wounds'**, 53:5) was not new.

The statement that he was **'stricken by God, smitten by him and afflicted'** (53:4) leads into the idea of satisfaction, for it raises the question why the Servant should be punished. The answer that Scripture provides is that sin (in this case ours, *not* the Servant's) cannot go unpunished. The justice of God demands that sin meet its deserved penalty: either in us or else in a substitute. It is the good news of the gospel that such a substitute is provided for us in Jesus Christ. The passage finds its fulfilment in the heart-rending cry of dereliction from the cross: 'About the ninth hour Jesus cried out in a loud voice, "My God, my God, why have you forsaken me?"' (Matt. 27:46).

> Jehovah lifted up his rod;
> O Christ, it fell on thee!
> Thou wast sore stricken of thy God;
> There's not one stroke for me.

It is this very idea of 'substitution through satisfaction' that lies behind the use of the New Testament word translated 'propitiation' in some versions of the English Bible (cf. 1 John 2:2, AV).

Stanza 4: The silent lamb (53:7-9)

Like the second stanza, this one tells of the Servant's sufferings, evoking his trial, death and burial. The mention of his burial in a rich man's tomb (53:9; cf. Matt: 27:57,60) is so precise that Bible critics insist that it cannot possibly be genuine! Despite the violence of his trial and death — **'oppressed', 'afflicted', 'slaughter', 'cut off from the land of the living'** — it is his silence that elicits the greater astonishment. 'When they hurled their insults at him, he did not retaliate; when he suffered, he made no threats. Instead, he entrusted himself to him who judges justly. He himself bore our sins in his body on the tree, so that we might die to sins and live for righteousness; by his wounds you have been healed' (1 Peter 2:23-24).

Stanza 5: Crowned with glory and honour (53:10-12)

Despite his own personal innocence, Christ was treated as a guilty man: **'Yet it was the Lord's will to crush him and cause him to suffer ... the Lord makes his life a guilt offering...'** (53:10).

Heaven itself accused Jesus of sins in those terrible hours on the cross: lusting and lying, cheating and coveting, destruction and deceit. In Luke chapter 23 there are five confessions of Jesus' total innocence (Luke 23:4,14,22,41,47), yet he was crucified as a common criminal. Isaiah's fourth Servant song tells us plainly that this is God's doing. Jesus was 'handed over' (cf. Matt. 20:19; 26:15; 27:2,18,26). It pleased the Lord to bruise his Son and put him to grief (53:10). This is what theologians have called 'Christ's passive obedience'; his obedience took the form of a willing acceptance of the will of the Lord. And he did so for sinners like you and me!

We cannot avoid the question: 'For whom did Christ die?' Isaiah depicts the Servant giving his life for **'the transgression of my people'** (53:8), and later on behalf of **'many'** (53:11 cf. 52:15). 'His people participate in the spoils of his victory,' comments Young.[9] It is not beyond the limits of exegesis at this point to conclude that the saving work of the Servant is undertaken directly on behalf of God's covenant people *and for them alone*.

Since substitution (as we have already noticed in commenting on verses 4-6 above) is the basic principle of atonement, it is consistent with the prophet's teaching to understand the saving work of the Servant as being altogther effective in that which it sets out to accomplish. Indeed, it is inconceivable — here in Isaiah 53, or elsewhere in the biblical revelation — to sustain an understanding of the redemptive process which in some way is rendered totally ineffective by the refusal of some to accept it.

The **'us'**, **'we'** and **'our'** which we noticed in verses 5-6 are clearly meant to signify believers: those who know that they are saved and therefore chosen by God. The prophet's way of thinking is thoroughly particularistic: he envisages a sovereign love saving, through a bona fide offer of the Servant to all mankind, those for whom, specifically and effectively, the Servant substitutes himself on the cross. They are, to be sure, many. At the same time, they are known to God beforehand through his electing love and specific covenant commitment. The thought is summarized by Jesus' words in John 10:14-15: 'I am the good shepherd; I know my sheep and my sheep know me — just as the Father knows me and I know the Father — and I lay down my life for the sheep' (John 10:14-15).

Other aspects of Christ's saving work are now mentioned: justification of many sinners (53:11), intercession on their behalf (53:12) and victory! The song concludes in triumph for the Servant.

He conquers the forces of darkness. The guilt of sin that bars fellowship with God is removed by the Servant's vicarious, substitutionary death on behalf of his people.

> **'Therefore I will give him a portion among the great,**
> **and he will divide the spoils with the strong,**
> **because he poured out his life unto death,**
> **and was numbered with the transgressors'**
> (53:12; cf. Col. 2:15; Heb. 2:14).

He conquers death (1 Cor. 15:26). This victory is achieved by his expiation of sin. 'His cross was the instrument which, in the lowest ebb of his human strength, he wielded with Almightiness, through the Eternal Spirit, as the weapon of his warfare and the means of his victory.'[10]

Summary

God's Servant would deliver his people from the bondage and misery of their sins by becoming their substitute. He would take the place of the sinner, taking the punishment that sin deserves. Isaiah 53 foretold that the iniquities of sinful men should be put away by the death of a righteous Servant of God in their stead. The background is that of the Old Testament sacrificial system, having at its heart the principle that atonement for sin can be made only by the death of a perfect substitute for the sinner. God's righteous Servant, says Isaiah, would be made an offering for sin (53:10-12). But where can such a victim be found? None qualified apart from the sinless Son of God.

36.
The covenant of peace

Please read Isaiah 54 and 55

One of the most characteristic phrases that Paul uses in the New Testament is 'in Christ Jesus' (1 Cor. 1:2; Eph. 1:1; Phil. 1:1; cf. Col. 1:2; 1 Thess. 1:1; 2 Thess. 1:1). Parallel with this is another emphasis: Christ is 'in' the believer (Rom. 8:10; Gal. 2:20; Col. 1:27). Together, these two concepts indicate the closeness of the bond between Christ and his people. According to the apostle, this truth — union with Christ — is something which God has made known to us by revelation: 'God has chosen to make known ... the glorious riches of this mystery, which is Christ in you, the hope of glory' (Col. 1:27). But where, in God's revelation, has Paul seen this truth? The answer lies, partly, in Isaiah 54.

The idea of union and communion lies at the heart of the Old Testament's understanding of God's relationship with his people. It is expressed by means of four word-pictures: the relationship of a father to his son (Deut. 1:29-31; Ps. 103:13-18); that of a master to a servant (1 Sam. 12:24); that of a shepherd to his sheep (Ps. 23); and that of a husband to his wife (54:5-8; Jer. 31:32).[1] It is the latter that Isaiah uses in this chapter: **'Your Maker is your husband'** (54:5). The God of Israel proves a faithful partner despite Israel's unfaithfulness.

Following the description of Calvary in Isaiah 53, in chapter 54 God, as the faithful Husband, assures future expansion to his unfaithful wife, his Old Testament church. The optimism of this chapter is built on the efficacy of the Servant's work in the previous chapter (53:10-12). Luther saw it this way: 'Even as in the preceding chapter the prophet had described Christ as the head of the kingdom, so here his body, that is the church, is described, as being oppressed, unfruitful and forsaken. But he comforts her and promises her great offspring.'[2]

Promises, promises

The chapter opens with a call to a **'barren woman'** to burst into song (54:1). The exile in Babylon reduced Israel considerably. Her condition was a wretched one; Isaiah describes it in terms of barrenness — a condition which incurred disgrace in the Old Testament (see 4:1). In that way, Israel's condition in the sixth century B.C. was similar to that of Abraham's wife, Sarah.

It is this picture of barrenness (and the allusion to Sarah) that causes the apostle Paul to cite this passage in Galatians 4:26-27. According to the apostle, there are two covenants and two Jerusalems. Since this chapter specifically mentions a covenant, **'the covenant of peace'** (54:10), this point needs some elaboration.

Abraham's two sons, Isaac and Ishmael, were to be symbolic of the way of faith and the way of unbelief. Ishmael, the son of the slave woman Hagar, represented Abraham's (and Sarah's) unbelief in God's promise of a son (see Gen. 16). The true son of promise was Isaac, born to Sarah in Abraham's ninety-ninth year (Gen. 21). Hagar and Sarah thus represented, by way of a convenient allegory, the two conditions of unbelief and faith respectively. The son of Hagar was the son of a slave — and thereby a slave himself. As such, 'born in the ordinary way' (Gal. 4:23), he represents the bondage of unbelief and the misery of sin. Abraham's involvement with Hagar was an attempt to gain the blessings of God by means of human initiative and effort. The whole affair was symbolic of a 'works' theology. Thus Hagar represents Mount Sinai and the earthly Jerusalem (Gal. 4:25). Isaac, on the other hand, 'born as the result of a promise' (Gal. 4:23), is symbolic of justification by faith alone. The birth of Isaac is a testimony to the fact that, though we may have to wait patiently for it, God's promise is sure.

It was precisely this faith — a faith which believes that great things are possible despite what outward circumstances may dictate — that Israel needed during its exile in Babylon. The time is coming, the prophet assures them, when God's Old Testament church will give birth to a great multitude. Revival is always a cause for singing!

The covenant with Abraham promised not only one son, Isaac, but an entire nation! (Gen. 12:2-3). We know that ultimately, this promise applies to the church (Gal. 6:16). It is in this sense that Isaiah reiterates it here:

> **'Enlarge the place of your tent,**
> > **stretch your tent curtains wide,**
> > **do not hold back;**
> **lengthen your cords,**
> > **strengthen your stakes.**
> **For you will spread out to the right and to the left;**
> > **your descendants will dispossess nations**
> > **and settle in their desolate cities'**

(54:2-3; cf. 49:19-20).

One has only to think of the way the church spread throughout Asia Minor in the decades following Pentecost to see the initial fulfilment of this prophecy.

Everything in Israel's experience pointed to the contrary. They were in fear of **'shame'**, **'disgrace'** and **'widowhood'** (54:4).The experience of Babylon was one of abandonment (54:7). The anger of God was intense: **'In a surge of anger I hid my face from you for a moment'** (54:8). There is the whiff of **'terror'** about (54:14). These were difficult and tense times brought about by Israel's sinful condition. It appeared as though Israel's Husband-Redeemer had issued a bill of divorce (cf. 50:1). But it never came to that. Along with the chastisement are words assuring Israel of his love:

> **'...The Lord Almighty...**
> **the Holy One of Israel is your Redeemer...**
> **The Lord will call you back...**
> **...with deep compassion I will bring you back...**
> **...with everlasting kindness**
> > **I will have compassion on you'**

(54:5-8).

Isaiah is fond of speaking about the compassion of God (30:18; 49:10,13; 51:3; 54:8,10; 60:10; 63:7).

The sign of the rainbow

The comparison with the days of Noah is a reference to God's promise never again to pour out his wrath upon mankind in the way he did at the time of the flood. The experience in Babylon may have appeared to signal a change in God's promise; but it was not so (54:9-10).

Two features of God's promise are singled out: his **'unfailing love'** and his **'covenant of peace'** (54:10). God may withdraw the light of his countenance for a while, but he will not abandon his church. The whole message of the Bible is shaped around God's coming to us in covenant love. The history of Israel had been an outworking of this promise from the first tangible promise in the Garden of Eden (Gen. 3:15). That is why Noah and his family had been saved. God had remembered his covenant (Gen. 6:18). Some have even suggested that the rainbow, shaped the way it is, is God's 'bow of war' thrown into the sky as a promise that he will keep his word. It is interesting that many generations later, the apostle John described the throne in heaven as having 'a rainbow resembling an emerald' above it (Rev. 4:3). God remembers his covenant! (Gen. 9:12-17).

Gems

The tent of verse 2 now gives way to the magnificent picture of Jerusalem studded with brilliant gems of **'turquoise', 'sapphires', 'rubies', 'sparkling jewels'** and **'precious stones'** (54:11-12). The picture is of the church's glory in heaven, and is one which the apostle John painted even more vividly: 'And he carried me away in the Spirit to a mountain great and high, and showed me the Holy City, Jerusalem, coming down out of heaven from God. It shone with the glory of God, and its brilliance was like that of a very precious jewel, like a jasper, clear as crystal ... The wall was made of jasper, and the city of pure gold, as pure as glass. The foundations of the city walls were decorated with every kind of precious stone. The first foundation was jasper, the second sapphire, the third chalcedony, the fourth emerald, the fifth sardonyx, the sixth carnelian, the seventh chrysolite, the eighth beryl, the ninth topaz, the tenth chrysoprase, the eleventh jacinth, and the twelfth amethyst. The twelve gates were twelve pearls, each gate made of a single pearl. The great street of the city was of pure gold, like transparent glass' (Rev. 21:10,18-21).

No matter how battle-weary the church militant may be, the church-triumphant is glorious!

The blacksmith

The church is composed of those **'taught by the Lord'** (54:13), and reckoned to be 'righteous' (54:14) through faith in the finished work of the suffering Servant of Isaiah 53. They have no need to fear the severing of their relationship with the Redeemer. They are 'in Christ' and nothing can undo that relationship (Rom. 8:28-39). No charges can be laid to the account of those whose trust is in Christ. 'Who will bring any charge against those whom God has chosen? It is God who justifies. Who is he that condemns?' (Rom. 8:33-34).

God is a **'blacksmith'** forging weapons to undo the attacker's aggression (54:16-17). Already the fires are hot and the swords are forged. **'No weapon forged against you will prevail'** is part of the truth that God's children need to hear the most in times like these (54:17). The only other occasion on which Isaiah refers to a blacksmith is in chapter 44. There the blacksmith is making gods (44:12), whereas here the blacksmith *is* God, forging weapons to destroy the false gods.

Darius thought he had fed Daniel to the lions. He expected, after a sleepless night, to come in the morning to a tomb (Dan. 6:18-19). To the question: 'Has your God ... been able to rescue you from the lions?' (Dan. 6:20), came the resounding 'Yes!' from God's servant. His faith had shut the lions' mouths! The kingdom of God cannot be shaken (Heb. 12:28). Luther's dynamic Reformation hymn contains the same triumphant thought in these lines:

And though this world, with devils filled,
Should threaten to undo us,
We will not fear, for God hath willed
His truth to triumph through us.

The Prince of Darkness grim,
We tremble not for him;
His rage we can endure,
For lo, his doom is sure,
One little word shall fell him.[3]

The gospel call (55:1-13)

The growing church of Isaiah 54 is followed by the gospel call of Isaiah 55. It is an urgent and passionate call to the lost. Isaiah 55 is God's own gospel sermon: the entire chapter is in the first person singular.

The offer is universal and sincere, directed to those who are hopeless:

> **'Come, all you who are thirsty,**
> **come to the waters;**
> **and you who have no money,**
> **come, buy and eat!**
> **Come, buy wine and milk**
> **without money and without cost'**
> **Why spend money on what is not bread,**
> **and your labour on what does not satisfy?**
> **Listen, listen to me, and eat what is good,**
> **and your soul will delight in the richest of fare'**
>
> (55:1-2).

It immediately reminds us of a similar expression used by Jesus in his encounter with the Samaritan woman at Jacob's well in Sychar. 'Everyone who drinks this water,' he said, 'will be thirsty again, but whoever drinks the water I give him will never thirst. Indeed, the water I give him will become in him a spring of water welling up to eternal life' (John 4:13-14).

Relieving hunger by supplying bread reminds us of Jesus' words at the occasion of the feeding of the 5,000: 'I am the bread of life ... But here is the bread that comes down from heaven, which a man may eat and not die. I am the living bread that came down from heaven. If anyone eats of this bread, he will live for ever. This bread

is my flesh, which I will give for the life of the world' (John 6:48-
51).

Three matters are worth noting.

1. The recipients of the call are needy

They have no money. Jesus' parable of the great banquet ends with
an invitation to 'Go out quickly into the streets and alleys of the town
and bring in the poor, the crippled, the blind and the lame' (Luke
14:21). Sinners have nothing with which to bargain with God for
their salvation. They are spiritually dead (Eph. 2:1).

2. God genuinely desires the salvation of all sinners

It is true that Isaiah has spoken of God's elective purposes (e.g.
43:1,20). Nevertheless, Isaiah began this prophecy with God's
invitation to sinners:

> '"Come now, let us reason together,"'
>   says the Lord.
> '"Though your sins are like scarlet,
>   they shall be as white as snow;
> though they are red as crimson,
>   they shall be like wool"'

(1:18).

God desires the salvation of all. 'Turn to me and be saved, all you
ends of the earth; for I am God, and there is no other' (45:22). 'Do
I take any pleasure in the death of the wicked? declares the
Sovereign Lord. Rather, am I not pleased when they turn from their
ways and live?' (Ezek. 18:23).

The will of God in the matter of the call, invitation, appeal and
command of the gospel is that all should turn to him and be saved.
Obviously, God has not *decreed* that all will be saved. Hell is not
empty. But he has made it clearly known that he *desires* the salvation
of all.

Little wonder that we are told in this chapter that there is a
mystery in understanding God (55:8-9). God 'expresses an ardent
desire for the fulfilment of certain things which he has not decreed

in his inscrutable counsel to come to pass ... a will to the realization of what he has not brought to pass, a pleasure towards that which he has not been pleased to decree. This is indeed mysterious...'⁴

3. Salvation is by grace alone

The needy are invited to purchase without money. *Sola Gratia*, by grace alone, was one of the watchwords of the Reformation. As such it was a call to go 'back to the Bible' and its clear statement that sinners 'are justified freely by his grace through the redemption that came by Christ Jesus ... apart from observing the law' (Rom. 3:24,28).

A necessary precondition

There are those who believe that salvation is obtainable no matter what work, or lack of work, may accompany it. Scripture, while insisting that works play no part in the obtaining of salvation, equally insists that works must accompany it. Paul's statement that 'God credits righteousness apart from works' (Rom. 4:6) is balanced by James' insistence that 'Faith by itself, if it is not accompanied by action, is dead' (James 2:17). Isaiah underlines this by suggesting that the insistence upon repentance is something which shows how different God's way of salvation is from that of man. 'The fact that God's thoughts are higher than ours (55:8-9) is not a statement about logic but about the way of salvation itself. Man's thoughts are to be brought into conformity with God's thoughts not by abandoning logic but by repentance.'⁵ Repentance, both negative ('forsake') and positive ('return'), must accompany salvation:

> '**Let the wicked forsake his way**
> **and the evil man his thoughts.**
> **Let him turn to the Lord, and he will have mercy on him,**
> **and to our God, for he will freely pardon**'
>
> (55:7).

'Unless you repent, you too will all perish' (Luke 13:5).

Muddled thinking

Ever since the seventeenth century the Western world has been
busily shrinking God to fit the minds of men. Deists taught that God
is remote from the world, so remote that we can effectively forget
all about him. In the eighteenth century Immanuel Kant suggested,
more or less, that it was confused and naive to think that God, if he
exists, communicates with men. Hence the Bible cannot be God's
Word. God was suitably silenced. The nineteenth century continued
the shrinking of God, arguing that God is no more than the highest
thoughts we have about him.

The result of all this has been a century of confused thinking
about God. Isaiah's word to Judah is therefore particularly relevant
today:

> '"For my thoughts are not your thoughts,
>   neither are your ways my ways,"
>   declares the Lord.
> "As the heavens are higher than the earth,
>   so are my ways higher than your ways
>   and my thoughts than your thoughts"'

(55:8-9).

The cause for the lack of shape in the lives of so many is the fact
that God means so little to them. There is nothing new under the sun!

The certain success of evangelistic labour

The mystery of God's will continues. It is obvious that God's
invitation is refused by many, but his decree as to the success of his
plan and purpose for the church cannot be thwarted:

> 'As the rain and the snow
>   come down from heaven,
> and do not return to it
>   without watering the earth
> and making it bud and flourish,

so that it yields seed for the sower and bread for
    the eater,
so is my word that goes out from my mouth:
It will not return to me empty,
but will accomplish what I desire
and achieve the purpose for which I sent it'
                                    (55:10-11; cf. 44:26; 45:23).

The certainty is based on the fact that the Word of God abides for
ever (1 Peter 1:25). It is inconceivable that the cross did not achieve
that which God intended. When a missionary was asked, as he was
about to set sail for China, 'Do you expect to make an impression
upon China?' he answered, 'No, but I expect that God will.'
The scale of God's work is cosmic.

'You will go out in joy
    and be led forth in peace;
the mountains and hills
    will burst into song before you,
and all the trees of the field
    will clap their hands.
Instead of the thornbush will grow the pine tree,
    and instead of briers the myrtle will grow.
This will be for the Lord's renown,
    for an everlasting sign,
    which will not be destroyed'
                                            (55:12-13).

The Bible envisages the 'regeneration' of the world (cf. Matt.
19:28; Titus 3:5). The day of the Christian's glorification will also
be the day when the universe will be transformed. The world is
wearing out like a garment and will be rolled away and changed (Ps.
102:26; Heb. 1:11-12). The church gives way in the end to a vision
which includes a new earth and a new heaven in which righteousness dwells (2 Peter 3:13; Rev. 21:1-4). Then 'The creation itself
will be liberated from its bondage to decay and brought into the
glorious freedom of the children of God' (Rom. 8:21). What a
contrast this is to the wasted vineyard of Isaiah 5!

Summary

Isaiah 54 has introduced the theme of a faithful husband's undying love and affection for his bride. God truly loves the church for which he gives the Servant as a Saviour and substitute. Thus, in a free and sovereign call, he gives a sincere invitation to all to partake of the feast he has prepared. And the perspective is wider still: Christ, having drawn the sting of death, makes salvation possible. He has dealt with the alienation that separates sinners from God and God from sinners. It is God's purpose that not only should God's children enjoy liberty from sin's dominion and presence, but that all creation should rejoice in his grace (55:12-13).

37.
Amazing grace

Please read Isaiah 56 - 59

A new section begins with chapter 56.[1] Chapters 40-55 were concerned almost entirely with events relating to the Babylonian captivity and consequent homecoming. The rest of Isaiah is devoted entirely to this homeland, considered in every aspect of it: from its present corruption (chapters 56-59) to its devastation when the Avenger comes for its destruction (chapters 63-64) and its eventual rescue (chapters 60-62) and glory (chapters 65-66).

There is, however, a connection with the preceding chapter. The requirement for repentance (55:7) leads the way to the need for holiness (**'justice'** and **'doing what is right'** 56:1) as a sign of its genuineness. 'The prophet,' says Calvin, 'shows what God demands from us, as soon as he holds out tokens of his favour, or promises that he will be ready to be reconciled to us, that our reconciliation may be secured. He demands from us such a conversion as shall change our minds and hearts, that they may forsake the world and rise towards heaven; and next he likewise calls for the fruits of repentance.'[2]

A house of prayer

Once more Isaiah raises expectations that Jesus' coming is near: **'My salvation is close at hand and my righteousness will soon be revealed'** (56:1; cf. 51:5). Consequently, those who have received God's blessing of salvation should be serious in their concern to be holy.

'**Doing what is right**' (56:1) and keeping one's '**hand from doing any evil**' (56:2) involve a concern for the fourth commandment. Keeping '**the Sabbath without desecrating it**' (56:2, 4,6) is something Isaiah will elaborate upon again in 58:13-14. Behind the principle of keeping one day in seven different from all the rest lie three ideas: it is, in part, a way of showing that God is Lord over our time (cf. Exod. 16:22-30); second, keeping the Sabbath holy is a way of showing love to God ('**to serve him, to love the name of the Lord, and to worship him...**' 56:6, the point of Isaiah 58:13); and third, it is a mark of loyalty to God's '**covenant**' (56:4); the Sabbath was itself a sign of the covenant (Exod. 31:13,17). This is covenant loyalty: 'You must observe my Sabbaths. This will be a sign between me and you for the generations to come, so you may know that I am the Lord, who makes you holy' (Exod. 31:13). 'If you love me, you will obey what I command' (John 14:15,21,23; 15:14). 'This is how we know that we love the children of God: by loving God and carrying out his commands. This is love for God: to obey his commands. And his commands are not burdensome' (1 John 5:2-3).

Once more, the salvation that is around the corner is not just for Jews: the '**foreigner**' will not be excluded (56:3; cf. 44:5). God's church will be bigger than they imagined:

'**The Sovereign Lord declares—**
    he who gathers the exiles of Israel:
"I will gather still others to them
    besides those already gathered"'

(56:8).

The '**eunuch**' (56:3-4), a representation of personal disability, is not cut off from the blessings either.[3] Rather, all who repent and believe this gospel of grace can expect something much better:

'**To them I will give within my temple and its walls**
    a memorial and a name
    better than sons and daughters;
I will give them an everlasting name
    that will not be cut off'

(56:5).

The eunuch's lack of posterity is answered by an 'everlasting name'. Because he had no sons, Absalom built a 'monument' (same Hebrew word) so that he would be remembered (2 Sam. 18:18). Christians can expect to be remembered for ever! The Lord will not forget them. The promise of 'everlasting life' assures them that their presence in heaven — a glorious, transformed place — will be 'for the Lord's renown' (55:13; again, the same word in Hebrew).

These — the poor, repentant ones who turn to the Lord — are promised a place in God's house, which is described as a **'house of prayer'** (56:7; Jer. 7:11; Matt. 21:13; Mark 11:17; 1 Tim. 3:15). This name reflects God's concern for holiness amongst his people. It was this concern — and, indeed, this verse — which caused Jesus to show such public anger at the way the temple was being desecrated in his day (Mark 11:12-33, especially verse 17). The house of prayer had become a commercial market-place. God's name, instead of being honoured and praised, was held in contempt. This situation could not be tolerated. The anger of Jesus, in turning over the tables and driving out the money-changers, was a glimpse of the Avenger, of whom Isaiah warned (63:1-3).

Dumb dogs (56:9-12)

The glimpse of the Avenger in the preceding section leads to a warning to the watchmen of the people (56:10), the shepherds of the flock (56:11). The theme is continuing: God demands evidence of holiness. But the pastors and teachers of ancient Israel are **'blind'**, **'lack knowledge'**, **'mute'**, **'love to sleep'** (56:10-11). They **'all turn to their own way, each seeks his own gain'** (56:11). Isaiah summarizes their attitude:

> **'"Come," each one cries, "let me get wine!**
> **Let us drink our fill of beer!**
> **And tomorrow will be like today,**
> **or even far better"'**

(56:12).

Those in leadership carry great responsibility (James 3:1). Israel's shepherds fell far short of the model of the true Shepherd's leadership. The watchmen were sleeping. At a later period Jeremiah was to express concern over false shepherds (Jer. 10:21; 12:10; 23:1-4; 50:6). In New Testament times there were 'shepherds who feed only themselves' (Jude 1:12).

Flagrant apostasy (57:1-13)

When the watchmen fall asleep (56:9-12) all kinds of evil flood in. Verse 1 of chapter 57 reminds us of Hezekiah's son, Manasseh, who persecuted the innocent (2 Kings 21:16): verses 5 and 9, with their reference to a revival of Molech-worship, may well allude to Manasseh's burning of his own son (2 Kings 21:6). It is difficult to imagine a greater reversal of character than that which took place when Manasseh succeeded his father. He is the only one of Judah's kings to be likened to Ahab (2 Kings 21:3). God was provoked to anger (2 Kings 21:6).

Tucked away in this chapter is a reassuring verse for God's children: they will die in peace (57:2; cf. Ps. 116:15). It is as though Isaiah wants to reassure his faithful readers, **'those who walk uprightly'**, as they read this chapter. False shepherds and sleeping watchmen are under severe scrutiny; they have cause to be afraid. But true believers can rest peacefully in the knowledge of God's love for them.

'But you...' brings us sharply back to the false shepherds and sleeping watchmen (57:3). 'As he had said that good men enjoy peace,' comments Calvin, 'so he threatens that the wicked shall have ceaseless war.'[4]

The evil that has come into the land includes sorcery (57:3), spiritual adultery (57:3), mockery (57:4), Canaanite sexual fertility rites (57:5), child sacrifice (57:5), idolatry — including the taking of pagan libations in the Hinnom Valley (57:6) — and further apostate rituals associated with the main Ammonite god, Molech (57:7-9). Nor do such apostates get wearied in their sinful ways (57:10).

God's response is to issue a challenge. Let them turn to their idols to save them from the coming peril:

> **'When you cry out for help,**
> **let your collection of idols save you!**

> The wind will carry all of them off,
> a mere breath will blow them away.
> But the man who makes me his refuge
> will inherit the land
> and possess my holy mountain'

(57:13).

The dwelling-place of God (57:14-21)

The previous section, filled as it was with threatening, ends with a brief statement of promise. It is this promise which is now taken up and elaborated upon. In form it is the opposite of the first section: filled as it is with promise, it ends with a terrible word of threatening.

God had taken Israel to court on many occasions for their crimes. He had **'accused'** (Hebrew *rib*, a technical word for a lawsuit) them before (57:16; cf. 3:13-14). He had grown **'enraged'** (57:17). But God's love for his people had revealed itself too, 'healing', 'guiding', 'comforting', and **'creating praise on the lips of the mourners in Israel'** (57:19). To these, the message is one of **'peace, peace'**; but along with it is the threat we have seen before **'"There is no peace," says my God, "for the wicked"'** (57:21; cf. 39:8; 48:22).

Blessed are the poor in spirit...

The basis of confidence in this chapter is once more underlined: it is rooted in the character of God and the nature of his relationship with his people:

> 'For this is what the high and lofty One says—
> he who lives for ever, whose name is holy:
> "I live in a high and holy place,
> but also with him who is contrite and lowly in
> spirit,
> to revive the spirit of the lowly
> and to revive the heart of the contrite"'

(57:15).

1. God dwells with his people

At the heart of God's covenant dealings with his children is the promise: 'I will be with you.' This was the experience of Joseph (Gen. 39:2) and was the promise given to Moses (Exod. 3:12; 33:14-16) and Joshua (Josh. 1:5,9; Deut. 31:6,8). It is repeated by Isaiah in chapter 43: 'When you pass through the waters, I will be with you... Do not be afraid, for I am with you' (43:2,5). Its consummate fulfilment is found in Isaiah's suffering Servant, who not only promised to be with his children at all times (Matt. 28:20), but whose name Immanuel means 'God with us' (7:14; 8:8; Matt. 1:23).

2. God dwells with the humble

Isaiah's reference to the **'contrite and lowly in spirit'** (57:15) is reminiscent of other passages in Scripture: 'The Lord is close to the broken-hearted and saves those who are crushed in spirit' (Ps. 34:18). 'He heals the broken-hearted and binds up their wounds' (Ps. 147:3). Jesus testified to this aspect of God's character in the beatitude: 'Blessed are the poor in spirit, for theirs is the kingdom of heaven' (Matt. 5:3). God dwells in broken hearts — hearts broken by sin.

3. God dwells in those whose faith is rooted in Christ

Behind all these beatitudes lies a passage in Isaiah 61:1-3, a reference to preaching good news to the 'broken-hearted'. Jesus, reading it in the synagogue in Nazareth, claimed that it was fulfilled in himself. The blessings of which this passage speaks find their accomplishment in Jesus Christ!

True and false worship (58:1-14)

The requirement for repentance continues (cf. 55:7). This point has already been made in the denunciation of Judah's leaders (56:9-12), and of the flagrant apostasy current in Judah (57:1-13). God, however, dwells with the contrite (57:14-21). Humility shows itself in a willingness to turn *away* from sin and *towards* God. This is a spirit which is obviously lacking in Judah's attitude to worship in

Isaiah 58, a chapter which contrasts true and false worship. 'The Lord does not look at the things man looks at. Man looks at the outward appearance, but the Lord looks at the heart' (1 Sam. 16:7). There are indications in the passage of a formal religion, but it is a religion with which God is displeased. Both negative and positive aspects are highlighted. First we see some of the negative ones.

1. Formal religion is not religion

There is an appearance of religion here: they seek after God day after day; they seem eager to know God's ways; they seem to desire to do what is right (58:1-2). They are going about the business of religion. They expect that God should reward them accordingly. They manage to convince themselves, but not God! They are even belligerent:

> **"'Why have we fasted," they say,
> "and you have not seen it?
> Why have we humbled ourselves,
> and you have not noticed?"'**
>
> (58:3).

This is all a reminder of how Isaiah began his prophecy (1:11-17). Judah's condition now, as then, is one of **'rebellion'** (58:1; cf. 1:2).

2. The essence of formal religion is doing as one pleases

Their observance of fasting (58:3) and the Sabbath (58:13) was characterized by self-pleasing. Fasting is by definition self-denial. The Sabbath, too, as Matthew Henry suggested, was made a day of rest so that it might be a day of holy *work*. Self-denial is at the heart of both: denying oneself legitimate fare (fasting), or time that one calls one's own (the Sabbath). But the formalists of Isaiah's time, while observing the letter of the law (fast days increased after the fall of Jerusalem, Zech. 7:5; 8:19), were unforgiving, impatient and proud (58:3-5). Formal religion is unrepentant religion. Its essence, self-pleasing, is as old as the Garden of Eden (Gen. 3:6). It is a sickening spectacle (cf. 1:15).

3. Formal religion is a hindrance to prayer

'You cannot fast as you do today and expect your voice to be heard on high' (58:4; cf. 1:15; 59:2). It was also the psalmist's belief: 'If I had cherished sin in my heart, the Lord would not have listened' (Ps. 66:18).

Positively, Isaiah makes further points.

4. True religion is heart religion

In the previous chapter, Isaiah had made the point clear:

'For this is what the high and lofty One says—
   he who lives for ever, whose name is holy:
"I live in a high and holy place,
   but also with him who is contrite and lowly in spirit,
to revive the spirit of the lowly
   and to revive the heart of the contrite"'

(57:15).

This is amplified in Isaiah's discussion on the purpose of fasting (58:6-9). The fast which God 'has chosen' (58:6), is to be a powerful aid to righteous living. There is no point in fasting, and expecting to win God's favour by doing so, if at the same time we are guilty of injustice, oppression, greed and insensitivity to the needs of others, as well as the absence of love, finger-pointing (accusation) and malicious talk (58:7-9) This issue was still a matter of concern in Jesus' day. Ostentatious Pharisees visibly paraded their fast days, disfiguring their faces (Matt. 6:16-18). Hand-in-hand with fasting, Jesus insisted, must go humility, confession of sin and meekness, as well as mercy (Matt. 5:3-9). 'Blessed are the pure *in heart...*'

5. True religion leads to true happiness

The list of things the righteous can expect is staggering: those who walk with the Lord will know an unclouded fellowship with him and answered prayer: **'You will call, and the Lord will answer; you will cry for help, and he will say: Here am I'** (58:9). They will receive a **'light'**, which speaks of prosperity and blessing (58:8,10), and guidance, which includes the provision of all things needful (58:11; cf. 57:18; Ps. 23:3).

The figure of a **'well-watered garden'** (58:11) is one Isaiah is fond of using (cf. 30:25; 33:21; 35:6,7; 41:17-18; 43:20; 44:4; 48:21; 49:10; cf. Jer. 31:12). In his opening chapter, Isaiah had described Israel's condition as 'like a garden without water' (1:30). 'It amounts to this,' comments Calvin, 'that this fountain of God's kindness never dries up, but always flows, if we do not stop its course by our own fault.'[5]

If we obey the Sabbath we shall be happy, says Isaiah (58:13). Doing what God intends us to do is never an irksome thing: God's yoke is easy and his burden is light (Matt. 11:28-30). To those prepared to follow this pathway, God promises **'joy'** (58:14). Newton once wrote,

Solid joys and lasting treasure
None but Zion's children know.[6]

Why some are not saved (59:1-21)

Isaiah 59 is darker than the previous chapter. It begins with a similar problem: sin is a hindrance to prayer (59:2; cf. 58:4). But whereas chapter 58 focuses on the blessings the righteous may expect, chapter 59 stresses the opposite: unrepentant sinners can expect none of them. To the former, there is the promise of light: 'Your light will rise in the darkness, and your night will become like the noonday' (58:10). To the latter there is darkness: **'Like the blind we grope along the wall, feeling our way like men without eyes'** (59:10). The gulf between believers and unbelievers is unbridgeable; darkness and light are the Bible's way of distinguishing the two (Eph. 5:8).

The chapter provides an answer to the question: why is it that some are *not* saved?

1. It is not through any lack of power in God

God's arm is not **'too short'**. Nor is God hard of hearing! There is no lack of power, or efficacy to save. Salvation has been effected by God's arm (59:16). The power of God in redemption manifests itself in the creation of Jesus' human body (Luke 1:35), in the strength constantly given to him during his earthly life (42:1), and in his resurrection from the dead (Acts 2:24). It also manifests itself in the application of redemption, including regeneration (1 Peter 1:23). God, who saved the dying thief (Luke 23:42-3), Saul of Tarsus (Acts 9:4-22), the adulterous woman of Samaria (John 4:7-26) and the slave Onesimus (Philem. 10; Col. 4:9) is *able* to save anyone. 'He is able to save completely those who come to God through [Christ]...' (Heb. 7:25).

2. *The cause is not anything in God, but in man*

It is *sin* that separates man from God:

> **'But your iniquities have separated**
> **you from your God;**
> **your sins have hidden his face from you,**
> **so that he will not hear'**
>
> (59:2).

Verses 3-8 describe vividly the spreading anarchy. Romans 3:15-17 picks up a part of it (59:7-8) as its own description of the sinfulness of mankind. Paul's summary of it is this: **'There is no fear of God before their eyes'** (Rom. 3:18). The truth about man is that poison, cursing and bitterness fill his mouth. Because they have known destruction and misery, they have not known peace. There is no exception to this analysis. Everyone falls under this condemnation.

'Let me put it plainly. If you do not accept this description of yourself apart from the cross of the Lord Jesus Christ,' argues Dr Martyn Lloyd-Jones, 'then there is no need to argue about it, you are just not a Christian. If you resent all this you are not a Christian, you are not yet convinced and convicted of sin, and you are not a believer in Christ, though you may have thought you were. If you in any way object to this, you are automatically putting yourself outside the kingdom of God and the Christian faith. This description of man in sin is the simple truth, the horrible truth. That is what sin has brought us to. Thank God there is a way out of it. ... "Oh wretched man that I am! who shall deliver me...? I thank God through Jesus Christ our Lord".'[7]

Sin obliterates all values. The casualties include justice, right-eousness and truth (59:14). Judah was the sort of place where, so long as you had enough money, you could get away with anything. Judicial corruption was rife. And God is **'displeased'** (59:15). His patience finally runs out.

The divine Warrior

When God's patience runs out he puts on his clothes and weapons of war. The well-known imagery of the Christian soldier in Ephesians 6:10-20 is based on Isaiah 59:15-17.[8] In the Old Testament, God appears as the divine Warrior appearing on his cloud war-chariot, riding into battle against his enemies:

'He parted the heavens and came down;
    dark clouds were under his feet.
He mounted the cherubim and flew;
    he soared on the wings of the wind.
He made darkness his covering, his canopy around him—
    the dark rain clouds of the sky.
Out of the brightness of his presence clouds advanced,
    with hailstones and bolts of lightning.
The Lord thundered from heaven;
    the voice of the Most High resounded.
He shot his arrows and scattered the enemies,
    great bolts of lightning and routed them.
The valleys of the sea were exposed
    and the foundations of the earth laid bare
at your rebuke, O Lord,
    at the blast of breath from your nostrils'

(Ps. 18:9-15).

'Praise the Lord, O my soul.

O Lord my God, you are very great;
    you are clothed with splendour and majesty.
He wraps himself in light as with a garment;
    he stretches out the heavens like a tent
    and lays the beams of his upper chambers on their waters.

He makes the clouds his chariot
and rides on the wings of the wind.
He makes winds his messengers,
flames of fire his servants'

(Ps. 104:1-4).

It is this image that Isaiah takes up now (and he will do so again in 63:2-3). The vision is the same one as John gives of Christ in Revelation 19:11-21, when he depicts him as the Warrior who comes to judge the world at the last day. God is displeased with injustice in the world. Putting on a breast-plate of righteousness and a helmet of salvation, he goes out to **'repay wrath to his enemies and retribution to his foes'** (59:18). The Christian's duty to go into battle against his enemies, equipped with the whole armoury of God, is merely a reflection of the Saviour himself. His enemies are our enemies (cf. John 15:20).

The divine Redeemer

Just as several previous chapters had ended with a word of warning (cf. 48:22; 57:20-21; 59:21), this one ends with a word of blessing to the repentant (59:20-21). The Redeemer, Jesus Christ, will come to save his people according the **'covenant'** of God (59:21). A number of important facts concerning the Redeemer and his atoning work are given.

Firstly, **'His own righteousness sustained him'** (59:16). What sustained Jesus was his attitude to obeying God's law. '"My food," said Jesus, "is to do the will of him who sent me and to finish his work"' (John 4:34). 'Father, if you are willing, take this cup from me; yet not my will, but yours be done' (Luke 22:42).

Secondly, part of the Redeemer's work is to judge, taking on the battle dress of a warrior (59:18). Retribution, as well as salvation, is the Redeemer's work.

Thirdly, the Redeemer's work is covenantal. Israel will be saved because God has promised as much. **'"My Spirit, who is on you, and my words that I have put in your mouth will not depart from your mouth, or from the mouths of your children, or from the mouths of their descendants from this time on and for ever,"** says the Lord'** (59:21). This is the verse Paul cites to back up the famous passage in Romans 11:26-27 which concludes: 'And so all Israel will be saved.' No place of origin (**'west'** or east, 59:19) will disqualify them from membership in the Redeemer's kingdom. The New Covenant, to which this is a reference, includes the promise of the Holy Spirit, as well as his word of truth (59:21). 'This Word and the Spirit will never depart from the Church, for the Church as the body of the Head is to declare the truth to all nations that the saving health of God may be seen by all.'⁹ The church is a nation of prophets (Num. 11:29; Joel 2:28).

Summary

God's church is to be marked by holiness and obedience to God's ways — things evidently lacking in the prophet's own day. The church that Isaiah knew was apostate. This provides the prophet with an explanation why it is that some will not be saved: they have chosen to live apart from God. To such there is the fearful warning of the coming of the Avenger. But once more, Isaiah speaks of the Redeemer: 'How sweet the name of Jesus sounds, in a believer's ear!' wrote John Newton. And he was right.

38.
The glory of God's church

Please read Isaiah 60-62

We are, of course, familiar with the fact that Gentiles comprise the majority in God's church. But in Isaiah's day, this was not so. Indeed, for many it was unthinkable. True, there had been folk in the kingdom like Ruth, a Moabitess, but they were a tiny minority. That is why we should attempt to catch the surprise and thrill of Isaiah's insistence of the coming influx of Gentiles into the church. It is a staggering fact that wise men 'from the east' were among the first to pay honour to the Redeemer (Matt. 2:1-12).

The closing chapters of Isaiah depict this influx, but go beyond it. The language is exalted, depicting things which transcend even our own experience of the kingdom. We should keep in mind the fact that Revelation 21, with its picture of the New Jerusalem, draws heavily on Isaiah 60.

There are those who take a view of Revelation 21 along fairly literal lines. It has been the consistent view of this book that this interpretation is invalid. The return of the dispersed Israelites to Jerusalem is first of all a description of the ingathering of the elect into the church. The reintroduction of sacrificial worship in a rebuilt temple in Jerusalem would, according to a literal interpretation, involve the sacrifice of **'rams'** (60:7). This is wholly unacceptable; it would involve a denial of the finished work of Christ (Heb. 10:1; 13:10-16; John 4:21-26). Ultimately, what we have here is a description of the glory of heaven itself. The prophet has 'heaven in his eye'.

Doves returning to their lofts (60:1-9)

The nations will walk by the light of the holy city, and the kings of the earth will bring their glory into it (60:3; cf. Rev. 21:24). This may be an allusion to the star that appeared over Bethlehem and the baby Jesus (Matt. 2:2).[1] The further references to the **'wealth'**, and **'riches'** (60:5), including **'gold'** and **'incense'** (60:6), together with **'camels'** from such far away places as **'Midian'** (in the Transjordan), **'Ephah'** (a son of Midian, Gen. 25:4), and **'Sheba'** (in southern Arabia — roughly, modern Yemen) may be an even clearer reference to the wise men who came 'from the east' to present their gifts to the young child, Jesus — gold suggesting royalty, incense divinity, and myrrh the passion and burial (cf. Ps. 72:10-11).[2]

Clearly, this passage is an announcement of God's intention to gather a worldwide harvest of the gospel. The **'sons ... and ... daughters'** (60:4) are of every nationality. The **'nations'** (60:3), **'islands'** and **'foreigners'** (60:10) comprise a large part of the church who **'honour the Lord'** (60:9). They are pictured as doves coming home to their lofts (60:8).

Conquered and not won (60:10-16)

The emphasis in 60:3-9 lies with the gifts coming from every quarter. In verses 10-12 the focus is on the many building projects undertaken by foreigners — traditionally the enemies of Israel. God, who had been angry with his people, now shows compassion. His anger does not last for ever towards those who are his (60:10). So great is the wealth streaming into Jerusalem that the caretakers of the city have no time to shut the gates after them, either by day or night (60:11). The apostle John makes use of this verse in his apocalyptic vision of the heavenly Jerusalem: 'On no day will its gates ever be shut, for there will be no night there' (Rev. 21:25).

Amongst those bearing gifts are various kings, coming in subjection to the only King of heaven and earth: 'They are escorted into the city, not against their will but freely and voluntarily, for they have been inwardly conquered and are true *douloi* (slaves) of the Lord.'[3] The rulers of the world are bowing to Christ. We may see here King

Artaxerxes, who issued a decree allowing Nehemiah to rebuild the walls of Jerusalem (Nch. 2:8). Others have also seen here the Gentiles so evidently building the New Testament church in Acts (Acts 15:14-16). Ultimately, the New Jerusalem is in view, filled as it will be with Gentile converts.

A glimpse of heaven (60:17-22)

Several features of the new Jerusalem now come into view.

1. Heaven is a place of true happiness

The transformation envisaged for Jerusalem will create an era of peace and prosperity (60:11-14), filled with **'joy'**, **'peace'** and **'righteousness'** (60:15-17). Again, John sees something similar (Rev. 21:1-5,21-27).

2. Its inhabitants are preoccupied with praise

The gates of this new Jerusalem are called **'Praise'** (60:18). As A. W. Pink once said, 'Praising and adoring God is the noblest part of the saint's work on earth, as it will be his chief employ in heaven.'

3. The theme of praise is salvation

The city walls are referred to as 'Salvation' (60:18). Isaiah's theme, from the opening verse, has been that the Lord saves.

> 'In that day this song will be sung in the land of Judah:
> We have a strong city;
>   God makes salvation
>   its walls and ramparts'
>
> (26:1).

4. The recipient of praise will be God himself

What makes heaven so wonderful is the presence of Christ. The presence of God, a promise which has been of the very essence of his covenant dealings with his people from the start, reaches its climax in heaven. There we shall see Christ (1 John 3:2). The light of Christ's glory, glimpsed briefly at the transfiguration, will then shine with dazzling brilliance. 'His clothes became as bright as a flash of lightning' (Luke 9:29; cf. John 1:14).

**'The sun will no more be your light by day,
nor will the brightness of the moon shine on you,
for the Lord will be your everlasting light,
and your God will be your glory.
Your sun will never set again,
and your moon will wane no more;
the Lord will be your everlasting light,
and your days of sorrow will end'**

(60:19-20).

Revelation 21:23 and 22:5 confirm that Isaiah's vision transcends anything that we have ever seen, or will see, here in this world. This is the glory of heaven; and he will return to it again and again before closing (e.g. 65:17-25).

5. *Only the righteous, the redeemed, will be in heaven*

Isaiah has made it clear that not all are saved. Some will be **'utterly ruined'** (60:12). The **'righteous'** (60:21) are those who have experienced what Isaiah 6 described when holy seraphim took the purging coals from the altar of sacrifice to take away Isaiah's sins. The righteous are those who trust in the Lord and his way of salvation (cf. 4:3). Heaven, though thronged with redeemed people, is only for those reckoned righteous through faith in Jesus Christ: 'God made him who had no sin to be sin for us, so that in him we might become the righteousness of God' (2 Cor. 5:21).

6. *This final state of existence is not far away*

Once more the prophet uses the expression **'swiftly'** (60:22) to describe what God is about to do. There are certain things which seem to us to be unnecessarily prolonged. Sometimes the work of God seems slow. Answers to prayer seem long in coming. But God

suddenly acts when men are least expecting it. Patience and faithfulness are what we need.

The everlasting covenant (61:1-9)

Isaiah's certainty with regard to the future is rooted in God's
covenant, which again surfaces in chapter 61. Chapter 60 has
described the future blessing. Chapter 61 goes on to describe the
One who introduces that blessing.

Here the covenant is referred to as **'an everlasting covenant'**
(61:8). Isaiah has mentioned it before (55:1-5). Jeremiah and
Ezekiel, both of whom use this same phrase, also call it 'the new
covenant' (Jer. 31:27-44; 50:4-5; Ezek. 16:60-63; 37:15-28). The
close connection between the 'everlasting covenant' and the 'new
covenant' in these passages reminds us that the 'newness' of the new
covenant is the quality of freshness and fulfilment. It is not that God
abandons what he has been doing and begins afresh. Rather, he
brings to a climax what has been there all along in the old. Several
features of the everlasting, or new, covenant are underlined in this
chapter; together they lead to the conclusion that Christians are **'a
people the Lord has blessed'** (61:9).

1. The Redeemer of the covenant: the Lord's Anointed

When Jesus took the Passover cup and said, 'This cup is the new
covenant in my blood, which is poured out for you' (Luke 22:20),
he saw himself, and his ministry, as the consummation of a lengthy
historical process of prediction and preparation. What had been
implicit in God's first covenant promise in Eden (Gen. 3:15), was
now fulfilled.

The **'me'** of the first verse is still the Lord who has been speaking
in the preceding chapter. Though the word 'servant' does not occur
in this section, we have here yet another song resembling the Servant
Songs (cf. 42:1-7; 49:1-6; 50:4-9; 52:13 - 53:12).

Jesus himself saw this passage as a crucial one in setting the
terms and mandate of his own mission. Following his baptism and
temptation in the wilderness, he entered a synagogue in Nazareth.
Along with a verse from an earlier chapter in Isaiah (58:6), he read

this passage, stopping, crucially, in the middle of the second verse (Luke 4:17-21).This demonstrates how fond he was of the book of Isaiah, but of even greater significance are his words that followed the reading of this passage: 'Today this scripture is fulfilled in your hearing' (Luke 4:21).

Jesus came to fulfil God's promise of a Saviour. Anointed as he was by the Holy Spirit (61:1; 42:1), Jesus claimed to have been endued with the unction, power and authority of the Spirit which would identify the Messiah; his works would be accomplished in the Spirit's power; their character confirms his identity (Luke 4:14). The poor, the prisoner, the blind, the bruised — those are the people who come under the power of his Spirit-filled ministry. Jesus is deeply aware of the needs of people. The Beatitudes, 'Blessed are the poor ... those who mourn...' (Matt. 5:1-12), comprising some of the earliest of Jesus' sermons after this incident, find many a reflection in this passage, especially in the eloquent phrases of verse 3:

'... **a crown of beauty**
 instead of ashes,
the oil of gladness
 instead of mourning,
and a garment of praise
 instead of a spirit of despair,
...**oaks of righteousness,**
 a planting of the Lord
 for the display of his splendour'

(61:3).

Little wonder that Jesus cited this passage to provide John the Baptist, in a moment of uncertainty, with convincing proof that he was indeed, as John had so valiantly proclaimed, the 'wonder-working Jesus' (Matt. 11:3-6).

2. The return of exiled Israel to the land of promise

Christians are kings and priests of the Lord. Once more, Isaiah depicts Israel's redemption in terms of the rebuilding of Jerusalem (61:4; cf. 35:1-10; 58:12). Though some expect a literal fulfilment,[4] this is misguided. The comforting of mourners (61:2) is the subject of one of the Beatitudes (Matt. 5:4). Jesus followed it with another: 'Blessed are the meek, for they will inherit the earth' (Matt. 5:5). So inheriting land is as much a New Testament expectation as it is an Old Testament one!

Jeremiah declared that God will bring his people 'back from captivity and restore them to the land' (Jer. 30:3; 32:37; 50:5-18; cf. Ezek. 37:21,26). When God made man, he created him to rule over his creation (Gen. 1:26-28). Greed led to the Fall and brought the earth under the curse of God, but throughout the Bible there are hints that this tragedy would be reversed and the promise of 'a land' restored.

Abraham was promised an inheritance in Canaan (Gen. 15:7), though, as Stephen pointed out, he never possessed any part of it (Acts 7:5; cf. Heb. 11:9-10). The 'land' which was promised to Abraham, and through him to all Christians, was one which the writer to the Hebrews describes as 'the city with foundations, whose architect and builder is God' (Heb. 11:10). It is the 'heavenly Jerusalem' (Heb. 12:22), 'the city that is to come' (Heb. 13:14), 'the new Jerusalem' (Rev. 21:2-4, 9-27) — of which Isaiah has yet 'many things to say' in the following chapters. The point is that we are meant to expect a literal fulfilment of this 'land — not in this world, but in the 'new earth'. That is indeed something worth anticipating!

3. The restoration of God's blessing upon his own people

Isaiah depicts a rebuilt Israel, served by foreigners (61:5), and fortified by those who had once been their enemies (61:6). This is a vivid description of the kingship and priesthood of all believers: **'and you will called priests of the Lord...'** (61:6; cf. 1 Peter 2:9-10; Rev. 1:6). Every Christian is someone else's priest, and we are all priests to one another. Since salvation is of grace rather than merit, there is no room for boasting (Rom. 3:27). Since we belong to the same family (or are 'slices of the same cake', as Martin Luther put it) we are called to serve one another (Gal. 6:2). As Luther once said, 'The fact that we are all priests and kings means that each of us Christians may go before God and intercede for the other. If I notice that you have no faith or a weak faith, I can ask God to give you a strong faith.'[5]

4. A robe of imputed righteousness

Isaiah's description of Israel's beauty, wearing the righteous garments which God has provided for her, is in stark contrast to her natural condition (61:10). The people whose sins were as scarlet are to become in Christ 'the City of Righteousness' (1:26). The righteousness which God's law demands can only be conferred from outside: 'This righteousness from God comes through faith in Jesus Christ to all who believe' (Rom. 3:22; cf. Rev. 6:11).

Those who have been 'reckoned' as righteous through faith in Jesus Christ (2 Cor. 5:21) are to pursue righteousness throughout their lives. Isaiah's assurance is that even this righteousness, the righteousness which belongs to the area of sanctification rather than justification, is a gift of God:

'For as the soil makes the young plant come up
    and a garden causes seeds to grow,
so the Sovereign Lord will make righteousness and praise
    spring up before all nations'
                                                (61:11; cf. Rom. 8:10).

Righteousness is concerned both with our relationship to God and with our ongoing commitment to a way of life that pleases him. This latter sense is just as much a gift of the Holy Spirit (1 Peter 1:2; 2 Peter 3:18; Eph. 4:14-16), changing us more and more, in mind and heart and life, into the image of Christ (Rom. 12:2; 2 Cor. 3:18; Eph. 4:23-24; Col. 3:10).

5. The vengeance of the covenant

The fact that Jesus stopped reading the passage halfway through the second verse is of great significance. What he omitted were the words: '[to proclaim] ... the day of vengeance of our God...' Israel had conveniently forgotten 'the vengeance of the covenant', the jealousy of God at work within the confines of his chosen people to punish transgression, to discipline them to greater holiness and to purge out evil.

The expression, used in Leviticus 26:25 (see also verses 14-45), is intended to remind us that even though God saves sinners, embracing them in his covenant, this is not to induce moral complacency.

As we have already seen, the covenant includes curses as well as blessings. Those who are merely pretending, as well as backslidden members of this covenant relationship, can expect the Lord to deal severely with them. Ultimately, this is a reference to the judgement of God upon the wicked at the end of time. Though the certainty of that judgement has been underlined (39:8; 48:22; 59:21; cf. Matt. 25:31-46; Acts 17:31; 2 Thess. 1:7-8), the Saviour's mission was a redemptive one (John 3:16-17).

'Come, let us sing unto the Lord...'

Such blessings as these are worth singing about! (61:10-11). In many ways it is a reminder of similar songs in chapters 12, 24-27.

> Come, thou fount of every blessing,
> Tune my heart to sing thy grace;
> Streams of mercy, never ceasing,
> Call for songs of loudest praise.
> Teach me some melodious measure,
> Sung by flaming tongues above;
> Oh, the vast, the boundless treasure
> Of my Lord's unchanging love!
>
> (Robert Robinson).

The beauty of Zion (62:1-5)

Chapter 62 opens with yet another poem (62:1-5). Commentators are divided as to who the 'I' is (62:1). Some think it may be Isaiah himself.[6] In this case, it means that the prophet will not rest until the things predicted have come to pass. Others argue that it is the Lord who is speaking here.[7] This would mean that God himself will not rest until what he has promised is fulfilled. Having spoken, he is eager to bring it to pass. God is always like that: anxious to show us that he can be trusted. He is utterly dependable. He will not rest until the salvation he has promised for his people is accomplished (62:1; cf. 42:4,14; 57:11; 65:6).

The righteousness of Zion, alluded to in the last verse of chapter 61, will shine out like the dawn (62:1). This is what Jesus does for sinners: he makes them shine (cf. Eph. 4:18; 5:8). The counterpart to this picture is Malachi's description of the coming of Christ, when he says, 'The sun of righteousness will rise with healing in its wings' (Mal. 4:2). 'The Bride's blush of joy is a response to his coming.'[8]

The redeemed church is Christ's bride; the figure used in chapter 54 is used again: **'As a bridegroom rejoices over his bride, so will your God rejoice over you'** (62:5; cf. Eph. 5:23-33). The wedding gown and jewellery of chapter 61:10 now make way for her change of name. We are familiar with the concept: new wives change their surnames. So it is here in Isaiah's prophecy. She will be called **'Hephzibah'** ('My delight is in her') as opposed to **'Deserted'**, and the land in which she lives will be called **'Beulah'** ('married') as opposed to **'Desolate'** (62:4). Little wonder that faithful believers pray earnestly that the Lord will bring forward the wedding day! (62:7).

Praying with all prayer and supplication...

Earlier (61:10-11) we were encouraged to sing. But singing is not enough; we are also called upon to pray that God's will might be done. Daniel no doubt knew of Isaiah's prophecy with regard to the besieging of Jerusalem (Dan. 1:1-2; cf. Isa. 39:6-7). It seems that he also knew Jeremiah's writings. Discovering a passage in Jeremiah 25:11-12, speaking as it did of the seventy-year length of the exile in Babylon — and realizing that sixty-eight years had already gone by — Daniel did not sit and wait for things to happen. He did not reason, 'Well, since God has predicted all of this, I do not need to pray.' Rather, he set himself to importunate prayer (Dan. 9:3-19).

Isaiah speaks of a similar response on the part of his companions in Jerusalem. Having predicted future glories, the Lord has urged the faithful to urgent, importunate prayer:

**'I have posted watchmen on your walls, O Jerusalem;
they will never be silent day or night.**

You who call on the Lord,
   give yourselves no rest,
and give him no rest till he establishes Jerusalem
   and makes her the praise of the earth'

(62:6-7).

'Some mercies,' said Spurgeon, 'are not given to us except in
answer to importunate prayer.' Some blessings are like ripe fruit in
autumn time ready for the picking; other blessings require the tree
to be shaken violently. Importunate prayer, as Jesus taught, is a vital
requirement of the Christian life (Luke 11:8; 18:7). Thomas Brooks
put it this way: 'He that would gain victory over God in private
prayer, must strain every string of his heart; he must, in beseeching
God, besiege him, and so get the better of him; he must be like
importunate beggars, that will not be put off by frowns, or silence,
or sad answers. Those that would be masters of their requests, must
like the importunate widow, press God so far as to put him to an holy
blush, as I may say with reverence; they must with an holy impu-
dence, as Basil speaks, make God ashamed that he cannot look us
in the face if he should deny the importunity of our souls.'⁹

And such faithful prayer warriors will not be disappointed. The
Lord assures them by an oath that his word can be trusted (62:8-9).
The covenant promises of grain and wine are part of the Old
Testament language of blessing (Deut. 28:8-12: cf. vv. 30-33). In
Babylon, the exiles were unable to celebrate their festivals, which
included bringing part of the harvest as a tithe to the Lord, and eating
it in God's presence (Lev. 23:39-40; Deut. 14:22-26). But all such
restrictions will be removed in the redemption God is accomplish-
ing. And even as Isaiah begins to describe this scene, he urges them
to get ready for what God is about to do (62:10-11). 'Claim your
liberty!' he exhorts them. Jesus is coming! And **'his reward'**, **'his
recompense'** (i.e. his redeemed people) **'is with him'** (62:11; cf.
40:10-11).

To add a finishing touch to the church's beauty, in addition to the
name Hephzibah, Isaiah mentions four more names:

'They will be called the Holy People,
   the Redeemed of the Lord;

> **and you will be called Sought After,
> the City No Longer Deserted'**
>
> (62:12).

This forms a wonderful climax to chapters 60-62.

Summary

Isaiah is contemplating a wonderful future for the church in these closing chapters. He has given us a glimpse of heaven. And we are meant to be in eager anticipation of it.

39.
The Warrior of heaven

Please read Isaiah 63:1 - 65:16

The Bible never leaves us in any doubt about the nature of God and his redemptive work. Whenever the glorious nature of things to come is revealed (as it has been in chapter 62) the warning is underlined once more. 'Consider therefore the kindness and sternness of God' (Rom. 11:22). Chapter 63 opens in a way which reminds of the divine Warrior going forth to battle in 59:15-21 and the 'day of vengeance' in 61:2-9. The future for the church is a glorious one; the future of the unrepentant is not. When God's patience runs out, he puts on his clothes and weapons of war. Like 59:15-21, the picture here is similar to John's portrait of Christ in Revelation 19:11-21 as the Warrior who comes to judge the world at the last day.

The blood-stained Warrior (63:1-6)

'**Edom**' and its capital city '**Bozrah**' (63:1) have typified the impenitent world before (34:6). Isaiah now displays his literary eloquence by reminding us that 'Edom' in Hebrew means '**red**', and 'Bozrah' is similar to a Hebrew word for 'grape-gatherer'. Red (crimson) is the colour of both blood and the juice of the grape. Isaiah had opened his prophecy with a description of Israel's sins as being 'like scarlet ... red as crimson' (1:18). Now he combines this metaphor with that of the process of making wine (63:3), in the course of which grapes were crushed by men and women in bare feet. The process resulted in a great volume of red liquid flowing

into a receptacle. It also meant that the clothes of those treading out
the wine were spattered with red stains.

This is not a picture of the cross, as some have thought, but of the
judgement of the wicked. There is hardly a more graphic portrayal
of God's wrath in the Bible than this one. John takes it up in
Revelation 14:17-20 and makes it clear that the divine Warrior is
none other than the Lamb, who will come on a white horse to
subjugate all enemies including Satan (cf. Rev. 19:11-20; 20:11-
15).

In the process of the final judgement of the wicked, the winepress
of God's wrath produces a great tide of blood; the land will be a
blood bath from end to end (cf. Rev. 14:20). 'Out of his mouth comes
a sharp sword with which to strike down the nations. "He will rule
them with an iron sceptre." He treads the winepress of the fury of the
wrath of God Almighty' (Rev. 19:15). Edom and Bozrah, represent-
ing the impenitent, will be destroyed (63:6; 34:6).

Friend or Foe? (63:7-64:12)

The Warrior of 63:1-6 is the **'enemy'** of 63:10. We have forgotten,
as had Isaiah's contemporaries, that our God can turn and become
our enemy. With all the talk of taking care not to fall into the power
of Satan we can forget a more dangerous course; it is possible to fall
out with God! He can turn and become our enemy.

Why was the church in Isaiah's day in the condition it was? It was
not because of any lack of power, or commitment in God:

> 'Surely the arm of the Lord is not too short to save,
>   nor his ear too dull to hear.
> But your iniquities have separated
>   you from your God;
> your sins have hidden his face from you,
>   so that he will not hear'
>
> (59:1-2).

The cause for Israel's condition — and Isaiah has the Babylonian
captivity in mind throughout all these chapters — is sin and
rebellion.

What the prophet does in the face of these two awesome truths is an eloquent example of biblical holiness: he engages in prayer and intercession. Isaiah turns to earnest intercession. God's sovereign character and promises of action in the future are never revealed in Scripture as excuses for personal indolence, but as urgent incentives for action. The fact that Jesus possessed all authority in heaven and earth did not mean the disciples could sit back and relax. On the contrary, it obligated them to go into all the world and preach the gospel. So here, Isaiah recognizes that God employs means to achieve his ends. Preaching the gospel is God's means by which Christ's rule over the nations is fulfilled; prayer for the restoration and renewal of Jerusalem is the means by which the Lord's promises are realized.

Isaiah's prayer calls for some comments.

True prayer is based on God's covenant promises

Isaiah calls to mind all the things God has done for him and his people in the lengthy history of Israel (63:7). What are they?

1. God's electing love

'Surely they are my people.' According to E. J. Young the words should be translated *'Only they* are my people...'[1] Israel were the covenant people of God. They had been set apart and made special by God's grace. Election, and the assurance of it in our hearts, is always a cause for rejoicing.

2. God's covenant formula

The expression 'my people' (63:8) is an essential part of the relationship that God has with believers. The husband-wife relationship of 62:4-5 now makes way for another covenant metaphor: the relationship of a father to a son (**'sons'**, 63:8; cf. 1:2,4). Sonship is the highest privilege of the Christian life.

3. God's sympathy

> **'In all their distress he too was distressed,**
> **and the angel of his presence saved them.**

> **In his love and mercy he redeemed them;**
> **he lifted them up and carried them**
> **all the days of old'**

(63:9).

Does the Lord really understand the way I feel? Of course he does — and sympathizes with it. The suffering in Egypt and during the period of the judges is probably in view: 'He could bear Israel's misery no longer' (Judg. 10:16). 'For we do not have a high priest who is unable to sympathize with our weaknesses... Let us then approach the throne of grace with confidence, so that we may receive mercy and find grace to help us in our time of need' (Heb. 4:15-16).

4. God's presence

Referring to incidents in the period of the Exodus (3:7; 19:4; 23:20-23; 33:14), Isaiah recalls the time when the 'angel of his presence' saved them from trouble. The angel of the Lord is none other than the Lord himself (Exod. 33:12). God had guided his people at every turn in the wilderness. In the wilderness of Babylon, he will do so again.

5. God's frequent interventions

'In his love and mercy he redeemed them; he lifted them up and carried them all the days of old' (63:9). The language is that of a mother carrying her little child with all the tenderness which that entails. God's interventions are of the most loving and tender sort.

6. God's chastenings

Even the scourgings of God are precious when they bring us back to God. Following the rebellion when they grieved the Holy Spirit, he turned and became their enemy (63:10). He withheld his interventions (63:15), hardened their hearts (63:17) and gave them over to their enemies (63:18). But when they return to the Lord, humbled by his chastening hand, what a welcome they can expect! Isaiah depicts horses descending into the valleys for rest and pasture (63:13-14). Anyone who has seen horses emerging from lengthy confinement into open spaces knows what delight and exhilaration they show. Bless God for his chastenings!

These are some of the loving-kindnesses of the Lord.

'Return, Lord ... we need you' (63:17 - 64:12)

At the heart of the prayer is the church's need for revival. **'Look down from heaven,'** he says (63:15). But what is revival? This passage brings out some important aspects of it.

1. The Lord makes known his presence and power, suddenly and dramatically

All revivals are marked by a mysterious, irresistible sense that God is near. His power is felt in an awesome way — like the way he had shown himself at the exodus of Israel from Egypt (63:11). Someone who witnessed a revival in Eastford, Connecticut in 1818 said, 'It was so evidently the work of God that not a dog dared move his tongue!'

2. A sense of holy fear

When God comes down, the nations tremble (63:2). Pride and arrogance are humbled. Unbelievers are convicted of their sins; believers are humbled and exalt the majesty of God. When God showed Moses his glory, Moses quickly bowed his face to the earth (Exod. 34:8). During the Great Awakening in the eighteenth century (in Britain and New England) entire nations were affected: leaders were raised up; laws were changed; patterns of life were altered; places of sin were closed. When God rends the heavens and come down, everything is affected by it.

3. Revival is a display of God's sovereignty

It is the impotence of the church that necessitates the cry for God's coming. Revival is a sovereign work of God. Unless he comes, and comes powerfully, there can be no revival. George Whitefield made thirteen trips to America in his lifetime, but only on one occasion, in 1740-2, did revival break out. William Charles Burns, after a period of unparalleled blessing in his preaching in Scotland, went to China and laboured faithfully for twenty-one years with little fruit. God is sovereign and prayer is needed for him to act.

4. Revival is a display of God's mercy

God had withdrawn. God was angry (63:10; 64:5). He had stood outside the door of the church (cf. Rev. 3:20). The people's hearts were hardened (63:17). They had grown insensitive to the demands of God. There was no fear of God in their lives. Moreover, they were downtrodden (63:18). They had reached a point where it had become impossible to distinguish them from their enemies. God's people cannot sink any lower than that! The church is, by turns, described as a **'desert'**, **'burned with fire'** and **'in ruins'** (64:10-11).

In contrast to the condition of the church, God's habitation is **'holy and glorious'** (64:11). The church had declared a truce with sin and had brought about God's displeasure. God's tenderness and compassion had been withheld from them (63:15). There could only be one remedy: the mercy of God. God would surely respond to this plea because he was, and is, a God who 'delights to show mercy' (Micah 7:18). **'You, O Lord, are our Father,'** pleads the prophet (63:16; 64:8). The covenant God is a Father. By his covenant he brings us into his family. Like any earthly father, God delights in the chatter of his little ones. Isaiah touches upon the heart of God's character, with his promise to be merciful.

5. During a revival there is a sudden conversion of sinners in great numbers

The concern for conversion is expressed in the plea:

> **'As when fire sets twigs ablaze**
> **and causes water to boil,**
> **come down to make your name known to your enemies**
> **and cause the nations to quake before you!'**

(64:2).

Only the heat of God's presence can set on fire the wood of our hearts and boil the water of the hearts of sinners. It is estimated that during a revival in New York in 1858 there were over a million conversions.

Revival is promised to those who **'wait'** on God! (64:4).

3. *True prayer is based on the needs of God's people*

Prayer for mercy and renewal can never ignore a frank confession of our sinfulness. Revival is a work of grace. Isaiah spreads out before God a frank confession of sin. He pours out a prayer of penitence on behalf of those who will heed his message (64:5-12).

Sin had rendered God's people **'unclean'** (64:6). Here Isaiah uses yet another graphic portrait not often understood in English translations: sin is like the stained cloths (**'filthy rags'**, 64:6) of a woman in her menstrual cycle. It is a condition of defilement (cf. Lev. 15:19-24). Sin makes us 'dirty'.

Sin is also a state of impotence. No one calls upon the Lord (64:7). It is also a state of wrath. God is angry (64:9). The Warrior (63:1-6) has gone forth against his enemies to do battle. Sinners are God's enemies (Rom. 5:10) and stand under his wrath (Rom. 1:18).

Isaiah was confident that the Lord is not indifferent to the needs of his people. He is a true Father (64:8). Isaiah had recalled how, at the time of the Exodus, God had said, 'Surely they are my people ... so he became their Saviour. In all their distress he too was distressed' (63:8-9). In the second 'exodus' which the prophet had foreseen (40:1-11) the Lord would deliver his people again. **'After all this, O Lord, will you hold yourself back? Will you keep silent and punish us beyond measure?'** (64:12).

Pray for revival!

God's answer (65:1-16)

The prayer for revival in the chapter 64 is answered in the opening verses of chapter 65. God's answer to Isaiah's prayer for revival is of such magnitude that we are meant to learn from it and be thankful. The church's moribund condition would not last for long — at least, not as God measures time (cf. 2 Peter 3:8). God's answers to our prayers are sometimes in ways that surpass our understanding. Even though we struggle to think his thoughts after him, his ways and thoughts are different from ours (55:8-9).

It is possible to see the remaining two chapters (65-66) as the answer to the prayer of 64:12: 'After all this, O Lord, will you hold yourself back? Will you keep silent and punish us beyond measure?' The answer, in part, is as follows: God will show himself to a multitude, larger than you can imagine. His church, though at present in a pitiful condition, will be restored to prosperity.

God's true church

Even though Israel had been chosen as God's special nation, not everyone in Israel was a true believer, 'for not all who are descended from Israel are Israel' (Rom. 9:6). What distinguishes the true church of God is not the division between Jew and Gentile, but between those who **'seek'** God and those who **'forsake'** him (65:10,11).

When the apostle Paul saw that far more Gentiles than Jews were believing on Jesus he faced a problem for which he needed a scriptural answer. He found it in Isaiah's predictions and said so in Romans 10:20-21, where he quoted Isaiah 65:1-2. The **'obstinate'** Jews of Isaiah's day, who were intent on pursuing their own ways (65:2) were to be cut off, whereas the Gentiles — **'a nation who did not call on [God]'** — were to be grafted in (cf. Rom. 11:22-24).

What is the cause of God's rejection of the Jews? The answer lies in their **'obstinate'** nature (65:2). They were a rebellious people (63:10). Jesus elaborated upon this in the parable of the tenants, when he said, 'Therefore I tell you that the kingdom of God will be taken away from you and given to a people who will produce its fruit' (Matt. 21:43; cf. Deut. 32:5-6,21).

Isaiah once more lists a catalogue of their sins. Rather than speaking of sin in general terms, Isaiah never seems to tire of preaching about particular sins. The list is appalling: a religion riddled with idolatry; ritualistic orgies in sacred gardens (cf. 1:29; 66:17); Babylonian customs of worship on brick-built altars; necromancy — consulting with the dead in graveyards; eating ceremonially unclean foods; all of which results in puffed-up, arrogant self-evaluation (64:2-5). Interestingly, as in our own day, Israel too worshipped the gods of luck and chance — **'Fortune'** and **'Destiny'** (65:11).

God cannot condone sin. He will not keep silent. He will pay back in full (65:6). The justice of God is never out of proportion to man's crimes against him. But neither is it less than they deserve: **'I will measure into their laps the full payment for their former deeds'** (65:7). In summary, they 'provoked' God to anger (65:3).

God's passionate pleas

The outstretched arms of God pleading on behalf of Israel are a poignant expression of the genuine quality of his compassion. God called them over and over again: **'I called but you did not answer, I spoke but you did not listen'** (65:12) 'When I called, no one answered, when I spoke, no one listened' (66:4). Similar expressions are found in Jeremiah (Jer. 7:13,16; 35:17). God opens his arms and his heart to the rebellious, as he calls them, but his summons seems to fall empty to the ground and meet with no positive response. They reject every overture of God. Such can expect no mercy; only the devastating images of slaughter and death await them (65:11-12).

But there is another call of God, a call which is effectual and elicits a response in the hearts and lives of those who hear it. From the midst of Israel there is a remnant according to the election of grace. Even in Israel's blight-stricken vineyard, there is **'some good in it'** (65:8; cf. ch. 5). To these, God promises peace and prosperity. Isaiah uses local geography to make his point. **'Sharon'** — a plain along the Mediterranean coast north of Joppa, known for its superb foliage and grazing land — and **'the Valley of Achor'** — a valley near Jericho — were on the western and eastern edges of the land respectively.

Calvin saw this as a picture of the church in the days to come: 'Although, in consequence of the banishment of her inhabitants into a distant country, she shall be forsaken and desolate, yet she shall at length be inhabited, so as to abound in flocks and herds, and have lands that are fertile and that are fit for pasture, and supply abundantly everything that is necessary for the food and support of men.'[2]

In verses 13-16 Isaiah underlines the sharp contrast between the fate of the wicked and the true remnant of God. The redeemed of the Lord can expect to **'eat'**, **'drink'**, **'rejoice'**, and **'sing'**; the future for unbelievers is the opposite: they will be **'hungry'**, **'thirsty'**, **'cry out with anguish'**, and **'wail in brokenness of spirit'**. These are the contrasting destinies of the sheep and the goats (Matt. 25:31-46). 'Whoever believes in the Son has eternal life, but whoever rejects the Son will not see life, for God's wrath remains on him' (John 3:36).

The blessed and the cursed

Isaiah passes the most damning sentence of all on unbelievers when he declares that their name will become a byword, an expression of the curse of God (65:15). The rebellious Israelites will be used as an example when curses are uttered. Believers, on the other hand, will be cited as examples of blessing. They will think of what **'the God of truth'**, the 'Amen', has done and they will have cause to rejoice in the faithfulness of God; whatever he has promised, he has done. There is coming a time when **'past troubles will be forgotten and hidden from my eyes'** (65:16).

Summary

Thoughts about heaven in chapter 62 have led the prophet to warn in the following chapter that there is a hell to be shunned, too. The picture of the blood-stained Warrior was meant to chill and solemnize. It was meant to drive the prophet's listeners, without delay, to Christ.

40.
The new heavens and the new earth

Please read Isaiah 65:17 - 66:24

Dr Martyn Lloyd-Jones once wrote, 'My whole outlook upon everything that happens to me should be governed by these three things: my realization of who I am, my consciousness of where I am going, and my knowledge of what awaits me when I get there.'[1] Isaiah wants to close his prophecy of encouragement to believers by drawing our attention upwards to heaven and what God is about to do. In the midst of present difficulties, the prophet urges us to look upwards.

Isaiah began his prophecy with a forthright declaration of Israel's condition: they were a 'sinful nation' (1:4-6). The formal, ritualistic worship of unbelieving hearts had sickened the Lord (1:11-14). The same abhorrence is reflected in the last chapter, where he likens their sacrifices to the breaking of an animal's neck (66:3 — a bloodless procedure and therefore ineffective as a sacrifice).

Throughout the book, the prophet has had cause to outline the particular nature of Israel's heinous crimes against the Lord. They had proved violators of the covenant and were liable to its curses. The Lord 'turned and became their enemy' (63:10). The Lord is a God of justice (30:18). The Warrior, clothed with battle dress, was coming for war.

But there were a remnant in Israel who remained faithful (65:8). Isaiah has finished praying on their behalf. He pleaded for mercy, saying,

'But when we continued to sin ...
    you were angry.

How then can we be saved?...
After all this, O Lord, will you hold yourself back?
Will you keep silent and punish us beyond measure?'
(64:5,12).

Isaiah's later chapters have been answering this question. God is in control, working out his purposes. His covenant to save his people will not, cannot, be abandoned (54:10; 55:3; 61:8). At the heart of this covenant is Jesus Christ himself (42:6; 49:8). The Saviour's coming into this world was, for Isaiah, only the beginning of the work of redemption. Calvary both removes the barrier of sin and shapes the people of God, making them fit for heaven — God's ultimate residence for his children. The darkness of so many of the prophet's pages now makes way for the brightness of the new heavens and the new earth. From the depths of sin, he rises to the heights of paradise.

A future millennial state? (65:17-25)

There is a problem of interpretation over these verses. The New Scofield Bible, for example, has the heading 'New heavens and new earth' over verse 17. The heading over verses 18-25, however, is 'Millennial conditions in the renewed earth with curse removed'. This view, which sees the passage as referring to a future 1,000-year reign of Christ on earth, obscures the fact that just as verse 17 clearly speaks of 'a new heavens and a new earth', verse 18 calls upon the reader to rejoice **'for ever'** — not just for 1,000 years. And verse 19 adds another detail which Revelation 21:4 understands as a mark of the final state: **'The sound of weeping and of crying will be heard in it no more.'** Dispensationalists draw our attention to verse 20:

> **'Never again will there be in it**
> **an infant who lives but a few days,**
> **or an old man who does not live out his years;**
> **he who dies at a hundred**
> **will be thought a mere youth;**
> **he who fails to reach a hundred**
> **will be considered accursed'**

(65:20).

Since death is mentioned in this verse, they insist, the passage cannot possibly refer to the final state.[2] Obviously, there can be no death in the final state; Isaiah has stated as much:

> 'He will swallow up death for ever.
> The Sovereign Lord will wipe away the tears
>   from all faces;
> he will remove the disgrace of his people
>   from all the earth.
>   The Lord has spoken'
>   (25:8; cf. Rev. 21:4).

Here in chapter 65 Isaiah is picturing in figurative terms the fact that the inhabitants of the new earth will live incalculably long lives. 'The point of *a hundred years old* (v. 20) is that in this new setting a mere century is shamefully brief, so vast is the scale.'[3] This interpretation is supported by the words of verse 22:

> **'For as the days of a tree,**
> **   so will be the days of my people;**
> **my chosen ones will long enjoy**
> **   the works of their hands.'**

In summary, the passage describes a new heavens and a new earth (65:17), calling upon the faithful to rejoice for ever (65:18) because it will be a condition where there is no weeping, or distress (65:19). There will be no death in heaven (65:20), or any kind of violence (65:25).

What an answer to the prayer of chapter 64! (64:5,12). Far from being 'angry for ever', God promises a paradise for his people. God often answers our prayers in a way that shames us for our unbelief. The Bible does not present an art of prayer; it presents the God of prayer, the God who calls before we answer and answers before we call (65:24). Far from prayer being man rising to God, it is man's response to what God has revealed. The basis of all prayer is what God has promised to do. This is, according to Calvin, 'the most valuable fruit of faith.'[4]

The dwelling-place of God (66:1-13)

The Lord, who is to bring about this new heavens and new earth, dwells in heaven. The present earth, which he created (66:2), is a footstool upon which he rests his feet (66:1). Isaiah is not going to finish his prophecy without reminding us of the God whose glory had shaken him to the core on a visit to the temple one day (ch. 6). Similar words are used in one of the psalms:

'Who is like the Lord our God,
　　the One who sits enthroned on high,
who stoops down to look
　　on the heavens and the earth?'

(Ps. 113:5-6).

The infinite greatness of God gives rise to the question how he can be present in any physical building (66:1). The temple which Solomon had built had served as a dwelling-place of God, but even he realized that God could not be localized in any man-made temple, magnificent though it might be (1 Kings 8:27; 2 Chron. 6:18). At ninety feet long and thirty feet wide the temple may well have been regarded as a 'great one' (2 Chron. 2:5), but it was not as great as all that! J. B. Phillips once wrote a provocative book called *Your God Is Too Small*. God is far too big to fit into our conception of him, too big for the irreverent worship of the contemporary church. He is the Gulliver in our Lilliputian world.

The answer to this tension between the transcendence and immanence of God lies in the manner of God's presence. He dwells in the hearts of those who humble themselves and acknowledge his greatness: **'This is the one I esteem: he who is humble and contrite in spirit, and trembles at my word'** (66:2). The Holy Spirit resides in the poor, humble and contrite (cf. 57:15-16).

1. Heaven is not yet

In a clear warning to his readers, who may well be euphoric at the thought of what God has done for them, but especially with what awaits them, Isaiah cautions them to expect persecution. The meek,

who tremble at God's Word, will be despised (66:5-6). Jesus warned
that his enemies are our enemies too (John 15:20). 'I have told you
these things, so that in me you may have peace. In this world you will
have trouble. But take heart! I have overcome the world' (John
16:33). There are persecutions to be endured (Mark 13:13). We need
to face that realistically. We cannot afford to be blinded to the
realities of heaven by a false hope (or wish) that life will be trouble-
free. There are battle scars to be borne by the warrior forces of the
Warrior King. But they who put the Lord to grief (53:3) will
themselves be put to grief (66:6). God is ashamed of those who are
ashamed of him and his people. The prophet urges us to listen to the
noise of the battle as the Judge goes forth to war against his (and our)
enemies (66:6).

2. A country born in one day

The things which God has promised in this book are so staggering
that many who first heard them (and we who read them) must have
wondered just how they would be brought about. So the Lord speaks
in terms of the birth of a new nation (66:7-11). The pregnant mother
figure gives birth, not only to a child, but to a nation. Theologians
love big words and one expression they sometimes use is
'gynomorphic imagery'! What they mean by this is simply this: God
is a mother giving birth to children. Perhaps the most peaceful,
contented scene we can ever witness in this world is that of a little
baby sucking at its mother's breasts. God assures the beleaguered
people of the Babylonian exile of a condition of pure joy. Who
hasn't been moved by a little child being comforted by a mother's
tender words? Such is God's care for his children (66:12-13).

The apostles on the Day of Pentecost must have thought of
passages such as this one as they witnessed thousands turning to
Christ. This extraordinary vision of an expanding church calls forth
a spirit of rejoicing (66:10,14). God's promises make us glad.

Larger and larger visions (66:14-17)

Isaiah is an evangelical prophet. His preaching both warned the
unrepentant and encouraged the righteous. In the midst of tender

portraits of a mother nursing her children, he gives a final warning of what awaits the wicked: **'With fire and with his sword the Lord will execute judgement upon all men, and many will be those slain by the Lord'** (66:16). Isaiah is a book of warning to those who will not bow down to the Lord. God wants us to be sure about this matter: **'fire'** and **'sword'** are part of God's wrathful character: 'When the Lord Jesus is revealed from heaven in blazing fire ... he will punish those who do not know God and do not obey the gospel of our Lord Jesus. They will be punished with everlasting destruction and shut out from the presence of the Lord and from the majesty of his power...' (2 Thess. 1:7-10).

The nations gathered in (66:18-24)

This book has interpreted the prophecies of Isaiah as spanning the first and second comings of Christ. The 'last days' begin with the ascension of Christ. Those who see these things differently have, by now, interpreted various sections of the prophecy according to their views. Those who expect a millennial reign of Christ on earth expect a full return of the Jews to Israel and the establishment of Jerusalem as the world's capital and centre of pilgrimage.

The closing verses of Isaiah are an example of passages which give rise to these different views. To be consistent with our understanding of the prophecy, we interpret what the prophet tells us in closing as being that the nations of the world, that is, *all the Lord's people from every tribe and nation* will be gathered into the church. God is intending to expand the church beyond the confines of the Jewish state. The nations of the world are to flood in.

Israel, as a theocratic state, will perish, but there will be survivors (66:19-21). They will come from the distant outposts of the world: **'Tarshish ... Libyans and Lydians (famous as archers), ... Tubal and Greece', and ... the distant islands that have not heard of my fame or seen my glory'**. All come flooding to Jerusalem bringing their offerings. E. J. Young summarizes the words of the prophet in this way: 'Well do I know the nature of the Jewish nation. Their deeds and their devices are not unknown to Me; hence the time has come when I shall in their place gather together the nations. In order to accomplish this I shall send out survivors of the judgement upon Israel who will proclaim My greatness and saving power among those nations which have never heard My Name nor seen My glory.'⁵

Isaiah speaks of a **'sign'** which will be set among God's people (66:19). It is none other than Jesus! (Acts 2:22). He is the One who gathers the people to God. He is the Redeemer of sinners!

But Isaiah cannot forget that just as there is a heaven, there is also a hell. How extraordinary that he ends the book this way! The church has forgotten about it, or prefers not to speak about it, but not Isaiah. He mentions the everlasting nature of heaven (66:22); he also speaks of the everlasting torment of hell. **'And they will go out and look upon the dead bodies of those who rebelled against me; their worm will not die, nor will their fire be quenched, and they will be loathsome to all mankind'** (66:24). The mention of the word 'rebelled' here brings us back to the very opening of Isaiah's prophecy (cf. 1:2). Like two book-ends, this charge against the Old Testament church encloses all that Isaiah has to say: they were living in rebellion and unless they repented they would suffer the consequences.

This is a verse which Jesus knew too. He preached on hell — the ultimate consequence of rebellion — more than any other, using this text to amplify its nature (Mark 9:48). The valley of Hinnom, south-west of Jerusalem, was a place where the refuse was burnt. From this valley the smoke of burning rubbish ascended. Every time a pilgrim came away from Jerusalem he would see it and be reminded of the end of the wicked. They are **'loathsome'** (66:24), a word which is translated 'contempt' in Daniel 12:2, where the picture is of unbelievers being raised from the dead, excluded for ever from the city of God. The picture is an abhorrent one. It is meant to be. Isaiah wants us to be in no doubt of the existence of hell.

But such is not the fate of the faithful whose trust is in the Lord's Messiah. They will **'endure'**. That is what the gospel is all about.

Summary

Having begun the prophecy with a statement of Israel's sinful and apostate condition, Isaiah closes with a vision of the new heavens and the new earth. The word of 'comfort' promised in 40:1 has by now reached its climax. George Adam Smith writes about this prophecy, that 'Throughout the exile the true Jew lived inwardly ... an inhabitant not so much of a foreign prison but of his own broken heart.'[6] The healing of that broken heart has come through the prophet's evangelical insistence on the centrality of Christ in the redemption of God's covenant people. Christ will come and provide the atonement necessary for sinners to be reconciled to God. God's sovereign purposes will be accomplished on a cosmic scale. His church will be gathered from the four corners of the world. The consummation will bring into being a new level of existence.

As the sovereign Lord of history, Isaiah has portrayed God as the supreme Creator of the universe, powerful and majestic. He made the very planets which ignorant men now worshipped. He knows the end from the beginning, sovereignly determining the outcome of the universe. The exile was no accident, but part of his plan. It was God's punishment for Judah's apostasy, but he had arranged a way back for the remnant who believed. He raised up Cyrus as a mere instrument in his powerful hands.

Yet, for all God's greatness, he is also tender and gracious. He is Israel's Lover (43:4), their Mother (49:15) and their Husband (54:5). It is inconceivable — blasphemous even! — to think that he would abandon his own people.

God, Isaiah tells his listeners, will do 'a new thing' (43:19) and restore his people to their land (49:8-26). It will be another exodus! (43:16-21). It will be an exodus that leads to a new land of unimaginable splendour (60:1 - 61:11) and cosmic proportions (65:17-25). In summary, Isaiah's message is: 'My righteousness draws near' (51:5). It is a way of salvation centred around God's Son (52:13 - 53:12). Through him the people would be healed.

The experience of restoration has been pictured in terms contrasting with their present condition. Currently they are apostate, and soon they will be exiles and servants. In the new age to come they will be prophets, kings and priests. They will bear a new name and emit a new beauty: the beauty of holiness (e. g. 52:1-12; 60:1-22; 61:4-7).

It is time to prepare the way of the Lord (40:3), to 'arise, shine, for your light has come' (60:1). It is time to think about heaven and whether or not we are prepared for it. Jesus taught his disciples to long for heaven (John 14:1-3). John Bradford, just a few months before his fiery entrance into heaven, could write thus: 'I am assured that though I want here, I have riches there; though I hunger here, I shall have fulness there; though I faint here, I shall be refreshed there; and though I be accounted here as a dead man, I shall there live in perpetual glory.

'That is the city promised to the captives whom Christ shall make free; that is the kingdom assured to them whom Christ shall crown; there is the light that shall never go out; there is the health that shall never be impaired; there is the glory that shall never be defaced; there is the life that shall taste no death; and there is the portion that passes all the world's preferment. There is the world that shall never wax worse; there is every want supplied freely without money; there is not danger, but happiness, and honour, and singing, and praise and thanksgiving unto the heavenly Jehovah, "to him that sits on the throne," "to the Lamb" that here was led to the slaughter, that now "reigns"; with whom I "shall reign" after I have run this comfortless race through this miserable earthly vale.'[7]

Only as we echo these words in our own hearts will Isaiah's message, 'Your God reigns,' become meaningful.

'Seek the Lord while he may be found' (55:6)

References

Preface
1. John Calvin, *Commentary on The Prophet Isaiah*, (Baker, 1981), vols VII and VIII; E. J. Young, *The Book of Isaiah*, (Eerdmans, 1965). (Unless otherwise stated all references to Calvin or Young are from these volumes.)

Introduction
1. See O. T. Allis, *The Law and the Prophets* (Presbyterian and Reformed, 1974), essay by Robert L. Alden, 'Isaiah and Wood', pp.377-87.
2. Timothy George, *Theology of the Reformation* (Apollos, 1988), p.103.

Chapter 1
1. See 24:20; 30:9; 36:5; 43:27; 46:8; 48:8; 50:5; 57:4; 58:1; 59:13; 63:10.
2. Cf. Heb. 3:8; 4:7; 12:5-28, where we are encouraged not to become hardened.
3. F. F. Bruce, *Israel and the Nations* (Paternoster Press, 1963), p.71 cited by David F. Payne, *Kingdoms of the Lord* (Paternoster Press, 1981), p.113.
4. This illustration will also be used by Isaiah in chapter 5.
5. *Macbeth*, Act 5, Scene 1.

Chapter 2
1. Cited by Sinclair Ferguson, *Daniel* (Word, 1988), p.147.
2. See the comments of Edmund P. Clowney, *The Doctrine of the Church* (Presbyterian and Reformed, 1969), pp.12-13.
3. Though in doing this the NIV might have unwittingly created or preserved the impression that the term 'latter days' is inappropriate for a reference to the near future.
4. Young, vol. 1, p.100.

5. Others include: Ps. 72:1-20; Isa. 11:1-9; 65:17-25; Jer. 23:5-6; Amos 9:11-15; Micah 4:1-4; Zech. 14:1-9, 16-21).

6. See notes in New Scofield Bible on this passage.

7. Norman Shepherd, 'Postmillennialism,' *Zondervan Pictorial Encyclopedia of the Bible*, IV, 823.

8. Note the way Isaiah uses this word 'come' in 2:5, reflecting a similar call in 1:18.

9. See G. Vos, *Biblical Theology* (Eerdmans, 1973), p.255. Vos says, 'Isaiah has a sarcastic term for naming the idols, *"elilim"*; this, though not of the same etymology with *El*, yet reminds of it, but by making out of the word a diminutive represents the pagan gods as "godlets", or (etymologically taken) as "good-for-nothing-ones".'

Chapter 3

1. The tree, in fact, is 'preserved' in the local museum and I guess, to be truthful, still remains!

2. Some believe that 'branch' here refers to Judah rather than Jesus. They point out that 'branch' is paralleled by 'the fruit of the land'. In that case the point is that Judah must be reborn. Though she is in a terrible state at the moment, a branch will emerge from her that will be his true people. From this branch Jesus will come.

Chapter 4

1. A. W. Tozer, *The Set of the Sail*, (Kingsway, 1987), p.34.

2. Cf. Rom. 9:22; 2 Peter 3:15, both of which speak of the patience of God with sinners. The NIV rendering of the 'unlimited patience of Christ' in 1 Tim. 1:16 is not accurate. The idea of 'long-suffering' does not imply that it is unlimited.

3. J. C. Ryle, *Holiness* (James Clarke, 1956), p.19.

4. Calvin, vol. 1, pp.176-7.

5. Young, vol. 1, p.219.

6. J. C. Ryle, *Expository Thoughts on the Gospels, John,* James Clarke, 1976), vol. 3, pp.113-114.

Chapter 5

1. Commentators disagree about the exact timing of Isaiah's call.

E. J. Young favours the view that Isaiah 6 gives an account of Isaiah's inaugural call. The first five chapters are then seen as a 'general introduction' to the message of the book, (see Young, vol. 1, pp.231-233), but 1:1 seems to imply that Isaiah was active *during* Uzziah's reign. Young is open to the idea that 1:1 is just a heading loosely attached to the book and not necessarily implying that Isaiah was ministering during Uzziah's reign (vol. 1, p.32).

J. I. Packer is of the view that this is Isaiah's conversion experience. Prior to this point he had been mistakenly of the opinion that he was accepted with God. The first five chapters were delivered by an unconverted man (see *Laid-Back Religion: A penetrating look at Christianity today*, IVP,1987, p.42).

Calvin sees the experience of Isaiah 6 as 'confirming' and 'strengthening' Isaiah in the discharge of his office (see Calvin, pp.198-9). This is the view adopted here. It is also the view of Sinclair Ferguson (see *A Heart For God* (Banner of Truth, 1987), p.86).

2. Ferguson, *A Heart For God*, p.85.

3. Calvin, p.203.

4. (1:4; 5:19,24; 10:20; 12:6; 17:7; 29:19; 30:11,12,15; 31:1; 37:23; 41:14,16,20; 43:3,14; 45:11; 47:4; 48:17; 49:7; 54:5; 55:5; 60:9,14).

5. Derek Thomas, *Serving The King* (Evangelical Press, 1989), p.9.

6. C. H. Spurgeon, *Lectures to my Students* (Marshal, Morgan & Scott), p.146.

7. Samuel Johnson, *Life of the English Poets* (Oxford U.P.), 2:365.

8. James Stewart, *Heralds of God* (Baker,1972), p.73. Actually, the words are by Archbishop William Temple, but Stewart used them to define preaching.

9. Christopher Catherwood, *Five Evangelical Leaders* (Hodder & Stoughton, 1984), p.174.

Chapter 6

1. The Arameans were descendants of Shem (Gen. 10:22-23). Syria did not become a political territory of its own until the fourth century B.C.; nevertheless, Aram is frequently referred to as 'Syria'. Aramaic was the language which Jesus spoke.

2. 'Aram' (see 7:1) is another name for Syria, and 'Ephraim' (see 7:2), being the largest tribe, is used here to denote the whole of Israel (see notes on chapter 17).

3. Ahaz did not possess the spiritual qualities of his father Jotham or grandfather Azariah. The list of his failures is quite staggering. He introduced the worship of the Canaanite god Molech and actually sacrificed his own children in the ceremonial fires (2 Kings 16:3). He not only permitted worship at the 'high places' but burned sacrifices there himself (2 Kings 16:4). He lost 120,000 Judean soldiers, 200,000 civilian hostages, and his own son in battle with Rezin and Pekah (2 Chron. 28). He surrendered the Judean port of Elath to the Syrians and later the Edomites (2 Kings 16:6). He spurned Isaiah's advice and turned to the Assyrians for help (Isa. 7:1-11). He closed down the temple, refusing to let the people worship there (2 Chron. 28:24). He removed the pavilion (a sheltered colonnade used by the priests in the temple) and bricked up the Upper Gate

of the temple, which his father had built (2 Kings 16:18). He confiscated the gold and silver treasures of the house of God and the royal palace to finance a bribe ('gift') to Tiglath-Pileser III (2 Kings 16:8). He placed a pagan altar in the central position in the temple, copied from a design he had seen in Damascus (2 Kings 16:10-11,15). He took the place of the priests, offering sacrifices himself. He also relocated the bronze altar built by Solomon, using it to examine the entrails of dead animals for a sign, thus introducing witchcraft into the temple.

4. Calvin, p.239.

5. Other uses of the word '*almah*' are in Ps. 68:25; S of S. 1:3; 6:8 and Prov. 30:19. Its use in this latter reference has occasioned the discussion that the word can mean a woman who is not a virgin. 'The way of a man with a maiden' seems to suggest that she is not a virgin. But the use of '*almah* elsewhere seems to be a clear reference to a virgin. In any case Matthew was in no doubt what he meant when he chose the word *parthenos*. He meant virgin! Luther offered 100 gulden to anyone who could prove *almah* meant 'married woman' (adding that the Lord alone knew where he would get the money!). Some have suggested that Isaiah could have used the Hebrew *bethulah* to suggest a young woman's unmarried, virgin condition, but there are at least two points to be made: though it can mean 'virgin', Joel 1:8 uses it for someone 'grieving for the husband of her youth'; and the Greek translation of the Old Testament (the Septuagint) always rendered *almah* by *parthenos*, a word which can only mean virgin. Since this translation was made in the third century B.C. the translators cannot be accused of manipulating the text to fit in with the birth of Christ.

6. The notes of the NIV Study Bible take this view. It is misguided.

7. Young, vol. 1, p.162.

8. See J. A. Alexander, *Commentaries on the Prophecies of Isaiah* (Zondervan, 1953), pp.168-73. Cf. the words of Willis J. Beecher: 'This prophecy falls into rank with most of the Messianic prophecies quoted in the New Testament, in that it is a repetition of the one great promise made to Abraham, to Israel, to David — that promise which was always being fulfilled in the older history, but always looking forward to larger fulfilment in the future.' See his essay 'The Prophecy of the Virgin Mother' in *Classical Evangelical Essays in Old Testament Interpretation*, compiled and edited by Walter Kaiser (Baker, 1972), pp.179-85 (esp. p.185).

9. Gerard van Groningen, *Messianic Revelation in the Old Testament* (Baker, 1990), p.534.

10. As well as Young, see E. W. Hengstenberg, *Christology of the Old Testament*, vol. 1 (Macdonald), p.420, and J. A. Motyer, 'Context and Content in the Interpretation of Isaiah 7:14', *Tyndale Bulletin 21* (1970): 118-25.

11. D. A. Carson, *The Expositor's Bible Commentary: Matthew* (Zondervan, 1984), p.79.

12. William J. Dumbrell, *The Faith of Israel: Its expression in the Books of the Old Testament* (Apollos, 1989), p.103.

Chapter 7

1. Some have insisted that 8:3 implies that this woman is Isaiah's *second* wife. (For this view, *see Messianic Revelation in the Old Testament*, by Gerard van Groningen, p.539). This would mean that his first wife died at the birth of Shear-Jashub. The idea behind this reasoning seems to be another speculation, namely, that the birth of Maher-Shalal-Hash-Baz is the initial fulfilment of the prophecy of Isaiah 7:14. If this is so, the 'prophetess' was at that time a virgin, who after marrying Isaiah, conceived and gave birth to a son. Two conjectures are present: firstly, that Maher-Shalal-Hash-Baz is the fulfilment of 7:14, something which is difficult to understand since he was *not called Immanuel*, and secondly, the death of Isaiah's first wife — something which is *not* mentioned in Isaiah!
2. Calvin, vol. 1, p.261.
3. Isaiah often changes his pictures quickly, e.g., 5:24; 9:17-21; 28:16,20.
4. J. C. Ryle, *Expository Thoughts on the Gospels: Matthew*, p.209.
5. The Hebrew Bible places the first verse of chapter 9 at the end of chapter 8.
6. The conquered regions of the kingdom of Israel were divided into three provinces, called by the Assyrians Dor (the Way of the Sea), Megiddo (Galilee of the Gentiles) and Gilead (Transjordan). Most of these newly created provinces remained intact without major changes for centuries, later being taken over by the Babylonians and then by the Persians.

Chapter 8

1. Manasseh ruled in Judah about sixty-five years after this time. This only goes to show that Isaiah's message went unheeded (cf. 53:1: 'Who has believed our report...?')
2. Young, vol. 1, p.333.
3. *Ibid.*
4. Translations are divided as to whether this constitutes one or two names: i.e. Wonderful Counsellor (NIV text) or Wonderful, Counsellor (NIV footnote, NKJV).
5. See Hengstenberg, *Christology in the Old Testament*, vol. 2, pp.434ff.

Chapter 9

1. Isaiah is perhaps standing at the gates of Jerusalem and imagining the coming of Sennacherib's armies from the north. In actual fact, they approached Jerusalem from the south (Lachish, cf. 36:2). This passage is only an attempt to suggest that when Assyria comes, she will take over the whole land. See map and comments on chapters 36-39.

Chapter 10
1. This is something we shall have to look at more closely when we examine Isaiah 42-43.
2. The word 'Meribah' ('quarrelled'), which was given to the place afterwards, means to 'file a lawsuit'. See Edmund Clowney, *The unfolding mystery: Discovering Christ in the Old Testament* (NavPress, 1988), p.121.
3. Calvin, vol. 1, p.398.
4. The NIV has lost this picture by using instead the word 'live' in these references.

Eschatology in the Old Testament
1. G. E. Ladd, *The Presence and the Future*, pp. 59-60, cited by A. A. Hoekema, *The Bible and the Future* (Paternoster, 1978), p.11.

Chapter 11
1. This was in 745/734 B.C. The prophecies recorded in chapters 13-27 are from a later time (apart from possibly chapter 20). Isaiah 14:28 gives us a clue as to the period: it is the year that Ahaz has died (715 B.C.) These chapters were then given some time after this date and some twenty or even thirty years after the first twelve chapters. It is not possible to be precise as to the dating of each individual chapter. It is quite possible that after the year 700 B.C. Isaiah went into retirement and put together the entire book as we now have it, adding some epilogues here and there.
2. Some have suggested that this section refers to Babylon during the Assyrian empire rather than the Neo-Babylonian empire. There is no new heading at 14:24, which begins a section on Assyria and it is therefore concluded that this entire section is actually against Assyria. It is true that from 729 B.C. onwards the Kings of Assyria also called themselves 'Kings of Babylon'. However, this does not adequately account for the mention of 'the Medes' in 13:17. Though the Medes were around during the Assyrian empire, this passage seems almost certainly to refer to Cyrus and the conquest of Babylon in 539 B.C.
3. Calvin, vol. 1, p.442.

Chapter 12
1. The Philistines had been Israel's first major enemy. Having originally come from Crete (cf. Gen. 10:14), they settled in the coastal plains, south-west of Canaan, roughly during the period covered by Exodus. In occupying Canaan the Israelites had taken deliberate steps to avoid 'the road through the Philistine country' (Exod. 13:17). In the time of the judges, relationships between Israel and the Philistines wavered. Samson married a Philistine wife, but his eventual capture and ridicule at their hands

revealed their mutual hostility. In Saul's time, it was the Philistines who captured the ark of the covenant (1 Sam. 4). They had by now occupied not just the coastal plains between Egypt and Gaza, but the Negeb and much of the hill country.

In particular, the Philistines were noted for their skills in iron and the making of weapons and chariots (1 Sam. 13:19-22). Saul's victory at the famous Battle of Michmash came only by means of divine intervention: a storm that caused the chariots to get bogged down (1 Sam. 14). David's victory over Goliath also revealed the hand of God (1 Sam. 17-18). Philistine power was seriously curtailed by another of David's victories (2 Sam. 5:25), but following his death their power once more increased. Isaiah has already mentioned the threat they posed during the reign of Ahaz (9:12).

2. The Moabites had family ties with Israel: Moab was the son born of the incestuous relationship of Lot and his eldest daughter (Gen. 19:36-7). They occupied the Transjordan area, east of the Dead Sea, and were constant enemies of Israel. One bright spot appears in their history when Naomi's widowed daughter-in-law, Ruth, professed faith and married Boaz and became the great-grandmother of King David (Ruth 4:17). Her appearance in the genealogy of Jesus in Matthew 1:5 marks her out as a trophy of God's grace to a Gentile in the Old Testament.

Despite this, their influence was an evil one. They encouraged sexual immorality in the practice of fertility rites, something in which Israel became involved during the time of Moses (Num. 25).

3. Calvin, vol. 1, p.473.

Chapter 13

1. Syria was also called 'Aram' (cf. 7:1,8). It was famous for its orchards and gardens, irrigated by the waters of the rivers Abana and Pharpar: 'Are not Abana and Pharpar, the rivers of Damascus, better than any of the waters of Israel?' (2 Kings 5:12). The city of Damascus formed a central meeting-point on the way from Egypt to the eastern states (the 'king's highway' ran through Damascus — Num. 20:17; 21:22).

A hundred years before Isaiah's time, Damascus had made a treaty with Ahab (the seventh king of Israel) to form a coalition of states to oppose Assyrian aggression (1 Kings 20:34). But these were troubled times between Israel and Damascus. Wars broke out which eventually resulted in Ahab's death (1 Kings 22:29-36). Both Elijah and Elisha prophesied in Damascus (1 Kings 19:15; 2 Kings 8:7). Hazael, the King of Syria, came to power by suffocating to death his predecessor, Ben-Hadad, with a wet cloth (2 Kings 8:15). His wars against Israel in Jehu's time were foreseen by Elisha, who shed tears over their particular cruelty and viciousness (2 Kings 8:12). Hazael had to face the Assyrian threat in 841 B.C.

Shalmaneser III attacked and Syria lost 16,000 men, 1,121 chariots and 470 cavalry. Hazael successfully retreated into Damascus, and after Shalmaneser's men had burnt the surrounding orchards they withdrew. However, this was the beginning of Syria's downfall.

Relationships between countries change quickly (as that of European countries with Germany in this century has shown). In Isaiah's day, King Rezin of Syria formed a treaty with Israel's king Pekah (ch. 7). Both were increasingly under an obligation not to offend the Assyrians. But in an attempt to revolt, they attacked Judah to try to gain its territory and support. Many Judeans were taken captive to Damascus and only released by the intervention of a prophet called Oded (2 Chron. 28). Ahaz, King of Judah, had been warned by Isaiah to trust in the Lord, but instead called upon Assyria to attack the northern states of Syria and Israel. In a series of raids lasting from 734-732 B.C. Rezin was killed, and Damascus was finally taken and plundered (Isa. 8:4). Many Israelite cities were also captured (9:1). Judah was to observe what happened to Damascus and take note (10:9-11).

2. After the division of the kingdom, the northern state of Israel was composed of ten tribes. Ephraim was always the more dominant and by the late eighth century B.C. the name 'Ephraim' became synonymous with 'Israel', in just the same way as the two southern tribes of Judah and Benjamin became known simply as 'Judah'. The fate of Ephraim (Israel) had, by Isaiah's day, become bound up with that of its neighbour, Syria, or Aram (see notes on chapter 7).

3. Nevertheless God continued to send prophets to Israel — men like Hosea and Jeremiah. Isaiah himself has already spoken of a day when the healing of the division would be brought about (11:13). Jeremiah says,

'They will come with weeping;
    they will pray as I bring them back.
I will lead them beside streams of water
    on a level path where they will not stumble,
because I am Israel's father,
    and Ephraim is my firstborn son'

(Jer. 31:9).

4. For more on the ungodly character of King Ahaz, the reader is referred to chapter 7, note 3 above.

5. Cush is the region south of Egypt sometimes called 'Ethiopia' (modern Sudan). At this point in the eighth century B.C., Cush had gained control of Egypt, and its fate was linked with that of Egypt in much the same way that Israel's was with Syria.

6. Dio Chrysostom (A.D.40-120), *11th Discourse*.

Chapter 14

1. All these events, the revolt of Babylon (which lies behind 14:28-32) in 715 B.C., and the sacking of Ashdod in 713 B.C. (which is the event recorded here in 20:1-6) are still in the future for Isaiah himself. None of these things has yet happened. After the fall of Israel in 722-721 B.C. King Hezekiah, who succeeded King Ahaz after his death in 731 B.C. (14:1), was under great pressure to look to Egypt and Cush for help against the Assyrians. Much of Isaiah's ministry was to warn against such a policy. He had to stand against the tide of public opinion and call for his leaders to trust in God. It was as difficult then as it would be now. This three-year period of semi-nakedness would probably have occurred somewhere after 721 B.C. and before 715 B.C.

2. The extent of Isaiah's nakedness is a matter of some dispute. Since there is a connection between Isaiah's action in verse 2, and the deportation of the people of Egypt and Cush **'with buttocks bared'** in verse 4, it is felt by some that Isaiah must also have been as naked as this (cf. Young, vol. 2, p.56). But others have insisted that even after the removal of the 'sackcloth' the prophet would still have worn some kind of loincloth (cf. Leupold, *Exposition of Isaiah*, (Baker, 1968) p.327: 'The claim that Isaiah, therefore, went about for a period of time stark naked can hardly be maintained.' See, too, Derek Kidner, *New Bible Commentary*, 'Isaiah' (IVP, 1970), p.602.

3. The conquest of Babylon by the Medo-Persian empire, under King Cyrus, did not take place until 539 B.C.

4. 'Elam' was one of Shem's sons (Gen. 10:22). The Elamites were part of the Persian army that conquered Babylon under Cyrus in 539 B.C. In 11:11 a remnant was seen coming back from Elam — a reference to the return under Zerubbabel, Ezra and Nehemiah: 'Now these are the people of the province who came up from the captivity of the exiles, whom Nebuchadnezzar king of Babylon had taken captive to Babylon (they returned to Jerusalem and Judah, each to his own town, in company with Zerubbabel, Jeshua, Nehemiah, Seraiah, Reelaiah, Mordecai, Bilshan, Mispar, Bigvai, Rehum and Baanah): The list of the men of the people of Israel: ... of Elam 1,254' (Ezra 2:1-2,7).

5. John may well have the fall of the Roman empire in mind in these references. Christians were being brutally persecuted when John wrote Revelation and they needed to know that Rome was not all-powerful. However, references to Babylon in Revelation are an allusion to evil in general — political and religious.

6. Martin Luther, 'A Mighty Fortress is our God' (1521), trans. Frederick H. Hedge (1853).

7. This is the view of Young, (vol. 2, pp.77-78).

8. This is the view of Leupold, *Exposition of Isaiah*, p.340.

9. See notes on Isaiah 7. This would also imply that this prophecy was given before 732 B.C. and not in the sequence given in Isaiah itself.

10. Arabs on camels, with only bows as weapons, were no match for the Assyrians. A relief from Ashurbanipal's palace in Nineveh shows Assyrian infantry on horseback pursuing Arabs fleeing on camels. On each camel there are two men, one guiding the animal with a stick and the other, a warrior, shooting arrows with a simple bow.

11. 'Phœnicia' is a word coined by the Greeks and is not found in the Old Testament. It is true that the NIV includes the word in verse 11 of this chapter, but the Hebrew is 'Canaan'. The inhabitants of Phœnicia called themselves 'Canaanites' in Old Testament times. Phœnicia is roughly the same as modern Lebanon.

12. Cf. 1 Kings 5:18; Ps. 83:7; Ezek. 27:9.

13. Outside Phœnicia some managed to maintain their identity and culture. One of Phœnicia's most famous sons is Hannibal of Alps and elephants fame.

14. 'At that time she will not lay up riches for herself, will not amass them by unlawful methods, but will employ them in the service of God, and will spend the produce of her merchandise in relieving the wants of the godly. When he used a word expressive of what was disgraceful, he had his eye on the past, but intimated that she would unlearn those wicked practices, and change her disposition.' Calvin, vol. 2, p.161.

Chapter 15

1. Calvin thinks the 'Valley of Vision' refers to the whole of Judea, rather than just the city of Jerusalem (vol. 2, p.109). As far as dates are concerned, most evangelical commentators place this prophecy during the siege of Jerusalem in Hezekiah's time, that is, at 701 B.C.

2. E. J. Young sees this chapter as referring to the destruction of Jerusalem by Nebuchadnezzar of Babylon, 150 years later. In that case, Isaiah 22 is not a report of the events, but a prophecy of the future. The view, as Young admits, is full of problems, because of the very clear references to Shebna and Eliakim, both of whom served under Hezekiah's administration. See Young, vol. 2, pp.87-8.

3. A fuller account of the siege of Jerusalem by Sennacherib will be given when we look at chapters 36-39.

4. Donald J. Wiseman, *Illustrations from Biblical Archeology*, 1958, pp.61-64.

5. Calvin, vol. 2, p.114.

6. The tomb is thought to have been discovered.

Chapter 16

1. Thomas Watson, *A Body of Divinity* (Banner of Truth, 1979), p.218.

2. Cf. Allan MacRae, *New Perspectives on the Old Testament*, edited by J.

Barton Payne, essay entitled 'Some principles in the interpretation of Isaiah as illustrated by chapter 24' (Word, 1970), pp.150-152.

3. Calvin, vol. 2, p.166.

4. Kidner, *New Bible Commentary*, 'Isaiah', p.604; Young, vol. 2, pp.146-66. He says, 'The judgement hitherto described has affected the entire world and not merely the land of Judah...' (p.163).

5. The depiction of a restoration of Israel in chapters 24-27 has led dispensationalists to expect the return of Jews to Palestine as part of biblical prophecy, and to see the emergence of the state of Israel in 1948 as its initial fulfilment.

6. Calvin takes the view that this covenant is the covenant of grace made with the Jews. This is in line with his general understanding of this chapter as a word to the Jews scattered throughout the known world of Isaiah's day (vol. 2, p.170).

7. Young, vol. 2, p. 158.

8. Palmer Robertson, *The Christ of the Covenants* (Presbyterian and Reformed, 1980), pp.277,284.

9. For a careful assessment of this idea, see Donald Macleod, *Behold Your God* (Christian Focus Publications, 1990), pp.106-109. See also comments on Isaiah 30:30-32.

10. Robert Murray M'Cheyne, *A Basket of Fragments* (Aberdeen, 1949), p.334.

11. That this is a reference to God, see NIV text: 'the righteous One'; also Calvin, vol. 2, p.178. E. J. Young, however, believes that this is a description of the (imputed) righteousness of the remnant (vol. 2, p.172).

12. Donald Macleod, *Behold your God*, pp.108-9

13. Richard Baxter, *The Reformed Pastor* (Banner of Truth), p.61.

Chapter 17

1. A. W. Pink, cited by J. I. Packer, *Knowing God* (Hodder & Stoughton, 1973), p.71.

2. Calvin, vol. 2, p.203.

3. Young, vol. 2, p.200.

4. *Ibid.*, vol. 2, p.205. 'None of these passages teaches that righteousness comes by good works' (p.205, n.6).

5. Calvin, vol. 2, p.217.

6. *Works*, vol. 14, p.260.

7. *Ibid.*

8. Leupold, *Exposition of Isaiah,* p.426f.

9. Young, vol. 2, p.247.

Chapter 18

1. Kidner, *New Bible Commentary*, 'Isaiah', p.606. The Hebrew shows the infantile nature of their response: *'Sav lasav, sav lasav, kav lakav, kav lakav.'*

2. Palmer Robertson, 'Tongues: Sign of Covenantal Curse and Blessing', *Westminster Theological Journal*, vol. XXXVIII, Fall 1975, p.44.

3. 'As a sign to unbelievers, they (tongues) bear primarily, although not exclusively, on unrepentant *Israel*.' Richard B. Gaffin, *Perspectives on Pentecost* (Baker, 1979), p.106.

4. Kidner, *New Bible Commentary*, 'Isaiah', p.607.

5. Calvin, vol. 2, p.321.

6. Owen, *Works*, vol. 7, p.534.

7. John W. Wenham, *The Enigma of Evil* (IVP, 1985), p.123.

8. John Calvin, *The Institutes of the Christian Religion*, 3.23.5.

9. Calvin, vol. 2, pp.338-39.

10. 'The perpetuity of the promise is foundational to the Messianic theology of the prophets, for if the promise ever came to an end, the Messianic hope would die.' Thomas Edward McComiskey, *The Covenants of Promise: A theology of the Old Testament Covenants* (IVP, 1985), p.26.

Chapter 19

1. John Stott, *I Believe in Preaching* (Hodder & Stoughton, 1982), p.310.

2. The hymn begins, 'Nothing either great or small...'

3. Thomas Watson, *The Doctrine of Repentance* (Banner of Truth, 1987, first pub. 1668), p.7.

4. See Donald Macleod, *Behold Your God*, pp.106-9, and earlier comments on Isaiah 24:14-23.

5. God is called 'spirit' in 31:3, but this has a different connotation from the usual theological significance of this word. G. Vos comments: 'It does not express immaterialness, but the energy of life in God. Its opposite is "flesh", signifying the innate inertia of the creature, considered apart from God. "Flesh" is not yet, as later in the N.T., associated with sin' (*Biblical Theology*, p.257).

6. Calvin, vol. 2, p.404.

7. Ryle, *Expository Thoughts on the Gospels: John*, vol. 3, p. 55.

Chapter 20

1. Jonathan Edwards, *Jonathan Edwards on Knowing Christ* (Banner of Truth, 1990), pp.159-160.

2. Young, vol. 2, p.414.

3. C. H. Spurgeon, *The Treasury of David*, vol. 1, p.186.

Chapter 21

1. See 'The covenant of grace and the doctrine of the remnant'.

2. Calvin, vol. 3, p.62.

3. C. S. Lewis, *Mere Christianity* (William Collins, 1970), p.172.

Chapter 22

1. See notes on chapter 22.
2. 'Field commander' (NIV) is regarded by the AV and NASV as a proper name rather than a title and translated 'Rabshakch'. The New King James Version says in the notes that this is a title and suggests 'Chief of Staff' or 'Governor' as possible translations.
3. C. F. Keil, *The Books of the Kings, Biblical Commentary on the Old Testament,* ed. C. F. Keil and F. Delitzsch, vol. 4 (Eerdmans, 1950), p.434.
4. See *Scripture and Truth,* edited by D. A. Carson and J. D. Woodbridge, essay entitled 'Scripture's Self-Attestation' by Wayne A. Grudem (IVP, 1983), p.21.
5. J. I. Packer, *I Want to be a Christian* (Kingsway, 1985), p.131.
6. Young, vol. 2, p.477.
7. Cf. Young, vol. 2, p.505
8. Payne, *Kingdoms of the Lord,* p.112
9. *Ibid.*

Chapter 23

1. This event occurred during the siege of Jerusalem, prior to the retreat of the Assyrian army and the murder of Sennacherib recorded at the end of the previous chapter.
2. I have written about Hezekiah's illness in Isaiah 38 and 39 and its close association with Psalm 30 in *Help for Hurting Christians* (Evangelical Press, 1991), pp.51-59.
3. Norman Anderson, *An Adopted Son* (IVP, 1985), p.230.
4. Keil and Delitszch, *Commentary on 2 Kings,* p.460; Young, vol. 2, p.513, n.11.
5. William Stanford La Sor, *The New Bible Commentary Revised, 2 Kings,* p.364.
6. Quoted by John Blanchard in *More Gathered Gold* (Evangelical Press, 1986), p.249.

Chapter 24

1. Young, vol. 3, p.17.
2. The Hebrew can mean 'to comfort, console, pity...' See F. Brown, S. R. Driver & C. A. Briggs, *Hebrew and English Lexicon of the Old Testament* (Oxford, 1975), p.637.
3. Technically, Isaiah was speaking to the southern kingdom of Judah. The ten northern tribes, collectively known as Israel, had by this time disappeared to the Assyrian invaders. After this period, the prophets would no longer speak in terms of 'Israel' and 'Judah', but often refer simply to 'Israel' as though the division had never taken place.
4. Anselm, *Cur Deus Homo,* Book ii.

5. Cf. Dirk H. Odendaal, *The Eschatological Expectation of Isaiah 40-66 with special reference to Israel and the nations* (Presbyterian & Reformed Publishing Co., 1970), pp.63-4.

6. Van Groningen, *Messianic Revelation in the Old Testament,* p.580.

7. Answer 87 of the *Shorter Catechism* to the question: What is repentance unto life?

8. Others had received God's Word too, e.g. the prophetess Anna (Luke 2:36).

9. Calvin, *Institutes,* I, III, i

Chapter 25

1. Charles Hodge, *Systematic Theology*, vol. 1 (James Clarke, 1960), p.367.

2. Isaiah spends a great deal of his time telling us about God's character in the closing pages of his prophecy. God is the Holy One (e.g. 40:25; 41:14,16,20; 43:3,14,15); the only God there is (40:18, 25; 45:5-6,18,21; 46:5); the everlasting One (40:28); the glorious One (42:8,12; 44:23); the righteous One (42:21; 51:5,8); the mighty One (49:26); the sovereign One (40:10; 49:22; 50:5,7,9); the Creator (40:28; 42:5; 43:1); the Sustainer of all things (40:22; 52:7); the Redeemer and Saviour of his people (43:1,11; 44:6; 49:26); the covenant Lord who does not forget his promise (42:6; 43:4,5; 55:1-5). Truly, Isaiah's prophecy is all about God!

3. Other translations have 'Spirit' for 'mind' at this point. There is no conflict, for as E. J. Young points out, 'The Spirit of the Lord is the Spirit of intelligence and understanding...' Young, vol. 3, p.44.

4. *Shorter Catechism,* Answer 11.

5. Young, vol. 3, p.57.

6. Martin Luther, *The Bondage of the Will*

7. Ferguson, *A Heart for God,* p.1.

Chapter 26

1. Elisabeth Elliot, *Loneliness* (Kingsway, 1990), p.20.

2. The Hebrew word is *qawah*: Brown, Driver & Briggs, *Lexicon,* p.875.

3. The Hebrew word is *yachal.*

4. Sinclair Ferguson, *Discovering God's Will* (Banner of Truth, 1981), p.106.

Chapter 27

1. Some commentators have interpreted the one who rises from the east as Abraham (e.g. the Jewish Targum) and others saw the figure as an allusion to Christ (e.g. Jerome). I have followed the interpretation given by E. J. Young in his commentary.

2. For some helpful insights into the world of fortune-telling, see Russ Parker, *The Occult: Deliverance from evil* (IVP,1989), ch.3; and Kevin Logan, *Paganism and the Occult* (Kingsway, 1988), chs 9-10.
3. Young, vol. 3, p.93.
4. B. B. Warfield, *Person and Work of Christ* (Presbyterian & Reformed), p.448.

The Servant of the Lord
1. Commentators differ widely as to the extent of the Servant Songs. We have adopted in this text the range of verses proposed by Gerard van Groningen (*Messianic Revelation in the Old Testament*, p.574). Others list the references as follows: 42:1-9; 49:1-13; 50:4-9; 52:13 - 53:12 (Kidner, *New Bible Commentary*, 'Isaiah', p. 612); 42:1-9; 49:1-7; 50:4-11; 52:13 - 53:12 (Leupold, *Exposition of Isaiah*, vol. 2, p.59). Others suggest the first song is 42:1-4 (e.g. Willis J. Beecher, 'The Servant', in *Classical Evangelical Essays*, ed. Walter C. Kaiser, Jr, p. 199).
2. For an in-depth study, there is a very helpful essay on this subject in *The Prophets and the Promise*, chapter entitled 'The Servant', by Willis J. Beecher (Baker), pp.263-88
3. The NIV has 'so he may worship me'. Though the idea of worship is undoubtedly present, that of service is uppermost.
4. Van Groningen, *Messianic Revelation in the Old Testament*, p.600.

Chapter 28
1. See N. B. Stonehouse, *The Witness of Matthew and Mark to Christ* (Philadelphia, 1944), p.62.
2. The word used for **'uphold'** is *'etmak-bo*, which can mean 'to grasp', to 'hold fast', or 'I hold him up.' The word for 'take hold of' (the Servant's hand) is *'essareka*, 'to watch, guard, or keep'.
3. George Smeaton, *The Doctrine of the Holy Spirit* (Banner of Truth), p.127.
4. For a most helpful elaboration upon this theme of the work of the Holy Spirit in the life of Jesus Christ, see Douglas MacMillan, *Jesus — Power Without Measure* (Evangelical Press of Wales, 1990).
5. Calvin, vol. 3, p.291.
6. The word 'departure' is *exodus* in Greek.
7. Louis Berkhof, *Systematic Theology*, (Eerdmans, 1941), p.266, (cf. Ps. 89:3).
8. Thomas Boston, *Complete Works*, vol. 1, p.333, cited by John Murray in *Collected Writings*, vol. 4 (Banner of Truth, 1982), p.237.
9. The NIV has 'kindness and sternness'.

Chapter 29

1. J. H. Bavinck, *An Introduction to the Science of Missions*, trans. David Freeman (Presbyterian and Reformed Publishing Company, 1960), p.11.
2. This expression, 'Immanuel principle' is used by Palmer Robertson in *Christ of the Covenants*, p.46.
3. Revised Scottish Metrical Version.
4. Brown, Driver & Briggs, *Lexicon*, p.355.

Chapter 30

1. The word 'Jeshurun' is assumed to be derived from the Hebrew verb *yasar*, 'to be straight, right'. Isaiah seems to depict Israel in their ideal state, the way they should be. Israel as Jeshurun are blessed and 'grow fat' with the riches God has bestowed upon them (Deut. 32:15).
2. See John H. Skilton, ed., *The Law and the Prophets, Old Testament Studies in Honour of O. T. Allis.* (Presbyterian and Reformed, 1974), essay entitled, 'Isaiah and Wood' by Robert L. Alden, pp.377-87. Of the four kinds of trees mentioned in 44:14, translated 'cedar', 'cypress', 'pine' and 'oak', two of the Hebrew words are unique to Isaiah. 'There is a similarity in the sounds of the Hebrew words of these two unknown trees with the two known ones. Isaiah is both poet and dendrologist' (p.379).
3. Calvin, vol. 3, p.376.

Chapter 31

1. See 'Cyrus in the Prophecies of Isaiah,' by John C. Whitcomb, Jr, in *The Law and The Prophets*, pp.388-401.
2. Young, vol. 3, p.206.
3. Josephus, *Antiquities*, xi. I, cited by Derek Kidner, *Ezra and Nehemiah* (IVP, 1979), p.33.
4. See van Groningen, *Messianic Revelation in the Old Testament*, p.597.
5. John Murray, *Collected Writings*, vol. 4, p.127.

Chapter 32

1. Thomas à Kempis, *The Imitation of Christ*, I, 19.
2. Quoted by Jerry Bridges, *Trusting God — even when life hurts* (NavPress, 1988), p.75.
3. Young, vol. 3, p.222.
4. Calvin, vol. 3, p.491.

Chapter 33

1. Sinclair Ferguson, *The Christian Life* (Banner of Truth, 1989), p.106.
2. *Westminster Confession*, ch. 18.
3. Calvin, vol. 4, p.62.

Chapter 34
1. See, Meredith Kline, *The Structure of Biblical Authority* (Eerdmans, 1971), pp.79f.
2. Calvin, vol. 4, p.84.

Chapter 35
1. Joachim Jeremias, *Eucharistic Words*, p.228, cited by John Stott, *The Cross of Christ* (IVP, 1986), p.145.
2. Mark 9:12, cf. Isa. 53:3; Mark 2:20, cf. Isa. 53:8; Luke 22:37, cf. Isa. 53:12.
3. Mark 14:8, cf. Isa. 53:9; Luke 11:22, cf. Isa. 53:12; Mark 14:61, cf. Isa. 53:7; Luke 23:34, cf. Isa. 53:12; John 10:11,15,17, cf. Isa. 53:10.
4. Stott, *Cross of Christ*, p.146.
5. Young, vol. 3, p.335
6. Van Groningen translates verses 14 and 15 this way:
    'Many were astonished...
        because he was marred
        because the people were sprinkled
    Just as [they admired him as the exalted One]
        Kings were dumbfounded
        because of what they saw and perceived.'
    (*Messianic Revelation*, p.625).
7. Verse 4 has sometimes been translated: 'Surely he has borne our sicknesses...' The verse is quoted in Matthew 8:17 in reference to Jesus' healing ministry. Some have used this verse to suggest that Christians should claim, not only forgiveness, but healing from the atoning work of Christ. 'Jesus died,' so the saying has it, 'to atone for our sicknesses as well as our sins.' A comparison is drawn with verse 12, 'He bore the sin of many...' If 'to bear' (Hebrew: *nasa'*) in verse 12 means 'suffer the punishment for', then it must have this meaning in verse 4 also. In popular idiom, the conclusion is put this way: all Christians should expect God to heal their bodies today, beacuse Christ died to atone for our sicknesses as well as for our sins. There are several problems with this view. John Stott summarizes them in this way: Firstly, the verb *nasa'* in Hebrew is used in several ways, some of which are far less technical than the meaning 'bear the punishment for'. For example, in Isaiah 52:11 the same word is used with reference to *carrying* the vessels of the Lord. Secondly, it is difficult to see what the penalty of sickness is. Sickness is itself a penalty. Thirdly, Matthew applies Isaiah 53:4 not to the atoning death of Jesus but to his healing ministry. Matthew is not suggesting that, if we are Christians, we can claim bodily healing from the atonement of Christ as a right; Matthew is simply saying that Jesus healed the sick as part of the way he fulfilled prophecy (see Stott, *Cross of Christ*, pp.244-5).

8. Leon Morris, *The Atonement: its meaning and significance* (IVP, 1983), p. 47.

9. Young, vol. 3, p.359.

10. Hugh Martin, *The Atonement*, p.250.

Chapter 36

1. See Derek Thomas, *Wisdom: the key to living God's way* (Christian Focus Publications, 1990), pp.11-26.

2. Cited by Leupold, *Exposition of Isaiah,* p.237.

3. Martin Luther, 'A Mighty Fortress is our God' (1521), tr. Frederick H. Hedge (1853).

4. John Murray, *Collected Writings*, vol. 4, p.131.

5. D. A. Carson 'Unity and Diversity in the New Testament' in *Scripture and Truth*, p.80.

Chapter 37

1. Liberals have detected in chapters 56-66 the work of yet another hand — Tritro-Isaiah! This mythical creature is supposed to have lived after the exile, having witnessed the rebuilding of the city of Jerusalem. This commentary accepts the view that Isaiah is the single author of the whole book.

2. Calvin, vol. 4, p.175.

3. Deuteronomy 23:1 tells us that a man who had been emasculated by choice (rather than by accident, or illness) was not to be granted admission to the assembly of the Lord. Behind this is the thought that such mutilation was a sign of cultic adherence to the Mesopotamian god, Ishtar. See P. C. Craigie, *The Book of Deuteronomy* (Eerdmans, 1976), pp.296-7.

4. Calvin, vol. 4, p.198.

5. Calvin, vol. 4, pp.238-9.

6. John Newton's hymn, 'Glorious things of thee are spoken' (1779).

7. D. M. Lloyd-Jones, *The Righteous Judgment of God: Exposition of Romans Chapters 2:1-3:20* (Banner of Truth, 1989), p.214.

8. See Tremper Longman III, 'The Divine Warrior' in *Westminster Theological Journal*, Fall 1982, pp.290-307.

9. Young, vol. 3, p.442.

Chapter 38

1. D. A. Carson, *Matthew*, in *The Expositor's Bible Commentary*, vol. 8, ed. Frank E. Gaebelein (Zondervan, 1984), p.82.

2. *Ibid.,* p.89.

3. Young, vol. 3, p.450.

4. See comments on Isaiah 35.

5. Cited by Timothy George, *Theology of the Reformers* (IVP, 1988), p.96

6. E.g. Willem A. VanGemeren, *Interpreting the Prophetic Word* (Zondervan, 1990), p.284.
7. E.g. Young, vol. 3, p.467.
8. Charles and Norma Ellis, *The Wells of Salvation: Meditations on Isaiah* (Banner of Truth, 1985), p.204.
9. Thomas Brooks, *The Privy Key of Heaven, Works*, vol. 2, pp.258-9.

Chapter 39
1. Young, vol. 3, p.480.
2. Calvin, vol. 4, p.389.

Chapter 40
1. D. Martyn Lloyd-Jones, *Studies in the Sermon on the Mount* (IVP, 1960), vol. 1, p.144.
2. Cf. A. A. Hoekema, *The Bible and the Future*, p.202.
3. Kidner, *New Bible Commentary*, 'Isaiah', p.624.
4. Calvin, vol. 3, p.405.
5. Young, vol. 3, p.532.
6. G. A. Smith, *The Book of Isaiah, The Expositor's Bible* (Hodder & Stoughton, 1889), vol. 2, (1990), p.63.
7. John Bradford, *The Writings of John Bradford* (Banner of Truth, 1979), vol. 1, p.267.